Commercial Cosmopolitanism?

This book showcases the wide variety of commercial cosmopolitan practices that arose from the global economic entanglements of the early modern period.

Cosmopolitanism is not only a philosophical ideal: for many centuries it has also been an everyday practice across the globe. The early modern era saw hitherto unprecedented levels of economic interconnectedness. States, societies, and individuals reacted with a mixture of commercial idealism and commercial anxiety, seeking at once to exploit new opportunities for growth whilst limiting its disruptive effects. In highlighting the range of commercial cosmopolitan practices that grew out of early modern globalisation, the book demonstrates that it provided robust alternatives to the universalising western imperial model of the later period. Deploying a number of interdisciplinary methodologies, the kind of 'methodological cosmopolitanism' that Ulrich Beck has called for, chapters provide agency-centred evaluations of the risks and opportunities inherent in the ambiguous role of the cosmopolitan, who, often playing on and mobilising a number of identities, operated in between and outside of different established legal, social, and cultural systems.

The book will be important reading for students and scholars working at the intersection of economic, global, and cultural history.

Felicia Gottmann is Senior Lecturer in History at Northumbria University, Newcastle. She is the author of *Global Trade, Smuggling, and the Making of Economic Liberalism: Asian Textiles in France 1680–1760* (2016) and, with Maxine Berg et al. editor of *Goods from the East, 1600–1800: Trading Eurasia* (2015). She held Fellowships at the Universities of Harvard, Warwick, Dundee, and Oxford, and is PI of the UKRI-funded Future Leaders Fellowship Project 'Migration, Adaptation, Innovation 1500–1800'.

Political Economies of Capitalism, 1600–1850

Series editors: Carl Wennerlind, Barnhart College, US, John Shovlin, New York University, US, and Philip J. Stern, Duke University, US

This series explores the many dimensions of early modern political economy, and especially the ways in which this period established both the foundations for and alternatives to modern capitalist thought and practice. This history is examined from a variety of perspectives—political, intellectual, cultural, economic, social, spatial, and others—and in contexts ranging from the local to the global.

Commercial Cosmopolitanism?
Cross-Cultural Objects, Spaces, and Institutions in the Early Modern World
Edited by Felicia Gottmann

Historicizing Self-Interest in the Modern Atlantic World
A Plea for Ego?
Edited by Christine Zabel

For more information about this series, please visit: https://www.routledge.com/Political-Economies-of-Capitalism-1600-1850/book-series/CARL

Commercial Cosmopolitanism?

Cross-Cultural Objects, Spaces, and Institutions in the Early Modern World

**Edited by
Felicia Gottmann**

LONDON AND NEW YORK

First published 2021
by Routledge
2 Park Square, Milton Park, Abingdon, Oxon OX14 4RN

and by Routledge
52 Vanderbilt Avenue, New York, NY 10017

Routledge is an imprint of the Taylor & Francis Group, an informa business

© 2021 selection and editorial matter, Felicia Gottmann; individual chapters, the contributors

The right of Felicia Gottmann to be identified as the author of the editorial material, and of the authors for their individual chapters, has been asserted in accordance with sections 77 and 78 of the Copyright, Designs and Patents Act 1988.

All rights reserved. No part of this book may be reprinted or reproduced or utilised in any form or by any electronic, mechanical, or other means, now known or hereafter invented, including photocopying and recording, or in any information storage or retrieval system, without permission in writing from the publishers.

Trademark notice: Product or corporate names may be trademarks or registered trademarks, and are used only for identification and explanation without intent to infringe.

A catalogue record for this book is available from the British Library

Names: Gottmann, Felicia, 1982- editor.
Title: Commercial cosmopolitanism?: cross-cultural objects, spaces, and institutions in the early modern world / edited by Felicia Gottmann.
Description: Milton Park, Abingdon, Oxon; New York, NY: Routledge, 2021. | Includes bibliographical references and index.
Identifiers: LCCN 2020043321 (print) | LCCN 2020043322 (ebook) | ISBN 9780367464615 (hardback) | ISBN 9781003028871 (ebook)
Subjects: LCSH: Economic history – 1600–1750. | Economic history – 1750–1918. | Cosmopolitanism – History.
Classification: LCC HC51.C63 2021 (print) | LCC HC51 (ebook) | DDC 330.9/03--dc23
LC record available at https://lccn.loc.gov/2020043321
LC ebook record available at https://lccn.loc.gov/2020043322

ISBN: 978-0-367-46461-5 (hbk)
ISBN: 978-0-367-71486-4 (pbk)
ISBN: 978-1-003-02887-1 (ebk)

Typeset in Times New Roman
by MPS Limited, Dehradun

In memory of Günther Gottmann (1931–2018)

Contents

List of illustrations	ix
List of contributors	x
Acknowledgements	xiii
Maps	xiv

Introduction: Commercial Cosmopolitanism?
Cross-cultural objects, spaces, and institutions in the
early modern world   1
FELICIA GOTTMANN

PART I
Cosmopolitan spaces, objects, and actors   21

1 Controlling the golden geese: Canton, Nagasaki and
the limits of hybridity   23
LISA HELLMAN

2 Trouble in the contact zone: Jeremias van Vliet in
seventeenth-century Ayutthaya   40
SVEN TRAKULHUN

3 Chinese commercial cosmopolitanism in the
eighteenth-century Mekong River Delta: the case of
Mạc Thiên Tứ   56
XING HANG

4 Money talks: confessions of a disgraced cosmopolitan
coin of the 1640s   72
KRIS LANE

viii *Contents*

5 'This whole business should be kept very Secret':
the English tobacco workhouses in Moscow   92
MATTHEW P. ROMANIELLO

6 Goods from the sea countries: material cosmopolitanism in Atlantic West Africa   108
BRONWEN EVERILL

7 From the Indian Ocean to the Atlantic: the commercial
ventures of Oman-Zanzibar   123
JEREMY PRESTHOLDT

PART II
Institutions, practices, and agents   **141**

8 Hats, furs and Indigenous traders in a global trade   143
ANN M. CARLOS

9 The social networks of Cosmopolitan Fraudsters: the
Prussian Bengal Company as a transnational
corporation   161
FELICIA GOTTMANN

10 Quasi-cosmopolitanism: French directors in Ouidah
and Pondicherry (1674–1746)   181
ELISABETH HEIJMANS

11 Commercial Cosmopolitanism? The case of the firm
De Bruijn & Cloots (Lisbon) in the eighteenth century   196
CÁTIA ANTUNES, SUSANA MÜNCH MIRANDA, AND
JOÃO PAULO SALVADO

12 The limits of cosmopolitanism: Ottoman Algiers in the
seventeenth and eighteenth centuries   212
MICHAEL TALBOT

13 Making Ireland poor: poverty, trade, and sectarianism
in the eighteenth century Atlantic   231
JAMES LIVESEY

Index   251

Illustrations

0.1	Overview of places discussed in this volume	xiv
0.2	Overview of places discussed in this volume	xiv
1.1	Island of Deshima, Dutch East India Company. Wellcome Collection	24
1.2	The Foreign Factories of Canton, about 1784–1785. 2002.6.6, Collection of The Corning Museum of Glass, Corning, NY	25
2.1	Map of Ayutthaya. In: Simon de La Loubère, *A New Historical Relation of the Kingdom of Siam* (London: F.L. for Tho. Horne, 1693). SB Berlin, Up 5520-1	41
2.1	Sakdina (simplified)	44
4.1	A 1644 Potosí Piece of Eight. Private Collection	74
4.2	Silver War Horse: A ca. 1650 Mexican Piece of Eight with Asian 'chop marks'. Private Collection	75
4.3	A 1647 Potosí Piece of Eight, Assayer 'Z'. Private Collection	75
4.4	A 1664 Potosí Piece of Eight with 1670s Flemish Countermark. Private Collection	76
7.1	The Sultana in London. Image from *The Illustrated London News* of 18 June 1842 entitled "Landing of the Queen's Presents." Courtesy of John Weedy, iln.org.uk	133
9.1	The Prussian Company employees' interactions upon arrival on the Coromandel Coast (spring & summer 1755)	169
9.2	The Prussian Company employees' commercial network in India: synchronic overview	170
9.3	Network adjusted to relative tie strength, indicating the frequency, duration, and relative importance of interactions	172

Contributors

Cátia Antunes is professor of the *History of Global Economic Networks: Merchants, Entrepreneurs and Empires* at Leiden University. Her interests lie in the Comparative History of Early Modern Empires, Merchant Culture and Entrepreneurial History and Empire Building. She has authored and edited numerous books in global history and has held fellowships and grants from the Dutch National Science Foundation (NWO), the European Research Council, the Marie Curie-ITN scheme, the Fulbright Programme, and Yale University amongst others.

Ann M. Carlos is professor emerita of Economics at the University of Colorado Boulder. She has worked extensively on aspects relating to the management of long distance trade by joint-stock companies in the early modern period, the impact of a commercial fur trade on the Indigenous economy in the eighteenth century and the standards of living of native communities in the eighteenth century. This work culminated in *Commerce by a Frozen Sea: Native Americans and the European Fur Trade* (2010) with Frank D. Lewis.

Bronwen Everill is a fellow of Gonville & Caius College, University of Cambridge and the author of *Abolition and Empire in Sierra Leone and Liberia* (2013), and of *Not Made By Slaves: Ethical Capitalism in the Age of Abolition* (2020). She has held fellowships at the Huntington Library, the John Carter Brown Library, and the Historical Society of Pennsylvania, and was the recipient of a Leverhulme Early Career Fellowship at King's College London.

Xing Hang is associate professor of History at Brandeis University. Together with Tonio Andrade he is editor of *Sea Rovers, Silver, and Samurai: Maritime East Asia in Global History, 1550–1700* (2016), and his monograph, *Conflict and Commerce in Maritime East Asia: The Zheng Family and the Shaping of the Modern World, c. 1620–1720* was published in 2016.

Elisabeth Heijmans (PhD Leiden University) is a post-doctoral researcher in history at the university of Antwerp. She is the author of *The Agency of*

Empire: Connections and Strategies in French Overseas Expansion (1684-1746) (2019). Her current research focuses on French merchants' perception of the future in the early modern period.

Lisa Hellman is leader for the research group 'Coerced Circulation of Knowledge' at the University of Bonn, and a Pro Futura Scientia XV Fellow at the Swedish Collegium for Advanced Study. She has formerly worked at Freie Universität Berlin and University of Tokyo, where she wrote her book *This house is not a home: European everyday life in Canton and Macao 1730–1830* (2019). She works in the intersection between social, cultural, maritime, and global history in East and Central Asia, with a special focus on gender.

Kris Lane holds the France V. Scholes Chair in Colonial Latin American History at Tulane University in New Orleans, USA. He is author of *Potosí: The Silver City that Changed the World* (2019), *Pillaging the Empire: Global Piracy on the High Seas, 1500–1750* (2015), *Colour of Paradise: The Emerald in the Age of Gunpowder Empires* (Yale, 2010), and *Quito 1599: City & Colony in Transition* (2002). He is currently working on a global history of the great Potosí mint fraud of the 1640s.

James Livesey is professor of History and Vice President for Research and Innovation at the National University of Ireland, Galway. He is author of *Making Democracy in the French Revolution* (2001) and *Civil Society and Empire: Ireland and Scotland in the Eighteenth-Century Atlantic World* (2009), and most recently of *Provincializing Global History. Money, Ideas, and Things in the Languedoc, 1680–*1830 (2020).

Susana Münch Miranda is research fellow at CSG/GHES, ISEG, University of Lisbon. Her current research interests comprise Colonial Governance (Iberian Empires), Fiscal History and Business History. With Leonor Freire Costa and Pedro Lains she is the author of *An Economic History of Portugal, 1143–2010* (2016).

Jeremy Prestholdt is professor of History at the University of California, San Diego. He is the author of *Domesticating the World: African Consumerism and the Genealogies of Globalization* (2008), which addressed East African demands for imported goods and how these shaped global exchanges in the nineteenth century; and most recently of *Icons of Dissent: The Global Resonance of Che, Marley, Tupac and Bin Laden* (2019).

Matthew P. Romaniello is associate professor of history at Weber State University and previously professor of history at University of Hawaii at Manoa. He is the editor of *Journal of World History* and author of *Enterprising Empires: Russia and Britain in Eighteenth-Century Eurasia* (2019), of *The Elusive Empire: Kazan and the Creation of Russia,*

xii *Contributors*

1552–1671 (2012) and has edited several volumes on material culture, consumption studies and transcultural encounters in global history.

João Paulo Salvado is research fellow at CIDEHUS, University of Évora. His work was funded by Fundação para a Ciência e a Tecnologia (Portugal) and POPH/FSE (EC) (SFRH/BPD/88967/2012). His current interests comprise State formation and Empire-building, Business History, and Merchant elites.

Michael Talbot (BA Cambridge, MA, and PhD SOAS) is senior lecturer in the History of the Ottoman Empire and Modern Middle East at the University of Greenwich. Prior to joining Greenwich, he was a researcher on the ERC-funded project, 'Mediterranean Reconfigurations' at Université Paris 1 Panthéon-Sorbonne. He is the author of *British-Ottoman Relations, 1661–1807: Commerce and Diplomatic Practice in Eighteenth-Century Istanbul* (2017), and in 2018 was selected as one of the BBC and AHRC's 'New Generation Thinkers'.

Sven Trakulhun is researcher and adjunct professor in history at the University of Konstanz having held posts at the Universities of Zurich, Hamburg, Potsdam, and Galway. He has published widely on the history of Thailand and its relations with Europe. He is the author of *Siam und Europa. Das Königreich Ayutthaya in westlichen Berichten (Siam and Europe. The Kingdom of Ayutthaya in Western Accounts)* (2006) and *Asiatische Revolutionen: Europa und der Aufstieg und Fall asiatischer Imperien (Asian Revolutions: Europe and the Rise and Fall of Asian Empires)* (2017).

Acknowledgements

This volume was conceived as part of a Leverhulme-funded research project (Early Career Research Fellowship 2014-396) and owes its existence to an initial conference and workshop generously funded and hosted by the University of Dundee's Scottish Centre for Global history in 2017. I am deeply grateful to both. Above all I am indebted to the chapter authors: they have been a pleasure, inspiration, and real honour to work with. I am particularly grateful to Cátia Antunes, Elisabeth Heijmans, Lisa Hellman, James Livesey, Sven Trakulhun, as well as to Julian Wright, who have all commented on various drafts of the introduction. I also would like to thank Robert Langham and Tanushree Baijal at Routledge and Philip Stern for suggesting this new book series.

This book has been a long time in the making. Since the first workshop the evolving manuscript and chapters have lived through turbulent times, politically and thanks to a global pandemic, but also in the lives of the various authors. A collaborative undertaking is always also the story of personal joys and losses, career moves, births, and bereavements. This one has seen its fair share of all of these. I lost my beloved father in early 2018. He was supremely uninterested in material possessions but he would just about have accepted a book. So this one is dedicated to him – as well as, of course, to my mother, whom he would never leave out.

Maps

Map 0.1 Overview of places discussed in this volume

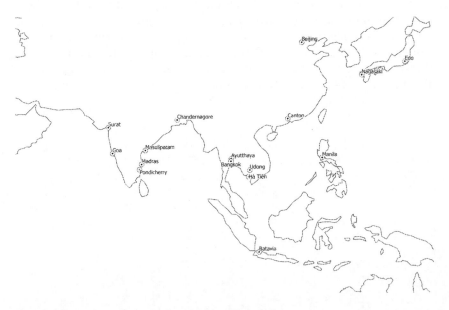

Map 0.2 Overview of places discussed in this volume

Introduction

Commercial Cosmopolitanism? Cross-cultural objects, spaces, and institutions in the early modern world

Felicia Gottmann

A foreigner who came to trade and settle in one of the many great commercial hubs of the Indian Ocean and China Seas in about 1700 would have had to learn and adapt to various local customs. To be truly successful he would have had to become a cosmopolitan. About 150 years later he (and indeed those traders continued to be almost exclusively male) could usually save himself the trouble. European colonialism and informal imperialism had imposed a much more uniform regime of trade regulations as well as extra-legal status for Europeans. If the nineteenth century was a globalised age, the early modern period was a cosmopolitan one.[1]

We define such 'lived' or 'practical' cosmopolitanism as the ability to adopt, adapt, and operate across two or more different cultural codes or 'vernaculars' simultaneously. In his work on cultural linguistics, Sheldon Pollock differentiated between periods of cosmopolitanism, based on a universalising *lingua franca*, and periods defined by bounded vernaculars.[2] When it came to commercial interactions, the early modern period certainly had its own *lingua franca*. Francesca Trivellato posited the existence of a 'truly global mercantile culture' in this era.[3] Cátia Antunes outlined its shared principles as the reciprocity inherent in the concept of exchange, the consequent recognition of debt and compensation to correct imbalances of payment in such exchanges, and finally the role of trust based on notions of honour and reputation.[4] However, in the early modern period this global commercial *lingua franca* was rudimentary and limited. Cultural misunderstandings and different local customs still required translation from one vernacular into another. The willingness and ability not only to master the universal *lingua franca* of early modern mercantile exchanges but to combine and creolise multiple vernaculars define what we call 'commercial cosmopolitanism'.

Commercial cosmopolitans often played on and mobilised a number of identities and operated in-between and outside of different established legal, social, and cultural systems. This could leave them vulnerable. However, as this volume shows, this very fragility was also a source of opportunity and power for cosmopolitan agents. Their ability to draw on different cultural codes gave them immense creative potential. They developed new trade routes, exchange mechanisms, and revenue streams, and inspired new and

2   *Felicia Gottmann*

hybrid objects, artworks, languages, and socio-economic or cultural practices which were themselves cosmopolitan. Cosmopolitan actors, objects, spaces, and institutions were thus not necessarily 'global' or 'transnational' – an anachronistic term for much of the world in this period. They were, however, always *transcultural* as they crossed and blurred linguistic, ethnic, and religious boundaries.

What this volume thus showcases is not the philosophical ideal of world citizenship or the intellectual recognition of a universally shared humanity, but rather the lived experience of cosmopolitanism across the world. On the theoretical concept, much ink has been shed, and, perhaps due to the current rise of militant nationalism, there has been a resurgence of scholarly interest in cosmopolitanism as a normative ideal and applied philosophical project.[5] Though often discussed only as part of the Western philosophical tradition, the ideal of the *Weltbürger*, 'citizen of the world' or Greek *kosmopolitēs*, exists in many cultures. It is a notable feature of Confucianism and, in perhaps a narrower religious sense, the *ummat al-Islām* has shaped a supra-national sense of global Islamic community for centuries.[6] In the West, cosmopolitan sentiment was a notable feature of Epicurean and Stoic philosophy and particularly blossomed in the European Enlightenment and its Republic of Letters, which, it ought to be said, remained well aware of other, non-European versions of cosmopolitanism.[7] Much has been written on the Enlightenment ideal itself, and nearly as much on its well-established link to commerce, which aspired to a world united and civilised by the shared give and take of peaceful exchange: a vision that did not survive long amid the brutal realities of global trade.[8]

Much less work has been done to investigate how the Enlightenment goal of commercial cosmopolitanism did – or did not – work in practice. In the late 1990s and 2000s, a number of works set out to address this: David Hancock, Margaret C. Jacob, and Alison Games all purported to show how early modern European traders were 'citizens of the world'.[9] Most of these accounts, however, were acutely Eurocentric. Jacob's cosmopolitans were all Europeans who never even left Europe, whilst Hancock's 'citizens of the world' were British citizens dealing with other British men elsewhere around the world. Games was an exception, analysing how late-sixteenth and early-seventeenth-century Englishmen in the Indian Ocean, Mediterranean, and Atlantic worlds adapted to, and adopted foreign cultures and customs as part of their survival strategy. Their cosmopolitanism was 'often a posture derived from weakness' which waned as soon as the English state grew powerful enough to impose centralised control over its colonial ventures.[10] The centrality of power relations to the deployment of commercial cosmopolitan tactics is confirmed by this volume's findings. Bringing together scholars working on early modern Africa, the Americas, Asia, and Europe, we analyse the functioning and characteristics of such strategies from multiple viewpoints across the globe.

Introduction 3

Cosmopolitan practice – theories, approaches, and the importance of methodological cosmopolitanism

To write a global history of cosmopolitan practice, such cosmopolitanism has to be reflected in our approach. To overcome what he called 'methodological nationalism', the late Ulrich Beck proposed social scientists change both their method and their object of study. He suggested researchers leave their national silos and focus on the transnational actors and processes that define the 'second' or 'reflexive' modernity of the twenty-first century. He maintained that these could only be grasped when studied across geographies and disciplines, by abandoning the intrinsic 'provincialism' that still defines many of our disciplines, in the social sciences just as much as in the humanities.[11] Early modernity, the period this volume focuses on, was characterised by very different kinds of transnational actors and processes, yet their understanding requires the same 'methodological cosmopolitanism' that Beck demanded.

To write a genuinely cosmopolitan history of transcultural commerce, we hence need to work across disciplinary and geographical boundaries. We also need to set certain boundaries ourselves when it comes to our definitions and objects of study. Not everybody engaging in early modern global trade was necessarily cosmopolitan. A British merchant, for instance, who only traded with other British merchants located elsewhere across the world, and who consequently did not display any ability or willingness to code-switch between different commercial cultures, does not fall in that category. On the other hand however, in our definition of cosmopolitanism, people are not the only possible cosmopolitan agents, nor did they have to consciously perceive themselves in these terms to fall into this category. Practices, spaces, and objects can also be cosmopolitan thanks to their openness to varying interpretations and their ability to move between, and even merge two or more vernacular traditions.

Polanyi and Curtin

Our focus on cross-cultural commerce is not, of course, without precedent. Indeed, the older literature on the topic is much less Eurocentric in approach than the later spate of works dealing with purported cosmopolitanisms. Karl Polanyi and Philip Curtin are the giants in this field.

Though much criticised, Polanyi's model of the 'Port of Trade' remains ubiquitously cited.[12] Ports of Trade, according to Polanyi, acted as neutrality and security devices for cross-cultural trade under early state conditions and, unlike competitive price-making markets, consisted of administered spaces in which 'native inhabitants provided organs for mediation and accountancy'. Before the establishment of true international markets, this was, he claims, 'the universal institution of overseas trade', and his list of examples includes several of the spaces under discussion in this

4 *Felicia Gottmann*

volume: Ouidah in the Whydah (later Dahomey) kingdom in modern-day Benin, a central node in the trans-Atlantic slave trade; Madras and Calcutta in India; and Canton in China. Scholars have since criticised his rather Eurocentric view of these regions and, by revealing the agency that commercial cosmopolitan practices could bestow on historiographically marginalised actors, contributions to this volume similarly challenge the rigidity of his assertions, revealing instead the hybrid forms of commercial and market-based exchange at work in Canton (Hellman, Chapter 1) or the North American fur trade (Carlos, Chapter 8).[13]

While Curtin's *Cross-Cultural Trade* was also a work of 'historic economic anthropology', his first commitment remained to history, with the focus on commercial practice.[14] Curtin posited the centrality of diasporas to the functioning of cross-cultural trade globally. He defined trade diasporas as 'socially interdependent but spatially dispersed communities' which, following the first rise of urban settlements, formed when commercial specialists removed themselves physically from their home community and went to live as aliens in another town. Members of such diasporas always lived in an asymmetrical relationship to the society surrounding them: they usually remained culturally distinct and politically marginalised, which permitted them to act as cultural brokers. Their very success also made them obsolete over time, as their mediation reduced cross-cultural differences and thereby the need for their brokerage. Curtin's model was flexible. It incorporated several types of power imbalances between foreign traders and hosts, from the supressed pariah traders, exemplified by much of the Jewish diaspora, to the independent, self-governing communities of the seventeenth- and eighteenth-century Jahaanke in West Africa, and the aggressive European trading-post empires in Asia. He also included different degrees of cultural blending between a diaspora being completely assimilated and a position of identitarian segregation; and he recognised the important impact diasporas had on host societies: economically, linguistically, and in terms of religious conversion. As such Curtin's *Cross-Cultural Trade* is one inspiration for this collection. However, a number of historiographical developments and methodological innovations have made a re-examination of the lived reality of cross-cultural trade decidedly necessary. This is what this volume offers.

Cultural history: hybridity and contact zones

Contact zones and the linked concepts of brokerage, go-betweens, hybridity, and transculturation have been amongst the most fertile and innovative fields of study in recent years. Emerging from postcolonial critical theory, they brought a new conceptual understanding of plural and hybrid spaces, such as frontiers, the middle ground, third space or the contact zone, in which identities are constantly negotiated and created and which differed completely from Polanyi's hermetic and controlled Ports of Trade.[15] The theorisation of such spaces has greatly benefitted from scholarship on

Introduction 5

cultural hybridity more broadly, which has analysed the multiplicity, versatility, and performativity of cultural and social identities.[16] This more nuanced view, which understands cultural identity as a performative act in which one individual can at the same time assume multiple changing and hybridised identities, contrasts sharply with Curtin's static and undifferentiated classifications, in which 'diasporic traders' assumed a fixed identity over time. Recent research in critical theory and cultural history has by contrast demonstrated how the translation and adaptation of different vernacular traditions created new hybrids, be those cultural, religious, or linguistic codes; practices of exchange, consumption, and production; or artistic and stylistic conventions. The results ranged from carefully negotiated hybrid practices of commercial exchange and the creole languages and cultures of the contact zone, to 'global objects' and 'global spaces of imagination' – all products of *métissage* and transculturation more than simple acculturation.[17] With perhaps the exception of global material culture studies, scholarship that investigates such processes of translation, adaptation and hybridisation, tends to focus not on commercial interactions but more on the unequal power relations in imperial and colonial regimes and on the brokerage involved in knowledge production.[18] Imperial expansion, warfare, and religious missions certainly were central mechanisms of cross-cultural contact in the early modern world, but trade was of at least similar importance and reached populations as yet unmolested by European colonialism. To study the mechanisms of commercial contact zones, cross-cultural economic brokers, cosmopolitan commercial spaces, transcultural objects, and hybrid practices of exchange, production, and consumption, this volume thus bridges the still-divided disciplines of cultural and economic history.

Economic history: institutional challenges of long-distance trade

In economic history, a more nuanced appreciation of the importance of organisations and institutions in the shape of New Institutional Economics has significantly advanced our understanding of the rules and practices underlying early modern commercial exchange, and offered a compromise in the formalist-substantivist debate that dominated in Polanyi's, and to some extent still in Curtin's days.[19] Research by economists, sociologists, and historians into the structural underpinnings of early modern long-distance trade has emphasised the persistent problem of principal-agent relations and of the increased transaction costs that came with imperfect or asymmetrical information flows and insufficient or biased formal enforcement mechanisms which could only partially be internalised through the reliance on kinship networks.[20] These are analysed by Ann Carlos in Chapter 8.

Chapters in this volume pay careful attention not only to organisations but also to the formal and informal institutional arrangements underlying the exchanges they study. This means that legal frameworks are just as

6   *Felicia Gottmann*

important as the socio-cultural norms in which commercial transactions were embedded.[21] The advantage commercial cosmopolitans had was their ability to understand, access, and play these different frameworks. As Chapters 11 and 13 by Livesey and Antunes et al. illustrate, the capacity to tap into different commercial networks and markets at once could give them a competitive commercial edge. It also gave them additional escape routes. Unlike the thousands of foreigners employed in armed services across the early modern world, who had to profess allegiance to their new masters, cosmopolitan traders could play both sides. Chapter 9 for example reveals how European East India Company agents in India on the one hand claimed extraterritorial rights that would exempt them from local taxation and legislation, but at the same time justified their private profiteering to their principals at home citing local customs.

The perhaps most cosmopolitan of all commercial activities in the period was smuggling.[22] Illicit traders sailed through the wide gap between actual commercial practice and the official rhetoric of 'closed systems' that insisted on administered and centrally controlled trade, be that in the form of Europe's mercantilist trade restrictions and monopolies over colonial trade, or China's Canton System and Japan's *sakoku* (closed-country policy) investigated by Lisa Hellman in Chapter 1.

Social networks

One particular socio-cultural structure that has received a much more robust analytical foundation in recent years is that of the social network. With the advent of social network analysis, historians have also adopted a more rigorous and critical use of the term.[23] Networks in the form of diasporas were central to Curtin's argument, but his diaspora concept lacked the analytical acuity that came with the advent of network studies. He falls prey to what Francesca Trivellato, building on the work of Rogers Brubaker, calls 'groupism', that is, the 'tendency to take discrete, sharply differentiated, internally homogenous, and externally bounded groups as basic constituents of social life.'[24] Such 'groupist' approaches to diaspora studies not only run counter to recent findings on hybridisation and transculturation in the realm of cultural theory, they also impede the study of cosmopolitan commerce. Cosmopolitans frequently act as bridges across networks, mobilising the creative potential of connections *between* established networks. They represent what Granovetter has termed the 'strength of weak ties', a term that also mirrors our commercial cosmopolitans' paradoxical position of both strength (as gatekeepers to separate networks they were able to leverage social and informational capital hermetic to those outside of that respective cultural, social, economic or legal system) and of weakness: mediating and moving across various cultures or networks, they did not fully belong to any one of them and thus frequently were objects of distrust and remained vulnerable to rejection or persecution by each one.[25] One role

Introduction 7

of the cosmopolitan is thus that of the oft-analysed broker, go-between or 'agent of transculturation' who serves as a connector between two or more primary groups with internally strong ties. They bridge what Burt has theorised as 'structural holes' in social networks and thereby gain social capital and the privileged access to good ideas from the other side of the hole.[26] However, whilst all cross-cultural commercial brokers were practical cosmopolitans, not all commercial cosmopolitans acted as brokers. Many were principals in their own right or simply members of self-organised horizontal cross-cultural economic networks.[27]

Social network analysis thus links with the literature on brokerage and the hybridity of contact zones: both are central to this volume. That the attempt to set up genuinely cosmopolitan social networks was not often successful however, is shown in Chapters 9 and 10 on European traders' relationships in early modern India and East Africa.

Spatial history and material culture

The model of the transcultural contact zone also plays an essential role in another field that has made significant analytical advances since its rudimentary use in Polanyi or Curtin: that of spatial history and theory. Space, whether physical, social, or cultural, has become much more rigorously theorised in recent research.[28] Critically informed understandings of space enrich this volume's investigations into the large urban arenas like Canton and Nagasaki (Chapter 1), Ayutthaya (Chapter 2), but also into smaller spaces, such as an Anglo-Russian warehouse (Chapter 5) or an Indian Ocean vessel (Chapter 7).

Next to spatial analysis, two further new directions in recent scholarship define this collection's methodology: global microhistory and global material culture studies. Cosmopolitan institutions, actors, and spaces are not the only focus of this collection. Following in the footsteps of the nascent approach of global material culture studies, we pay close attention to the material objects of commerce, which, polyvalent and subject to symbolic and physical reappropriation, could themselves become cosmopolitan.[29] Certain types of transcultural objects are well known, such as Chinese porcelains adapted for the Middle-Eastern or European market, and once again copied and transformed there.[30] Some are famous to this day, such as the Spanish 'pieces of eight', perhaps the first ever global currency (Chapter 4 by Lane). Some are less familiar to us, such as Russian cigars rolled with English techniques, containing American or Ukrainian tobacco (Chapter 5 by Romaniello). Beyond tangible objects, commercial cosmopolitanism also generated new practices of production and consumption, like the new ways of understanding, clustering, and consuming goods in Atlantic West Africa explored by Bronwen Everill (Chapter 6).

8 *Felicia Gottmann*

Microhistory and subaltern agency

One of the weaknesses of traditional world history, freely acknowledged by Curtin, was that 'the price to be paid' for establishing broad connections and patterns across the globe was 'a decided neglect of [...] the affairs of individual men and women'.[31] An innovative way of avoiding this high cost is the newly emerging approach of global microhistory.[32] Combining case studies with microhistorical insights allows contributors to this collection to bring back individual agency to global history. Indeed, the agency that marginalised or subaltern actors could reclaim by adopting cosmopolitan commercial strategies is one of this volume's central concerns. Effective global history, the kind that is empirically evidenced and grounded in lived reality, requires equal expertise in local and regional history. This is especially true of global microhistory. In the best kind of global microhistory, John-Paul Ghobrial claims, 'the close study of a global life drags us back necessarily to a deep, local history'.[33]

Many of the contributions thus explore, on a microlevel, the complex relationship cosmopolitan actors had with established socio-cultural, legal, and economic institutions. As Curtin pointed out, alien traders appeared doubly suspicious to their host societies. They evoked both the sempiternal distrust of foreigners and misgivings about merchants more broadly, who, in most societies, combined low social status with high wealth in a high-risk environment.[34] In this volume we demonstrate that it was not only the combination of filthy lucre and the whiff of foreignness that made commercial cosmopolitans suspicious, it was their subversive potential: the opportunities inherent in the ambiguous situation of the commercial cosmopolitan could afford individual actors without any formal powers a greater potential for autonomous agency. Chapters in this volume reveal how adopting commercial cosmopolitan strategies increased the margin of opportunities available to subaltern subjects, such as concubines and prostitutes from low-status ethnic groups in Siam or China (Chapters 1 and 2 by Hellman and Trakulhun).

Power and vulnerability are doubly intertwined in the position of the commercial cosmopolitan. On the one hand, this volume confirms the assertion made by Games with reference to early modern English subjects abroad: cosmopolitanism was a strategy often adopted from a position of weakness. Pursuing cosmopolitan tactics allowed vulnerable actors to increase their margin of action, be these the subaltern groups just mentioned, European agents trading outside direct colonial control in Southeast India and West Africa, independent Sino-Vietnamese trading communities in the Gulf of Thailand, or indeed a Sultanate seeking to navigate the increasing Anglo-American economic and imperial dominance (Chapters 3, 7, and 10 by Heijmans, Hang, and Presthold respectively). On the other hand, however, the very in-betweenness that gave commercial cosmopolitans increased room for manoeuvre also made them more vulnerable: they might be able to

Introduction 9

play both sides, but both sides could also turn on them. The situation cosmopolitans found themselves in thus always remained dangerously fragile. Little wonder then that when conflicts were brewing between Chinese officials and the European merchants in Canton, the Chinese compradors, interpreters, and servants fled from the foreign ships and factories as soon as possible.[35]

Taken together, global microhistory, global material culture studies, New Institutional Economics, advances in social network analysis, spatial theory, and New Cultural History's theorisation of hybridisation and transculturation in contact zones provide us with a new methodological apparatus that allows us to push our analysis further than was possible for Curtin and Polanyi. With these analytical tools we are able to discern the operational structures, practices, frictions, and overlaps within and between commercial communities in the early modern world. For the period between around 1500 and 1800 presents a crucial and unique era in the history of world trade and globalisation.

The early modern as a period of multiple commercial cosmopolitanisms

What we term 'commercial cosmopolitanism' is an age-old phenomenon: next to war, trade is perhaps the oldest cross-cultural connector and it has linked Eurasia and Africa for millennia. For most of this time Europe had not played a particularly important role in early Eurasian and African trade. By the time the Europeans rounded the Cape of Good Hope in 1488, Persian and Armenian merchants had been established in China for centuries, while the commercial nodes of the Indian Ocean world and great trading cities of the Islamic empires, such as Cairo, Aleppo or Constantinople, hosted multinational, multi-ethnic, and multi-faith commercial communities as a matter of course.[36] However, the early modern period presents a step change in the history of globalisation. Driven in part by exports of New World silver, the Spanish-Ameircan silver pesos discussed by Lane in Chapter 4, this period saw an hitherto unprecedented level of global connections.

While quantifiable economic globalisation in terms of price convergence may only have occurred in the nineteenth century, the early modern period was the first in history in which all heavily-populated landmasses were connected through sustained and systematic trade, with far-reaching consequences for all involved.[37] Following individual commodity chains reveals the interconnectedness of the early modern world. Silver and precious metals, mined in South America by enslaved peoples from West Africa, were shipped to Europe and to Asia to pay for spices, tea, and fine manufactured goods such as porcelain, cottons, and silk textiles, which in turn attracted consumers in Africa, the Americas, and Europe.[38] However, even though it was Europeans who provided the logistics of the transcontinental trade, they did not determine its logic. Rather, this was driven by East Asian fiscal

10   *Felicia Gottmann*

policy and the resulting demand for silver just as much as by the sophisticated preferences of African consumers.[39] In most of the global markets on which the Europeans operated, they were unable to dictate terms. What Bayly calls an age of 'proto-globalisation' was by no means a world of European hegemony.[40]

Even where limited by European colonisation, subaltern agency persisted: African slaves cultivated and traded new world foods, both in the Americas and in Africa, while Asian lascars were indispensable to the functioning of European ships trading the Indian Ocean. Moreover, in most parts of Africa and Asia where Europeans sought to trade, their position remained fragile and contested. They faced difficulties inserting themselves into regional trade networks, markets, and long-established commercial cultures in Asia and the Indian Ocean world but also in satisfying the demands of discerning consumers in East and West Africa. Whether in Africa, the Levant, or East Asia, Europeans were usually forced to abide by the terms set by local rulers, bankers, and merchants. Just like the many other trading communities they met there, they had to develop various different cosmopolitan strategies and behaviours to be able to ply their trade. In such spaces, Europeans were just one of many groups and individuals who sought to exploit the risks and opportunities inherent in cross-cultural trade. Given this multipolar character of the early modern world, the period thus saw different types of commercial cosmopolitanism, which differed substantially from those deployed under the later regimes of European imperialist hegemony. The assumption of this hegemony was geographically and temporarily uneven. It certainly coincided with the rise of Russia and the decline of the Safavid, Mughal, and Ottoman Empires, but it was not universally established until well into the nineteenth century – as illustrated by Jeremy Prestholdt's chapter, a study of Zanzibar's independent cosmopolitan commercial missions of the 1830s and 1840s, which provide the end point to this volume.

If cosmopolitanism was frequently born out of vulnerability and was always an act of mediation or compromise, it ceased as soon as the willingness or ability to compromise diminished. This could be due to a rise in sectarianism, as Livesey detects in Ireland (Chapter 13), but it could also be a simple question of power balance. Michael Talbot shows in Chapter 12 how insufficient institutional infrastructure and the lack of consular representation left North African merchants in a vulnerable situation in eighteenth-century European courts. Talbot's case studies form part of a wider trend also evident in Romaniello's chapter: once Western Europeans attained a dominant economic, military, and colonial position, their willingness to adapt to local commercial institutions diminished drastically. As soon as European powers had the ability to violently impose their own preferred modes of exchange together with the associated legal, political, and diplomatic institutions, they did so, be that in eighteenth-century North America and Bengal, or in nineteenth-century China and Japan. The economic institutions Europeans imposed were by no means solely those of free-market

Introduction 11

exchange and production. Monopolies persisted and were sometimes even strengthened under European control, particularly in Asia. Just as the Dutch VOC had jealously controlled export and production of spices on the Moluccas, the take-over by the British East India Company in Bengal, for instance, led to sustained attempts to impose monopolistic control over textile production.[41]

The great diversity of forms of production and exchange in the early modern period makes it impossible to apply clear labels such as 'capitalist', 'free-market', 'administered', 'trade' or 'tribute'. Polanyi already acknowledged that the commercial centres on the Malabar coast did not fit into his model of either free-market exchange or administered Ports of Trade. In this volume, Carlos and Hellman demonstrate that, thanks to the cosmopolitan commercial conventions in place, neither did Canton and Nagasaki, or the North American fur trade (Chapters 1 and 8). Before the advent of Western imperial hegemony, the early modern world was a multipolar one, with a plethora of different commercial practices and institutions, which in turn engendered diverse commercial cosmopolitan strategies. Today, when debates about free trade, fair trade, protectionism, and the sustainability of capitalism are raging once again and the world is again becoming increasingly multipolar, it is vital to understand such strategies.

This volume

Rather than providing mere narrative accounts of the various characteristics of commercial cosmopolitanism in different geographical, cultural, and political settings, this volume analyses the operational structures, practices, frictions, and failures of commercial cosmopolitanism in the early modern world. We do not argue that there was a single discernible type of cosmopolitan strategy but instead seek to appreciate them in all their complexities. Common to all forms of commercial cosmopolitanism, however, were two things. The first was the creative potential arising from the combination of various vernaculars. The results were new avenues for profit-making and value creation as well as new and hybrid objects, practices of consumption, production, and exchange. The second was the fundamental paradox of cosmopolitan practice: the cosmopolitan actor's ability to bridge two or more commercial cultures afforded them a competitive edge, and those in vulnerable or subaltern positions often found that adopting cosmopolitan commercial strategies was an effective means to expand their margin of opportunity. At the same time, the very hybridity and institutional in-betweenness that empowered commercial cosmopolitans also left them particularly vulnerable. The power and fragility of commercial cosmopolitanism at the same time as its – often unrealised – immense creative potential are at the heart of this book.

To explore this double aspect the contributions centre their analysis around five poles of investigation: cosmopolitan spaces, actors, objects,

12 *Felicia Gottmann*

practices, and institutional arrangements. Drawing on recent advances in spatial history, cultural theory, global material culture studies, and micro-history, chapters in Part I, 'Cosmopolitan Spaces, Objects, and Actors', investigate the multifaceted material objects of commerce which, symboli-cally and physically reappropriated, were themselves cosmopolitan. Some of these are the type of goods well-known to historians of global and inter-cultural trade such as textiles, ceramics, or tobacco. Some are much less obvious: North American furs, Dutch family portraits, or Chinese bibles. Finally, some objects become cosmopolitan only in their local use and combination: as Bronwen Everill demonstrates, practices of clustering cer-tain globally-traded and locally-produced goods allowed consumers along the Upper Guinea Coast to turn their homes and bodies into sites of a distinctive commercial cosmopolitanism. Spaces can be just as cosmopolitan and hybrid as objects. The often highly contested spaces in which the multicultural commercial interactions took place have previously been theorised as frontiers, contact zones, third spaces or 'middle grounds' and defined as loci of hybridisation and transculturation. As chapters in this section demonstrate, such spaces were characterised by the agency not only of cosmopolitan objects but also of individual actors whose subaltern status has so far eclipsed their commercial interventions: slaves, servants, concubines, prostitutes, and wives, all found strategies to leverage their intercultural and material capital.

In Part I, scholars working on early modern global trading routes and centres with multinational commercial communities thus investigate how their cosmopolitan spaces functioned, how they were policed, subverted, and exploited by the authorities, the individual actors, and the objects they traded. Lisa Hellman's chapter focusses on the enclosed but cosmopolitan commercial spaces of eighteenth-century Canton and Nagasaki, offering a multi-group comparison that evaluates the difficulties of balancing stability and profit, all the while paying close attention to the polyvalent material objects that underlay and accompanied this trade.

Similarly sensitive to the politics of space, Sven Trakulhun's contribu-tion investigates the role of Dutch East India Company (VOC) merchants in the vibrant cosmopolitan capital of Siam, analysing in particular the writings of one Company official, Jeremias van Vliet, which provide a unique insight not only into the history of early modern Thailand but also into the various social, political and economic entanglements that shaped his life.

In Chapter 3 Xing Hang investigates how Hà Tiên, located on what is now the Cambodian-Vietnamese border, came to flourish under the leadership of the Sino-Vietnamese creole Mạc Thiên Tứ in the eighteenth-century, not only as a multi-ethnic entrepôt for international trade but also as a site of cultural production and political intermediation.

Kris Lane traces the entangled story of perhaps the most cosmopolitan of all traded goods: the Spanish piece of eight. Minted in Spanish America and

Introduction 13

in peninsular Spain beginning in the late sixteenth-century, the silver peso of eight reals or 'piece of eight' became a truly global currency early in the seventeenth century. However, just like any other cosmopolitan actor, cosmopolitan objects like these coins could prove untrustworthy, causing immense damage to all who relied on their intermediation. When word spread of a huge fraud in the Spanish Empire's most important money supply, the royal mint at Potosí, modern-day Bolivia, the impact on trading networks stretching from Italy to India and the Philippines was immediate.

Still focussing on objects of trade, on tobacco in general and cigars in particular, in Chapter 5 Matthew Romaniello explores the history of a failure of what could have been a productive space of commercial cosmopolitanism. Early modern Russia had a long history of inviting foreign experts to establish commercial concerns within its borders. The tobacco workhouse set up by English traders to produce cigars in early eighteenth-century Moscow could have served as a cosmopolitan space of technological exchange between English specialists and a Russian labour force. Instead, the English government's instructions to recall the specialists in questions and destroy all tools reveals how easily political and diplomatic concerns could overrule cosmopolitan collaborations.

From the consumption of tobacco, grown by enslaved Africans in America and exported by English merchants to Russia, the next chapter turns to the bustling port cities of eighteenth-century West Africa, which, as Bronwen Everill argues, experienced the development of a newly Atlantic-inflected material cosmopolitanism. The region's engagement with global trade led to the incorporation of new consumer goods, arranged in characteristic combinations, into daily formal and informal rituals.

In this section's closing chapter Jeremy Prestholdt investigates how in the 1830s, in a time of increasing Anglo-American hegemony, one particular commercial practice – the trading voyage – and one particularly cosmopolitan commercial space and object, the Indian Ocean vessel that sailed from Zanzibar to New York in 1840, served to leverage the economic and political capital of the Sultanate of Oman and Zanzibar.

The volume's second part, 'Institutions, Practices, and Agents', focuses on the underlying structures of early modern cosmopolitanism, drawing on advances in business history, New Institutional Economics, and social network analysis. Institutional and legal frameworks were crucial to the functioning of international trade. In line with recent scholarship emphasising the role of strong states in economic development, Talbot demonstrates how the lack of diplomatic back-up left North African traders in a vulnerable position vis-à-vis European courts.[42] At the same time, cross-cultural commercial interactions could offer new opportunities for risk-takers thanks precisely to the lack of institutional control. Chapters in Part Two analyse how different types of firms, networks, and business organisations evolved to exploit legal loopholes and commercial in-between spaces in Europe, Asia, the Middle East and Africa. Commercial cosmopolitans could

14   *Felicia Gottmann*

exploit their weak links to multiple and fragmented networks to access new markets and opportunities, bridging national and religious divides while innovating and adopting more advanced practices in the process, as Antunes et al. and Livesey illustrate. Not all of these practices were crowned with success: next to inevitable principal agent problems, tensions between different legal frameworks and established cultural groupings meant that failures of cosmopolitan interactions and ideals were at least as prevalent as their success.

In Chapter 8 Ann Carlos investigates the workings of the multinational trade in furs, sourced in sub-Arctic Canada and made into hats in Europe. Providing an institutional analysis of the structures used by the Hudson's Bay Company to manage the classic agency problems of any long-distance trade, the chapter argues that the taste, preferences and demands of Indigenous actors structured the trade not merely in terms of their cultural practices but more importantly in terms of the prices received for their products. Indigenous traders, Carlos concludes, must be seen as equal partners in this trade.

The typical principal-agent problems of cross-cultural long-distance trade are also a central concern of Chapter 9. Using the example of the multinational team in charge of the first trading voyage sent out by the 1750s Prussian East India Company to Bengal, the study employs a mixture of thick description and social network analysis to investigate the specific challenges a small multi-national trading enterprise faced when operating across different legal frameworks.

The prevalence of cross-imperial networks and the necessity for European commercial agents to adapt to local political and legal frameworks are also a prevalent concern of Elisabeth Heijman's chapter which compares the operational structures of French commercial agents on the Coromandel Coast in India and the Bight of Benin in West Africa. Both Chapters 8 and 9 find that opportunistic inter-imperial collaboration between European agents abroad did not automatically entail genuine commercial cosmopolitanism.

The same cannot be said of the Dutch firm De Bruijn and Cloots operating from Lisbon that forms the subject of Chapter 11 jointly authored by Catia Antunes, Susana Münch Miranda and João Paulo Salvado. The Dutch traders' commercial cosmopolitanism, that is their ability to adapt their comparatively advanced mercantile knowledge and ways of conducting business to the workings of the Lisbon market, gave them an edge both over the Portuguese competition whose methods were less sophisticated and over their Dutch rivals who did not have the same access to Portuguese overseas colonies and markets.

The last two chapters, however, tell stories of the failures of cosmopolitanism towards the end of the early modern period. Using documents from the French, British, Ottoman, and Algerian archives, Michael Talbot's chapter charts the later eighteenth-century erosion of commercial cosmopolitanism in the Western Mediterranean. The articles of Algerian treaties,

Introduction 15

concluded between the Ottoman regencies of the Barbary coast and European powers such as Britain and France in the seventeenth and eighteenth centuries, had instated multi-layered legal and diplomatic frameworks facilitating peaceful commerce even in wartime. However, increasingly these were challenged and ignored by northern European powers intent on asserting their power in the region.

The final chapter by James Livesey investigates eighteenth-century Ireland, whose commercial elites' cosmopolitan strategies allowed them to operate across both the Catholic Empires of France and Spain and, via representation in London-based banks, also in trade with Protestant North America and the European continent. Livesey analyses how Irish elites nevertheless represented themselves as culturally divided and ultimately lost the cosmopolitan – and extremely profitable – ability to bridge different cultural spheres.

These final failures demonstrate how 'anti-cosmopolitanism', whether expressed as sectarianism or xenophobia, impoverishes societies: not only economically, but, by foreclosing the immense creative potential inherent in sustained peaceful transcultural interactions, also socially, culturally, and intellectually.

Notes

1 On nineteenth-century globalisation see C. A. Bayly, *The Birth of the Modern World, 1780–1914: Global Connections and Comparisons* (Oxford: Blackwell, 2004); Jürgen Osterhammel, *The Transformation of the World: A Global History of the Nineteenth Century*, trans. Patrick Camiller (Princeton: Princeton University Press, 2014).
2 Sheldon Pollock, 'Cosmopolitan and Vernacular in History', in *Cosmopolitanism,* ed. Carol A. Breckenridge, Sheldon Pollock, Homi K. Bhabha, and Dipesh Chakrabarty (Durham and London: Duke University Press, 2002), 15–53; idem, 'India in the Vernacular Millennium: Literary Culture and Polity 1000–1500', in *Early Modernities,* ed. Shmuel Eisenstadt, Wolfang Schluchter and Björn Wittrock, special issue of *Daedalus* 127, no. 3 (1998): 41–74. For a take on 'vernacular cultures' from the perspective of the history of knowledge, see 'AHR Forum: Vernacular Ways of Knowing', *American Historical Review* 123, no. 3 (June 2018).
3 Francesca Trivellato, *The Familiarity of Strangers. The Sephardic Diaspora, Livorno, and Cross-Cultural Trade in the Early Modem Period* (New Haven: Yale University Press, 2009), 178.
4 C.A.P. Antunes, 'Cutting corners: when borders, culture and empire do not matte' (Inaugural lecture at Leiden University held Friday, 9 June 2017), 6. https://openaccess.leidenuniv.nl/bitstream/handle/1887/51550/oratieAntunesENG.pdf?sequence=1 [accessed 14 Sept 2018]
5 See for instance Martha C. Nussbaum, *The Cosmopolitan Tradition: A Noble but Flawed Ideal* (Cambridge, Massachusetts: The Belknap Press of Harvard University Press, 2019); Anthony Appiah, *Cosmopolitanism: Ethics in A World of Strangers* (London: Penguin, 2007).
6 Philip J. Ivanhoe, 'Confucian Cosmopolitanism', *Journal of Religious Ethics*, 42 (2014): 22–44. Seema Alavi argues for a differentiation between the medieval

16 Felicia Gottmann

Ummah and a newly emergent 'Muslim Cosmopolitanism' as part of a counter-strategy to European imperial expansion: Seema Alavi, *Muslim Cosmopolitanism in the Age of Empire* (Cambridge Mass & London: Harvard University Press, 2015). Khairudin Aljunied, *Muslim Cosmopolitanism: Southeast Asian Islam in Comparative Perspective* (Edinburgh: Edinburgh University Press, 2017) provides a contemporary perspective. For a philosophical analysis and justification of cosmopolitanism see Appiah, *Cosmopolitanism.*

7 Eric Brown, 'Hellenistic Cosmopolitanism', in *A Companion to Ancient Philosophy*, ed. Mary Louise Gill and Pierre Pellegrin (Oxford: Blackwell, 2006), 549–58. On the link between the two see Martha C. Nussbaum, "Kant and Stoic Cosmopolitanism," *Journal of Political Philosophy* 5, (1997): 1–25.

8 On the Enlightenment ideal of on trade as promoting peaceful cosmopolitanism see: Thomas Schlereth, *The Cosmopolitan Ideal in Enlightenment Thought: Its Form and Function in the Ideas of Franklin, Hume and Voltaire, 1694–1790* (Notre Dame and London: University of Notre Dame Press, 1977); Karen O'Brien, *Narratives of the Enlightenment: Cosmopolitan History from Voltaire to Gibbon* (Cambridge: Cambridge University Press, 1997); and David Adams and Galin Tihanov, eds. *Enlightenment Cosmopolitanism* (Oxford: Legenda, 2011); Margaret C. Jacob, *Strangers Nowhere in the World: The Rise of Cosmopolitanism in Early Modern Europe* (Philadelphia: University of Pennsylvania Press, 2006). On the *philosophes'* awareness of the difficult relationship of trade to colonisation and warfare see: Sankar Muthu, *Enlightenment against Empire* (Princeton: Princeton University Press, 2009); Sunil M. Agnani, *Hating Empire Properly: The Two Indies and the Limits of Enlightenment Anticolonialism* (New York: Fordham University Press, 2016); Anoush Fraser Terjanian, *Commerce and its Discontents in Eighteenth-Century French Political Thought* (Cambridge: Cambridge University Press, 2016); Felicia Gottmann, "Intellectual History as Global History: Voltaire's *Fragments sur l'Inde* and the Problem of Enlightened Commerce," in *New Global Connections: India and Europe in the Long Eighteenth Century,* ed. Gabriel Sanchez, Simon Davies, and Daniel Roberts (Oxford: Voltaire Foundation, 2014), 141–55.

9 David Hancock, *Citizens of the World: London Merchants and the Integration of the British Atlantic Community, 1735–1785* (Cambridge and New York: Cambridge University Press, 1997); Alison Games, *The Web of Empire: English Cosmopolitans in an Age of Expansion, 1560–1660* (Oxford: Oxford University Press, 2008); Jacob, *Strangers Nowhere.* Cf. *Cosmopolitan Networks in Commerce and Society 1660–1914*, ed. Andreas Gestrich and Margrit Schulte Beerbühl (London: German Historical Institute, 2011).

10 Alison Games, *The Web of Empire,* 10.

11 Ulrich Beck, "Varieties of Second Modernity and the Cosmopolitan Vision," *Theory, Culture & Society* 33, no. 7–8 (2016); Ulrich Beck, *Weltrisikogesellschaft: Auf der Suche nach der verlorenen Sicherheit* (Frankfurt am Main: Suhrkamp, 2011), 285–374. See also Anders Blok and Sabine Selchow, "Special Theme Introduction: Methodological Cosmopolitanism Across the Socio-cultural Sciences," *Global Networks* 20, no. 3 (2020).

12 Originally developed in Karl Polanyi, Conrad M. Arensberg, Harry Pearson, eds. *Trade and Market in the Early Empires: Economies in History and Theory* (New York: Free Press, 1957), the model is best summarised in Polanyi, "Ports of Trade in Early Societies," *The Journal of Economic History*, 23 (1963): 30–45.

13 See the contributions by Ann C. Carlos and Lisa Hellman in this volume. For a critique of Polanyi's characterisation of trade organisation in Ouidah see Robin Law, *Ouidah: The Social History of a West African Slaving Port, 1727–1892* (Athens: Ohio University Press, 2005).

Introduction 17

14 Philip Curtin, *Cross-Cultural Trade in World History* (Cambridge and New York: Cambridge University Press, 1984), ix.

15 Richard White, *The Middle Ground: Indians, Empires, and Republics in the Great Lakes region, 1650–1815* (Cambridge and New York: Cambridge University Press, 1991); Mary Louise Pratt, *Imperial Eyes: Travel Writing and Transculturation* (London, New York: Routledge, 1992); Homi K. Bhabha, *The Location of Culture* (London, New York: Routledge, 1994); Sebastian Jobs and Gesa Mackenthun, eds. *Agents of Transculturation Border-Crossers, Mediators, Go-Betweens* (Münster: Waxmann, 2013).

16 For a brief overview see Peter Burke, *Cultural Hybridity* (Cambridge and New York: Cambridge University Press, 2009).

17 Anne Gerritsen and Giorgio Riello, "Spaces of Global Interactions: the Material Landscapes of Global History," in *Writing Material Culture History*, ed. Gerritsen and Riello (London and New York: Bloomsbury, 2015), 111–13. Idem, "Introduction: The Global Lives of Things. Material Culture in the First Global Age," in *The Global Lives of Things: The Material Culture of Connections in the First Global Age*, ed. Gerritsen and Riello (London: Routledge, 2015), 1–28.

18 On colonial power-relations see White and Pratt above. For intermediation in knowledge-production see Kapil Raj, *Relocating Modern Science: Circulation and the Construction of Knowledge in South Asia and Europe, 1650–1900* (Basingstoke: Palgrave Macmillan, 2007) and Simon Schaffer, Lissa Roberts, Kapil Raj, and James Delbourgo, eds. *The Brokered World: Go-betweens and Global Intelligence, 1770–1820* (Sagamore Beach, MA: Science History Publications, 2009). However, see Cátia Antunes, Leor Halevi, and Francesca Trivellato, eds. *Religion and Trade: Cross-cultural Exchanges in World History, 1000–1900* (Oxford: Oxford University Press, 2014) and to some extent also Jobs and Mackenthun, eds. *Agents of Transculturation*.

19 On the New Institutional Economists' debt to Polanyi see: Douglass C. North, "Markets and Other Allocation Systems in History: The Challenge of Karl Polanyi," *Journal of European Economic History* 6 no 3, (1977): 703–16; Keith Hart, "Karl Polanyi's Legacy," *Development and Change* 39, no. 6 (2008): 1135–43.

20 Emily Erikson, *Between Monopoly and Free Trade: The English East India Company* (Princeton: Princeton University Press, 2014). Ann M. Carlos, "Principal-Agent Problems in Early Trading Companies: A Tale of Two Firms." *The American Economic Review* 82, no. 2 (1992): 140–5. Cf. *Merchants and Trade Networks in the Atlantic and the Mediterranean, 1550–1800. Connectors of Commercial Maritime Systems*, ed. Manuel Herrero Sánchez and Klemens Kaps (London and New York: Routledge, 2017).

21 Amongst the New Institutional Economists, Avner Greif's explicit incorporation of social norms and beliefs into the concept of institutions are particularly helpful in this regard. See Avner Greif, *Institutions and the Path to the Modern Economy: Lessons from Medieval Trade* (Cambridge: Cambridge University Press, 2006), for a historically-sensitive critique of his findings see Trivellato, *The Familiarity of Strangers*, 13–15.

22 On the multicultural nature of smuggling see Alan L. Karras, *Smuggling: Contraband and Corruption in World History* (Lanham, MD: Rowman and Littlefield, 2009). Cf. Silvia Marzagalli, "Was Warfare Necessary for the Functioning of Eighteenth-Century Colonial Systems? Some Reflections on the Necessity of Cross-Imperial and Foreign Trade in the French Case," in *Beyond Empires: Global, Self-Organizing, Cross-Imperial Networks, 1500-1800*, ed. Cátia Antunes and Amélia Polónia, 253–77; and Jurre Knoest on Japanese

18 Felicia Gottmann

smuggling, Michael Kempe on global piracy, and Bram Hoonhout on smuggling in the Guyanas in the same volume.
23 For an overview see Joanna Innes, "Networks in British History," *East Asian Journal of British History* 5 (2016): 51–75.
24 Brubaker cited in Trivellato, *The Familiarity of Strangers*, 11.
25 Mark S. Granovetter, "The Strength of Weak Ties," *American Journal of Sociology* 78, no. 6 (1973): 1360–80.
26 Ronald S. Burt, "Structural Holes and Good Ideas," *American Journal of Sociology* 110, no. 2 (2004): 349–99. Cf. Burt, *Structural Holes: The Social Structure of Competition* (Cambridge, MA: Harvard University Press, 1992).
27 *Beyond Empires: Global, Self-Organizing, Cross-Imperial Networks, 1500–1800*, ed. Cátia Antunes, and Amélia Polónia (Leiden, Boston: Brill, 2016). Ana Sofia Ribeiro, *Early Modern Trading Networks in Europe: Cooperation and the Case of Simon Ruiz* (Abingdon, New York: Routledge, 2016).
28 Barney Warf and Santa Arias, eds. *The Spatial Turn: Interdisciplinary Perspectives* (London: Routledge, 2008); Mathias Middell and Katja Naumann, "Global History and the Spatial Turn: from the Impact of Area Studies to the Study of Critical Junctures of Globalization," *Journal of Global History* 5 (2010): 149–70; Beat Kümin and Cornelie Usborne, "At Home and in the Workplace: A Historical Introduction to the 'Spatial Turn'," *History and Theory* 52, no. 3 (2014): 305–18.
29 For an introduction see Riello and Gerritsen, "Spaces of Global Interactions," in Riello and Gerritsen, eds. *Writing Material Culture History*; and Riello and Gerritsen, eds. *The Global Lives of Things: The Material Culture of Connections*.
30 Robert Finlay, *The Pilgrim Art: Cultures of Porcelain in World History* (Berkeley, CA: University of California Press, 2010); Anne Gerritsen, *The City of Blue and White: Chinese Porcelain and the Early Modern World* (Cambridge: Cambridge University Press, 2020).
31 Curtin, *Cross-Cultural Trade*, x.
32 Tonio Andrade, "A Chinese Farmer, Two African Boys, and a Warlord: Toward a Global Microhistory," *Journal of World History* 21, no. 4 (2010): 573–91; Natalie Zemon Davis, "Decentering History: Local Stories and Cultural Crossings in a Global World," *History and Theory* 50 (2011): 188–202; Sanjay Subrahmanyam, *Three Ways to be Alien: Travails and Encounters in the Early Modern World* (Waltham, Mass: Brandeis University Press, 2011).
33 John-Paul A. Ghobrial, "The Secret Life of Elias of Babylon and the Uses of Global Microhistory," *Past and Present* 222, no. 1 (2014): 51–93 (p. 59).
34 See Curtin, *Cross-Cultural Trade*, 6.
35 Li Chen, *Chinese Law in Imperial Eyes: Sovereignty, Justice, and Transcultural Politics* (Publisher: New York: Columbia University Press, 2018), 30.
36 Ronald Findlay and Kevin H. O'Rourke, *Power and Plenty: Trade, War, and the World Economy in the Second Millennium* (Princeton, NJ: Princeton University Press, 2007). Anthony Reid, *Southeast Asia in the Age of Commerce, 1450–1680*, 2 vols (New Haven, Yale University Press, 1988–93). James D. Tracy, ed. *The Rise of Merchant Empires: Long-Distance Trade in the Early Modern World, 1350–1750* (Cambridge: Cambridge University Press, 1990); Curtin, *Cross-Cultural Trade*, 90–135.
37 Dennis O. Flynn and Arturo Giráldez, "Born Again: Globalization's Sixteenth-Century Origins," *Pacific Economic Review* 13, no. 3 (2008): 359–87. Cf. Flynn and Giráldez, "Cycles of Silver: Global Economic Unity through the Mid-Eighteenth Century," *Journal of World History* 13, no. 2 (2002): 391–427; Kevin O'Rourke and Jeffrey G. Williamson, "After Columbus: Explaining Europe's

Overseas trade boom, 1500–1800," *Journal of Economic History* 62, no. 2 (2002): 417–56.

38 For case studies on specific commodity chains see Maxine Berg, Felicia Gottmann, Hanna Hodacs, Chris Nierstrasz, eds. *Goods from the East. Trading Eurasia 1600–1830* (New York and Basingstoke: Palgrave Macmillan, 2015); Sidney W. Mintz, *Sweetness and Power: The Place of Sugar in Modern History* (New York: Viking, 1985); Kris Lane, *Colour of Paradise: The Emerald in the Age of Gunpowder Empires* (New Haven: Yale University Press, 2010); Finlay, *The Pilgrim Art*; Woodruff D. Smith, "Complications of the Commonplace: Tea, Sugar, and Imperialism," *Journal of Interdisciplinary History* 23, no. 2 (1992): 259–79; Giorgio Riello, Cotton: The Fabric that Made the Modern World (Cambridge: Cambridge University Press, 2013); Sven Beckert, *Empire of Cotton: A New History of Global Capitalism* (London: Allen Lane, 2014) as well as Flynn and Giráldez above.

39 Shogo Suzuki, Yongjin Zhang, and Joel Quirk, eds. *International Orders in the Early Modern World: Before the Rise of the West* (London New York: Routledge, Taylor & Francis Group, 2016). Jeremy Prestholdt, *Domesticating the World: African Consumerism and the Genealogies of Globalization* (Berkeley and Los Angeles: University of California Press, 2008). Serge Gruzinski, *L'Aigle et le Dragon. Démesure européenne et Mondialisation au XVIe siècle* (Paris: Fayard, 2012).

40 C.A. Bayly, "'Archaic' and 'Modern' Globalization in the Eurasian and African Arena, c. 1750–1850," in *Globalization in World History*, ed. A. G. Hopkins (New York: W. W. Norton & Company, 2002), 47–73. Cf. Bayly, *The Birth of the Modern World*.

41 Hameeda Hossain, *The Company Weavers of Bengal: The East India Company and the Organization of Textile Production in Bengal, 1750–1813* (Oxford: Oxford University Press, 1988).

42 A similar case is made by Sebouh Aslanian with regard to the increasingly precarious position of Armenian merchants in relation to the British East India Company: Aslanian, "Trade Diaspora versus Colonial State: Armenian Merchants, the English East India Company, and the High Court of Admiralty in London, 1748–1752," *Diaspora: A Journal of Transnational Studies* 13, no. 1 (2004): 37–100. On the importance of the State and institutional support in global history more widely see Peer Vries, *State, Economy and the Great Divergence. Great Britain and China, 1680s–1850s* (London: Bloomsbury, 2015); and Prasannan Parthasarathi, *Why Europe Grew Rich and Asia Did Not: Global Economic Divergence, 1600–1850* (Cambridge and New York: Cambridge University Press, 2011).

Part I

Cosmopolitan spaces, objects, and actors

1 Controlling the golden geese

Canton, Nagasaki and the limits of hybridity

Lisa Hellman

From the late seventeenth century to the late eighteenth century, Nagasaki and Canton constituted the two primary zones for maritime trade with Europe in Japan and China respectively. Both constitute classic examples of early modern maritime encounters between East Asia and Europe in which the Europeans did not hold the upper hand, and were also conceived of as typical Ports of Trade, according to Karl Polanyi, as being natively administered spaces, as opposed to competitive price-making markets.[1] In the case of Canton, this categorisation is tied to an outdated idea of the Qing government as somewhat disinterested in foreign trade.[2] Indeed, to see these ports as primarily administered exaggerate the difference as being one of kind, rather than just of degree, between how European and East Asian international markets were regulated: in these ports, local Asian monopolies on maritime trade met European monopoly companies. Instead, Canton and Nagasaki can be placed within the framework of global history as gateways to globalisation not entirely unlike other harbours.[3] Doing so stresses how they were vibrant contact zones, with a mix of ethnic, cultural and economic groups. The global history perspective also brings to the fore that while the European trade was hugely profitable, it was not the driving force: Nagasaki's largest trading group were the Chinese, and Canton had been an international port for centuries before the Europeans arrived.

These two harbours were regulated in a number of ways, based on the aim to balance profit and control. These systems placed the Europeans in just the position of weakness that Alison Games argues was the point from which cosmopolitan strategies were adopted.[4] However, despite being trading hubs, their asymmetric power relations, and the diversity of groups active there, neither of these ports serve as a good example of assimilation as a commercial strategy. Rather, these hubs showcase the limits of hybridity. Therefore, to compare the European commercial activities in Canton and Nagasaki, in light of the heterogeneity of local actors and the multitude of hierarchies of power, can further our discussion of power and vulnerability in transcultural trade and illuminate the diverse power relations that cosmopolitan strategies both exploited and created. Nagasaki and Canton illuminate friction between East Asian and European discourses of good commercial practices, as well as the

Figure 1.1 Island of Deshima, Dutch East India Company. Wellcome Collection.

connection between the political, economic, and cultural factors that lay behind the ways these ports were policed.

China and Japan had similar regulations of their maritime trade with Europe. These were established in the early seventeenth and eighteenth centuries, respectively. Trade was restricted to the foreign quarters outside the city walls in Canton, and to Deshima and the Chinese quarters in Nagasaki. The policing of the international trade in Nagasaki began in the early 1600s. Whereas the year 1661 saw the peak of the trade, it was followed by a clampdown on, and increased control of, the trade. In 1715, new regulations again reduced the trade volume. The time frame for the strictest regulations, if not the bulk of the trade, are similarly mirrored in China. In Canton, practices for controlling this trade evolved during the first half of the eighteenth century, and were later codified in 1761.[5] The regulations were the result of gradual processes, but by the mid-eighteenth century both harbours had well-established rules on foreign trade.

There is a broad range of studies on these ports, as well as comparisons between them. They represent interesting examples of early modern hubs of globality and zones for intercultural entanglements outside European colonial control. Researchers increasingly stress the multiplicity of groups and actors active there, as well as the importance of placing them in an Asian mercantile and cultural framework – even if the actors studied and worked within a European trading company.[6] Moreover, these commercial spaces are only comprehensible when placed within certain systems of political and religious discourses. There had been European Christian missions in both Japan and China, but by the early eighteenth century, Christian missions were forbidden – and missionaries persecuted. The officials in both China and Japan drew inspiration from each other on how to relate to Europeans and other foreign traders – specifically how to keep trade flourishing without relinquishing political control or destabilising the coastal towns.[7] As a result, Chinese and Japanese authorities consciously

Figure 1.2 The foreign factories of Canton, about 1784–1785. 2002.6.6, Collection of The Corning Museum of Glass, Corning, NY.

worked to prevent foreign traders from settling, and Canton and Nagasaki were set up far from the capitals of Beijing and Edo.

Part of these similarities can be tied to these countries' internal political situation. When establishing these systems, Japan and China had just suffered from a civil war and a foreign invasion respectively, and the countries were fraught with ethnic, political, and religious tensions. In response, the governments attempted to control the administration, the military groups, the culture of the elites, the women, and the Christian missions – anything that could be considered a threat to internal stability. The policies regarding trade should be set in relation to national policies attempting to establish an overarching control, rather than expressing some form of xenophobia or a desire for national seclusion. The Chinese and Japanese administrations had a clear idea what type of contact zone they wanted: one focused on trade, rather than political interaction, and open attempts at cultural integration were perceived as threats to this stability rather than as commercial strategies.

The similarity in the control mechanisms in Canton and Nagasaki (regulations on international maritime trade, a ban on Christianity, and a wary view of the presence of the foreign traders), in the way these trading contacts were interpreted in Europe, and in the connections between them, constitute good reasons to study them together during the eighteenth

26   *Lisa Hellman*

century: they offer a possibility to study European cosmopolitan commercial practices in East Asia and the limits of such strategies. Environments with asymmetric power relations such as these encouraged cosmopolitan tactics for vulnerable actors but, here, we can trace to what degree cosmopolitanism were tactics in the face of weakness, or rather fit with imposed expectations. From received comparative frameworks, it is clear that an analysis of the commercial relations in Canton and Nagasaki must consider the spatial construction as well as the legal frameworks, but also the linguistic and gendered contacts.[8] This comparison follows not only the conditionality of the commercial interaction, but also resulting group constructions and power relations. Here, rather than becoming zones for cultural hybridity, alterity was used more as acquiescence than subversion.

Multiplicity of groups and limits of hybridity

There is a deep-rooted myth that Tokugawa Japan and Qing China have been 'closed' or isolated countries, a narrative connected to the idea of the 'Sakoku' or as 'Eastern xenophobia' and has long since been disproved.[9] While the reality was a varied – but regulated – contact with other countries and cultures, this discourse of closedness make the ports particularly exciting venues in which to study cosmopolitan commercial practices. In addition, a closer look at the trading spaces in Canton and Nagasaki show not just zones for regulation or, in Polanyi's terms, administered, but zones of multi-party organic interaction.

From 1635, the Chinese were allowed to trade in Nagasaki. Once the Qing had switched to an active trade policy, by 1684, the number of ships had increased. Soon, more than 100 Chinese ships per year sailed to Nagasaki, a number the European vessels never came close to. The increased control of the Dutch also applied to the Chinese trading group: from 1689, they were housed in a separate quarter in Nagasaki, and from 1715 there were stricter controls on the amounts of trade and the issuance of licenses to trade there. The Dutch began their trade operation in Japan in the port of Hirado. In the early sixteenth century, the Japanese government constructed the fan-shaped island of Deshima in Nagasaki. This island was initially intended to house the Portuguese traders in Japan, who were treated with increasing suspicion because of their connection to the Christian missions. When the Portuguese were banned from Japan in 1639, the Dutch were made to move to Deshima.[10] From 1613 to 1623, the British East India Company attempted to establish themselves in Japan, during which time they were deeply involved with the Chinese trading houses in Nagasaki.[11] The ties between the Chinese and the British are a good sign of how the Nagasaki trade primarily was a China trade; indeed, the Dutch company trade in Japan was aimed more at the intra-Asian than the European market. Neither the 'Dutch' nor the 'Chinese' label denote a homogenous group. Even if a ship was formally Dutch, far from everyone on board was, while the Chinese group also included, for example, Vietnamese traders. The most important distinction from the Japanese point of view was not which group of foreigners they belonged to, but whether they settled. If they chose to establish a domicile in Nagasaki, as indeed some of the Chinese interpreters did, they could fall under a different jurisdiction.[12]

Canton offered a no less of complex mix of groups. The Qing government promoted trade from 1685, and from around 1720 European trade was concentrated to the foreign quarters outside of Canton. Canton was open to trade with all foreign groups – and commonly they were treated the same, something that rankled the large trading companies and groups, but benefited the smaller. Side by side in foreign quarters that were just a few hundred metres long lived and worked traders from European monopoly companies, as well as Jewish, Parsi, Armenian, and Muslim traders.[13] Canton and Nagasaki did not constitute contact zones for a meeting between two homogenous groups, but cooperation and conflicts between various groups of locals and foreigners, and their most successful strategy was that of separation.

Only a few Japanese and Chinese merchant houses were allowed to take part in the main part of the foreign trade in both of their native countries – it was a monopoly system on the Asian as well as the European side. The spatial conditions were not only intertwined with an imposed similarity between groups, but also the creation of difference within them – for example, of class. In Canton, the only people to live in the foreign quarters were the handful of supercargoes and their servants and slaves. The largest group of foreigners, the sailors, spent most of their time in the harbour of Whampoa a few kilometres down the river. In Nagasaki, the only people who stayed in Deshima were the *opperhoofden*, or chief traders, while the sailors lived on board the ships. That spatial class difference would not differ much back in China or Europe, and it was upheld as much by the foreign officers as by the local authorities, both wanting a smooth trading season.[14]

The hierarchies within the trading groups could be extreme. In both Canton and Nagasaki, there were slaves arriving with the Europeans from Africa or South Asia. The role of these slaves in the commercial interactions, not the least from smuggling, needs more research, but apparent from their appearance in the court records from Deshima and the Canton is the variety of the tasks the slaves carried out, as well as their mobility.[15] The relationship between slavery and cosmopolitanism was not an easy one at this time. While cosmopolitan thinkers in Europe criticised slavery as part of their humanistic agenda, the same processes of globalisation preserved European slavery, for example in the Caribbean, a contradiction remarked upon at the time.[16] While several European company traders criticised oriental slavery and subjugation, everyday life for the officers in Canton and Nagasaki included being waited on by slaves. In Nagasaki in particular, the number of slaves far exceeded that of foreign traders. Slaves were very commonly depicted in Japanese paintings of Deshima.[17] Both in

28 Lisa Hellman

Japan and China, the slaves were considered typical for the European trading spaces.

Another important feature of the foreign spaces in China and Japan is the matter of religion. In China, the mission was still going on by the 1720s, when it had been banned in Japan almost a hundred years before. By the 1730s, Christianity was strictly forbidden in both China and Japan, and missionaries and converts were extradited or even executed. In China, the focus was not primarily on restricting Christian texts but rather on people, and there is a striking lack of Christian activity or missions for much of the eighteenth century.[18] In Japan, written material on Christianity was banned, and the ships were searched for such material. As the Japanese authorities had established, traders could be Christians 'in their hearts' as long as they did not attempt any outwards demonstrations. All Japanese residents had to register at a temple, to confirm their adherence to the ban on Christianity. After a Chinese temple had been erected in the Chinese trading quarters in Nagasaki, the Chinese traders were subject to the same system of control. Most who got caught carrying bibles were Chinese Christian traders, not Dutch. In the same vein, while the Chinese traders were made to tread on pictures of the Holy Virgin, a practice called *fumi-e*, to prove that they were not Christian, the Dutch were exempt from the practice.[19] While the Chinese were primary suspects for being Christian, Dutch trade representatives presented themselves as anti-Catholic, and against the 'Popish religion'.[20] These spaces can neither be comprehended as a two-party-encounter, nor as melting pots: practices of cultural mergers were seen as threatening stability.

It is also in relation to the harmony of the trade that one should view the policing of female presence: women were seen as a destabilising factor in both Canton and Nagasaki. Therefore, foreign men and local women (of a similar class) were strictly separated, and foreign women were either discouraged or forbidden to come to the harbour. Women were considered to be the key to settling, and to integrating into another society, and neither the Japanese nor the Chinese authorities wanted to encourage that – the goal was profit, not hybridity. In other early modern ports, women played a crucial role as linguistic and cultural go-betweens. In Canton and Nagasaki, the separation between men and women were a key part of how the space was policed, and how limits were put on hybridity.[21]

There were, however, differences to how this gender separation was carried out. Some foreign women came to Canton, but before the beginning of the nineteenth century, they were preciously few. In addition, there were contacts with local prostitutes, in particular of the boat people minority, Tanka, living on the Pearl River. However, Tanka were marginalised in the Chinese society, which might be a reason for why this contact was, if not allowed, then ignored. As the contact was formally forbidden, local women in Canton who did meet foreign men could not openly play the role of broker. In Japan, contrastingly, there was a formalised system for interactions between foreign, both Dutch and Chinese, traders and the Japanese women who were their prostitutes and companions, the *yūjo*. From 1630, there were regulations on mixed children from these marriages, and from 1715 these regulations became even more strict. These women were the only Japanese allowed to visited the foreign compounds, making them both cultural and practical go-betweens. It is not entirely certain what position these women held in society. The foreign liaisons were bound to end after a few trade seasons, and mixed children were not allowed to leave Japan. Consequently, while some of these women seem to have been able to return home to their families, meaning that they were not all ostracised, they were still in a vulnerable position, with little room for manoeuvre.[22]

There are several ways in which one might interpret the position of these women, as well as other marginal actors of the foreign compounds such as slaves. The special position they were placed in by the Japanese administration could make them stakeholders in the trade.[23] The ambiguous position of the cosmopolitan could potentially afford those with little formal influence a greater agency, but it might equally be true that in Canton and Nagasaki the local societal marginalisation, for example of certain groups of women, was a presupposition for the cosmopolitanism practices and cultural brokerage of the male traders. Consequently, while the fluidity of cosmopolitanism could potentially be both empowering and precarious, is not entirely clear which groups these cosmopolitan practices were rewarding.

Both Canton and Nagasaki were, in effect, arenas for interactions between diverse foreign and local groups. As Francesca Trivellato rightly points out, such groups consistently changed, and were also constructed in and as an effect of their interaction.[24] During the height of the control of the trade – that is, the first half of the eighteenth century – the foreign traders did remain culturally distinct and politically marginalised, just as Philip Curtin suggests a successful cross-cultural trader would.[25] However, doing so did not necessarily permit them to act as cultural brokers, nor did the contact over time reduce the need for brokerage. In these circumstances, the success of the foreign traders relied on an acceptance of their relative weakness, just as elsewhere in Asia, but the most useful strategy was one of cultural distance.

This comparison also underlines the need to use the concept of hybridity with caution.[26] Homi Bhabha's concept of hybridity is heatedly debated, one concern being that instead of a field of 'productive play' between cultures, it risks becoming a fixed, stable identity descriptor itself – in the worst case, hybridity is simply a new kind of transcendental signifier, one that presumes that cultures produce alterity when meeting, and that there is an inherent and political drive for change in that entanglement.[27] Feminist criticism of Bhabha's coupling of hybridity and cosmopolitanism stress how the idea of a 'hybrid culture' as a prerequisite for cosmopolitan competence is deeply problematic, as it places immigrants, mixed marriages, and their potential children in a particular position as forces of change that produce alterity, which is inherently tied to counter-culture.[28] In both Nagasaki and Canton

30 *Lisa Hellman*

there was, rather than conscious use of alterity, an imposed homogeneity of diverse foreign groups, in which they were forced to share a space – simultaneous with their forced separation from most of the locals – as well as a conscious use of class and gender hierarchies to uphold the order in this separate system. Hybridity might even have been forced upon local groups considered marginal enough not to cause potential disruption.

Language

A successful trader either needed access to a go-between with language skills, or know multiple languages himself. This stress on languages would have been even stronger for actors identifying as cosmopolitans. In the eighteenth-century European intellectual debates on cosmopolitanism, languages played a special part, as they represent the potential to create a universal conversation, and how and which languages should be learned was debated.[29] The regulations of the trading quarters of Canton and Nagasaki show clearly that the Chinese and the Japanese administration shared this view of the importance of languages. As the goal was to keep the harmony of the foreign quarters while retaining profit, that is to guard the golden goose, the effect, however, was a strictly regulated access to language learning. Rather than being results of preconceived and set groups, the division between foreign traders and locals were that of a continuously upheld difference and imposed separation, also in terms of language.

Foreigners were not allowed to learn Chinese or Japanese, and communication was supposed to rely entirely on official interpreters. The three groups of interpreters (the ones in the Canton, the Dutch, and the Chinese quarters) worked as go-betweens. The sources available to us provide a lot more information about the interpreters in Nagasaki, than about those in Canton. The latter did not play the same role as cultural and scientific broker as the interpreters in Nagasaki did. This system simultaneously provided control, and facilitated the trade – the two matters did not necessarily contradict each other. The control enabled bridging the space, albeit in very particular ways.[30]

In Nagasaki, there were specialised translators both to Chinese and to Dutch. The Dutch language functioned as a symbol for this foreign trade, and on paintings depicting the island of Deshima it was common to copy Dutch words or phrases.[31] However, Chinese was also considered an exotic and foreign language. In scholarly circles in China, there was an increased interest in the Japanese language during the late Ming dynasty.[32] On the ground in Japan, however, the traders largely remained dependent on the interpreters. And while Chinese knowledge, that is both knowledge about China and knowledge in Japanese, had a special role within the Japanese society, very few Japanese could actually speak Chinese, especially not the traders' dialect.[33] Instituted already in the beginning of the seventeenth century, and parallel in the different domains, these positions eventually became hereditary. While they initially were assigned the position as interpreters, the scope of their assignment eventually expanded. In 1751, when a board of control of the Chinese quarters was instituted, the responsibility of the interpreters included knowledge of the other countries, religious control and general responsibility of the Dutch and Chinese foreign quarters respectively. By the end of the Tokugawa era there was a group of naturalised Chinese in Nagasaki, and a Chinese language school was instituted; thereby, they might be the closest thing to a 'classic' hybrid group that this port environment can offer.[34] In general, however, the diversity of language in these commercial zones was used by the authorities as much as a tool for cultural separation as it was used for integration by the traders themselves.

In Canton, Pidgin English gradually developed as a joint language for international communication in the foreign quarters. It was a language common to many different groups, including Chinese merchants and dock workers, but excluding the officials.[35] This very language was a hybrid: Cantonese Pidgin English has been called the 'mother of all pidgins' as the word 'pidgin' is derived from the word 'business' in Cantonese.[36] What it reflects, however, is not a merger, but a layer of imposed control and homogeneity. In time, the production of Chinese-Pidgin vocabularies strengthened the perception in China of the foreigners as a homogeneous group speaking one language. Eventually, the language further policed the potential for cultural or ethnic hybridity: Pidgin was the key to life in Canton, but rather than opening the doors to mainland China, it restricted foreigners to contacts with the Chinese in the foreign quarters. As the Governor-General Li Shiyao explained in the mid-eighteenth century, foreign traders should have no need for interactions, nor thus a vocabulary, beyond that needed for selling and buying goods.[37] Pidgin English – while being an essential communication tool between Chinese and foreign traders – eventually served the aims of the Chinese language policy. European missionaries in China argued that Pidgin English distorted the Sino–foreign contact and eventually the language became a symbol of the foreigners' confinement.[38]

There is also a gender and ethnic aspect to these language skills. In Canton, Tanka women interacted with the Europeans far more openly and far more often than any other group of local women, and there are also records of these women speaking pidgin.[39] Similarly, the prostitutes in Nagasaki, the *yūjo*, are recorded as having spoken Dutch, as well as Chinese, and in effect thus acting as cultural and local interpreters. However, they were not welcome to invest in the commercial interactions. In both cases, there is little sign of the women commonly knowing how to read and write these foreign tongues. To the contrary, an eighteenth-century satirical Japanese verse about the *yūjo* and their quarter read:

Maruyama —

32   Lisa Hellman

> where letters come to women
> which they cannot read[40]

It was the marginalised position of these women that made it possible and necessary for them to acquire linguistic skills, whereas the cosmopolitan traders could not.

Language did not only constitute an imposed difference in these trading environments, it was also the basis for similarity. In contrast to the self-assigned universalism of the cosmopolitan ideal, however, sameness was imposed on foreigners in both Canton and Nagasaki. In Canton, a notion of the foreigner as a joint group was used increasingly often from the end of the seventeenth century. The first term used was that of 'foreigner', *yi*, which applied to all who were non-Chinese. This goes into the general Qing discourse of barbarian/civilised, where the key difference was 'Chinese or not', not subdivisions thereof. Eventually, a notion of the European/Western also developed, although that was not so much an ethnic distinction but a practical one, applying to any non-Chinese traders in Canton regardless of religion, ethnicity, or nationality. Eventually, the use of a joint term for all foreigners, such as *fangui* (which the Europeans translated as 'foreign devils') became a way to argue for Chinese xenophobia.[41] Foreigners took an active role in spreading the idea that all foreigners were seen as the same by the Chinese. The American trader William Hunter wrote of his stay in the early nineteenth century, 'by the Chinese all foreigners were called "Fan Kwaes," or "Foreign Devils"', and then mentioned a pamphlet for Pidgin English that he said was called 'Devils' Talk', and continued, 'I have often wondered who the man was who first reduced the "outlandish tongue" to a current language'.[42]

There was a similar development of a joint term for all foreigners in Japan. The character for Tang, *tō*, was used broadly for all people and things that generally came from China or the surrounding region. In the late Tokugawa period the word *tōjin* could be applied to all foreigners, regardless of origin. Words such as *morokoshi* or *kara* could be taken to mean both 'strange', 'foreign', and 'Chinese', depending on context. Similarly, the word *Oranda* could apply to a group of Dutch traders, but it could equally often denote foreignness – commodities or people that were called Oranda were from diverse origins.[43] It is important to be careful not to translate these complex words as denoting a single and specific nationality, whether Chinese or Dutch.

Instead of creating a personal meeting and a bridge, the language diversity of these harbours reflect gendered and classed differences in how the interaction was policed, and conscious separation between the foreign traders and the rest of the countries. Furthermore, the creation of a word and a concept of a foreign group, that resided in a particular port, imposed a layer of meaning on the foreigners. Rather than a sign of bottom-up hybrid

Controlling the golden geese 33

commercial and cultural practices, terms such as *fangui* and *tōjin* represent a homogeneity imposed by the administrators.

Doux commerce and cosmopolitanism

There were multiple varieties of cosmopolitanism in eighteenth-century Europe and Asia. They did, however, commonly assume that their imagined ideal would be allowed to be practiced, as inherent in the 1755 definition from Samuel Johnson's *Dictionary of English Language*, where a cosmopolitan is 'at home in every place'.[44] Commercial and humanitarian cosmopolitanism may have been conflated in discussions on violence in international trade and the moral position of merchants, but the two varieties might have differed in relation to assumption of power. In various trading spaces throughout the Indian Ocean, Mediterranean, and Atlantic worlds, European merchants used adaptation as a commercial strategy, and the resulting cosmopolitanism was a result of their vulnerable position.[45]

The asymmetrical power relations affected both how that relationship played out on the ground – and how it was talked about afterwards. Francesca Trivellato has argued for the existence of a global mercantile culture in the early modern world, one that depended on cooperation, trust-formation, and complex social relations.[46] In contrast, Cátia Antunes has proposed that the global merchant networks shared a common conceptual framework.[47] Whether well-functioning intercultural trade was primarily an effect of the building of trust or the gradual synchronisation of trade practices, China is particularly interesting as an example, being used as an argument in eighteenth-century debates on political economy and commerce. It gave rise to reports from the trade on the ground. In such journal and travel writings, from China and Japan, there is a debate on the very commonalities and the trust that Trivellato and Antunes argue for the importance of.

The texts from the interaction in these contact zones do not exactly paint a rosy picture. There was constant talk of smuggling, bribery, and corruption. Across the board, among the Dutch as well as the Chinese in Nagasaki, among the Europeans in Canton, and among the Chinese merchants in Canton, the arguments put forward are strikingly similar: the other trade group was cheating, and greedy, and did not know how to trade in a civilised fashion.[48] Complaining that the other trade groups did not comprehend the practices of *doux commerce*, that they were cheating and greedy, presented an excuse to adapt to local practices – including smuggling and rule-breaking.[49] The rules were never completely adhered to in either port; rather, smuggling, disobedience, and rule breaking were rampant.[50] Japanese traders illegally purchased products from the Dutch and the Chinese, and established their own trade routes to other regions in East Asia. Much smuggling made use of established routes and spaces and was

34   Lisa Hellman

carried out by the same actors as the official trade; while the smuggling did gradually undermine the system, particularly in Canton, it also ran parallel to it.[51]

While this type of rule breaking was well known, it was far from accepted. Rather, there was constant tension between when Chinese and Japanese authorities' acceptance of minor transgressions, and their enforcement of these rules. In Nagasaki, it was the go-betweens who got punished when any case of smuggling was found out.[52] Also, in Canton, there were several groups of go-betweens who could be held responsible for the behaviour of the foreign traders. Still, in 1831, an edict of the governor decreed that should the foreigners break the rules again, not only would the traders be punished, but: 'I will take the Hong merchants who did not keep them under strict control, and the Linguists and Compradores who taught and instigated *them*, one and all, and punish their crimes with a heavy hand'.[53] Notably, the adherence and subversions to the rules was tension that not only applied to the foreign traders, but also included local traders, officials, interpreters and others working in these contact zones.

In general, the ways that the trade was policed also made it function smoothly. That the Japanese and Chinese officials provided go-betweens, a space, as well as routines can also be seen as simplifying the commerce. In that sense, that the European traders were stressing the particular circumstances of this space, presented an excuse to use certain local practices. In Nagasaki, the Dutch traders were painfully aware of the dominant role of the Japanese authorities, as was the role of the Chinese authorities in Canton. In both ports, the solution for them and the other foreigners was most often acquiescence.[54] It did mean that a rational tradesman in this context had to be culturally flexible, which in China as well as Japan meant having intercultural capital for a merchant group and could be about adapting to and staging cultural differences; rather, effecting change or cultural integration.

While foreign traders might express frustration at the idea of all being crammed into one place and being treated as one and the same, that could also be to the foreign traders' advantage. In Canton, they also acted as a joint group at times, for example when negotiating with officials turn into conflict.[55] Complaining about the fact that the European traders had to act differently, they actually circulated knowledge about how to do well, albeit disguised as complaints and discourses of Oriental despotism. In that sense, travel writings and ship's journals can be considered as commercial cultural handbooks, not only as sources for creating a discourse of Orientalism.[56] As soon as European powers had the ability to impose their preferred modes of exchange, they did so; but that was not yet an option in eighteenth-century East Asia. Rather, in Canton and Macao, they adapted by keeping apart, and created trust through at least the appearance of obedience.[57]

Conclusion

The multiplicity of groups in Canton and Nagasaki simultaneously made cosmopolitanism here as much a case of imposed homogeneity and the re-creation of difference and set boundaries as it was about mediating between groups.

While hybrid practices have elsewhere been shown to destabilise power structures, the cases of Canton and Nagasaki rather illuminate the limits of hybridity. Some actors taking part in this interaction, the foreign traders, were consciously barred from such practices. Other and even more vulnerable groups, such as the prostitutes, had the position of broker, and practices that placed them in the tension fields between cultures imposed upon them. The marginalised groups were perhaps primarily used to attain just cultural co-herence enough to make the trade run smoothly, a strategy used by local authorities and accepted and made use of by the cosmopolitan actors.

Cosmopolitan commercial practices formed part of many different cultures in the early modern world, as indeed several contributions in this volume have shown.[58] A classic criticism against global history is its focus on trade contacts, based on the idea that these highlight cooperation and integration rather than asymmetric power relations and violence.[59] What the comparison between Canton and Nagasaki can show, however, is that sometimes, a successful adaptation as a citizen of the world meant not in-tegration, nor practices of hybridity, but rather an acceptance of imposed difference, and a creation of such difference was a sign of European political weakness, not strength or ambition.

Notes

1 This categorisation is still used for Canton. See Emily Erikson, *Between Monopoly and Free Trade: The English East India Company, 1600–1757* (Princeton: University Press, 2014), 129–30.

2 Loren Brandt, Debin Ma, and Thomas Rawski, "From Divergence to Convergence: Reevaluating the History Behind China's Economic Boom," *Journal of Economic Literature* 52, no. 1 (2014): 45–123.

3 Patrizia Carioti, "17th-Century Nagasaki: Entrepôt for the Zheng, the VOC and the Tokugawa Bakufu," in *Gateways to Globalisation Asia's International Trading and Finance Centres*, ed. François Gipouloux (Cheltenham: Edward Elgar, 2011).

4 Alison Games, *The Web of Empire: English Cosmopolitans in an Age of Expansion, 1560–1660* (New York: Oxford University Press, 2009), 10.

5 W.E. Cheong, *Hong Merchants of Canton: Chinese Merchants in Sino-Western Trade: [1684–1798]* (Richmond: Curzon, 1997); Osamu [恬] Ōba [大庭], *Nagasaki tōkan-zu shūsei* [長崎唐館図集成] (Suita: Kansai Daigaku Shuppanbu [関西大学出版部], 2003); Louis Cullen, "The Nagasaki Trade of the Tokugawa Era: Archives, Statistics, and Management," *Japan Review* 2017, no. 31 (2017): 69–104.

6 See for example Evert Groenendijk, Cynthia Viallé, and Leonard Blussé, eds. *Canton and Nagasaki Compared, 1730–1830: Dutch, Chinese, Japanese Relations: Transactions* (Leiden: Institute for the History of European Expansion, 2009); Leonard Blussé, *Visible Cities: Canton, Nagasaki, and Batavia and the Coming of*

36 *Lisa Hellman*

the Americans (Cambridge: Harvard University Press, 2008); Masashi Haneda, "Canton, Nagasaki and the Port Cities of the Indian Ocean: A Comparison," in *Asian Port Cities, 1600–1800: Local and Foreign Cultural Interactions*, ed. Masashi Haneda (Singapore and Kyoto: NUS Press in association with Kyoto University Press, 2009), 13–23; Hiroji [博二] Harada [原田], "Nagasaki to Kōshū [長崎と広州]," in Nihon no taigai kankei 6 *Kinseiteki sekai no seijuku* [日本の対外関係6 近世的世界の成熟], eds. Yasunori [泰典] Arano [荒野], Masatoshi [正敏] Ishii [石井], and Shōsuke [章介] Murai [村井] (Tokyo: Yoshikawa kōbunkan [吉川弘文館], 2010); Angela Schottenhammer, "Empire and Periphery? The Qing Empire's Relations with Japan and the Ryūkyūs (1644–c. 1800), a Comparison," *The Medieval History Journal* 16, no. 1 (2013): 139–96.

7 Blussé, *Visible Cities*.
8 Masashi Haneda, "Introduction: Framework and Methods of Comparative Studies on Asian Port Cities in the Seventeenth and Eighteenth Centuries," in *Asian Port Cities, 1600–1800: Local and Foreign Cultural Interactions*, ed. Masashi Haneda (Singapore and Kyoto: NUS Press in association with Kyoto University Press, 2009), 1–12.
9 Henry D. Smith, "Five Myths about Early Modern Japan," in *Asia in Western and World History: A Guide for Teaching*, ed. Ainslee Embree and Carol Gluck (Armonk, NY: M. E. Sharpe, 1997).
10 Blussé, *Visible Cities*, 21–22.
11 See Richard Cocks and Edward Maunde Thompson, *Diary of Richard Cocks, Cape-Merchant in the English Factory in Japan, 1615–1622: With Correspondence* (London: Printed for the Hakluyt Society, 1883).
12 Carioti, "17th-Century Nagasaki"; Ōba [大庭], *Nagasaki tōkan-zu shūsei* [長崎唐館図集成]; Haneda, "Introduction: Framework and Methods of Comparative Studies."
13 Paul A. Van Dyke, *Merchants of Canton and Macao: Politics and Strategies in Eighteenth-Century Chinese Trade* (Hong Kong: Hong Kong University Press, 2011).
14 Van Dyke, *Merchants of Canton and Macao*; Matsui [松井] Yōko [洋子], "Dejima to kakawaru hitobito [出島とかかわる人々]," in *Nichiran kankeishi o yomitoku (jō) tsunagu hitobito* [日蘭関係史をよみとく(上)つなぐ人々], ed. Matsukata [松方] Fuyuko [冬子] (Kyoto: Rinsen Shoten [臨川書店], 2015), 146–80.
15 See Leonard Blussé et al., eds. *The Deshima Diaries: Marginalia 1740–1800* (Leiden: Brill, 2015).
16 Pauline Kleingeld, "Six Varieties of Cosmopolitanism in Late Eighteenth-Century Germany," *Journal of the History of Ideas* 60, no. 3 (1999): 505–24; Ingvild Hagen Kjørholt, "Cosmopolitans, Slaves, and the Global Market in Voltaire's *Candide, Ou l'optimisme*," *Eighteenth-Century Fiction* 25, no. 1 (2012): 61–84.
17 Isabel Tanaka-van Daalen, "Dutch Attitudes towards Slavery and the Tardy Road to Abolition: The Case of Deshima," in *Abolitions as a Global Experience*, ed. Hideaki Suzuki (Singapore: NUS Press, 2016), 73–112; Lisa Hellman, *Navigating the Foreign Quarters: Everyday Life of the Swedish East India Company Employees in Canton and Macao 1730–1830* (Stockholm: Department of History, Stockholm University, 2015), 90–92; Ichirō [一郎] Ōtani [大谷], *Nagasakihanga to ikoku no omokage* [長崎版画と異国の面影] (Tokyo: Itabashi kuritsubijutsukan [板橋区立美術館], 2016).
18 John W. Witek, "Catholic Missions and the Expansion of Christianity, 1644–1800," in *China and Maritime Europe, 1500–1800: Trade, Settlement, Diplomacy, and Missions*, ed. John E. Wills Jr. et al. (Cambridge: Cambridge University Press, 2010); Susumu [進] Murao [村尾], 'Kōshi o risanka suru –

kaien-eki jūsan-gyō Makao [港市を離散化する － 懐遠駅・十三行・澳門]',
Tenridaigaku kokusai bunka gakubu chūgokugo kōsu kenkyūshitsu [天理大学国際
文化学部中国語コース研究室] 25 (2009): 1–12.

19 Takayuki [孝右] Shimada [島田] and Yuriko [ゆり子] Shimada [島田], *Fumi-e: Gaikokuhito ni yoru fumi-e no kiroku* [踏み絵: 外国人による踏み絵の記録] (Tokyo: Yūshōdōshuppan [雄松堂出版], 1994); Marius B. Jansen, *China in the Tokugawa World* (Cambridge, MA: Harvard University Press, 1992).

20 Blussé, *Visible Cities*, 21–22.

21 Douglas Catterall and Jodi Campbell, eds. *Women in Port: Gendering Communities, Economies, and Social Networks in Atlantic Port Cities, 1500–1800* (Leiden: Brill, 2012).

22 Yoko (洋子) Matsui (松井), "Nagasaki to Maruyama yūjo chokkatsu bōeki toshi no yūkaku shakai [長崎と丸山遊女 [直轄貿易都市の遊廓社会]," in *Santo to chihō toshi* [三都と地方都市], eds. Ashita (朝) Saga (佐賀) and Nobuyuki (伸之) Yoshida (吉田) (Tokyo [東京]: Yoshikawakōbunkan [吉川弘文館], 2013); Yoko Matsui, "The Legal Position of Foreigners in Nagasaki during the Edo Period," in *Asian Port Cities, 1600–1800: Local and Foreign Cultural Interactions*, ed. Masashi Haneda (Singapore and Kyoto: NUS Press in association with Kyoto University Press, 2009), 24–42; Paul A. Van Dyke, "Floating Brothels and the Canton Flower Boats 1750–1930," *Revista de cultura* 37 (2011).

23 Compare to the idea of social groups being singled out by the state as presented in Regina Grafe and Alejandra maria Irigoin, "A Stakeholder Empire: The Political Economy of Spanish Imperial Rule in America," SSRN Scholarly Paper (Rochester, NY: Social Science Research Network, 2012).

24 Francesca Trivellato, *The Familiarity of Strangers: The Sephardic Diaspora, Livorno, and Cross-Cultural Trade in the Early Modern Period* (New Haven: Yale University Press, 2009), 10–12.

25 Philip D. Curtin, *Cross-Cultural Trade in World History* (Cambridge; New York: Cambridge University Press, 1984).

26 Mary Louise Pratt, "Arts of the Contact Zone," *Profession* (1991): 33–40; Homi K. Bhabha, *The Location of Culture* (London, New York: Routledge, 1994).

27 Antony Easthope, "Bhabha, Hybridity and Identity," *Textual Practice* 12, no. 2 (1998): 341–48; Ulrike M. Vieten, *Gender and Cosmopolitanism in Europe: A Feminist Perspective* (Farnham: Ashgate, 2012), 102–5.

28 Vieten, *Gender and Cosmopolitanism in Europe*, 105–10.

29 Michael Scrivener, *The Cosmopolitan Ideal* (London: Routledge, 2015), 62–63; Kleingeld, "Six Varieties of Cosmopolitanism in Late Eighteenth-Century Germany."

30 Keisuke Yao, "The Fundamentally Different Roles of Interpreters in the Ports of Nagasaki and Canton," *Itinerario* 37, no. 3 (2013); Matsukata [松方] Fuyuko [冬子] , "Tsūyaku to 'yottsu no kuchi'" [通訳と「四つの口」,] in Nihon no taigai kankei 6 kinsei-teki sekai no seijuku [日本の対外関係6　近世的世界の成熟], eds. Yasunori [泰典] Arano [荒野]荒野泰典, Masatoshi [正敏] Ishii [石井] and Shōsuke [章介] Murai [村井] (Tokyo: Yoshikawa kōbunkan [吉川弘文館], 2010).

31 Nagasaki-shi Dejima shiseki seibi shingikai [長崎市出島史跡整備審議会] (curator), *Deshima-zu – sono keikan to hensan* [出島図──その景観と変遷] (Nagasaki: Nagasaki-shi [長崎市], 1987).

32 Joshua A. Fogel, *Between China and Japan: The Writings of Joshua Fogel* (Leiden: Brill, 2015), 299.

33 Jansen, *China in the Tokugawa World*; Ōba [大庭], *Nagasaki tōkan-zu shūsei* [長崎唐館図集成].

34 Yao, "The Fundamentally Different Roles of Interpreters in the Ports of Nagasaki and Canton"; Taichi [太一] Wakaki [若木], *Nagasaki: Tōzaikōshōshi no*

38 *Lisa Hellman*

butai gekan Min Shin jidai no Nagasaki shihai no kōzu to bunka no shosō [長崎：東西交渉史の舞台　下巻　明・清時代の長崎　支配の構図と文化の諸相] (Tokyo: Benseishuppan [勉誠出版], 2013).

35 Kingsley Bolton, *Chinese Englishes: A Sociolinguistic History* (Cambridge, New York: Cambridge University Press, 2003), 153–59; Phil Benson, "The Origins of Chinese Pidgin English: Evidence from Colin Campell's Diary," *Hong Kong Journal of Asian Linguistics* 10, no. 1 (2005).

36 Michelle Li, Stephen Matthews, and Geoff P. Smith, "Pidgin English Texts from the Chinese English Instructor," *Hong Kong Journal of Asian Linguistics* 10, no. 1 (2005): 79.

37 Li Chen, *Chinese Law in Imperial Eyes: Sovereignty, Justice, and Transcultural Politics* (New York: Columbia University Press, 2016), 76–77.

38 Jia Si, "Breaking through the 'Jargon' Barrier: Early 19th Century Missionaries' Response on Communication Conflicts in China," *Frontiers of History in China* 4, no. 3 (2009).

39 Lo-shu Fu, *A Documentary Chronicle of Sino-Western Relations (1644–1820)* (Tucson: The University of Arizona Press, 1966), I: 408.

40 Frits Vos, "Forgotten Foibles: Love and the Dutch at Dejima (1641–1854)," *East Asian History* 39 (2014): 144.

41 Aili (爱丽] Li [李], "Baiqian yinü fen chengqun 'yu' shui liao ren duo zhanglihua (百千夷女纷成群"与"谁料人多张丽华)," in *Haojing ying xichao: pingbi yu huanchong zhong de qingdai aomen zhongxi jiaoliu* [蠔镜映西潮: 屏蔽与缓冲中的清代澳门中西交流], ed. Xiang [湘] Zhou [周] and Aili [爱丽] Li [李] (Beijing: Shehui kexue wenxian chubanshe [社会科学文献出版社], 2013); Lydia He Liu, *The Clash of Empires: The Invention of China in Modern World Making* (Cambridge, MA: Harvard University Press, 2004).

42 William C. Hunter, *The 'Fan Kwae' at Canton Before Treaty Days, 1825–1844* (London: Kegan Paul, Trench, and Co., 1882), 64–65.

43 Jansen, *China in the Tokugawa World*, 85; Keiko Suzuki, "The Making of Tōjin Construction of the Other in Early Modern Japan," *Asian Folklore Studies* 66, no. 1/2 (2007): 83–105.

44 Kleingeld, "Six Varieties of Cosmopolitanism in Late Eighteenth-Century Germany."

45 Games, *The Web of Empire*, 10–15.

46 Trivellato, *The Familiarity of Strangers*, 178.

47 Catia Antunes, "On Cosmopolitanism and Cross-Culturalism: An Enquiry into the Business Practices and Multiple Identities of the Portuguese Merchants of Amsterdam," in *Cosmopolitanism in the Portuguese-Speaking World*, ed. Francisco Bethencourt (Leiden: Brill, 2017).

48 Lo-shu Fu, *A Documentary Chronicle of Sino-Western Relations (1644–1820), Vol. II* (Tucson: The University of Arizona Press, 1966), 144–78; Paul A. Van Dyke and Cynthia Viallé, eds. *The Canton-Macao Dagregisters, 1763* (Macau: Instituto Cultural do Governo da R.A.E. de Macau, 2008); Cynthia Viallé, "'To Capture Their Favour": On Gift-Giving by the VOC', in *Mediating Netherlandish Art and Material Culture in Asia*, ed. Thomas DaCosta Kaufmann and Michael North (Amsterdam: Amsterdam University Press, 2014); Yong Liu, "The Commercial Culture of the VOC in Canton in the Eighteenth Century," in *Asian Port Cities, 1600–1800: Local and Foreign Cultural Interactions*, ed. Haneda, Masashi (Singapore and Kyoto: NUS Press in association with Kyoto University Press, 2009), 122.

49 Manhoung Lin, *China Upside Down: Currency, Society, and Ideologies, 1808–1856* (Cambridge: Harvard University Asia Center, 2006); David Mervart,

"Republic of Letters Comes to Nagasaki: Record of a Translator's Struggle," *Transcultural Studies* 6, no. 2 (21 December 2015): 8–37.

50 Masashi Haneda, "Common and Different Characteristics of Canton and Nagasaki Compared with Port Cities in the Indian Ocean," in *Canton and Nagasaki Compared, 1730–1830: Dutch, Chinese, Japanese Relations: Transactions*, ed. Evert Groenendijk, Cynthia Viallé, and Leonard Blussé (Leiden: Institute for the History of European Expansion, 2009).

51 Louis Cullen, "The Nagasaki Trade of the Tokugawa Era: Archives, Statistics, and Management"; Paul A. Van Dyke, "Smuggling Networks of the Pearl River Delta before 1842: Implications for Macao and the American China Trade," in *Americans and Macao. Trade, Smuggling and Diplomacy on the South China Coast*, ed. Paul A. Van Dyke (Hong Kong: Hong Kong University Press, 2012); Jurre Knoest, "'The Japanese Connection": Self-Organized Smuggling Networks in Nagasaki circa 1666–1742', in *Beyond Empires: Self-Organizing Cross-Imperial Economic Networks vs Institutional Empires, 1500–1800*, ed. Cátia Antunes, and Amélia Polónia (Leiden: Brill, 2016).

52 Haneda, "Common and Different Characteristics of Canton and Nagasaki Compared with Port Cities in the Indian Ocean," 21–28.

53 *East India Affairs China Correspondence* (Parliamentary Papers, House of Commons, 1832), 86–87.

54 Blussé Leonard, "Divesting a Myth: Seventeenth Century Dutch-Portuguese Rivalry in the Far East," in *Vasco Da Gama and the Linking of Europe and Asia*, ed. Anthony R. Disney and Emily Booth (New Delhi: Oxford University Press, 2000); Adam Clulow, *The Company and the Shogun: The Dutch Encounter with Tokugawa Japan* (New York: Columbia University Press, 2013); Van Dyke, *Merchants of Canton and Macao.*

55 Hellman, *Navigating the Foreign Quarters*, 64.

56 Miles Ogborn, "Writing Travels: Power, Knowledge and Ritual on the English East India Company's Early Voyages," *Transactions of the Institute of British Geographers, New Series* 27, no. 2 (2002): 155–171.

57 Clulow, *The Company and the Shogun.*

58 Kleingeld, "Six Varieties of Cosmopolitanism in Late Eighteenth-Century Germany"; Minghui Hu and Johan Elverskog, *Cosmopolitanism in China, 1600–1950* (New York: Cambria Press, 2016).

59 Frederick Cooper, "What Is the Concept of Globalization Good for? An African Historian's Perspective," *African Affairs* 100, no. 399 (2001): 189–213.

2 Trouble in the contact zone

Jeremias van Vliet in seventeenth-century Ayutthaya

Sven Trakulhun

In her book on *Travel Writing and Transculturation*, Mary Louise Pratt defined *contact zones* as spaces in which "peoples geographically and historically separated come into contact with each other and establish ongoing relations", mostly in colonial contexts.[1] Contact zones can be regarded as specific sites of transition, as "third spaces", where cultural and social differences are being constantly negotiated. Pratt used the term to counter diffusionist accounts of European conquest and domination so familiar to historians of the European overseas expansion. By contrast, the idea of contact zones highlights interaction, cross-cultural exchange and hybridity. While the concept lends itself well to overcoming simple colonial/non-colonial dichotomies, it remains vague without tangible empirical data on the ways in which interlocking understandings and practices took place in contact zones. Investigations of these interactions often depend on case studies. This essay looks at the Siamese capital of Ayutthaya as a cosmopolitan space, where cultural and social differences were being constantly negotiated. Eventually, it explores the life and writings of the Dutch East India Company officer Jeremias van Vliet (1602–1663), who lived in Ayutthaya between 1633 and 1642. Van Vliet occupies a peculiar place in the history of Thailand. There is no other European traveller, merchant or missionary in the seventeenth century who wrote more extensively on the kingdom. Van Vliet's four books on Siam, written between 1636 and 1640, provide valuable insights into the various social, political, and economic entanglements that shaped a Dutch company man's life in Siam.[2] At the same time, Van Vliet is a good example for exploring both the functioning of a multinational trading community and the limits of cross-cultural exchange.

Trading patterns and social order in seventeenth-century Ayutthaya

When Van Vliet arrived in Siam in 1633, Ayutthaya was a cosmopolitan port city hosting a large number of foreign trading communities. After long and disastrous wars with Burma in the sixteenth century, the Siamese kingdom was reviving its economy to participate in the expansion of trade in Southeast Asia.

During the reign of King Songtham (r. 1610–1628), Ayutthaya emerged as an important entrepôt in the region where goods from East Asia, India, and Persia were imported, stored, and traded. To this merchandise were added local forest products, elephants, dyes, and rice, as well as metals such as copper, lead, and tin. Among the different ethnic groups residing in Ayutthaya were merchant families from different Asian and European countries who settled in separate quarters of the city (Figure 2.1).

Asian commercial centers like Ayutthaya attracted great numbers of foreign merchants and were considerably larger than European colonial settlements in the East.[3] According to the Dutch traveller Jan Janszoon Struys, the Siamese kingdom was especially open to foreigners:

> They [the Siamese] are of a very liberal nature, and civil to converse with all, but especially to Strangers. English, Portugueezes, Hollanders, and Moors, without respect to their Profession, have liberal access to enter, inhabit and traffic in the Land, by order of the King; and enjoy as much

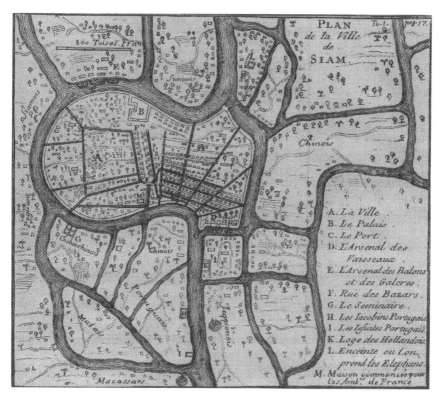

Figure 2.1 Map of Ayutthaya. In: Simon de La Loubère, *A New Historical Relation of the Kingdom of Siam* (London: F.L. for Tho. Horne, 1693). SB Berlin, Up 5520-1.

42   Sven Trakulhun

> Liberty, and benefit of the Law, as his own natural subjects; which draws abundance of Foreigners, from all Countreys, who come thither, either upon the account of Commerce, or to seek Protection.[4]

The Siamese state depended on external assistance in many ways. The government required assistance of foreigners to deal with the already ethnically diverse population in the country and the capital, sought their linguistic skills in diplomatic intercourse, benefited from their expertise in military technology, and employed foreign merchant networks in international trade. Most royal junks were manned with Chinese sailors and navigators, while Portuguese mercenaries and Japanese bodyguards featured prominently in the Siamese army. A number of key positions in the administration were usually in the hands of non-Siamese officials, particularly in the office of the *Phra Khlang*, the Siamese ministry responsible for commerce, international relations, and the conduct of crown trade. For example, the "Department of Eastern Maritime Affairs and Crown Junks" (*Krom Tha Sai*) was controlled by Chinese harbormasters, while the "Department of Western Maritime Affairs of the right" (*Krom Tha Khwa*) was headed by South Asian Muslims.[5]

For Europeans, Ayutthaya and other ports in the Gulf of Siam were instrumental to the maintenance of important trading routes between China and Japan in the East, and India and Persia in the West. The Portuguese had settled in the country since around 1511 and continued a modest presence as merchants, mercenaries, and intermediaries.[6] The Spaniards had been familiar with the Gulf of Siam at least from the early 1590s, when they unsuccessfully tried to establish a foothold in Mainland Southeast Asia.[7] English traders of the *East India Company* opened a godown in Ayutthaya in 1612 to inquire about the Siamese market and seek openings for English goods. However, English relations with the Siamese court seriously deteriorated in 1687 when about one hundred Englishmen died in a clash with Siamese troops in the city of Mergui on the Tenasserim coast.[8] French attempts to gain influence in the kingdom began in the 1660s during the reign of King Narai, but spectacularly failed after his dethronement and death in 1688.[9]

The Dutch *Vereenigde Ost-Indische Compagnie* (VOC) was the dominant European power in Southeast Asia throughout the seventeenth century. The Dutch were hoping to get access to the markets of China and Japan by establishing trading posts along the sea routes to East Asia. Siam became a major supplier of rice for Batavia and provided the Dutch with sappanwood, black lac, cloths, and deer hides for sale in Japan in exchange for silver. The Company maintained an almost continuous presence in Ayutthaya from 1608 until the siege and destruction of the city in 1765–1767. During this long period, relations between the VOC and the Siamese state were predominantly peaceful, but there was also an enduring

Trouble in the contact zone 43

struggle over the terms of trade, the political role of the Dutch in Siam, and the rules and norms of community life.

In theory, the VOC aimed at acquiring a monopoly of certain key commodities of Eurasian trade (such as spices and textiles), but in reality still much of its economic success depended on the extent to which Company merchants managed to participate in intra-Asian trade. To their great displeasure, however, Siamese commercial policy was no less monopolistic than their own. Trade in Ayutthaya was firmly controlled by the king, whose junks were sailing as far west as Mocha and as far east as Nagasaki.[10] The Dutch also faced competition from established Muslim and Chinese merchants, who maintained close connections to the court and especially to the *Phra Khlang*. Dutch merchants were not in a position to change commercial patterns according to their wishes. All they could do was negotiate trade concessions with the Siamese court. To this end, they carefully fostered diplomatic relations with the Siamese kings, who regularly received letters and gifts from the Governor-General of Batavia and the Prince of Orange in The Hague. On several occasions, the Dutch warranted military assistance against potential aggressions of the Iberian powers and rebellious Siamese tributary states of Cambodia and Pattani (although with little effect), and were afterwards rewarded for their goodwill with exclusive trade privileges.[11]

Siamese kings have established an administrative system to exercise control over native proto-entrepreneurial groups and the growing influx of foreign merchants. This system was inclusive rather than exclusive, integrating native subjects as well as foreign residents into a common hierarchy of titles and ranks. While the majority of people in Ayutthaya belonged to the *Munnai-Phrai* category (officials and commoners) or ranked as slaves (*that*), there was a small class of nobles (*Khunnang*), of which some were appointed officials by the king.[12] Like in many land-abundant, labor-scarce economies, the power and charisma of a Siamese monarch was based on manpower. Siamese kings were constantly attempting to augment the population of the country in wars and slave raids.[13] There was a well-developed social-administrative system of hierarchy and bureaucratic control over labor. Thai officials registered the whole population, as well as the number of rice fields, fruit trees, and many other taxable resources. They developed complex sets of social grading, of which the most sophisticated was the *Sakdina* system (Table 2.1). In theory, this system encompassed the whole population of the kingdom, from high-ranking nobles at the top of the social ladder, down to beggars and slaves. The dignity of the various grades of nobility was measured in terms of land units (*rai*).[14] *Sakdina* is a compound word combining the Sanskrit *Sak-thi* (power) and the Thai *Na* (paddy field). It could be translated as "field power" or "land status" or "status as shown by land". Although the *Sakdina* system must have reflected rights over real land, however, in the fully-evolved administrative system the allocation of land was only symbolic.[15]

44   *Sven Trakulhun*

Table 2.1 Sakdina (simplified)

Sakdina of Princes	Land units (rai)
King	unlimited
Uparat	100.000
Chao fa Prince (*krom*)	40.000–50.000
Member of the royal family (krom)	11.000
lower members of the royal family	1.500–7.000
lowest members of the royal family	500–1.000
Sakdina of the Nobles	
Highest Ministers (*Somdet Chao Phraya*)	30,000
Ministers (*Chao Phraya*)	10.000
Heads of lesser ministries (*Phraya*)	1.000–10.000
Senior administrators (*Phra*)	1.000–5.000
Lower-ranking administrators (*Phan*)	100–400
Other Social Classes	
Skilled workmen, supervisors	25–30
Heads of households, some menial workers	20
Most commoners	15
Base-level commoners	10
Beggars, slaves	5

The *Sakdina* made no distinction between "foreign" and "native" subjects. The adoption of foreigners into the hierarchy could be most advantageous for those who permanently settled in the country and had special service to offer, particularly access to foreign markets, goods and trade networks. The most famous example for how successful assimilation worked in Ayutthaya is the powerful Bunnag family. The Bunnags are of Arabo-Persian descent whose ancestors immigrated to Siam in the early seventeenth century.[16] They climbed up the social ladder, built up close ties with the royal Thai family both by intermarriage and steady diplomatic service, adopted Buddhism during the eighteenth century to permanently secure their position at court, and produced in this manner at least five state ministers (*Chaophraya*) until the end of the Ayutthaya period (1351–1767).[17] Their influence on Thai politics further grew under the kings of the Chakri dynasty in Bangkok. Since the reign of King Rama II (1809–1824), several members of the Bunnag family have occupied prominent positions in the Siamese administration.[18]

Dutch Company directors too were from early on vested with ranks, titles, and insignia, because of their importance as customers of Siamese crown trade and potential allies in times of war. Dutch sources state that at least the directors and one or two of the next-ranking Company administrators held official positions in the *Sakdina*. Van Vliet reportedly held the rank of *Okluang* and later rose to the dignity of an *Okphra*, which marked him out as a person of authority in the Siamese administration. Inclusion in the Thai

Trouble in the contact zone   45

official order was important for the Dutch as it allowed at least the directors of the Company to participate in some of the king's council meetings. This was a great advantage, because it enabled them to address the Siamese king with issues of interest for the VOC that otherwise might have been ignored.[19]

Mestizo cultures and the politics of segregation

Social integration also worked on a personal level, albeit in a rather informal way. As there were virtually no Dutch women migrating to the East Indies in the seventeenth century, Company employees of all ranks had relationships with local women, mostly from other migrant communities such as the Mon from Lower Burma or the Lao from the northern mainland.[20] Under favorable circumstances, these family arrangements could have some mutual benefits. Women dominated the domestic markets in Siam and could act as mediators between their foreign partners, local traders, and Siamese officials, while in turn their husbands could offer their own goods, expertise, and trading networks. Since many of these mixed couples had children, the Dutch settlement came to have a strong mestizo element. However, the main problem was that Dutch merchants usually did not come to stay in Siam. The idea was to save enough money to repatriate to the Netherlands and enjoy an early retirement at home. Only few company agents settled permanently in Siam, and, as in other parts of Southeast Asia, cohabitation of Dutchmen with Asian women were mostly only temporary affairs.[21]

The number of Eurasian families grew over the decades, and so did the number of mestizo children in the Dutch camp in Ayutthaya. The Siamese king valued manpower as a precious resource and would rather not dispense with Eurasian offspring, so in principle it was forbidden to take children out of the country. Most children probably remained in Siam after the departure or death of their fathers. According to Gijsbert Heeck, a Dutch company surgeon who visited the Siamese kingdom in 1655, many parents abandoned their Eurasian children and took them into care of a kind of orphanage located near the Dutch lodge in Ayutthaya.[22] However, when family conditions were more favorable, children of mixed birth could enter the service for the VOC or find employment at the Siamese court. A good example is the Company physician Daniel Brochebourde, who married a local woman with whom he had four children. In 1672 he was employed by King Narai as a court physician and was succeeded by his son Mozes, who then handed the post to his son Jeremias in 1724.[23]

Van Vliet, too, had mestizo offspring. He lived in concubinage with Osoet Pegua, a Mon woman of humble descent who bore him three daughters and probably assisted him in collecting and reading Thai manuscripts for the composition of his books. She grew up in the Dutch settlement in Ayutthaya and played a prominent role in Siamese-Dutch trade. Osoet became the wife or concubine of three Dutchmen. She had a son with Jan van Meerwijck, a

46   *Sven Trakulhun*

free trader who lived in Siam in the early 1630s. Some years later, she started a second family with Van Vliet and finally took up with Jan van Muijden, the director of the Dutch factory in Siam from 1646 to 1650. According to Rijckloff van Goens, the Dutch Commissioner to Siam in 1650, Osoet was well-connected to the royal palace and especially to the wife of the powerful official Okya Sombatthiban, who was then one of the closest advisors of king Prasatthong of Siam.[24] She used her language skills to successfully work as a broker in Dutch-Siamese trade, supporting her husbands in secretly buying tin, arranging for loans from wealthy Siamese nobles when the Company was short of cash, or obtaining export licences for the Dutch for rice and other commodities that where otherwise difficult to obtain in greater quantities.[25]

Since there were various ways in which foreigners could find entrance into local trade networks and society, historians often describe Ayutthaya as a multi-cultural space, where different ethnic and religious groups were living together in an "almost-ecumenical" manner.[26] Social integration naturally required a willingness on the part of the newcomers to acknowledge indigenous social rules and cultural practices. Dutch merchants in Siam were sojourners rather than immigrants, with a cultural identity that remained firmly rooted in a European Calvinist tradition. It is even more striking, therefore, to see how they managed over the years to learn the language of Siamese diplomacy, and how eager many Dutchmen were to become incorporated into the Thai social system. To please the Siamese government, VOC officials carefully observed the rules of gift-giving and courtly protocol, frequently participated in official state ceremonies, and occasionally even donated for the building or renovation of "pagan" Buddhist temples. From the point of view of their ability to conform to Siamese customs and behavior patterns, the Dutch were certainly the most successful European group in early modern Siam.[27]

At the same time, there were limits of cross-cultural entanglements set by the external conditions under which the Dutch were operating in Siam. The Siamese government clearly understood that a Dutch Company director owed first allegiance to his Governor-General in Batavia, while his loyalty for the Siamese king would only last as long as he dwelled and traded on Siamese territory. Dutch officials therefore never achieved higher positions at the Siamese court, although some of them served as economic or military advisors in the local administration. The temporary nature of their presence in Siam also raised a number of legal questions, especially those pertaining to the legal status of Dutch-Siamese offspring. Although Siamese policy was far from consistent in this regard, a number of laws issued in the seventeenth century indicate a tendency to separate foreign communities from the native population. A first provision on cross-cultural marriage was introduced by King Prasatthong in 1633. The clause was annexed to the *Phra aiyakan atya luang* (Law on offences against the state, dated AD 1352). It strictly prohibited the cohabitation of Siamese or Mon women and European or other non-Buddhist foreigners (including Muslims). It provided sanctions at six levels, ranging from the payment of fines for minor offences to the beheading of the convict for serious infringements. The law was reiterated and even amended by King Narai in 1663. The legislators, it seems, were primarily concerned with religion and espionage. The law should prevent women from being "converted to hold wrong beliefs, outside the "holy [Buddhist] religion", and preclude the fathers and their children from informing foreigners of "state affairs".[28]

Siamese distrust was not entirely unfounded. The Dutch repeatedly expressed their worries about mestizo children growing up in Siam without a Christian education. When Van Vliet was returning to Batavia in 1642, he asked the Siamese court for permission to send the three daughters he had with Osoet Pegua to a Dutch school in Batavia. However, his former wife wanted them to stay in Siam and successfully obstructed Van Vliet's request until she died in 1658. Batavian officials later tried to come to a general agreement with the Siamese court and in 1664 obtained permission for children under seven years to leave the country when their Dutch fathers relocated or returned home.[29] Of course, there has always been a huge difference between theory and practice in everyday life. Segregation in Siam was in fact less strict than it appeared on paper. Despite the harsh penalties imposed on intermarriage, no case is known in which a severe penalty has been imposed for transgressing the laws. Yet, at least in legal terms, Siamese society became a salad bowl rather than a melting pot, divided along ethno-religious lines and with little room for connections between the different cultural groups.

Writing commercial cosmopolitanism: Van Vliet and his work

It was also true that the Dutch did their best to thoroughly describe and study the peculiarities of the Siamese kingdom. Company authorities strongly encouraged their employees to collect information about the countries in which they were operating. For the VOC, an ideal commercial cosmopolitan was indeed both a candid merchant and a spy, constantly gathering local intelligence wherever he was posted. There was a growing demand for knowledge in the Netherlands (and elsewhere in Europe) about Asian markets, new goods, and products traded in the East. The success of the VOC in the seventeenth century was closely linked to the structure of information-handling that evolved in Amsterdam as a by-product of the operations of its commercial networks.[30]

A number of careers in the East had proven that demonstrating intimate knowledge of the places where the VOC had factories could open up a way to the highest posts in the Company's service. The first Dutch author to write more extensively on the Siamese kingdom was Cornelis van Neijenrode, director of the VOC factories in Ayutthaya and Pattani between 1617 and 1621. When he left Siam, he submitted to his head office an

48   *Sven Trakulhun*

elaborate description of the country, including an exhaustive list of Siamese imports and exports. In 1623, van Neijenrode became Governor of the trading post in Hirado, a position he held until his death in 1633.[31] Another example is Joost Schouten, who served as the director of the Dutch factory in Ayutthaya from 1633 to 1636. In 1638, Schouten, who published a highly-acclaimed description of the kingdom of Siam, was sent by the VOC to several diplomatic missions in Southeast Asia in subsequent years. In 1640, he became a member of the *Council of the Indies* in Batavia.[32]

Jeremias Van Vliet was an even more ambitious writer and added a wide range of new material to the Company's colonial archive. His first work on Siam is a detailed report of events that happened in Ayutthaya in 1636, when eight drunken Dutch Company assistants and a sub-merchant were arrested by the Siamese authorities for rioting in front of a Buddhist temple. The next day, they were taken to the court of King Prasatthong, who obviously received such a distorted view of events that he considered having the delinquents trampled to death by elephants. Van Vliet was, at that time, in charge of the VOC office in Ayutthaya and managed to relieve his employees only by signing a humiliating declaration in which he confessed his guilt and promised to carefully observe the laws of the kingdom in the future.[33]

The diary of the "picnic incident" (as historians call this episode today) was first published in Dutch in 1647 and provides insight into some of the complexities of Ayutthaya's multicultural society. Van Vliet's negotiations with the Siamese court were difficult because Dutch authorities were still ignorant of Siamese political etiquette and court language. A few months prior to the events, an official Netherlands embassy had arrived in Ayutthaya with hundreds of fully armed Company soldiers, which led Prasatthong to imagine they had been sent "to frighten him with the power of the Netherlands."[34] Moreover, the Ambassador carried a letter from Governor-General Antonio van Diemen in which he openly criticized Siam's trade policy. The translators were apparently unable to render the Governor's "harsh and resolute" tone into appropriate royal language (*ratchasap*) and thus offended the king and his court.[35] Some of the interpreters spoke neither Portuguese nor Malay, while others only knew the Siamese and the "Moorish" (i.e. Persian) languages. Facing an almost Babylonian confusion of tongues, Van Vliet meticulously reported in his diary how communication between the court and the Company failed on various occasions, putting all the blame on the interpreters who, in his eyes, were either incompetent or plotting against the VOC.[36]

The Dutch were also still unfamiliar with local jurisdiction. As a senior Company merchant, Van Vliet was considered by the Siamese as the head (*munnai* or *nai*) of the Dutch community in Ayutthaya and was accountable for the conduct and decent behavior of his employees. Good conduct was of course defined by Siamese laws, as was the use of fines, fees, and punishment in case of misconduct. When King Prasatthong finally pardoned the

Trouble in the contact zone 49

prisoners and lifted the restrictions he had imposed on Dutch trade during the conflict, he did so only under the condition that Van Vliet was responsible for any faults his fellow-merchants may commit in the future.[37] Van Vliet's account was meant as an apology, because after hearing about the incident, Governor-General Antonio van Diemen in Batavia accused Van Vliet of having humbled himself, crawling "along the floor like a delinquent, begging forgiveness for your crimes, which you then accepted gratefully as if it came from God Himself."[38] The political message his journal conveyed fitted well in a time when the Netherlands was at war with Spain. Van Vliet described a paradigmatic case of arbitrary rule, in which a king could decide on the life and death of his subjects at his whim and without being bound to a trial. When Van Vliet's diary appeared in print in 1647, Holland was a federal republic with *stadtholder* William II, Prince of Orange, at its head. The revolt of the Netherlands against Spanish rule still dominated political debates, so it was hard for Dutch readers not to see the parallels between the unlimited authority of Siamese kings and Spanish despotism.[39]

Van Vliet argued that a tyrannical form of rule was an almost inevitable consequence of Siam's recent history. A central theme of his work is the corruption of ancient Siamese laws and the kingdom's constitution. According to Van Vliet, the Siamese empire had enjoyed political stability until the outbreak of military conflicts with Burma in the second half of the sixteenth century, when decades of constant warfare began to undermine the foundations of the state. He regarded King Prasatthong as the latest example for a longer period of political decline in Siam that over the past century had thrown the kingdom into despotism. In his *Description of the Kingdom of Siam* he summarized:

> Since the time that the Kingdom of Siam was established, the king has always had almost sovereign power, but according to the written laws His Majesty had to consult the imperial council, and where His Majesty used bad judgment, partiality, or exaggeration, the mandarins had the power to check him. But when the empire [...] began to decay, more and more power and privileges were given to the king, as the people believed that by doing so the other nations would fear them more. The kings have ruled over a long period as monarchs with entire authority over peace, war, treaties, justice, remission of penalties, and all other affairs concerning the empire and the population. The kings could make laws and prescriptions as they pleased, and they did not consult or ask the counsel of the most influential men or nobles nor of the different classes of the people, unless His Majesty of his own free will thought it advisable to consult them.[40]

In many respects, the *Description* does resemble Schouten's work written some years earlier. Yet Van Vliet had a more clearly expressed political

50   *Sven Trakulhun*

intention, perhaps even a colonial agenda.[41] His account foreshadows many of the ideas that would later become constitutive for the European concept of "oriental despotism", stressing the unrestricted power of Asian kings and the servile nature of their subjects.[42]

Van Vliet's notion of oriental rule was naturally shaped by a peculiar Dutch mindset and therefore prone to prejudice, but it was also informed by contemporary Siamese views on history-as-decline. This becomes clearer in his most unconventional text, the *Cort Verhael van't naturel eijnde der vollbrachter tijt ende successie der Coningen van Siam* written in 1640. The chronicle is a pioneering work since it was the first European study of the history of a Southeast Asian country almost exclusively based on indigenous sources. A large part of the *Cort Verhael* is concerned with the reigns and achievements of Siamese kings, perhaps because of the nature of the Siamese chronicles from which he derived his information. Van Vliet sometimes adopted the style of storytelling prevalent in the royal chronicles of Ayutthaya, while at the same time borrowing from European literary genres such as travel literature, historiography, and classical drama. Van Vliet declared to hold rational ideas of historical plausibility, separating fables from truth, and presenting his superiors with a reliable account of the "succession, names and nature of the Siamese kings ... [that] have never been brought to light by our predecessors."[43]

However, the major source of his narrative is the Pāli chronicle *Sangitiyavamsa*, a piece of traditional Buddhist historical writing with a religious rather than political purpose.[44] Despite the many details the *Sangitiyavamsa* contains on dynastic chronology, it construed the history of Siam not simply as a succession of kings and dynasties, but as a constant struggle for purity of the teachings of the Buddha. The history of Buddhism was molded as one of a continuous pollution of the original doctrine over a long period of time. According to the *Sangitiyavamsa*, the teachings of Buddha would endure five thousand years before inexorably vanishing from the world of men. The decline of the faith would proceed in five successive stages, during which the knowledge of the Scriptures, the observance of the Buddhist precepts, and finally the corporeal relics of Buddha will disappear. People imagined the final period of religious degeneration as a dark age (*kala-yuga*) affected by greed, poverty and violence; religious decline and political turmoil were thus intrinsically connected. It is possible that Van Vliet derived his concept of Siamese history from this eschatology, repeatedly stressing the corruption of ancient Siamese laws and the kingdom's constitution.[45]

Van Vliet's final work on Siam is entitled *Historiael Verhael der Sieckte ende Doot van Pra Interra-Tsia 22en Coninck in Siam* (Historical Account of the Illness and Death of Pra Interra-Tsia, 22nd King of Siam). Written in 1640, it first appeared in 1663 in an abridged French translation compiled by the Dutch-French diplomat and scholar Abraham de Wicquefort. He has altered the original in various ways and provided his readers with a rather

Trouble in the contact zone 51

narrow portrait of an Oriental tyrant, who has seized the throne against law and convention. The text describes the royal succession from the illness and death of King Songtham in 1628 to the rise to power in 1630 of Sri Worawong, the later King Prasatthong. For Van Vliet, Prasatthong was a usurper whose struggle for the throne entirely consisted of a long series of murder, intrigues and deceptions. Van Vliet argued that the dynastic history of Siam was marked by usurpation and bloody coups d'état throughout the seventeenth century, plotting the recent Siamese past as a constant process of political and economic degeneration.[46]

However, since political government is always embedded in *realpolitik*, Prasatthong's lack of inherited legitimacy did not constitute an insurmountable obstacle to ruling the kingdom. In a curious conclusion (not included in the French version of 1663), Van Vliet reflected in an almost Machiavellian fashion on some fundamental issues of dynastic change, comparing Prasatthong's rise to power with that of the Roman Emperor Caracalla in the third century AD and of the Emperor Phocas, the first usurper of Byzantine history in the seventh century. After listing a range of other usurpers from ancient European history, Van Vliet concluded that "in matters relating to government and well-being of his Kingdom, His Majesty [Prasatthong] has been a wise, careful, and mighty Prince, who has possessed his Kingdom in prosperity and peace."[47] Van Vliet argued that even a violent usurper could transform into an able political leader once all his contenders were eliminated and the government was brought under control. Moreover, every usurper had to legitimatize his rule through royal virtue, constantly striving towards the welfare of the state. After all, even an oriental despot depended on the consent of his people.

Conclusion

Van Vliet's works are "hybrid texts", capturing crucial moments of transculturation: they are interspersed with anecdotes from indigenous chronicle writing, contain translations from Siamese manuscripts and, perhaps unwittingly, adopt Buddhist conceptions of historical change. At the same time, Van Vliet remained deeply rooted in European literary traditions and was always aware of the limits of cross-cultural exchange. He proposed a balance between cultural adaptation, political neutrality, and social segregation that turned out as an effective strategy to maintain a continuous presence in Siam. The degree to which a foreign community conformed to Thai expectations was a key factor for economic success or failure. Such a strategy required a degree of local knowledge that only a skilled commercial cosmopolitan like Van Vliet could provide. Collecting reliable information about Asian countries called for an appropriate understanding of the functioning of local markets, the rules of local politics, and knowledge of Asian languages. Go-betweens who possessed such skills were therefore necessary, indeed indispensable for the VOC's business in the *Indies*.

52   Sven Trakulhun

However, the position of a cross-cultural broker was also highly vulnerable and ambiguous. While it took years to acquire sufficient knowledge of a foreign culture to ensure successful trade, living abroad for too long could also undermine a Dutchman's morality. Far away from home and constantly tempted by the shady allures of the East, Company servants became notorious in Europe for sexual debauchery and moral misbehavior. Dutch merchants in Siam were no exception in this regard. The most famous example is Joost Schouten, whose brilliant career ended in a most ignoble manner. In 1644, he was found guilty of "gruesome sodomy", which he confessed to have started in Siam. Schouten was convicted by the Dutch judiciary of "devilish lechery" and then "strangled and burnt to ashes" in Batavia.[48]

Others were accused of enriching themselves by smuggling or fraud. The salaries of the great majority of VOC employees were so meager that virtually nobody could live only on official payment. Although private trade was strictly limited in volume by Company law, "everyone from Governor-General to cabin-boy traded on side and everyone else knew it," as Charles Boxer has noted.[49] When Cornelis van Neijenrode died of alcohol abuse in Hirado in 1633, he left a fortune of roughly f 23,000. It seemed obvious to the Company authorities that he could not have amassed such a sum only from his salary. The Court of Justice in Batavia resolved that Van Neijenrode had enriched himself with "unfaithful actions or illicit and private trade" and confiscated his complete inheritance.[50]

Jeremias van Vliet met an almost similar fate. His monthly income as a Company merchant was approximately 60 guilders. When he left Siam in 1642 he had accumulated a fortune of about f 30,000, equivalent to roughly 2–2.5 Million USD. In 1646, he was found guilty of corruption, suspended from office, and forever banned from service in the Company. Fortunately for Van Vliet, he was married at that time to Catharina Sweers, the sister of Solomon Sweers who was a member of the Dutch Council of the Indies and ensured that his brother-in-law was repatriated to Holland under the most honorable conditions. Van Vliet resettled in Schiedam, his birthplace, where he led the quiet life of a wealthy rentier until his death in 1663.[51] His name has left no mark in the chronicles of Ayutthaya. He owes his fame not to the part he played in the history of Thailand, but to the contribution he made towards its recording.[52] Yet his life in Siam can illuminate how cultural mediation and social finesse enabled the Dutch to survive in a socio-political environment that ultimately remained "foreign".

Notes

1 Marie Louise Pratt, *Imperial Eyes. Travel Writing and Transculturation* (London/ New York: Routledge, 1992), 6.
2 For an English translation of Van Vliet's writings, see *Van Vliet's Siam,* ed. Chris Baker, Dhiravat Na Pombejra, Alfons van der Kraan and David K. Wyatt

Trouble in the contact zone 53

(Chiang Mai: Silkworm Books, 2005). Quotations from Van Vliet's work are from this edition.

3 Anthony Reid, *Southeast Asia in the Age of Commerce 1450–1680. Vol. 2: Expansion and Crisis* (New Haven/London: Yale University Press, 1988–93), 62–77. Reid's figures are based on European travel reports and should be used with caution.

4 John Struys, *The Perillous and Most Unhappy Voyages of John Struys; through Italy, Greece, ... Media, Persia, ...*, *and other places in Europe, Africa and Asia* (London 1683), 41.

5 Bhawan Ruangsilp, *Dutch East India Company Merchants at the Court of Ayutthaya: Dutch Perceptions of the Thai Kingdom, c. 1604–1765* (Leiden/Boston: Brill, 2007), 13–14.

6 Maria da Conceição Flores, *Os Portugueses e o Sião no Século XVI* (Lisbon: Imprensa Nacional Casa de Moeda, 1995).

7 Dhiravat Na Pombejra, "Conflicts and Rivalries Along the Coasts of Siam: Ayutthaya's Relations With the Portuguese, the Spaniards, and the Dutch in the 1620s and 1630s", in *500 Years of Thai-Portuguese Relations. A Festschrift*, ed. Michael Smithies (Bangkok: Siam Society, 2011), 142–60.

8 John Anderson: *English Intercourse with Siam in the Seventeenth Century* (London: Kegan Paul, Trench, Trubner & Co, 1890); on the "Mergui massacre" see 335–63.

9 Dirk van der Cruysse, *Siam and the West, 1500–1700* (Chiang Mai: Silkworm Books, 2002).

10 Jeremias van Vliet, "Description of the Kingdom of Siam 1638," in *Van Vliet's Siam*, ed. Chris Baker, Dhiravat Na Pombejra, Alfonsvan der Kraan and David K. Wyatt (Chiang Mai: Silkworm Books, 2005), 167. Royal monopolies changed from reign to reign, however; see Dhiravat na Pombejra, "A Political History of Siam under the Prasatthong Dynasty 1629–1688" (PhD Diss., London, SOAS, 1984), 38–40.

11 Dhiravat na Pombejra, "Political History", 176–185.

12 Warangkana Nibhatsukit: "The Emergence of Proto-entrepreneurial Groups in the City of Ayutthaya During the 17th–18th Centuries." *Silpakorn University International Journal* 6, no. 1–2 (2006): 91–121.

13 David Feeney, "The Decline in Property Rights in Men in Thailand, 1800–1930." *Journal of Economic History* 49, no. 2 (1989): 285–96.

14 1 rai = 1,600 square meter.

15 Barend J. Terwiel, *Thailand's Political History. From the Fall of Ayutthaya to Recent Times* (Bangkok: River Books, 2011), 45–53.

16 See David K. Wyatt, *Studies in Thai History. Collected Articles* (Chiang Mai: Silkworm Books, 1994), 90–97.

17 Mohammed Ismail Marcinkowski deals at some length with early Iranian-Siamese contacts in *From Isfahan to Ayutthaya: Contacts Between Iran and Siam in the 17th Century* (Singapore: Pustaka Nasional, 2005).

18 See Akin Rabibhadana, *The Organization of Thai Society in the Early Bangkok Period, 1782–1873* (Ithaca, NY: Cornell Univ. Pr., 1970), 147–54.

19 George Vinal Smith, *The Dutch in Seventeenth Century Thailand* (Detroit: The Cellar Bookshop, 1977), 106–7; 144; Dhiravat Na Pombejra, "VOC Employees and their Relationships with Mon and Siamese Women: A Case Study of Osoet Pegua.", in *Other Pasts. Women, Gender and History in Early Modern Southeast Asia*, ed. Barbara W. Andaya (Honolulu: University of Hawai'i at Mânoa, 2000), 195–214, here 206.

20 This type of liaison appears to have been widespread in Southeast Asia; see Sven Trakulhun, *Siam und Europa. Das Königreich Ayutthaya in westlichen Berichten, 1500–1670* (Hannover-Laatzen: Wehrhahn Verlag, 2006), 166–79.

54   Sven Trakulhun

21 Barbara Watson Andaya, *The Flaming Womb. Repositioning Women in Early Modern Southeast Asia* (Chiang Mai: Silkworm Books, 2008), 123–7.
22 Barend J. Terwiel, *A Traveler in Siam. Extracts from the Journal of Gijsbert Heeck* (Chiang Mai: Silkworm Books, 2008), 57. Heeck's account is published in full in *Terug naar de Oost. De reis van VOC-chirurgijn Gisjbert Heeck, 1654–1656.* Bezorgd en ingeleid door Barend Jan Terwiel en Peter Kirsch (Zutphen: WalburgPers, 2017), here 234.
23 Dhiravat Na Pombejra, "Ayutthaya as a Cosmopolitan Society: A Case Study of Daniel Brochebourde and His Descendants", in *Court, Company, and Campong: Essays on the VOC Presence in Ayutthaya* (Ayutthaya: Historical Study Centre, 1992), 25–42.
24 Alfons van der Kraan, "On Company Business. The Rijckloff van Goens Mission to Siam, 1650." *Itinerario* 22, no. 2 (1998): 42–84, here 63–65.
25 See Dhiravat, "VOC Employees," 196.
26 Bhawan, *Dutch East India Company Merchants*, 45.
27 Smith, *The Dutch*, 109–14.
28 Dhiravat, "VOC Employees," 209–10.
29 Margot E. van Opstall, "From Alkmaar to Ayudhya and Back." *Itinerario* 9/2 (1985): 108–20.
30 Jan de Vries, "Understanding Eurasian Trade in the Era of the Trading Companies", in *Goods from the East, 1600–1800: Trading Eurasia.* ed. Maxine Berg, Felicia Gottmann, Hanna Hodacs, Chris Nierstrasz (Houndsmills: Palgrave Macmillan, 2015), 7–43.
31 Cornelis van Neijenrode, "Vertoog van de Gelegenheid des Koningrijks van Siam." *Kroniek van het Histoorisch Genootschap, Gevestigd te Utrecht* 27/2 (1872): 279–318.
32 Joost Schouten, "*Beschrijvinge van de Regeeringe, Macht, Religie, Costuymen, Traffijcquen ende andere remercquable saecken, des Coninghrijcks Siam*", in Isaac Commelin, ed. *Begin ende Voortgang vande Vereenigde Neederlandtsche Geoctroyeerde Oost-Indische Compagnie*, 4 Vols. (Amsterdam: Jansonius, 1646), Vol. 4, 203–17. The account was later translated into English, French, German and Latin.
33 Jeremias van Vliet, "Report and Historical Account of the Event", in *Van Vliet's Siam*, 45–88. The historical context of the affair has been described in more detail in Han Ten Brummelhuis and John Kleinen, *A Dutch Picnic in Ayutthaya, 1636* (Amsterdam: University Amsterdam, 1984).
34 Van Vliet, "Report," 63.
35 The group of translators and intermediaries involved in the case consisted of Ian Iaclins (a mestizo from the Dutch lodge), an unidentified 'Pecap', three court interpreters named Okmun Wichit Phasa, Okluang Pith Parap and Alexander Pinieur, a Chinese called Tjoucko, a VOC interpreter named Trompanidt, and a Javanese Muslim merchant referred to as Radie Ebrehem; Van Vliet, "Report," 48–54, passim.
36 Van Vliet, "Report," 61; 71. Interpreters and translators were in a particularly vulnerable position when cross-cultural communication failed. Characteristically, the Trompanidt was later put in prison, while Radie Ebrehem was put to death shortly after the incident; Smith, *The Dutch*, 30.
37 Van Vliet, "Report," 81–84.
38 Quoted in Alfons van Kraan, "Introduction," in *Van Vliet's Siam*, 40.
39 Jeremias van Vliet, "*Verbael ende Historisch verhael van't gene des Vereenighde Nederlandtsche Geoctroijeerde Oost-Indische Companies Dienaers onder de directie van Jeremias van Vliet, in den Jaren 1636 ende 1637 [...]*," in François Pelsaert,

Trouble in the contact zone 55

Ongeluckige Voyagie, van't Schip Batavia, naer de Oost-Indien (Amsterdam: Jan Janz, 1647), 61–108.

40 Van Vliet, "Description of the Kingdom of Siam," in *Van Vliet's Siam*, 111 (first publ. as *Beschrying van het Koningryk Siam*, Leiden 1692).

41 See Chris Baker, "Van Vliet's *Description* and its Design," in *Proceedings of the International Symposium "Crossroads of Thai and Dutch History,"* ed. Dhiravat na Pombejra (Bangkok: Seameo-Spafa, 2007), 151–61.

42 For a nuanced assessment of the concept see John-Pau Rubiés, "Oriental Despotism and European Orientalism: Botero to Montesquieu," *Journal of Early Modern History* 9, no. 1–2 (2005): 106–80.

43 Jeremias van Vliet, "The Short History of Occurrences in the Past and the Succession of the Kings of Siam," in *Van Vliet's Siam*, 195.

44 Vickery, Michael, "Review of Jeremias van Vliet: The Short History of the Kings of Siam," *Journal of the Siam Society* 64, no. 2 (1976): 207–36, here 214; 219.

45 For an interpretation of the 1789 version of the *Sangitiyavamsa* see Craig J. Reynolds, *Seditious Histories. Contesting Thai and Southeast Asian Pasts* (Seattle and London: University of Washington Press, 2006), 143–60.

46 Van Vliet, "Historical Account of the Illness and Death of Pra Interra-Tsia, 22nd King of Siam [...]," in *Van Vliet's Siam*, 255–322.

47 Van Vliet, "Historical Account," 321.

48 Heeck, *Terug naar de Oost*, 37v.

49 Charles Ralph Boxer, *The Dutch Seaborne Empire 1600–1800* (London: Penguin Books, 1965), 225–6.

50 Leonard Blussé, *Strange Company. Chinese Settlers, mestizo women and the Dutch in VOC Batavia* (Leiden: Koninklijk Instituut voor Taal-, Land- en Volkenkunde, 1986), 184.

51 Baker et al.: "Introduction," in *Van Vliet's Siam*, 29–30.

52 Han ten Brummelhuis, *Merchant, Courtier, and Diplomat: A History of the Contacts between the Netherlands and Thailand* (Lochem/Gent: Uitgeversmaatschappij de Tijdstroom, 1987), 31.

3 Chinese commercial cosmopolitanism in the eighteenth-century Mekong River Delta: the case of Mạc Thiên Tứ

Xing Hang

How did Hà Tiên, today a sleepy town on the Vietnam–Cambodia border, flourish as an enclave of Chinese commercial cosmopolitanism in maritime East Asia during the eighteenth century? The port's prosperity rested upon a confluence of regional and global economic trends. These include commercialization in China, fueled by population expansion and resource shortages, and Southeast Asia's sparse demographic density and abundant endowments. Chinese merchants and settlers, taking advantage of the Qing Dynasty's (1644–1911) relaxed policies on trade and travel abroad, flooded into Southeast Asia in numbers unprecedented in past history. Their reach extended from bustling port cities to the remotest jungle, and their junks connected different parts of the region with each other and China. They mingled and, in some cases, intermarried with the native population. Their commercial preeminence has led scholars, such as Carl Trocki and Leonard Blussé, to speak of the eighteenth century as a "Chinese century" in maritime East Asia.[1] Yet warfare and geopolitical competition threatened to upset or redirect trading networks and goods. So did conflicts among Chinese immigrants from different provinces, classes, and occupational groupings, and interethnic strife with natives and European colonial authorities.

Hà Tiên and its ruler, Mạc Thiên Tứ (Mo Tianci, d. 1780), embodied the opportunities and tensions generated by a commercially cosmopolitan environment. Himself the son of a Chinese father and Vietnamese mother, he struggled to maintain a balance of power between a complex set of interested parties to ensure the continued survival and prosperity of his port polity. He paid vassalage to the Nguyễn lords of Cochinchina in southern Vietnam but also promoted Hà Tiên as a neutral mediator in the fierce, protracted struggle between Cochinchina and Siam for influence over the Cambodian throne. Despite his background as a descendant of a Ming loyalist who fled Manchu rule, he actively cultivated ties with the Qing court and elites. He welcomed to his realm, with open arms, merchants, missionaries, and scholars. Yet, he and his predominantly Leizhou/Hainan community engaged in a zero-sum competition with their Chaozhou counterparts in neighboring Siam to dominate the trade routes of the Gulf of Thailand.

Chinese commercial cosmopolitanism 57

The fortunes of the port polity highlights the commercial cosmopolitanism of eighteenth-century maritime East Asia, which made possible a transnational Chinese civic sphere outside of established state structures and political arrangements. The situation provided tremendous power and leverage to men like Mạc Thiên Tứ, whose very marginality in a marginal frontier setting allowed him to successfully navigate and mediate among a complex conjunction of interests. Nonetheless, the order that he established rested on fragile foundations. Fundamental changes to the regional configuration of power and international trade flows in the last quarter of the eighteenth century led to his downfall and spelled the end of Hà Tiên's autonomy. This chapter examines the how this polity rose, flourished, and declined, and explores the broader ramifications for Chinese commercial cosmopolitanism in maritime East Asia.

Ming loyalism and the founding of Hà Tiên

The commercially cosmopolitan setting of Hà Tiên derives, in part, from its own geographic marginality. The port lies at a crossroads; toward its east is the Mekong River Delta, with its swampy forests and vast, intricate network of waterways. Two large branches of this river, in turn, divide the delta into an eastern and western portion, with Hà Tiên lying at the westernmost extremity. Moving farther to the west, the landscape changes into dry flatland that extends through most of present-day coastal Cambodia up to Sihanoukville (Kampong Som). It is a narrow strip of land, bounded by the Cardamom and Elephant ranges, which effectively cut it off from the rest of Cambodia, including the key population centers of Phnom Penh and Udong to the north, and the border with Thailand to the west.[2] Besides fertile land suitable for rice cultivation and export, the entire area had access to the shipping and trade routes on the Gulf of Thailand that connected to the China Seas and the rest of maritime East Asia. The monsoon winds and ocean currents made the entire coastal area from the Saigon area to Bangkok an ideal transit point for ships, given the technology of that period.[3] Navigational handbooks written in the mid-Qing period always include the area in their compass guides for ships traveling between Japan and the China coast, and the Malay Peninsula and the Indonesian Archipelago.[4]

Hà Tiên's favorable location made the formation of a separate polity conceivable. Indeed, during the late seventeenth century, its hinterlands constituted a marginal, sparsely populated frontier nominally under Cambodia. Besides scattered original Khmer settlements and more recent settlers, landless Vietnamese from Cochinchina began to flow in through the eastern Mekong River Delta from farther north. Both groups opened up new land for agricultural cultivation or fished near the sea.[5]

The situation in China, namely the downfall of the Ming Dynasty (1368–1644) and its replacement by the Qing, caused a flood of refugees

58 *Xing Hang*

loyal to the former dynasty to take refuge in Southeast Asia. These immigrants usually uprooted their entire clans from their native places, while former Ming commanders brought along their units. They preceded the subsequent wave of Qing traders and settlers after the court in Beijing legalized private trade and travel in 1684. The dynastic transition profoundly altered the course of historical development in the Gulf of Thailand littoral as well. Mo Jiu (Mạc Cửu, 1655–1735), a Ming loyalist adventurer from the Leizhou Peninsula of Guangdong, went to Cambodia in 1680 and was appointed by the king to serve as the headman of the Chinese community. He was a typical example of someone who emigrated because he "could not bear the disorder wrought by the barbarian hordes upon China."[6]

With the blessing of the royal court at Udong, he acquired a base at Hà Tiên and opened it up as a free port for international trade.[7] However, he soon grew uncertain of Cambodia's ability to protect his realm on its own. The court in Udong was plagued with internecine succession struggles, an unstable situation that invited frequent interference from neighboring Siam. Fearful of Siamese power, Mo sought protection from its competitor, Cochinchina, which was expanding into the Mekong River Delta and increasing its influence over Cambodia. In 1708, he sent two of his trusted retainers to Huế and submitted as a vassal to the Nguyễn lord. The ruler bequeathed the name of Hà Tiên (River Spirit) garrison (*trấn*) upon Mo's realm, after a local legend of a fairy that supposedly roamed its waters. Mo was given the position of regional commander (*Tổng binh*).[8]

In 1728 and 1729, Mo dispatched two envoys to Japan, and received authorization to trade in Nagasaki. In 1729, he evidently overcame whatever of his own ideological baggage remained and opened up trading linkages with the Qing via Guangzhou.[9] He further undertook administrative reforms, dividing the hinterlands of the port into seven villages and recruiting landless Vietnamese to settle and farm the land to provide more revenues and support the needs of his port.[10] When he passed away at the ripe old age of 80 in 1735, Mo had established sound political and economic foundations for his realm.

The economics of commercial cosmopolitanism

Mạc Thiên Tứ, the eldest son of Mo's marriage with a Vietnamese woman, built upon the promising beginnings laid down by his father to dominate Hà Tiên for the next four decades. In 1739, just four years after his ascension to power, a Siamese-backed Cambodian force attempted to seize the port. After a fierce conflict, Tứ managed to rout the invaders. It was a significant victory, for Hà Tiên would face no more major threat to its existence until the 1770s.[11] He also took advantage of the fierce rivalry between Siam and Cochinchina over Cambodia to significantly expand Hà Tiên's hinterlands. In 1757, through deft diplomacy, he acquired control over five Cambodian provinces. His realm now stretched from the Cà Mau Peninsula on the southern shore of the Bassac (Hậu Giang), a branch of the Mekong River, across the Gulf of Thailand littoral to the present-day Cambodian-Thai border. His acquisition allowed him privileged access to the Mekong Delta and close proximity to the Chaophraya Plain, the two largest rice-producing areas in Southeast Asia. He proceeded to recruit settlers and promote the opening of new land for agriculture and resource extraction.[12]

Commercialization in China worked to further enhance the prominence of Hà Tiên. Steady population growth in the Qing over the eighteenth century gradually ran up against ecological limits, especially in the southeastern coastal provinces of Fujian and Guangdong. More than ever before, the country relied heavily upon interregional and international linkages to support its elaborate commercial infrastructure.[13] As the Chinese coastal areas grew increasingly deficient in food supplies, the Qianlong Emperor (1711–1799, r. 1735–1796) took measures in 1743 to encourage rice imports, including the reduction of duties for ships carrying 10,000 *dan* (500,000 kg) or more, and ranks and titles for merchants based upon their contribution.[14]

Taking advantage of its ideal geographical location and abundant natural resources, Hà Tiên became a leading exporter to the Chinese market of copious quantities of rice, produced in the Mekong River Delta and parts of Cambodia and Siam. After 1758, Hà Tiên increasingly took on the functions of a trading emporium. Between the 1760s and 1770s, an era undoubtedly marking the height of Tứ's power, it handled as much as half of all shipping in the China trade.[15] Tin replaced rice to became Hà Tiên's preeminent export. The metal was an essential component in the production of canisters to store and maintain the freshness of tea leaves, a product that was rapidly becoming the biggest component of China's foreign trade, especially with the West.[16] Some of it was produced locally, but the majority came from the mines of Bangka, farther south. Instead of going to Guangzhou, rice was exported to Bangka to supply the needs of another leading Chinese export: her vast supply of surplus labor in the form of immigrant tin miners.[17] By the middle of the eighteenth century, Mạc Thiên Tứ had successfully controlled the flow of a sizable share of products from the China–Japan, China–Southeast Asia, and the China–South Asia–European trading networks.

The geopolitical context of commercial cosmopolitanism

Besides transforming the main port of his realm into a regional trading emporium, he aimed to maintain and expand this profitable enterprise. Accordingly, he retained and modified the civil administration forged under his deceased father.[18] Although very little documentation exists about these institutions and their personnel, they probably remained in a rudimentary state. Otherwise, he apparently relied primarily upon military garrisons to rule over his realm, a situation not unlike that of neighboring Cochinchina.[19] He also possessed a sizable number of warships. In 1767, at

60   *Xing Hang*

the height of his power, one of his commanders led 50,000 men and over a hundred ships in a major campaign against Siam.[20]

Despite the vast resources and manpower at his disposal, Tứ seemed ambiguous about clearly defining the nature of his polity. Sakurai and Kitagawa conclude from their innovative transnational comparison of historical sources that Hà Tiên was a polity with "two faces: one for the Khmer people and another for the Chinese, as well as two faces for internal and external affairs." On the one hand, Tứ subscribed to the Confucian model of clearly defined administrative and ritual obligations. Following in his father's footsteps, he rendered vassalage to Cochinchina. In 1736, soon after his accession, he sent envoys to Huế, which granted him the right to inherit the rank of regional commander. The Nguyễn lord further bequeathed new ranks and titles upon him, including the Tông Đức marquis and the position of commissioner-in-chief (Đô đốc). Cochinchinese settlers, primarily landless peasants, continued to flood into his realm, forming a demographic majority in the countryside around the urban ports, where the Chinese congregated.[21] Moreover, the Nguyễn lord stationed a hundred soldiers in Hà Tiên.[22] Additional garrisons in Saigon and other parts of the Mekong River Delta stood ready to defend him if he came under attack from Cambodia or Siam.[23]

At the same time, however, Tứ was influenced by the more decentralized, Indic-inspired Southeast Asian conception of space prevalent in Cambodia. Here, political order resembled a mandala, characterized by overlapping, concentric spheres of power in which their rulers recognized one or several main overlords.[24] Within each realm, a city situated at the mouth of a river served as the main power center, with the hinterlands upstream serving as political subordinates supplying the tribute and products necessary for its sustenance.[25] Hà Tiên, which boasted its own commercial ports and agriculturally rich interior, was typical for the Southeast Asian political scene. Mạc Thiên Tứ's role was simply an expansion of his father's role as a *shahbandar*, or harbor master, an ancient institution in Southeast Asia and other parts of the world. At port cities, places where mercantile communities of many different ethnic groups congregated and plied their wares, local rulers would designate prominent merchants to administer the affairs of their respective diasporas. They enjoyed extraterritorial privileges, such as their own living quarters and the right to enforce the laws and customs of their ancestral countries. In exchange, they would represent their respective communities in dealing with the rulers and merchants of other ethnicities.[26]

From the perspective of the court in Udong, Tứ, known in the records as Preah Sotoat, qualified, at most, as one of several regional strongmen. Indeed, the immediate environs of Hà Tiên never ceased to remain under the authority of the Cambodian governor of Banteay Meas Province, who, after 1756, received the royal title of Okna Reacea Sethei.[27] The same goes with the five other provinces that Mạc Thiên Tứ appropriated for his realm in 1757. In contrast to the Vietnamese sources, which consider it an unalterable

Chinese commercial cosmopolitanism 61

alienation of land, the Cambodian records make no mention of such a significant loss of territory. Local administrators remained in their places and continued to derive their legitimacy from the Udong court, except they now worked more closely with Tử. He depended heavily upon these governors in matters related to the Khmer population, an overwhelming majority especially on the Gulf of Thailand rim, and mobilize them for military service.[28]

Although an excellent starting point for grasping the character of Mạc Thiên Tử's enterprise, the "dual political structure" proposed by Sakurai and Kitagawa only applied in the external context to his interactions with Cambodia and Cochinchina. Many contemporary visitors from other parts of the world reveal yet another side to this polity. Qing observers unambiguously referred to it as the Gangkou Kingdom (*guo*) and to Mạc Thiên Tử by name as a "king" who lived in a Chinese-style palace.[29] As it turns out, Tử deliberately crafted this image toward countries outside his immediate neighborhood. Intriguingly, the letters that he sent to the Japanese port of Nagasaki along with two missions in 1740 and 1742 established his credentials as the king of Cambodia. The full title used to preface his greeting to the shogun and request for normalized trading relations reads: Supreme Commander of Land and Naval Forces Charged with All Matters in the Land of Zhenla, Rewarded with the Noble Title of Nak Samdec Preah Sotoat, King Mạc of Cambodia (柬埔寨國大總制統理水陸軍務帶管真臘通國地方進爵六參烈巴司哲王鄚).[30]

As can be seen, there are a multiplicity of definitions of Hà Tiên's status, whether from political actors, observers, and scholars. Tử himself added fuel to the fire by giving contradictory claims of his role in the governance of his realm. In reality, the different faces that he put on for different audiences merely served as means toward his ultimate aim: to maximize the profit from the exploitation of agricultural resources and trading routes. In other words, Tử's polity operated more like a business enterprise than a fully-fledged state. For this reason, the French philosopher and adventurer Pierre Poivre, who either visited or heard extensively about Hà Tiên during his travels in Southeast Asia, claims that Tử personally "disdained" the title of king. He "never pretended to reign but only to establish an empire of reason" and was "very content to be the chief laborer and merchant of his realm."[31] Poivre makes him out to be an apolitical entrepreneur committed solely to economic growth and prosperity for his people.

Besides the tolerant political climate toward overseas trade in China, geopolitics in Southeast Asia provided another impetus for Hà Tiên's ambiguous autonomy. As Liam Kelley and John Wong correctly point out, Tử was situated in a complex and volatile geopolitical environment, and therefore had to constantly negotiate his identity and allegiances to maximize his interests and legitimacy at any given time.[32] Tử shared much in common with Chinese communities elsewhere in maritime East Asia, including Cochinchina and the Dutch East India Company's Asian

62 *Xing Hang*

headquarters at Batavia, on Java. Their emergence had much to do with the lack of resources and manpower on the part of European colonies and native states to fully administer their realms, along with the absence of a strong, committed outside power in the region. The authorities welcomed and, in some cases, actively recruited the Chinese as partners in their projects at domestic consolidation.[33] Oftentimes, especially in the vast, sparsely populated frontiers, the co-colonizers could, through superior numbers and organization, break free of their original patrons to forge their own quasi-governmental enterprises. Hà Tiên served as a fitting example of this process.[34] In the face of a complex, multipolar regional order, along with the challenges of administering a multiethnic polity in a vast, sparsely settled frontier, Mạc Thiên Tứ thus put on different faces before different audiences to legitimate his rule.

A transnational civic sphere

Tứ took advantage of Hà Tiên's hazy status to position it as a transnational civic sphere, a meeting ground for the relatively unhindered exchange of ideas and information. China's growing integration with the global economy allowed for increased ease of accessibility and more frequent bilateral contact with the ancestral land. Hà Tiên saw an influx not only of merchants from China, but also members of the educated elite. They tended to be impoverished lower-level gentry who struggled to make ends meet for themselves back home and sought better opportunities overseas. Liang Zhongluan, for instance, was "a poor Confucian" from Guangdong and "at seventy, did not have any offspring." He sailed to Hà Tiên and served as an instructor in the schools, a service for which Tứ rewarded him lavishly.[35]

To facilitate regular diplomatic and commercial exchange with the Chinese and neighboring Cochinchina, both of which subscribed to a common cultural framework, he established the Academy for the Selection of Worthies (Chiêu Anh Các) in 1735. It served the purpose of a social club and literary society. Under its auspices, Tứ would gather with key associates and invited scholars to compose and exchange poetic verses in drinking parties and festive occasions. The most famous and only surviving output of the academy was a published anthology centered upon Tứ's celebration of the ten most prominent landmarks of his realm. The over 360 poems in the "Hà Tiên thập vịnh (Ten verses of Hà Tiên)," undoubtedly made up a small portion out of hundreds or possibly thousands more that failed to survive the vicissitudes of historical change.[36]

Only a handful of the 30-odd poets who contributed to this anthology were local to Hà Tiên.[37] Around 25 came from the Chinese provinces of Fujian and Guangdong, and six to seven from Cochinchina. Of these, many never stepped foot onto Hà Tiên but maintained correspondence from afar, sending their own compositions onboard merchant vessels during each monsoon season. The academy thus became a primary venue for forming

Chinese commercial cosmopolitanism 63

and maintaining an active international dialogue with literati, statesmen, and merchants from both countries. In addition to the poets mentioned above, Tử maintained a lively exchange of letters with Nguyễn Cư Trinh (1716-1767), commander of the Nguyễn expeditionary force in Cambodia, and Lê Bác Bình, a native of the Saigon area who became a Confucian scholar in Huế.[38]

Besides showing himself to be a man of letters, Mạc Thiên Tứ also proved to be a generous patron of religion. He donated to the establishment and upkeep of several Buddhist temples in Hà Tiên, including the purchase of statues and other religious implements from China. Tử treated Western missionaries with equal kindness. Upon his invitation, the French bishop of Ayutthaya in Siam stayed with him at Hà Tiên while on the way to Huế. The bishop later recalled to Pierre Poivre that Tử was "a man of character." In addition, he welcomed the French and Franciscans from Manila to establish permanent missions in his realm.[39]

Despite his eclectic outlook, Mạc Thiên Tứ heavily emphasized the Chinese character of his polity, at least in the urban centers, where his administration was most direct and the diaspora population most concentrated. Qing observers wrote with admiration that the residents of the port "all lived in houses made of tiles and bricks," just like in China, and not the stilt structures common to Southeast Asia. Tử further took care to ensure generational continuity, particularly among his fellow cohort of immigrant diaspora and their descendants. He maintained a network of schools that taught the Confucian Classics, poetry, and literature. Promising students, as well as impoverished ones unable to care for themselves, would be selected to serve as teachers at his expense. He established a shrine to Confucius in the center of town for "the king and every person on down to pay their respects" to the great sage.[40]

However, the Chinese identity that Tử featured differed drastically from the Chineseness of the ancestral land. Travelers to Hà Tiên from the Qing expressed shock at witnessing "the dress and institutions of the previous dynasty," referring to the Ming. The residents, they noted, grew out their hair long, in contrast to the shaven pates and queue imposed by the Manchu rulers in China on pain of death, and wore loose, flowing robes with wide sleeves rather than the tight riding jackets of the Qing.[41] From the perspective of these travelers from the ancestral land, Tử's realm may have contained a more pristine and primordial form of Chineseness. It was precisely the shared experience of a traumatic dynastic transition and an anti-Manchu narrative that underlay an unprecedented crystallization of a Chinese identity outside China.[42]

This emphasis on the maintenance of Chinese norms was not unique to Hà Tiên but also other concentrated diasporic settlements across Southeast Asia, including Spanish Manila, Batavia, and the Cochinchinese port of Hội An. Nonetheless, it was an identity that absorbed many local elements through intermarriage and cultural borrowing. As a result, these places

64 *Xing Hang*

witnessed the rise of a creolized elite community consisting of the descendants of the original immigrants from China. They went by a variety of classifications, such as Peranakan in Batavia, mestizo in Manila, and Minh Hương (people of Ming descent) in Cochinchina.[43] Tứ himself was a fitting example of the latter, being of mixed Sino-Vietnamese parentage. As Anthony Reid has shown, this creolization stood in sharp contrast to the Chinese immigrants of previous centuries, who became completely absorbed into a native urban elite within one or two generations.[44]

Neutrality and mediation

In keeping with the effort to establish the reputation of Hà Tiên as a bastion of culture, Tứ actively sought to define his realm as a politically neutral space, and himself a disinterested mediator for the contentious warring parties in his neighborhood. In 1755, when Cochinchinese troops invaded Cambodia to unseat the pro-Siamese King Ang Sngoun (r. 1749–1755), the beleaguered ruler fled to Hà Tiên to seek refuge under Tứ. As a result of Tứ's efforts, the Nguyễn lord agreed to withdraw his troops and restore the throne to the status quo ante in exchange for the cession to Huế of Cambodian territory around present-day Mỹ Tho, adjacent to the south of the Saigon area.[45]

Within a matter of months, however, more turbulence ensued when Ang Sngoun passed away. The deceased's uncle returned from Siam to succeed to the throne, only to be assassinated by one of his nephews six months later. The usurper then plotted to eliminate his rival, Ang Ton (r. 1758–1775), the grandson of the murdered king. He also happened to be the adopted son of Mạc Thiên Tứ. Upon discovering the conspiracy, Ang Ton fled to Hà Tiên. As Cochinchinese forces amassed to enter Cambodia and remove the pro-Siamese faction from the throne, Tứ again stepped forward to mediate a solution. In 1757, he successfully persuaded the Nguyễn lord to recognize Ang Ton as the new ruler, and arranged for the cession to Cochinchina of more Cambodian territories, this time the entire northern part of the Mekong River Delta up to Châu Đốc in the west, as compensation. Tứ then escorted Ang Ton to Udong to ensure a peaceful ascension to the throne.[46] Through these series of negotiations, the Siamese maintained their influence over their neighbor, while Cochinchina obtained vast tracts of territory that it had always coveted. Yet, without doubt, Tứ had become the new kingmaker in Cambodian politics. The contenders who sought refuge with him in both 1755 and 1757 were ultimately chosen to rule, and Ang Ton was able to sit on the throne without much incident until 1775.

Because of his successful mediation, Tứ's sphere of influence reached its height, with much of the Gulf of Thailand littoral owing primary allegiance to him. The centrality of Hà Tiên in the region as a neutral space and sanctuary once again became apparent in 1767, when Burmese forces overran Siam and sacked the capital of Ayutthaya. The king died of anxiety,

Chinese commercial cosmopolitanism 65

while the invaders carried off the crown prince and women and booty back to their country. Only two royal princes, along with their entourage of several hundred, fled to Hà Tiên, where Tứ built a house for them to reside.[47]

The Burmese invasion transformed Hà Tiên into a regional clearinghouse for news and information. Trusted merchants from the port served as ideal spies, given the transient nature of their business and since their vessels sailed to all of the major destinations in Southeast Asia. In fact, the Qing came to depend upon Tứ for confidential intelligence related to Siam and Burma. Every year between 1766 and 1770, Li Shiyao (d. 1788), the governor-general of Guangdong and Guangxi, dispatched several military officials at the rank of patrolling admiral (*youji*) to board merchant ships bound for Hà Tiên. They interviewed Tứ in person about the latest developments, and had him forward to Siam and Burma the Qianlong Emperor's pronouncements. On his part, Tứ sent special missions led by relatives or close confidants to Guangzhou. They carried onboard detailed descriptions of Burma, compiled from Chinese gazetteers, translations from Southeast Asian narratives, and firsthand observations. They also furnished detailed navigational charts and compass routes of the Gulf of Thailand zone.[48] As a reward for his assistance, the Qianlong Emperor invited Tứ's envoys for a personal audience in Beijing. He feasted the entourage for five days and bestowed upon them lavish gifts, and ordered several officials to sail with the mission back home.[49]

A sudden downfall

By the late 1760s, Hà Tiên had reached the height of its influence and prestige as a transnational zone of neutrality and a center of culture and military intelligence. Yet, Mạc Thiên Tứ's commercial cosmopolitanism would also lead to his rapid undoing once the geopolitical situation became unbalanced. Events in Siam touched off this process of decline. Merchants and immigrants from Chaozhou, in eastern Guangdong, had settled in large numbers in the eastern frontier of Siam. They established a competing emporium at Chanthaburi, just to the west of Tứ's sphere of influence, and attempted to obstruct his business by establishing bases on the islands in the Gulf of Thailand and launching piratical raids against his shipping. However, Tứ managed to suppress their activities through several naval campaigns in the 1750s and 1760s.[50]

However, the Burmese invasion of Siam in 1767 changed everything. The fall of the Ayutthaya Dynasty made possible the meteoric rise of a dynamic, vigorous ruler: Taksin (b. 1734, r. 1767–1782), himself a creolized Chinese, the son of a Chaozhou tax farmer and a Thai princess. He received support and financing from his compatriots in the Chaozhou mercantile community, providing him the means to expel the Burmese and reestablish control over Siam and its dependencies.[51] In exchange, Taksin supported their

66 *Xing Hang*

commercial activities, both at their base of Chanthaburi and his new capital, Bangkok. Within just a few years after its establishment, Bangkok grew rapidly into a major rival to Hà Tiên for the shipment of rice and other transshipment services.[52] Tứ witnessed these developments with alarm. In 1769, he abandoned the wise policies of neutrality and mediation that had served his realm so well for the past three decades. Instead, he decided to initiate a showdown by launching a full-scale invasion of Chanthaburi in an attempt to root out Chaozhou power. Although Hà Tiên troops captured the city, devastating epidemics soon decimated the ranks and made it impossible for them to proceed. Unable to sustain further losses, Tứ ordered a withdrawal. Out of a total of 50,000 men deployed in the campaign, only 10,000 of them returned.[53]

Even worse, his actions invited the direct retaliation of Taksin, who amassed a huge army that overran and laid waste to Hà Tiên in 1771. Tứ barely escaped with his life and, with some of his followers, took refuge at Trấn Giang (present-day Cần Thơ), a port on the eastern edge of the Mekong Delta.[54] Taksin's forces proceeded to forge a path of destruction through Cambodia before striking Cochinchina. After months of fighting, accompanied by negotiations, he and the forces of the Nguyễn lord reached a truce. As part of the settlement, Siamese forces agreed to withdraw from Hà Tiên and restore the city to Tứ.[55] However, this recovery was shortlived. The Tây Sơn rebels, who were fighting against Cochinchina, cut through the defenses of the Saigon garrison and advanced deep into Tứ's realm. Once again, Hà Tiên fell, this time to the rebels, and was put to the torch. The rebels would go on to unite all of Vietnam over the next decade.

In an ironic twist of fate, Mạc Thiên Tứ, his relatives, and officials fled to Bangkok, where Taksin welcomed them with open arms. The threat posed by the Tây Sơn rebels now brought these formerly bitter enemies, together with the embattled Nguyễn, into the same cam.[56] However, old differences die hard. At first, Taksin treated the exiles with great generosity and kindness. Despite the genuine attempt at reconciliation, he presently suspected them of plotting to overthrow him and seize the Siamese throne. In a fit of rage, he personally confronted the entire entourage during a court audience with the supposedly incriminating evidence of their involvement. Forlorn and embittered, and unable to move Taksin despite the most earnest pleas of innocence, Mạc Thiên Tứ committed suicide by drinking poison in 1780. He was seventy years of age. Taksin then had Tứ's sons and grandsons, and wives and concubines, a total of 36 members of the Mạc family, beheaded. Others were exiled to the remote frontiers.

The tragedy marked the definitive end of the Hà Tiên port polity's heyday as an trading entrepôt and an independent political actor in maritime East Asia. Over the course of the nineteenth century, it became incorporated, into successive stages, into a unified Vietnam under the Nguyễn. Nonetheless, surviving members of the Mạc family, descended from the sons of Tứ's concubines, still served as the head of Hà Tiên on a hereditary basis. They

Chinese commercial cosmopolitanism 67

enjoyed some autonomy in administration as well as revenue collection and military within a much-reduced realm. Only after the French occupied Hà Tiên in 1867 and imposed colonial rule, as with the rest of Indochina, did these privileges come to a definitive end.[57]

Conclusion

The emergence of Hà Tiên as a crucial emporium for maritime East Asian trade in the eighteenth century had as much to do with structural factors as the dynamic personality of Mạc Thiên Tứ. China's dependence upon foreign trade, combined with the vast frontier spaces in Southeast Asia, provided the conditions for a stable, creolized diaspora that combined, usually through intermarriage, the cultural elements of the ancestral and adopted lands. The sparsely settled Gulf of Thailand littoral, in particular, created the ideal conditions for the full development of Chinese political and economic power in the form of autonomous polities.

Mạc Thiên Tứ took advantage of Hà Tiên's geographic location at the crossroads of the maritime East Asian trading lanes to transform his enclave into a profitable commercial entrepôt. He ensured its continued prosperity and survival by projecting multiple representations of his rule, from Confucian notions of hierarchy and territory to the more disperse Southeast Asian mandala networks. He sought to transform Hà Tiên into the hub of a transnational civic sphere by patronizing literature and religion, and highlighting the Ming Chinese character of his realm. His cautious approach toward diplomacy, characterized by neutrality and mediation, maximized the benefits for his realm under the existing geopolitical arrangements.

In fact, Tứ's rule over Hà Tiên fulfilled Curtin's categorization of an autonomous, self-governing mercantile community characterized by "a self-conscious pacifism and neutrality toward all political struggles."[58] However, his realm did not exactly reach the level of the European colonial outposts in Asia, such as the Dutch, British, or French East India Companies. Instead, Hà Tiên can be more aptly characterized as a transnational transplantation of Chinese local society during the Ming and Qing periods. As the works of Timothy Brook, William Rowe, and Melissa Macauley show, semi-formal grassroots organizations proliferated across the country over this period, ranging from clans and native-place associations to merchant guilds and shrine and temple management. They provided much-needed services to local societies at a time when population growth and commercialization severely strained the resources of the regular bureaucracy. Gentry played a leading role, serving on the board of directors of the grassroots organizations and acting as mediators between their communities and governmental authorities above. In addition, they adjudicated most legal disputes, operated charities and schools, built roads and bridges, and maintained clan shrines. The basis of their power derived from land ownership and certification of their status through the civil service examinations.[59]

68 Xing Hang

Seen in this context, Mạc Thiên Tứ's actions resembled those of a gentry elite set loose on a sparsely populated frontier with minimal control from state authorities. He was able to create effective institutions that ensured the proper governance and defense of his realm, while profiting from the lucrative trading networks of maritime East Asia. The different faces that he put before the rulers of different lands represented efforts at mediation within a complex, multiethnic geopolitical environment. His establishment of Confucianism as an orthodoxy, combined with his poetry clubs and friendships with Qing and Cochinchinese elites, allowed him to accumulate cultural capital and legitimacy where no institutionalized mechanism for certification existed, in particular, the civil service examinations.

Yet, Tứ never appeared to have moved beyond a utilitarian approach to governance as a means rather than the establishment of a territorial state as an end in itself. All of the mainland Southeast Asian powers – Vietnam, Siam, and Burma – underwent this process, which resulted, by the late eighteenth century, in powerful, consolidated kingdoms. In the words of Victor Lieberman, they were "implacably hierarchic, anti-entropic, obsessed with innumerable particularities of status and privilege determined by one's distance from the sovereign."[60] Tứ's passivity in this regard, and the resulting lack of a coordinated bureaucratic rationalization, ultimately subjected him to the decisions and contingencies of his increasingly powerful neighbors. At the same time, like the semi-formal local organizations in China, the core of his realm rested upon particularistic ties of shared dialect and native place, which his commercial cosmopolitanism could never supplant. As a result, he and his Leizhou/Hainan inner circle engaged in a bitter rivalry with the Chaozhou merchants of Siam, a contest that would ultimately spell the doom of Hà Tiên and autonomous Chinese regimes in mainland Southeast Asia.

Notes

1 Leonard Blussé, "The Chinese Century: The Eighteenth Century in the China Sea Region," *Archipel* 58 (1999): 107–29; and Carl Trocki, "Chinese Pioneering in Eighteenth-Century South Asia," in *The Last Stand of Asian Autonomies: Responses to Modernity in the Diverse States of Southeast Asia and Korea, 1760–1840*, ed.Anthony Reid (New York: St. Martin's Press, 1997), 83–102.

2 Sakurai Yumio, "Eighteenth-Century Chinese Pioneers on the Water Frontier of Indochina," in *Water Frontier: Commerce and the Chinese in the Lower Mekong Region, 1750–1880,* ed. Nola Cooke and Li Tana (Lanham, MD: Rowman and Littlefield, 2004), 36–39; Kitagawa Takako, "*Kampot* of the Belle Epoque: From the Outlet of Cambodia to a Colonial Resort," *Southeast Asian Studies* 42, no. 4 (2005): 395–96.

3 Barbara Watson Andaya, *To Live as Brothers: Southeast Sumatra in the Seventeenth and Eighteenth Centuries* (Honolulu: University of Hawai`i Press, 1993), 123.

4 Xiang Da, ed. *Liangzhong haidao zhenjing* (*Two Kinds of Compass Guides to the Sea Routes*) (Beijing: Zhonghua shuju, 1992). See, for instance, 35–36, 50–51, 82–83, 174–75.

Chinese commercial cosmopolitanism 69

5 Minh Vũ, "Vai trò họ Mạc trong việc khai khẩn đất Hà Tiên," *Xưa và Nay* (Spring 1999): 30.
6 Vũ Thế Doanh, ed. *Hà Tiên trấn Hiệp trấn Mạc thị gia phả* (Hanoi: Nhà Xuất Bản Thế Giới, 2006), 93.
7 Chin Keiwa (Chen Ching-ho), "Kasen Maku-shi no bungaku katsudō, toku ni Kasen Jūei ni tsuite," *Shigaku* 40.2/3: 315; Trương Minh Đạt, "Họ Mạc thời kỳ đầu khai sáng đất Hà Tiên," *Nghiên cứu lịch sử* 2.3–4 (2001): 10–14.
8 Doanh, *Gia phả*, 93, 94, 97.
9 Trần Kinh Hòa (Chen Ching-ho), "Họ Mạc và chúa Nguyễn ở Hà Tiên," *Văn hóa Á châu* 10 (1958): 33–34.
10 Trịnh Hoài Đức, *Gia Định thành thông chí* (Hanoi: Nhà xuất bản Giáo dục, 1998), 304–5; Sakurai Yumio and Kitagawa Takako, "Hà Tiên or Banteay Meas in the Time of the Fall of Ayutthaya," in *From Japan to Arabia: Ayutthaya's Maritime Relations with Asia,* ed. Kennon Breazeale (Bangkok: Toyota Thailand Foundation, 1999), 158–59.
11 Xu Wentang and Xie Qiyi, eds. Da Nan shilu *Qing-Yue guanxi shiliao huibian* (Taipei: Academia Sinica, 2000), 21.
12 Đức, *Thông chí*, 309.
13 Ramon H. Myers and Wang Yeh-chien, "Economic Developments: 1644–1800," in *The Cambridge History of China*, vol. 9.1: The Ch'ing Empire to 1800, eds. Denis Twitchett and John King Fairbank (Cambridge, UK: Cambridge University Press, 2002), 564; Anthony Reid, *Southeast Asia in the Age of Commerce, 1450–1680: The Lands Below the Winds* (New Haven, CT: Yale University Press, 1990), 25–26.
14 Zheng Yangwen, *China on the Sea: How the Maritime World Shaped Modern China* (Leiden: Brill, 2011), 103–9.
15 Li Tana and Paul van Dyke, "Canton, Cancao, and Cochinchina: New Data and New Light on Eighteenth-century Canton and the Nanyang," *Chinese Southern Diaspora Studies* 1 (2007): 12.
16 Li and van Dyke, "Canton, Cancao, and Cochinchina," 11.
17 Andaya, *To Live as Brothers*, 185, 191, 291; Li Tana, "Eighteenth-Century Mekong Delta," 150.
18 Đức, *Thông chí*, 307–10.
19 John K. Whitmore and Brian A. Zottoli, "The Birth of the State of Vietnam," in *The Cambridge History of China*, vol. 9 pt. 2: *The Ch'ing Dynasty to 1800,* ed. Willard J. Peterson (Cambridge, UK: Cambridge University Press, 2016), 206–7.
20 Doanh, *Gia phả*, 111.
21 Phan Huy Lê, "Về việc đánh giá họ Mạc ở Hà Tiên," in *250 năm Tao đàn Chiêu Anh Các (1736–1986)* (Rạch Giá: Sở Văn Hóa Thông Tin Kiên Giang, 1986), 43.
22 Pierre Poivre, "Journal d'un voyage à l'Indochine," in *Revue de l'Extrême-Orient,* ed. Henri Cordier (Paris: E. Leroux, 1887), vol. 3, 414.
23 Đức, *Thông chí*, 305–6.
24 Kenneth R. Hall, *A History of Early Southeast Asia: Maritime Trade and Societal Development, 100–1500* (Lanham, MD: Rowman and Littlefield, 2010), 22–29.
25 Sakurai and Kitagawa, "Hà Tiên or Banteay Meas," 169.
26 Philip Curtin, *Cross-Cultural Trade in World History* (Cambridge, UK: Cambridge University Press, 1984), 130.
27 Sakurai and Kitagawa, "Hà Tiên or Banteay Meas," 157–59.
28 The mandala model is explained in greater detail in Owen W. Wolters, *History, Culture, and Region in Southeast Asian Perspectives* (Ithaca, NY: SEAP Publications, 1999), 27–40.
29 Zhang Tingyu et al. (com and ed.), *Qingchao wenxian tongkao* (Shanghai: Commercial Press, 1936), 7463.

70 *Xing Hang*

30 Kondo Morishige, *Gaiban tsūsho*, in *Kondo Seisai zenshū* (Tokyo: Kokusho kankōkai, 1905), vol. 1, 271. Zhenla is the traditional Chinese name for Cambodia. When Kondo transcribed this document, he wrote down the surname of Tứ as Trịnh (鄭), which is quite easily confounded with Mạc (鄚).

31 Pierre Poivre, *Ouevres complettes* (Paris: Chez Fuchs, 1797), 142.

32 Leonard Blussé, *Strange Company: Chinese Settlers, Mestizo Women, and the Dutch in the VOC Batavia* (Dordrecht: Foris, 1986), 135–8; G. B. Souza, *The Survival of Empire: Portuguese Trade and Society in China and the South China Sea, 1630–1754* (Cambridge, UK: Cambridge University Press, 2004), 87–168. John D. Wong, "Improvising Protocols: Two Enterprising Chinese Migrant Families and the Resourceful Nguyễn Court," *Journal of Southeast Asian Studies* 50.2 (2019): 246-247, 253; and Liam C. Kelley, "Thoughts on a Chinese Diaspora: The Case of the Mạcs of Hà Tiên," *Crossroads: An Interdisciplinary Journal of Southeast Asian Studies* 14.1 (2000): 90.

33 Tonio Andrade originally applied the concept of co-colonization to talk about the role of Chinese settlers in Taiwan under the auspices of the Dutch East India Company. See Andrade, *How Taiwan became Chinese: Dutch, Spanish, and Han Colonization in the Seventeenth Century* (New York: Columbia University Press, 2008), 115–32.

34 Chen Ching-ho, the pioneering scholar of overseas Chinese studies, compares the Mo/Mạc to other Chinese statebuilders, such as Taksin (1734–1782, r. 1767–1782), king of Siam, Wu Rang, the autonomous lord of Songkhla in southern Thailand, and the West Borneo mining federations led by Luo Fangbo (1738–1795). See Chin (Chen), "Kasen Maku-shi," 312–13.

35 Luo Tianchi, *Wushan zhilin*, in *Qing dai Guangdong biji wuzhong*, ed.Wu Qi (Guangzhou: Guangzhou People's Publishing House, 2006), 58.

36 Mạc Thiên Tứ, *An Nam Hà Tiên thập vịnh*, Institute of Hán-Nôm Studies A. 441, n.; Xu and Xie, *Da Nan shilu*, 20; Đức, *Thông chí*, 306–7. For a detailed study of how Tứ utilized the academy and its poets to forge a transnational Chinese literary space, refer to Claudine Ang Tsu Lyn, *Poetic Transformations: Eighteenth-Century Cultural Projects on the Mekong Plains* (Cambridge, MA: Harvard University Press, 2019), 121-190.

37 Tứ, *Thập vịnh*, n.; Doanh, *Gia phả*, 102; Xu and Xie, *Da Nan shilu*, 20; Đức, *Thông chí*, 306.

38 Lê Quý Đôn, *Phủ biên tạp lục*, in Nguyễn Khắc Thuần (ed.), *Lê Quý Đôn tuyển tập*, pt. 2 (Hanoi: Educational Publishing House, 2008), 348–49; Tứ, *Thập vịnh*, n.; Xu and Xie, *Da Nan shilu*, 60.

39 Pierre Poivre, "Journal d'un voyage," 414.

40 Zhang et al., *Qingchao wenxian tongkao*, 7463.

41 Ibid., 7463.

42 Reid, *Age of Commerce*, vol. II, 314.

43 Philip Kuhn, *Chinese Among Others: Emigration in Modern Times* (Lanham, MD: Rowman and Littlefield, 2008), 70–71; James Wheeler, "Cross-cultural Trade and Trans-regional Networks in the Port of Hoi An: Maritime Vietnam in the Early Modern Era" (PhD diss., Yale University, 2001), 150–1.

44 Reid, *Age of Commerce*, vol. II, 314–15.

45 Đức, *Thông chí*, 209–10; Xu and Xie, *Da Nan shilu*, 21.

46 Đức, *Thông chí*, 211–12; Xu and Xie, *Da Nan shilu*, 8.

47 Doanh, *Gia phả*, 108; Sakurai and Kitagawa, "Hà Tiên or Banteay Meas," 174–75.

48 Doanh, *Gia phả*, 131–133; *Gaozong chun huangdi shilu*, vol. 11 (Beijing: Zhonghua shuju, 1986), 201; Li Qingxin, "Mao shi Hexian zhengquan ('Gangkou guo') jiqi duiwai guanxi," *Haiyang shi yanjiu* 5 (2013): 133–35.

Chinese commercial cosmopolitanism 71

49 Doanh, *Gia phả*, 132.
50 Đức, *Thông chí*, 307–8; Xu and Xie, *Da Nan shilu*, 21.
51 Puangthong Rungswadisab, "War and Trade: Siamese Interventions in Cambodia, 1767–1851" (PhD diss., University of Wollongong, 1995), 73–79.
52 Zheng, *China on the Sea*, 113–14.
53 Doanh, *Gia phả*, 115–17.
54 Doanh, *Gia phả*, 118–119; Xu and Xie, *Da Nan shilu*, 11; Đức, *Thông chí*, 319.
55 Doanh, *Gia phả*, 123–4; Xu and Xie, *Da Nan shilu*, 12–13; Đức, *Thông chí*, 320–21.
56 Doanh, *Gia phả*, 136–7; Xu and Xie, *Da Nan shilu*, 23; Đức, *Thông chí*, 330.
57 For a detailed, precise narrative of Hà Tiên after Mạc Thiên Tứ's death, see Nicolas Sellers, *The Princes of Hà-Tiên (1682–1867): The Last of the Philosopher-Princes and the Prelude to the French Conquest of Indochina: A Study of the Independent Rule of the Mạc Dynasty in the Principality of Hà-Tiên, and the Establishment of the Empire of Việtnam* (Brussels: Editions Thanh-Long, 1983), 81–84, 127–39.
58 Curtin, *Cross-Cultural Trade*, 5.
59 See, for instance, Timothy Brook, *Praying for Power: Buddhism and the Formation of Gentry Society in Late-Ming China* (Cambridge, MA: Harvard University Press, 1993); William T. Rowe, "Social Stability and Social Change," in *Cambridge History of China*, vol. 9.1; Melissa Macauley. *Social Power and Legal Culture: Litigation Masters in Late Imperial China* (Stanford, CA: Stanford University Press, 1998).
60 Victor Lieberman, *Strange Parallels: Southeast Asia in a Global Context, c. 800–1830* (Cambridge, UK: Cambridge University Press, 2003), vol. 1, 41.

4 Money talks

Confessions of a disgraced cosmopolitan coin of the 1640s

Kris Lane

The choice was perhaps arbitrary, but the physical properties of gold and silver lent themselves to coining. Both metals are fusible, malleable, shiny, and rare. Today it is estimated that gold is some twenty-five times rarer than silver in the earth's crust, yet its value relative to silver has fluctuated over time (ca. 110:1 as of this writing). World cultures have disagreed about these metals' relative values, but not about their absolute values. Both remain 'precious', and therefore dangerous.

Turning raw silver or gold into a border-crossing money – a cosmopolitan currency – required more steps. An issuer of some stature, for example a queen, offered a stamp of approval, a brand. Standard weight and purity were expected, but a truly cosmopolitan currency did not have to be tested at every border. Put another way, a piece of metal had to become an appealing metaphor, backed by a convincing narrative.[1] Such were the Venetian silver ducat and gold 'sequin' or *zecchino* of late medieval times. In part, their consistency guaranteed success abroad, but so also did the reputation of Venice.[2] It spoke volumes.

These first 'world trade' coins were relatively small, a reflection of general scarcity. With the American silver bonanza of the sixteenth to eighteenth centuries, the scope and scale of world money markets was suddenly transformed. This was the era of 'big money'. As Carlo Cipolla noted, sizable silver coins of about an ounce, crudely struck and alloyed with seven percent copper, flooded global markets a few decades after the discovery of the world's richest silver deposit in Potosí (Bolivia) in 1545, especially after its mint opened in 1574.[3] The opening of the Potosí mint coincided with the creation of the transpacific 'Manila galleon' trade, but most silver flowed across the Atlantic before reaching Asia.

Minted in Mexico and peninsular Spain as well as in Potosí, the silver peso of eight reals or 'piece of eight' quickly became the world's first globally accepted trade coin. Stamped with the Habsburg coat of arms and the Cross of Jerusalem interspersed with castles and lions – plus the king's name and his assayer's and mint's initials – the *peso de a ocho* rode on its reputation well into modern times. For the most part, people trusted the Spanish king

Money talks 73

to make good money since (in theory) he possessed the silver mountain of Potosí. His name and arms were guarantees.

Yet the piece of eight was to suffer grave misfortunes never experienced by the Venetian ducat. Around 1640, word of massive fraud inside the royal mint at Potosí, the Spanish empire's most active one, wreaked havoc on world markets, revealing not only the limits of global trust but also the depths of world dependency on Spanish-American silver in an age of crisis. Ugly, misshapen, and, during the 1640s, debased and underweight, the beleaguered Potosí peso was a 'lying, cheating' commercial cosmopolitan. What story had to be told, what metaphors deployed, to restore confidence in the world's first global money?

The *Seahorse*

Near the end of July 1644, the *Seahorse*, a tiny ship sailing for the English East India Company, anchored in Cavite, port of Manila. A 'black Portuguese' interpreter and former Manila resident named Pedro de Brito had urged English merchants to sail several thousand miles to the Philippines from Surat, a bustling cosmopolitan port on India's northwest coast. The company men hoped to trade samples of Gujarat's prime cotton fabrics for silver brought across the Pacific from Spanish America.

In the 1640s, England was at war with itself but at peace with Spain. Wary, Philippine governor Don Sebastián Hurtado de Corcuera held off despite his reputation for graft and smuggling. The English merchants and their interpreter were certainly spies, and, for all he knew, pirates. In an age of violent competition for precious commodities, global traders used every trick and wile to evade monopoly trade restrictions, and when peaceful evasion failed, blades were drawn. Cosmopolitan crews with forged documents and fluid loyalties wandered freely among the Iberian colonies in the 1640s, and a few clever charlatans charmed their way into vice-regal circles, raising alarm.[4]

Spain's brief peace with England stood in contrast to its long war with the Dutch, winding down after nearly eighty years of hostilities. But peace hardly seemed imminent in 1640s Philippines. When the *Seahorse* arrived, diverse Spanish subjects were reeling from a string of Dutch attacks, mostly carried out by agents of the United East India Company or VOC.

Philippine defenses held, but between 1643 and 1648 VOC vessels blockaded the supply of arms and cash from Acapulco brought by the annual Manila galleon. Even without the Dutch, several great ships had been lost to storms and sandbars. Pious churchmen bewailed added afflictions: earthquakes, volcanic eruptions, disease epidemics, and finally skirmishes among native Filipinos, resident Chinese merchants, and armed penal exiles. The 1640s were tough all over thanks to climate change, but many interpreted this as divine wrath.[5] In 1645, the Archangel Michael, flaming sword held high, became the embattled Philippines' patron saint.

Figure 4.1 (a) and (b) A 1644 Potosí piece of eight. Private collection.

In response to the English merchants' request for permission to trade Indian textiles, the Philippine governor demanded guns, iron, saltpeter, and ships' cables. Amid war, he said, his subjects had no need of cloth. This was likely untrue, since trade with Portugal had been severed by the Braganza revolt of 1640 (albeit after a nearly two-year news delay). Contraband was never entirely pinched off, but with the Dutch blockade cottons from India were likely in short supply in Manila.[6] Alternative fabrics from China, engulfed in civil war, were also scarce.

The Dutch had driven the Spanish from their last outpost in Taiwan in 1642. Soon after, beginning in 1644, all trade with the mainland was disrupted by the lumbering collapse of the Ming Dynasty.[7] These baleful events might be dismissed as mere surface ripples, but in retrospect one sees that deeper economic and political tides were turning. Just before the Manchu invasions the exchange rate for silver had nearly evened out between Europe and China, rendering arbitrage, a major stimulus for global trade, less profitable (Figures 4.1–4.4).

Even so, China's hunger for silver was not sated. English and Italian merchants visiting Macao in the late 1630s found the demand for Spanish (American) pesos very high, holding a premium over Japanese silver. Japan was a rare Asian alternative source of the white metal, and Portuguese merchants in Macao clutched both their Japanese and Spanish silver lifelines on the eve of expulsion from the islands and their own rebellion against Spain. Aspiring 'fidalgos of the Far East', these colonial outliers were deeply in debt to bullion traders in both Manila and Kyushu.[8]

East and Southeast Asian trade was rich, varied, and complex, and the peso, the default global trade coin, lubricated most interregional exchanges. VOC records show how silver pieces of eight or 'rials,' as the Dutch and

Figure 4.2 Silver war horse: A ca. 1650 Mexican piece of eight with Asian 'chop marks'. Private collection.

Figure 4.3 (a) and (b): A 1647 Potosí piece of eight, Assayer 'Z'. Private collection.

English called them, fit into South China's inter-island and coastal trade as the Iberians pulled back. A junk going from Quinam (Vietnam) to Changchou captured in August 1633 carried exotic commodities including pepper, ambergris, rhino horn, ivory, ebony, sandalwood, sappanwood, 'eagle wood,' dragon's blood, cardamom, birds' nests, horsehair, tortoise shell, and camphor, along with more ordinary goods like ox hides, copper ingots, and rice. Also confiscated were 3,266 pieces of eight, many no doubt minted in Potosí.

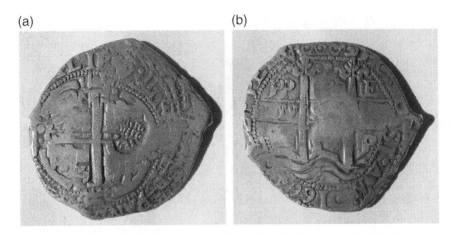

Figure 4.4 (a) and (b) A 1664 Potosí piece of eight with 1670s Flemish countermark. Private collection.

In 1636, VOC official Jost Schouten described Siamese silver portrait coins made from smelted pieces of eight, along with ingots equivalent to 48 pesos or 20 taels. The *peso de a ocho* was also the default accounting unit. Throughout Southeast Asia, Chinese fabrics were priced at so many 'reals of eight' per picol (133.5 lbs.), and pesos remained in demand as mainland bronze and copper cash was recalled in the early 1640s.[9] Perhaps the peso's rough appearance made it seem more trustworthy or more like a raw commodity than the finely milled but slightly less silver-rich Dutch *rijksdalers* and variants, many also made from Potosí silver.

China's 'silver century', as Richard Von Glahn has called the years 1550 to 1650, ended badly. The so-called Kangxi depression following the 1644 Qing invasion reversed older monetary trends, which included periodic debasements.[10] It is likely that amid the shocks of famine, war, and epidemic disease that struck China in the 1640s few noticed the declining quality of silver coins with the Potosí mint mark. A Chinese merchant resident in Dutch Batavia described the crux year of the Qing takeover thus:

> The Shunzhi emperor was the son of the Mude deity, therefore he was vigorous in spring and obtained the world. Dust storms and terrible rains were then raging in China. At night tens of thousands of horses and wild animals fought with each other, their shrieks spread everywhere, snow and ice were almost one foot thick. It is said that the footprints of giants and elephants were observed.[11]

Clearly, China in 1644 faced graver challenges than suspect foreign money. Yet despite the 'Ming-Qing cataclysm', it is unlikely that much Andean

Money talks 77

silver got far beyond China's borders in the form of debased coins anyway. As in India, discussed below, Chinese coastal merchants smelted most incoming money.

Rather than strike a standard coin like the Indian rupee, Chinese merchants stocked bullion in the form of high-grade, horse hoof-shaped ingots (*yuanbao*). Ordinary Chinese coinage was mostly copper and bronze, more or less backed by silver (or silver futures), a multi-tiered system not so different from seventeenth-century Castile's. But that was in ordinary times. With the fall of the Ming, everyone who could do so hoarded and exchanged bits of *hacksilber* ranging in size from a few hundredths of a tael to the five-ounce *ding*. For the terrified citizens of cities like Yangzhou, which fell to Qing troops in May 1645, a few slivers of silver hidden in a garment and used to placate invading soldiers proved the difference between life and death.[12]

Silver grew increasingly scarce after 1644, and monetary changes in the early Qing era led some to question whether silver was wealth itself or just an arbitrary trade medium, an illusion. This is not to say that no one missed silver. In hard times, one could hardly help but long for it. Writing decades later, the provincial governor of Jiangning, Mu Tianyan mused:

'I still remember that in 1649–50, before maritime trade was proscribed, the marketplaces were filled with foreign goods. Buyers and sellers primarily used foreign silver coins as the medium of exchange, and thus these coins circulated widely in every province. But nowadays not a single foreign coin is to be had. This is clear evidence that the fountain of fortune has been sealed up.'[13]

When the *Seahorse* merchants reached Cavite in 1644, Manila's extra-mural Chinese community was recovering from a 1639 massacre. In Japan, the Tokugawa Bakufu expelled all Europeans by 1639, allowing only a single Dutch factor to live on Deshima Island near Nagasaki. The Dutch in these uncertain years were obsessed with Japanese silver, too.[14] Amid sharp reorientations, merchants such as the Englishmen on the *Seahorse* would have to be extremely clever if they were to establish far-flung networks and alliances in these troubled seas. Even the better-placed Dutch had to remain flexible, on watch for new predators and parasites.

The English factors who reached Manila from Surat in 1644 were further weakened by the fact that they had no guns or powder to spare the Philippine governor. For fear of Dutch inspectors, their charter forbade them from selling such items. As it was, the Surat merchants were at the end of their tether, acting without permission from the London office. They had not even bothered to check in with fellow factors at the pepper station of Bantam, on the western tip of Java.

Manila's governor stalled, then gave signs of hope. Hurtado said to wait for his successor, Diego Fajardo Chacón, due to arrive any day from Acapulco. Stuck, the *Seahorse* traders withered in the humid heat of Cavite, worried they would lose their cotton cargo to mold and mildew. Just as the

78   *Kris Lane*

last chance to catch the monsoon back to India via Makassar was fading, the new governor authorized sale of the Gujarati cottons - on condition that the English return the next year with iron and saltpeter, anything to help fight the Dutch.

Thus in early December 1644 the *Seahorse* returned to India with a small but valuable cargo of silver coins and bullion, plus some dyewood and sugar. When the little ship reached Surat in March 1645 the EIC's resident factors were surprised to realize a profit despite the long delay and enormous distances traveled. Indeed, the *Seahorse*'s return from such a voyage in troublous times itself occasioned joy. This was especially true in a decade of tentative English probing in the wake of the VOC.[15] One fact on which all could agree was that in the vast monsoon trade circuit of Asia, East Africa, and Arabia, silver remained the lifeblood of commerce. As the Chinese in Manila said: 'Plata es sangre,' 'Silver is blood.'

Surat

The English factory in Surat was miserable in the 1640s, according to both merchants and visitors. The city itself was recovering from a devastating 1631 famine. As they sweated and swatted, company factors dreamt of tapping a trickle of Mughal wealth. Unlike the Ming, the Mughals were on the ascent. Shah Jahan may have been the richest man on earth, yet exchange rates were tight at empire's edge. One could not trade with foreign coins or bullion.

Writing their directors in London, Surat's Company men complained that certain Spanish-American silver coins were being heavily discounted by the Mughal's intermediaries, the *serrafs* responsible for converting foreign money and bullion into rupees or their equivalent in merchandise. The English, like the Dutch and Portuguese before them, found they had little to offer South Asians besides precious metals. Gold proved tricky, leaving silver as the commodity of choice.

The EIC's Surat directors were delighted to discover high-quality Spanish-American silver among the goods brought from Manila by the *Seahorse* merchants. In addition to several thousand 'rials of eight,' the English got silver ingots for their cloth. The Spanish called these ingots *piñas*, or pinecones. The English described them thus: 'the 26 peaces made up triyangle wise called virgin silver, the purest sort that is brought to these parts. The like, we believe, weare never seene in Suratt, for there is no mixture of any other metal in it, and very little loss in the melting thereof.'[16]

We know from other records that compact, pure, untaxed silver ingots of this type, typically weighing 20–30 lbs., were secretly exported from Potosí and other Andean mining districts throughout the seventeenth century. Contraband *piñas* left Peru's Pacific ports of Callao and Arica; others left the South Atlantic port of Buenos Aires.[17] Even if they originated in the mines of Mexico, which were struggling in the 1640s, the triangle-shaped

Money talks 79

ingots had reached the Philippines illegally. Perhaps the new governor himself had brought them.

The eight-real silver coins, meanwhile, if they came from Potosí's mint, may have been debased, although the English documents do not say. The money was set aside as the Surat factors went on about the ingots: 'the bullion the finest that ever yet was seen in these parts, and indeede so fine that wee shall be enforced to melt it and mix it with the rials to make it of a fit alloi for these sheroffs, who will not exceed a rupee the *tola* in price.'[18]

Pure silver ingots were most welcome as Surat's English factors faced stacks of debased 'rials of eight' sent from England. The merchants did not yet connect the suspect coins to Potosí, where debasement was rampant, yet going back a few years one finds a 27 January 1642 letter to the directors from Suvali or 'Swally Marine', Surat's offshore anchorage, noting that Spanish-American silver coins sent from London were mysteriously dropping in weight and purity. A few Dutch *rijksdalers* were entirely false, but this was a fluke; the chronic problem was with debased 'Spanish rials'. A 'rial of eight' was to be just under an ounce (27 g) of 930 fine silver.

Gujarat's 'shroffs' or *serrafs* could be quite powerful. The EIC relied heavily on the Bania merchant Virji Vora by the 1640s, and he had been important to the VOC since the early 1620s. As Ghulam Nadri notes, Vora bought up VOC and EIC imports, especially Mediterranean coral, which he traded for pepper.[19] Crucially, when both companies were short of cash Vora advanced them rupees by the tens of thousands, to be repaid (overwhelmingly) in Spanish-American 'rials'.

Virji Vora leveraged his lending power to demand free freightage to the Persian Gulf and Red Sea on European vessels. In 1643, when the EIC was struggling to find ready money, Vora was busy trading cotton goods and opium for pepper in Calicut, on India's southwest coast. The pepper came back to Surat, sold at substantial mark-up to the English. Without local brokers like Vora there would be no trade, yet their power cut deeply into EIC profits. The English in 1640s India were in a position to dispute the strength of weak ties.

The Dutch had a similar, more formalized relationship with the Bania serraf brothers Tulsidas and Tapidas Parekh, trading silver and coral for pepper but also relying on the two men for credit and cash advances. Tulsidas Parekh was the VOC's primary money changer in the 1640s and 1650s, and both brothers received a stipend from the VOC as an incentive to stay true. Another Surat-based Bania broker heavily involved in Indian Ocean shipping was Mohandas Naan, for whom trust was similarly negotiable. For Surat's 'shroffs,' only good silver could seal a deal. Whereas the coin used to speak for itself, it was now – increasingly – the smelting fire.

Throughout the 1640s, EIC factors in Surat complained that the rial/rupee exchange rate bent against them. By 1645, the serrafs were loath to accept any peso bearing the telltale mintmark 'P' for Potosí. Not all Potosí

80   *Kris Lane*

pieces of eight were debased, but there were enough bad ones to erode trust. Accused of sending unsound money to India, EIC directors in London complained that Surat's factors were wrong about the coins. They charged company accountants with embezzling funds or at least being fooled by the serrafs. The problem was in India, they said, not England.

Where were the EIC's directors getting their Spanish-American 'rials of eight,' good and bad? Most likely it was from England's so-called carrying trade with Spain toward the end of the Thirty Years War. As Spain fought France and the Netherlands, peace with England enabled English carriers to transport silver to troops in Flanders, but also to engage in complex webs of contraband trade.[20]

Between 1633 and 1648 the English shipped silver coins from Cádiz to Dunkirk via Dover. In part as a result of this cash surge, considerable wool got picked up at Bilbao. A 1645 treaty gave English merchants better terms, shielding them from Philip IV's periodic silver confiscations. A portion of American treasure thus took a detour to London, where some pieces of eight were smelted and reminted but most were re-exported as trade coins to the Baltic, Mediterranean, or South Asia. All the trading companies grappled for them.

Though English factors and directors bickered loudly over shoddy Potosí pesos, their problems were, in relative terms, miniscule. EIC traders in the 1640s were gossamer threads, capillaries in a complex, world-encompassing circulatory system that fed Spanish-American silver to East and South Asia through dozens of maritime and overland routes. The quantity of money and merchandise handled by the EIC in these years paled beside competitors, particularly regional merchants. The factors complained in the same 27 January 1642 letter from Swally Marine that they could barely sell their *good* rials to Surat's serrafs. They had been forced to queue up behind a crowd of Indian and Arabian merchants just arrived from Mocha on a monsoon-driven fleet.[21]

Many of these 'country traders,' as the English called them, linked Mediterranean markets to the Indian Ocean via the Red Sea. In this instance, they reportedly brought over 1.7 million pieces of eight to exchange for cloth and other goods at Surat. The flood of all this Spanish-American silver forced the English to wait 33 days to process their mere hundred thousand or so coins.[22]

London kept pushing. In March 1642, the directors said they were sending another 200,000 pesos, a vital cash infusion if the EIC in Surat were to survive. The Surat factors held their breath, but an English merchant who sold coral at Goa in July 1643 reported that the peso's value was still up in the Portuguese colonial capital: a cause for hope.[23]

Yet suspect coins kept coming from London, most acquired through a mix of legal and contraband trade with Spain. Exasperated, Surat factory president Francis Breton wrote the directors on 27 January 1644, complaining that: 'Of the rials received this time the shroffs objected to 13,300,

Money talks 81

and would not (after exact tryall made of there alloy in the Kings mint, your own and the Customers houses) bee induced to buy them, unless wee would submitt to part with them at 205 rupees per 100 rials'.[24] The English rejected this steep discount and took their coins south to Goa and north to Ahmadabad. They managed to get the old rate but only after absorbing transport costs.

In his letters, President Breton remained puzzled by the peso's dropping intrinsic value. He suggested the king of Spain had reduced the weight and purity of his coins due to his 'necessities'. Philip IV had plenty of necessities in the 1640s, but as will be seen, intentionally debasing the bedrock silver coinage of the Indies, indeed of the world, was inconceivable.

Exchange rates for older pesos remained high in India, but these coins soon disappeared. The 'new' silver pesos were by contrast everywhere, and a growing percentage tested badly. Desperate merchants and moneychangers were now calling for gold coins such as the venerable Venetian sequin, anything trustworthy.

Unmoved by Breton's complaints, London EIC officials shot back in a 29 March 1644 letter: 'Wonder that the rials should be found short in tale [purity], and suspect some trickery on the part of the shroffs'.[25] Surely the king of Spain was not to blame for fluctuating Indian exchange rates, but rather local cheats, and probably unscrupulous company men as well. Surat's assayers and counting-house men were to be watched more carefully.

President Breton responded in an angry letter of 28 November 1644 defending his employees: 'Resent the imputation that they do not attend properly to the weighing and counting of the money received: It is a business that passeth not in private, but is constantly done in your warehouse, wher your rials etc. are first told [assayed] and then weighed; whereupon two or three of your servants are constantly attendant, whereof your Acommptant is usually one, or (if he be upon any occasion absent) some one of the Counsel or of trust is entrusted therewith…'[26]

Vigilance was not the issue, nor was it a failure of interpersonal trust. President Breton fired back harder at the directors: '[I] Have previously complained of the lightness and coarseness [impurity] of the rials sent [from London]; and now find the last consignment much worse than any before received. The proportion brought to Surat contained only 560 Civill [Seville] or of the best sort: 14,727 Mexico: and 3,333 of the course or new sort ['Peru' in the margin]. The two former kinds were sold at the usual rates; but the third they are keeping for some other occasion, rather than part with them at 208 1/4 rupees [per hundred], which is the highest price offered, either here or at Ahmadabad'.[27]

Here, in late 1644, English East India Company factors struggled to carry on their entire India trade with Spanish 'rials of eight' from three mints: Seville, Mexico City, and Potosí. There was a premium on Seville coins, whose mintage was closely watched by royal officials. Mexican ones were nearly as dependable, although some were mildly deficient. It was only the

82   *Kris Lane*

pieces of eight of Potosí or 'Peru' that were now unwanted, or so heavily discounted that EIC factors faced considerable losses.

Money fears were mounting just as the *Seahorse* returned from Manila with its small cargo of pure silver ingots and not-yet-tested, transpacific 'rials of eight'. The Surat factors were so keen for more such extra-fine 'triangle-shaped' ingots that they launched a second voyage to Manila in April 1645 in the ship *Supply*. The slightly larger vessel returned to Surat in the spring of 1646 with 40,000 'rials of eight' worth of cash and merchandise, but also with a note from the Spanish governor saying not to try again: an order from Philip IV had closed this tempting 'back door' to the silver of Spanish America.

Surat's English merchants had again carried only Indian cotton cloth to Manila, a wise decision since their ship had been duly examined by Dutch VOC officials before entering Manila Bay. Had guns, iron, or powder been found, the voyage would have been a total bust. There is no mention of more pure silver ingots 'the likes of which hath never been seen,' and Surat's factors returned to the fight over debased coins. By 1648, the EIC president reported to London that the serrafs refused Peruvian 'rials' altogether.

Genoa

Tucked up against the lush hills of Liguria, the gritty city known as La Superba was on its heels. Exasperated Genoese treasury officials banned Spanish America's famous *pezzi da otto* or pieces of eight in February 1642. The decrees suggested a sudden emergency, but signs of trouble went back to the 1630s.[28] Rumors of debased Spanish-American silver bars reached Genoa in the mid-1620s and talk of bad coins appeared in official correspondence by 1637.

The hammer came down in 1641, when Genoa's city council and mint overseers began outlawing suspect coins and calling them in for exchange. Initially, Mexican pesos were equally suspect, but Genoese officials soon zeroed in on the real problem: the coins of 'Peru', or Potosí. Many coins were so crudely struck that not even the telltale 'P' was visible.

Once the Mediterranean's commercial powerhouse, Genoa faced crisis in the 1630s. Plague hit in 1630; in 1635, the outbreak of the Franco-Spanish war. More trouble came in the form of sputtering Spanish currency and bullion flows, long the lifeblood of the republic. Well before Columbus, Genoese merchants had forged close ties with Spain's monarchs, nurturing a banking elite to rival and eclipse the great south German families. They did so while maintaining a long-established and well-armed political independence, an expensive if understandable conceit.

By the time of Philip II, the Hispanic Monarchy relied on Genoese lenders to maintain its far-flung armies, particularly those in Flanders but also in Milan and elsewhere in Italy. Many a soldier's payroll flowed through Genoa, a portion of it consisting of pieces of eight minted in Potosí. The

Money talks 83

king of Spain also paid Genoese merchants millions of pesos in Potosí silver to supply troops with arms, food, and transport. By contrast, Genoa's main export to Spain was paper. The Spanish empire consumed it by the ton.[29]

Payment in debased silver was only one of the many risks of lending to the Habsburg kings of Spain. Royal defaults and payment delays grew more frequent after 1620 just as transatlantic silver flows grew less certain. Causes for this worry included Spanish America's general mining crisis, but there were also shipwrecks and corsair attacks to vex the king and his creditors. Most silver fleets arrived as hoped, but they came only once a year. Meanwhile, colonial defense costs soared even as smuggling and other forms of corruption and subterfuge ate away at the king's share.

The wise and well-connected found ways to profit in hard times, but new competitors, many of them Portuguese New Christians encouraged by the Count-Duke of Olivares, plus the royal favorite's capricious fiscal policies, added new uncertainties. Genoese bankers, long the Spanish Habsburgs' lifeline, were by 1640 struggling to keep their heads above water. Ancient family firms were failing, their coats-of-arms dissolving in the acid rain of sovereign debt.

If silver was the blood of early modern world commerce, it was just as surely the sinews of global war. The Asia trade absorbed great quantities of American silver, but so did Europe's perennial religious, dynastic, and other conflicts. The end of the Thirty Years War, which coincided with Potosí's mint fraud, brought Spain's fiscal-military crisis to a head. Faced with declining silver production throughout the Americas, Philip IV struggled to maintain his already vast war machine, much of it concentrated in the Low Countries.

Davide Maffi explains that between 1634 and 1660 the war in Flanders alone cost the Spanish treasury over 75 million escudos.[30] This was equivalent to over 121 million silver pesos of eight reals. For comparison, registered coin production at Potosí's mint was almost exactly 100 million pesos between 1634 and 1660. This included the peak years of the 1640s, when debasement was rampant. Even if a constant stream of all the coined silver coming out of Potosí had actually reached Cádiz and then Brussels, it would not have covered the annual costs of war in Flanders. The flow of silver was instead the promise that kept Castile in hock, barely covering interest payments. And Flanders was just the most expensive of Spain's multiple European battlefronts.

A multi-front war with France, religious obligations to Habsburg relatives in Austria and Germany, and a string of internal conspiracies and rebellions forced Spain's ministers to deploy troops all around Europe and also within Iberia. Compared with Spain's multiple European and domestic crises, the Potosí mint fraud appeared at first a minor concern, a blip or anomaly. Yet this was a time when only pure silver could pay bills abroad. As the debasement's scope became clear in the form of pink cash, panic over Habsburg solvency and the world's formerly most trusted currency spread.[31]

84   Kris Lane

Facing tough times in an era of Dutch competition and French military ascendancy, La Superba's relationship with Spain was strained. By 1638 Genoa's oligarchs created the Our Lady of Liberty Company to launch a fleet of galleys to protect its Mediterranean merchant convoys, many of them carrying Spanish bullion and coin.[32] The *nuovo armamento* relied on paid oarsmen, and was therefore costly, as was maintenance of the Tunisian island outpost of Tabarka, run by the Lomellini family.

The point of the 'Lady Liberty' fleet was to revive Genoa's declining commercial fortunes. French pirates and Barbary corsairs were a constant menace, made worse by Spain's withdrawal from Mediterranean defense. The fleet company died with the Peace of Münster in 1648, but not without leaving a massive hole in the city's budget. Other revivalist projects included the formation of an abortive East India Company.[33]

As for money shipments in these changing times, Gian Carlo Calcagno found record of 68.75 million 'pieces of eight' transported from Spain to Genoa between 1600 and 1639. Surviving registries are incomplete, so this is but a taste.[34] In a 1638 manual, Genoese merchant-banker Domenico Peri noted that: 'the pieces of eight of Spain that require a test of purity and weight are traded by weight as if they were raw, uncoined silver and they are sold according to their purity'.[35] If Peri's advice were followed, La Superba could act as a monetary firewall against debased *pezzi da otto*, much like Surat. Apparently, its merchants had not been so cautious.

Genoese treasury officials banned Potosí coins as early as 1641, repeating their orders throughout the decade and even into the early 1660s.[36] The earliest bans were copied in Milan, at this time subject to Spain. Both Genoa and Milan minted their own coins, but as in much of coastal Asia, no coin was as cosmopolitan as the Spanish piece of eight. It was just as common in Livorno and other Italian ports as it was in Surat.[37] To everyone's surprise, soon after 1640 it was suddenly suspect, often light and impure.

In addition to published broadsides, some of the earliest Genoese bans went out in the form of handwritten decrees to regional governors.[38] La Superba's treasury and municipal officials called on all Ligurians to collect and remit suspect coins to the mint, where they would be scrapped by weight and exchanged for local currency.

Mint and treasury records for the 1640s and 1650s suggest that members of Genoa's city council, the Collegio Maximo, and board members of the Bank of San Giorgio were deeply vexed by the problem of bad coins, but that after some groping and contradictory decrees they hit upon a winning solution, formalized by 1648 if not earlier. By then the problem had been narrowed to recently minted 'Peruvian' pieces of eight, but the solution was to cast a broader net in order to address the city's acute bullion shortage.

As early as March 1642, officials worried that total bans on 'Spanish' pieces of eight would drive both silver and gold currencies out of Genoese territory. There were not enough good local coins to fill the void and bronze or copper billon issues (plus false coppers, allegedly from Corsica) were yet

Money talks 85

another headache. To boot, there were other bad coins circulating besides the 'Spanish' ones. These included ducatoons and other denominations from Venice, Milan, Bologna, Parma, Naples, Florence, and Savoy. Bans on these coins prompted retaliatory decrees. Any type of money 'di buontà solita' or proper quality was hard to find. Even bad Genoese *soldi* were popping up.[39]

Yet Genoa's mint assayers singled out pesos of eight reals from Peru for their 'bassa liga' or deficient alloy as of 11 December 1641, drawing closer attention in May 1642. A new published broadside or *grida* followed, complete with engravings of suspect coin designs to guide the perplexed. Another decree from 9 March 1643 again pointed to bad Peruvian coins, but 1644 spot assays of 'Spanish' pesos from Mexico, Toledo, Seville, and Potosí (here labeled 'Peru') found many coins to be fine and weighty. Clearly the decrees of 1641–1642 had not eliminated these pieces of eight from circulation.

The trick was how to find and hold onto 'Li pezzi da otto reali di bouna stampa della solita buontà e peso' or 'The true-weight, good pesos of eight reals with the proper mint marks'. A council member opined in a letter of 30 June 1643 that pieces of eight could be reduced to commodity (*mercancia*) status, scrapped as bullion without a total ban. The city simply had to set up a less punitive trade-in policy.

Progress was slow or halting. A 1645 decree provided new guidelines on bad 'Spanish' coins, offering exchange rates along with harsh words. A flurry of opinions on how to stabilize Genoa's currency woes followed. Genoa was short of change and of money in general. Mint officials, the 'sindico della Camara de la Zecca,' were at a loss.[40] The 1645 decree was nevertheless read all over Liguria and the Riviere by town criers, each local official reporting the date of 'publication'. Residents of San Remo, Rapallo, Savona, and other towns could not claim ignorance of the law.

Genoese officials tried something new in 1647, to take effect in the following year. Amid the 'joy' of the Peace of Münster, 1648 turned out to be a year of confiscations, continuing in 1649 and 1650 and cascading for more than a decade into the 1660s. The records are jammed with seizure orders across the years 1648–1650, entirely focused on 'banned reals' (*reali prohibiti*). Genoese officials re-issued earlier bans that included coins from Mexico, although the core problem consisted of certain 'Peruvian reals with the old design'.[41]

It appears that customs officials stationed on Liguria's borders and in its ports, especially the port of Genoa itself, began to confiscate *all* Peruvian and Mexican coins carried by *all* travelers and shippers. Since the Peruvian ones were already notorious and subject to loss without compensation, they rarely appear in the confiscation papers. Smart people knew better than to get caught with them.

But by enforcing the older blanket bans in 1648, Genoese officials caught almost everyone carrying Mexican coins, most of them sound, by surprise. Captains, crew, and passengers on ships from England, Flanders, Hamburg,

86   *Kris Lane*

and many other places were stripped of all Spanish-American silver coins in exchange for receipts.[42] The English ship *Gran Loggi* (or *Luigi*) was searched on 10 November 1648, producing many mostly Mexican coins. A Spanish galley from Naples was searched on 27 February 1649 yielding a whopping 1,146,181 *reali* or pieces of eight, mostly from Mexico but some from Potosí.[43] Also taken from the galley were 60 bars of silver weighing some 110–120 marks (55–60 lbs.) each.

No one was safe. Typical was a tiny merchant vessel from Majorca, yielding only a few coins and leaving behind in the archive only a brief and faded receipt. Larger ships caught in the new confiscation dragnet included the *Concord*, the *Blue Eagle*, and *St. Bernard*. Several ships carried nearly 300,000 pesos, a reminder of the significance of hard money transfers by sea. The ship *Arabella*, under Capt. Jack Goody ('Jacomo Gooddy'), carried consignments of pieces of eight in the tens of thousands each. The consignees' names and coin totals were dutifully copied from the ship's manifest as officials hauled in the treasure. Pesos taken from the ship *Scipione* were promptly smelted in Genoa's Zecca.

Even La Superba's petty traders were put under surveillance. Anyone dealing in pesos, especially Peruvian ones, risked not only confiscation but jail. If we can trust the archive, the years 1648–1650 look like a money inquisition, with Potosí's *pezzi da otto* as heretics and their Mexican cousins as fall guys. Impure Potosí coins were not yet gone; they had to be sniffed out one by one. One poor fellow was caught on 7 April 1649 for trying to buy something with a few 'Peruvian' pesos taken from his mother's purse. A larger fish was Ambrosio Grendi, caught buying up suspect Potosí pesos from anyone needing to be rid of them.

The great Potosí mint fraud was of course the root of all this monetary uncertainty, yet it also provided an excuse for Genoese high officials to try and ameliorate their larger money problems by confiscating huge amounts of Mexican currency that was probably good or only slightly light or underfine. With some notable exceptions, it appears that bad Potosí coins were by this time largely flushed out of the Ligurian marketplace, yet they were subject to repeated, specific decrees in 1648. La Superba was looking a lot like Surat.

Spanish ambassador Pedro Ronquillo wrote to Philip IV from Genoa on 2 October 1648, saying:

> Among the silver brought in two ships just arrived from Cádiz that I reported to Your Majesty there arrived a great quantity unregistered, and they found many chests of reals made in Peru of such inferior quality that these bankers (*hombres de negocios*) have remitted 70 chests of them to Venice, expecting a 25% loss, and some quantity more has been collected in Venice with the intention of smelting them, which in turn has spurred the Genoese to have them returned, offering to give them some other quantity in good money - assuming they can get it -

Money talks 87

seeking to escape from those [bad Peru coins] by some other path, trying to avoid the worst damage this incident has caused, such that the piece of eight does not circulate at all nor does anyone want them...[44]

The problem of debased Potosí coins was not new, but the situation had grown dire by 1648. Ronquillo claimed that Genoa was gripped by a currency shortage after shipping considerable coin to the Levant and then to France (specifically pieces of eight) to buy wheat. Wheat and bread shortages all over Italy were driving up prices after a failed harvest. Like money, bread loaves were light and 'debased' with suspicious ingredients.

Ronquillo predicted troubles, obliquely reminding the king of the huge 1647 Naples rebellion. The French, having enjoyed a good harvest, were said to be demanding silver before sending any wheat or flour. Although their king had outlawed Spanish silver coins for all the reasons known, 'those of Provence' were demanding them anyway, the only currency they would take, which in turn drove down the value of the Genoese soldi to never-seen levels.

Taken together, the Genoese confiscation orders stretching from 1647–1650 are a telling reminder that 'Spanish' pieces of eight remained the default currency in the Mediterranean. They circulated by the millions, speaking across frontiers. Despite being stamped with the cross of Jerusalem even the Barbary corsairs preferred them as ransom payment – with the disclaimer 'Minted by the enemy of religion, the Christian. May God destroy him!'[45]

Genoa's rejection of Peruvian pieces of eight sent from Spain to supply troops in 1648 probably also forced Philip IV to reconsider his own tolerance of these coins, culminating in a series of royal decrees calling in and devaluing Potosí money throughout the year 1650. The 1650 decrees caused a new wave of panic throughout the Spanish realms, from Buenos Aires to Guatemala, only to be followed by more-or-less copycat decrees as far away as Königsberg.[46]

A cosmopolitan coin

Knowing that money talks, the king of Spain ordered the Potosí peso redesigned after the main fraudsters were executed in 1650. Restored to its full weight and purity, the coin was to tell the truth about itself with more dates and initials and a new image: the recycled image of the Pillars of Hercules and the beckoning waves of the Atlantic. Added to this was the long-dead Emperor Charles V's motto: *Plus Ultra*, 'Further Beyond'. Would it be enough?

It was understood that the Potosí piece of eight was not destined for Spain or even Europe but rather for the rest of the world, to do as it had always done: to lubricate trade and finance war. As a container of value it had to reassert its ability to speak a universal language. Yet it took a generation for the 'P' to be forgiven. As late as the 1670s, pieces of eight used to pay

88 Kris Lane

soldiers in Flanders had to bear a countermark with the emblem of the Golden Fleece, and those 'rials' used to buy pepper in Sumatra in the same decade had to be assayed like scrap metal or they would be rejected. This venerable cosmopolitan coin had betrayed more than a few trusting traders, and their confidence would not be easily regained.

Notes

1 On commercial money, I follow anthropologist Stephen Gudeman, *Economy's Tension: The Dialectics of Community and Market* (Oxford: Bergahn, 2008), 134–36.
2 See Alan M. Stahl, *Zecca: The Mint of Venice in the Middle Ages* (Baltimore: Johns Hopkins University Press, 2000).
3 Carlo Cipolla, *Conquistadores, pirati, mercatanti* (Bologna: Il Molino, 1996). I have used the Spanish ed.: Cipolla, *Conquistadores, piratas, mercaderes: La saga de la plata española*. trad. Ricardo González (Buenos Aires: Fondo de Cultura Económica, 1999). The first ounce-size coin appeared ca.1495 at Joachimsthal, Germany, giving rise to the term 'thaler' or 'dollar'. As central Europe's mining boom faded, large Spanish-American coins filled the gap. For more on the Potosí mint, see Kris Lane, *Potosí : The Silver City that Changed the World* (Oakland : University of California Press, 2019), 84–86; 127–36.
4 This section relies mostly on Serafin D. Quiason, *English Country Trade with the Philippines, 1644–1765* (Quezon City: University of the Philippines Press, 1966), 3–16; William Foster, ed. *The English Factories in India, 1642–1645: A Calendar of Documents in the India Office, Westminster* (Oxford: Clarendon Press, 1913), 144–45, 165–67, 174–81, 206–09, 212, 218–26, 249–50, 272–73, 278; and K.N. Chaudhuri, *The English East India Company: The Study of an Early Joint-Stock Company, 1600–1640* (London: Frank Cass, 1965). See also D.K. Bassett, "The Trade of the English East India Company in the Far East, 1623–1684: Part I, 1623-65," *Journal of the Royal Asiatic Society of Great Britain and Ireland* 1/2 (Apr. 1960): 32–47. For Philippine governor Hurtado, see William J. McCarthy, "Cashiering the Last Conquistador: The *Juicio de residencia* of don Sebastián Hurtado de Corcuera, 1639–1658," *Colonial Latin American Historical Review* (Winter 2013): 1–26. On other English adventurers in the Indian Ocean in these years, see Alison Games, *The Web of Empire: English Cosmopolitans in an Age of Expansion, 1560–1660* (New York: Oxford University Press, 2008). For an outstanding case of 1640s charlatanism, see Ryan D. Crewe, "Brave New Spain: An Irishman's plot for Mexican Independence," *Past and Present* 207, no. 1 (2010): 53–87.
5 Geoffrey Parker, *Global Crisis: War, Climate Change, and Catastrophe in the Seventeenth Century* (London: Yale University Press, 2013).
6 Emma H. Blair and James A. Robertson, eds. and trans. *The Philippine Islands, 1493–1898*. 55 vols. (Cleveland: Arthur H. Clark, 1903–1911), 35: 209–77, 354–57. See also W.L. Shurz, *The Manila Galleon* (New York: E.P. Dutton, 1939).
7 José Eugenio Borao Mateo, *The Spanish Experience in Taiwan, 1626–1642: The Baroque Ending of a Renaissance Endeavor* (Hong Kong: Hong Kong University Press, 2009).
8 C.R. Boxer, "Plata es Sangre: Sidelights on the Drain of Spanish-American Silver in the Far East, 1550–1700," *Philippine Studies* 18, no. 3 (1970): 457–78 (463); and Boxer, "The Swan-Song of the Portuguese in Japan, 1635-39," reprinted in Boxer, *Portuguese Merchants and Missionaries in Feudal Japan, 1543–1640*

Money talks 89

(London: Variorum, 1986), ch. 2. The silver, advanced in bonds called *respondencias*, one of which Boxer found in prewar Japan, was used to buy silk in Canton to resell in Nagasaki. On Taiwan, see Tonio Andrade, *Lost Colony: The Untold Story of China's first Great Victory over the West* (Princeton: Princeton University Press, 2011).

9 Cheng Wei-Chung. *War, Trade and Piracy in the China Seas, 1622–1683* (Leiden: Brill, 2013), 329. Other items captured from trading junks this year included deerskins, 'silver nuggets', benzoin, nutmeg, and lacquer. A table (332) shows the fluctuating value of the piece of eight 1625–60 at Batavia and Taiwan in *stuivers*. It appears the *real* was overvalued 1648–55, then dropped. See also C.R. Boxer, ed., *A True Description of the Mighty Kingdoms of Japan and Siam by François Caron and Jost Schouten* (London: Argonaut Press, 1935), 52–53, 64–65.

10 Richard Von Glahn, "Cycles of Silver in Chinese Monetary Policy," in *The Economy of the Lower Yangzi Delta in Late Imperial China: Connecting Markets, Money, and Institutions,* ed. Billy K. L. So (New York: Routledge, 2012), 17–71.

11 Leonard Blussé and Nie Dening, eds. *The Chinese Annals of Batavia, the Kai Ba Lidai Shiji and Other Stories (1610–1795)* (Leiden: Brill, 2018), 70.

12 Lynn A. Struve, ed. *Voices from the Ming-Qing Cataclysm: China in Tigers' Jaws* (New Haven: Yale University Press, 1993), 32–48, 61–71.

13 Richard Von Glahn, *Fountain of Fortune: Money and Monetary Policy in China, 1000–1700* (Berkeley: University of California Press, 1996), 217.

14 Adam Clulow, *The Company and the Shogun: The Dutch Encounter with Tokugawa Japan* (New York: Columbia University Press, 2014). See also Willem C.H. Robert, ed. *Voyage to Cathay, Tartary and the Gold- and Silver-Rich Islands East of Japan* (Amsterdam: Philo Press, 1975).

15 Robert Parthesius, *Dutch Ships in Tropical Waters: The Development of the Dutch East India Company (VOC) Shipping Network in Asia, 1595–1660* (Amsterdam: Amsterdam University Press, 2010), 32, 49, 141–42.

16 Quiason, *English Country Trade*, 11.

17 Margarita Suárez, *Desafíos transatlánticos. Mercaderes, banqueros y el estado en el Perú virreinal, 1600–1700* (Lima: FCE/PUCP/IFEA, 2001).

18 Foster, ed., *The English Factories in India, 1642–1645*, 252. Letter from Surat Factory president Breton and others to Company, 31 March 1645.

19 Ghulam A. Nadri, "The English and Dutch East India Companies and Indian Merchants in Surat in the seventeenth and eighteenth centuries: Interdependence, competition and contestation" in *The Dutch and English East India Companies: Diplomacy, Trade and Violence in Early Modern Asia,* eds. Adam Clulow and Tristan Mostert (Amsterdam: Amsterdam University Press, 2018), 125–49.

20 Stanley J. and Barbara H. Stein, *Silver, Trade, and War: Spain and America in the Making of Early Modern Europe* (Baltimore: Johns Hopkins University Press, 2000), 62–63. The Steins draw from Harland Taylor, "Trade, Neutrality and the 'English Road,' 1630–1648," *Economic History Review* 25, no. 2 (May 1972): 236–60.

21 Foster, *The English Factories in India, 1642–1645*, 7:28.

22 For the bigger picture see Hans Walther van Santen, *De Verenigde Oost-Insische Compagnie in Gujarat en Hindustan, 1620–1660*. Ph.D. dissertation, University of Leiden (Meppel: Krips Repro, 1982), 76, 210. Santen demonstrated the relative strength of Dutch traders at Surat vs. other merchants who had only silver (mostly pesos) to offer.

23 Foster, *The English Factories in India, 1642–1645*, 107.

24 Foster, *The English Factories in India, 1642–1645*, 144–45.

25 Foster, *The English Factories in India, 1642–1645*, 174.

26 Foster, *The English Factories in India, 1642–1645*, 209.

90 *Kris Lane*

27 Foster, *The English Factories in India, 1642–1645*, 209.
28 'Having encountered in the pieces of eight with markings from Mexico and Peru notable shortcomings in quality and purity, such that many of them are considerably inferior to what they should be, [it is ordered that] those coined in Mexico and Peru remain banned and prohibited, either by possession or in any form of exchange whatsoever'. Decree published in Genoa, 14 February 1642, quoted in Cipolla, *Conquistadores, piratas, mercaderes*, 69 (my translation).
29 Roberto Blanes Andrés, "Aproximación a las relaciones comerciales marítimas entre Génova y Valencia en el reinado de Felipe IV (1621–1665)," in *Génova y la Monarquía Hispánica (1528–1713)*. 2 vols., eds. Manuel Herrero Sánchez, Yasmina Rocío Ben Yessef Garfia, Carlot Bitossi, and Dino Puncuh (Genoa: Società Ligure di Storia Patria, 2011): 1:171–90. Paper varieties exported to Spain were dizzying (pp. 181,184): 'marca mayor moreno, blanco, negro, fino, cotralla; ordinario, de protocolo, de escribir, de imprenta, de estraza, grueso, mediano, de naipes, de escritura de la ribera, papel ferro, azul, estampado, del Final, del Piamonte'. On the factories themselves, mostly near Voltri, see Manlio Calegari, *La manifattura genovese della carta (sec. XVI-XVIII)* (Genoa: ECIG, 1986).
30 Davide Maffi, *En defensa del imperio: los ejércitos de Felipe IV y la Guerra por la hegemonía europea, 1635–1659* (Madrid: Editorial Actas, 2013), 432.
31 Although some historians now downplay the importance of American silver by stressing innovative credit arrangements, I follow an older school of thought that suggests these financial innovations would not have been possible without a steady stream of American silver. American silver, however insufficient at a given moment, provided liquidity. See, for example, Stanley J. and Barbara H. Stein, *Silver, Trade, and War: Spain and America in the Making of Early Modern Europe* (Baltimore: Johns Hopkins University Press, 2000), especially ch.2, "The European Diaspora of Silver by War." For the mid-seventeenth century, the Steins followed the arguments and statistics provided by Antonio Domínguez Ortiz, Frank Spooner, Geoffrey Parker, and a few others.
32 Thomas A. Kirk, *Genoa and the Sea: Policy and Power in an Early Modern Maritime Republic, 1559–1684* (Baltimore: Johns Hopkins University Press, 2005), 147.
33 Sanjay Subrahmanyam, "On the Significance of Gadflies: the Genoese East India Company of the 1640s," *Journal of European Economic History* 17, no. 3 (1988). Another company, the San Giorgio (named for the bank) was formed in 1656 to trade with Brazil, but it also failed. Genoese investment in the Spanish-American slave trade also had its ups and downs, but this was a private rather than a state project.
34 Kirk, *Genoa and the Sea*, 87–88.
35 Giovanni Domenico Peri, *Il negotiante* (Genoa: 1638), 73–74 (my translation).
36 Cipolla, *Conquistadores, piratas, mercaderes*, 69–72. Cipolla flubs a few details, for example referring to 'Francisco Nestares Rocha' on p. 70, but his analysis is mostly solid.
37 Corey Tazzara, *The Free Port of Livorno and the Transformation of the Mediterranean World, 1574–1790* (New York: Oxford University Press, 2017). A good piece of eight traded for about 6 Tuscan *lire*.
38 Archivio di Stato de Genoa (ASG), Monetarum Diversarum/Zecca Antica, hilera 38, 1641–1642. The decrees continue in hileras 39, 40, 41, 42, and 43.
39 ASG, Finanzas, parte/zecca antiga, Monetarum diversarum, see 9 November 1644 *grida* on how to spot them, hilera 39.
40 Ibid., hilera 40. Marco Aurelio Spinola led the opinion campaign.
41 Ibid., hileras 41 and 42. "reali di Peru di stampa antica."
42 See examples in hilera 41.

Money talks 91

43 Ibid., hilera 42. The galley's captain was Juan Pereyra Gutiérrez.
44 Archivo General de Simancas (AGS): Hacienda (AJH) 939-I-23, 1,2 (my translation).
45 Sevket Pamuk, *A Monetary History of the Ottoman Empire* (Cambridge: Cambridge University Press, 2000), 110.
46 Kris Lane, "The Hangover: Global Consequences of the Great Potosí Mint Fraud, ca.1650–1675," in *Potosí y el mundo,* eds. Rossana Barragán and Paula Zagalsky (Leiden: Brill, forthcoming, 2021).

5 'This whole business should be kept very Secret'

The English tobacco workhouses in Moscow

Matthew P. Romaniello

In February 1705, Charles Whitworth, the newly-appointed English envoy to the court of Russia, arrived in the border town of Smolensk as he travelled overland to Moscow from the Baltic coast. In a letter to the foreign secretary, Whitworth observed that he had passed '50 to 60 sleds loaden with Tobacco which is planted in Ukraine, and I am informed that 2 or 300 hundred of the same usually pass every year' on its way to the ports of Königsberg and Riga. One of Whitworth's tasks in Russia was to resolve the outstanding issues with the tobacco contract signed by the tsar with a group of English merchants. The merchants had identified Ukrainian (or 'Circassian') tobacco as one of the primary impediments to their potential sales. Whitworth's report was the beginning of his investigation into the current tobacco market. His verdict on Ukrainian tobacco was not kind: 'This tobacco is extreamly bad but not costing about a penny a pound, find [s] considerable vent amongst the poor Peasants of Lithuania, who provided they can have the smoke at a cheap rate are not nice as to the smell'.[1]

Whitworth arrived in Russia at a pivotal time. Throughout most of the seventeenth century, the Russian government had banned the importation of tobacco into its borders 'on pain of the death penalty'.[2] Tsar Petr Alekseevich (Peter the Great, r. 1682–1725) reversed this prohibition in 1696, granting a one-year monopoly on tobacco sales to one of his merchants. In 1697, he sold the tobacco licence to a foreign merchant for the first time. With an opportunity available, the English Board of Trade and Plantations advised the crown later that year that discussing the tobacco trade with the tsar was a top priority for their upcoming meeting in the Netherlands.[3] As a result of the two sovereigns' negotiations, a group of English merchants signed a contract for an export monopoly of tobacco to Russia for two years beginning in 1699. According to the contract, the monopoly would remain in force until all the imported tobacco was sold. Despite the hopes of the contract, the deal was not successful with most of the imported leaf sitting unsold in Moscow several years later.[4]

In an attempt to salvage the tobacco contract, a few of the contractors established a facility in Moscow in 1705 to produce rolled tobacco from the unsold leaf. Two English craftsmen from London managed these new 'workhouses', and were responsible for importing the necessary tools and additives ('liquors') to manufacture the luxury product. The craftsmen supervised a local Russian workforce to produce the rolled tobacco. The workhouses, therefore, were a cosmopolitan space for a technological exchange between foreigners and locals; this was a typical situation in Russia. Numerous foreign experts from both east and west established enterprises in Russia, including textile mills and mines. Many English specialists, such as physicians, military officers, and shipwrights, entered Russian service in the previous decades, and, by the beginning of the eighteenth century, served in greater numbers than ever before.[5] However, the English reaction to the export of a tobacco production technique to Russia was not positive. Both the Board of Trade and Plantations and merchants in London raised alarm over the potential loss of the Russian market if these Russian workers learned how to prepare the 'extreamly bad' Ukrainian leaf as if it was England's specialty product.

By time Whitworth reached Moscow in the spring of 1705, he had two tobacco-related tasks. The first was to resolve the outstanding issues with the tobacco contract, assisting the tobacco contractors with the final sale of their unsold product. The second was to destroy the workhouses and the imported equipment, and then remove the craftsmen from Russia before the local authorities could intervene. The destruction of the tobacco workhouses was a unique moment in Russia's history of foreign exchanges. The English government chose to eliminate its own merchants' business interests abroad, rather than allow the potential loss of a production technique. No other government intervened inside Russia's borders; no other English craftsman was prevented from having an independent career in Russia. This chapter will examine why this event, and no other, threatened England's tolerance for the cosmopolitan careers of its subjects.

The tobacco workhouses

Tsar Peter the Great met King William III in Utrecht in 1698, signing a series of agreements concerning the relationship between the two countries, including the contract for the exclusive right to export tobacco to Russia.[6] The contract required the English merchants to export 3,000 hogsheads of tobacco to Russia (3 million pounds) in the first year (1699), and 5,000 hogsheads in the second. After the second year, the contract was renewable annually for another 5,000 hogsheads, for up to seven years. Under the terms of the contract, tobacco could be sold anywhere in the kingdom (a later point of contention), and the tsar agreed to ban all other tobacco imports, which was hardly a concession as no other supply of tobacco was legally allowed into Russia. The tsar agreed that Ukrainian-grown leaf would not enter Russia from Poland-Lithuania to preserve the English monopoly on sales in European Russia.[7]

94   *Matthew P. Romaniello*

The Board of Trade and Plantations strongly endorsed the new contract. While the expansion from zero legal imports to 3 or 5 million pounds of leaf per year was an optimistic assessment of the market, the board's estimate of tobacco imports in the other 'northern' states indicates this number was within the consumption level of Russia's neighbours. According to information gathered by the board in 1696, just before the Russian contract, Denmark and Norway imported approximately 2.5 million pounds per year and Sweden imported 4.[8] With a larger population than its neighbours, the figure for Russia was not unreasonable. However, the transition from no legal consumption to a comparable level with countries with an established habit in two years was unquestionably ambitious.

Despite the board's prediction and the merchants' hopes, the tobacco imported in the first year was largely unsold, remaining in the contractors' Moscow warehouses. Public criticism in England was inevitable from the contractors' failure to sell tobacco at the expected rate. Following more than fifty years of smuggling tobacco into Russia, the tobacco contractors seemingly wasted the opportunity to import tobacco to Moscow.[9] The contractors themselves fuelled the criticism at home by publishing a broadsheet in 1700 that predicted tobacco sales in Russia would be at least £150,000, turning 'the Balance of all of Our Northern Trades in Our favour', even though they had not succeeded in selling the first year's imports by the end of the second year.[10] The unsold tobacco sitting in Moscow confirmed the contractors had failed, and even required the assistance of the government to salvage their initial investment in the new business.

England's envoy Charles Whitworth arrived in Moscow in February 1705 to resolve two significant issues: resolving the tobacco contract and negotiating a trade agreement between Russia and England. Both goals had the support of the English merchants operating in Moscow, 'because hitherto they onely carried on their Trade by the bare permission of the Czar, without having any publick authority, whereon they could ground their Liberties and privileges, except the contract with the Tobacco Company, which had already been violated in most its articles'.[11] While the tobacco imported in the first year (1699) still sat in Moscow's warehouses, whether the contract itself had been violated was a matter of dispute. The merchants offered two arguments. The first was that the genuine market for tobacco was in Siberia, not European Russia, and therefore the tsar's refusal to allow sales in Siberia prevented potential success. The second was that Ukrainian ('Circassian') tobacco was being regularly smuggled into Russia from Poland-Lithuania. Early in 1705, the contractors protested that 'In the Army's Circassian Tobacco hath been publickly Sold, and Last Year not only hundreds in the sailes, but the Company's Servts imprison'd, & their Tobacco taken away by the Government without payment'.[12] Despite the contractors' complaints, the Russian government had honoured the contract's terms. Siberia was a separate kingdom from European Russia, therefore the English right to sell anywhere in Russia was never included in

'This whole business' 95

the original agreement.[13] In fact, the Russian government passed a new law in 1701 that no tobacco from Siberia could be sold in Moscow because its market belonged to the English, reinforcing the terms of the contract.[14] Furthermore, Ukrainian tobacco was illegal to sell anywhere in Russia until 1727, when Russia legalised its sale following Russia's acquisition of some of the tobacco-producing regions of Ukraine.[15] In other words, only when Ukrainian tobacco became domestic was its sale permitted, long after the English lost the monopoly.

Therefore, Whitworth's first, formal report on the state of English trade may have accurately reflected the merchants' complaints about their treatment in Russia, but also reiterated their own flawed conclusions on Russia's actions. In his letter to the foreign secretary summarizing the situation, Whitworth did not believe there was hope of salvaging the trade.

> I think it my duty to acquaint you, that the Czar is about taking the Whole Tabacco Trade into his own hands, and having it carried on by the Burgermeister of this City who accordingly a few days ago has agreed for 5 or 6 pude [1 pud = 36 lbs.] with Mr Martin and Speelman two factors of the Russian Company, who at the same time had undertaken to get over from England persons capable to dry cut and spin the Tabacco, by whose help the Moscovites may in a little time learn to dress up that which grows Circassia and either put it off, or at least, mount it with the English, which practice cannot but in time prove of a very ill consequence to that part of our Commerce, which is almost the one beneficial trade that can be expected here.[16]

Whitworth's observations noted two concerns. The first was that all future sales were endangered if the tsar monopolised the entire trade, which was a surprising worry in light of the failure of the English monopoly to produce any sales. The second was that two of the contractors, Joseph Martin and James Spilman, had hired tobacco craftsmen to establish a new facility to prepare tobacco leaf. While Whitworth considered the former a greater issue than the latter, the reaction in London was quite different.

Whitworth began negotiations with the Russian government to resolve the tobacco issues before his first letter would reach London. The results of these early discussions challenged the position of the tobacco merchants. His second report on tobacco sales to the foreign secretary, sent in May 1705, revealed that the Russian government had restricted all sales of Ukrainian tobacco in Russia, but noted the Russians had no ability to prevent Ukrainian tobacco from being sold in Ukraine, as it was Polish territory. More troubling, according to the Russian government, the original contract had not given permission to sell tobacco in Siberia for three years, which could have allowed that right in 1702, except the Russian government was aware the English had never imported the full amounts required in the first and second year of the contract, and therefore the contract itself was not in force.[17]

96   *Matthew P. Romaniello*

Though Whitworth's news from Moscow was poor, there was increasing alarm in London about the idea of establishing a tobacco workhouse in Moscow under the direction of English craftsmen. The tobacco contractors had a clear divide. Martin and Spilman hired the craftsmen, and purchased their equipment, while several of the other tobacco contractors asked the Board of Trade and Plantations to stop this plan. Though Whitworth would later report the goal had been to prepare the tobacco leaf sitting in the contractors' warehouse, the London-based merchants believed that Martin and Spilman had purchased Ukrainian tobacco to use in their new enterprise. Having locally-sourced tobacco, allowed the 'Muscovites who are numerous Industrious & work cheap be thus assisted & instructed by our own manufacturers. They will in a few years have great Quantities of their own growth and manufacturing & may in time Supply all the Northern and Eastern parts of the World much cheaper than England & then the Crown of England will of necessity by the decay of Customes share with the generall misfortunes of the Subjects if timely care be not taken to prevent it'.[18] The Board of Trade agreed, urging the foreign secretary to intervene immediately to prevent the Russians from becoming 'equally skilled in that Mystery with any of your Majesty's Subjects dealers in Tobacco, Which proceedings being of most pernicious consequence to the Trade of your Majesty's Subjects and Welfare of Your Plantations'.[19]

Following the recommendations of the board, the Queen's secretary notified the foreign secretary to prepare the necessary warrants to remove the two tobacco craftsmen from Moscow in May 1705. In addition, the foreign secretary was instructed to notify Whitworth that he must 'cause the said Engines and Materials already there to be broken and destroyed in His Presence in the most private and effectuall manner that may be'. In addition, the two merchants who organised the new facility, Martin and Spilman, were cited for 'making a contract without Her Majesty's knowledge and allowance in a matter so injurious to Other Her Majesty's Subjects'. Furthermore, no merchant would be allowed 'to send any persons into Muscovy versed in the Mystery of Spinning and Rowling Tobacco or any Instruments or Materials for the same or to employ any Persons therein as they tender Her Majesty's displeasure and will answer to the Contrary at their Perills'.[20]

On 1 June, the foreign secretary ordered Whitworth to 'destroy those materials brought from hence to Mosco for the carrying on the manufacture' and 'order the Persons concern'd there in forthwith to return home'.[21] Once those tasks were accomplished, Whitworth should inform the tsar that Queen Anne had demanded these actions. The foreign secretary instructed Whitworth to assure the tsar that the English shipwrights, artificers, and 'volunteers' in service to tsar would not be recalled, if there was any 'alarm [in] the Court of Mosco' over the possible loss of those English specialists.[22]

'This whole business' 97

Whitworth's first response was to provide an accurate account of the facility in Moscow. He was slightly confused by his new instructions, having been directed 'to transmit the fullest account ... of the numbers, names, & of the persons concern'd in the manufacturing Tobacco'. However, he replied 'there is no Tobacco manufactur'd here, except as that belongs to the English Company for which purpose they have onely two persons, Francis Peacock a Tobacco cutter, and Peter Marshall a Tobacco Spinner. These prepare the Tobacco before and after it is cut and spun, which method they entirely keep to themselves a secret, but in the laborious parts of the work, at spinning, rolling, and cutting they employ above 200 Russians'.[23]

Though his correspondence reveals some ambivalence about his instructions, Whitworth did carry out the directives, reporting his actions to the foreign secretary on 18 July. His letter takes an odd tone, first criticizing the foreign secretary for the delay in notifying him until a letter date 1 June – a full month after the Privy Council's decision. He then noted that while Peter Marshall had been extracted from Moscow, Marshall's wife would not be accompanying him (as instructed) because she died one month earlier. Whitworth then set about destroying the facility without achieving the notice of its 200 Russian employees. This required the removal of Marshall from Moscow without alerting him to true state of affairs. Marshall had taken the appointment in Russia under 'apprehension of his being prosecuted by the Government for some misdemeanours and undue practices in his Trade. He had likewise of several occasions sho'd an inclination of entering unto the Czars service and is so much accused of Intemperance and indiscretion that I had all reason to suspect he might discover what was on foot, and under protection of the government hinder me from fulfilling my Commission'. To handle Marshall, Whitworth relied on the assistance of the tobacco cutter, Francis Peacock, who had 'the Character of a sober and discreet person', to take Marshall away from Moscow, where he was presented with a letter instructing him to 'return to England on the pain of her Majesties highest displeasure'.[24]

In the letter presented to Marshall after his removal, Whitworth refrained from the more explicit threats recorded in his letter to the foreign secretary. He began positively, noting 'As Loyal and Fine Subjects [you] will receive and execute Her Majesties will with all due obedience and as little noise as possible'. The latter part may have been the more important, as 'this whole business should be kept very Secret'. Furthermore, despite the royal command to immediately leave Russia, 'on your arrival in England you shall receive all fitting incouragement and protection from the Government, and I shall also take care to command you to one of Her Majesties principall Secretary of State'.[25] Whitworth's concern about Marshall's untrustworthy character undoubtedly led to the kinder words about his potential future in London.

Once the craftsmen left Moscow, Whitworth acted quickly. All of the Russian workmen were dismissed, because no work could proceed without

98 *Matthew P. Romaniello*

the masters supervising the enterprise. Then Whitworth, his secretary, and four servants went to dismantle the workhouses. They destroyed

> several Instruments & materials, some whereof were so strong that they oblidged us to make a great noise in pulling them to pieces. There were eleven barrels about a quarter full of the Tobacco Liquor in several degrees of preparation, which I caused all to be let out; and destroy'd 5 parcells of Ingredients which are used in the Composition tho' indeed I could have wished that some of them might have been removed & saved. ... I likewise broke the great Spinning wheel, and above threescore reels for rowling, I then destroyed three engines ready set up for cutting Tobacco, and took away the plates & Cranes for two more, several large engines for preparing the Tobacco into form have been pull'd to pieces, their forms split, the wooden poles broke, the Copper carried away, and about 20 fine sives cut to pieces nor is the least thing left standing, except some great plain wooden presses (wherein they put the Tobacco after it is roled and wetted) & some ordinary wooden tables. The next day my Servants returned & burnt all of the remains of the wood which wee had broke & my Smith is now working in my house on the rest of the iron and copper machines.[26]

While Whitworth executed the destruction of the workhouses as instructed, he had regrets over this turn of events. Following his description of the action, he was uncertain if the contractors' business could survive. 'It were very much to be wished both for the good of England, and the Interest of the persons concern'd, that this Contract or Monopoly had never been made but since it has been done, the apparent ruine of the Company may possibly deserve some consideration'.[27]

Unfortunately for Whitworth personally and Anglo-Russian relations in general, the tsar's government had discovered the destruction of the workhouses only two days after the rollers had been sent on the road to Arkhangel'sk, leaving Whitworth to wait apprehensively for the consequences. According to Whitworth, a group of Moscow's merchants had become suspicious when Marshall left town, and 'Sent Some people to visit the workhouses in the night, who enter'd at the windows, ... and soon perceived that all was removed or broken'. The break-in had been led by a former servant of the previous English consul, who had been 'turned away for many misdemeanours, accused his Master to the [Russian] Government if Severall unfair practices in Trade'.[28] While his initial accusations that led to his dismissal had not been proven, the destruction of the workhouse was proof of English malfeasance. Within two weeks, Whitworth reported to the foreign secretary that 'I am fully convinced that her Majesty's Resolution to recall the Tobacco Cutters had given rise to the report of Her designing to withdraw all Her other Subjects from the Czar's service'. Nor was it only the Russians who believed this rumour, but also the Englishmen currently working in the tsar's government. Whitworth noted that 'Mr. Stiles who having engaged to bring over some Ship Carpenters hither, was apprehensive that his proceeding might likewise draw upon himself Her Majesty's Displeasure'.[29] Whitworth had no choice but to meet with several representatives of the tsar's government during August to assure them that more English shipwrights for the tsar's service would be arriving in Arkhangel'sk shortly, in hopes of easing relations between the countries. Whitworth added that the queen had no intention of recalling any English subjects from Russian service.[30]

The foreign secretary, the Board of Trade and Plantations, and Whitworth all believed the destruction of the workhouses to be necessary to protect English interests from the potential of a trained Russian workforce utilizing the machinery to prepare Ukrainian tobacco as if it was the better quality, but more expensive, Virginian leaf. Whitworth arrived in Russia having already criticised the poor quality of the potential imported leaf from Poland-Lithuania. However, state authorities in London, particularly the Board of Trade, believed the affordable price of Ukrainian tobacco over-rode a concern for quality in northern Europe. While Russian tobacco habits may have been relatively recent, Whitworth was concerned that they were pleased to 'chop their tobacco with axes on the ground' in order to prepare it, which made both Virginian leaf and the elaborate manufacturing process unnecessary.[31] The English masters brought not only new flavours to disguise the poor quality of Ukrainian leaf but also a cleaner and quicker process for turning raw leaf into rolled cigars. If any part of the workhouses had been left functioning, the English would have had little to offer the unsophisticated consumers of Russia, who were not willing to pay a premium for the English-imported leaf.

Russia's reaction

Russia had a history of welcoming foreign specialists to work in the country, well before the tobacco workhouses were built. In the second half of the seventeenth century, English diplomats exploited Russian interests as an opportunity to improve relations between the two countries. Samuel Collins, for example, was an English doctor who became the tsar's personal physician, serving in Moscow for nine years until 1666. He was recruited for his position by the current envoy, John Hebdon. Collins later published his observations of the Russian court, its government, and commercial opportunities in a well-known text, *The Present State of Russia*.[32] Numerous English and Scottish officers were recruited for the Russian army, including General Patrick Gordon, who served in Russia from 1661 until his death in 1699.[33] Neither was Russia's interest in foreign specialists limited to the British Isles, nor entry into the tsar's service a prerequisite for a career in Russia. Dutch merchants had a well-established role in the Russian mining industry.[34] Indian merchants supervised the production of textiles in

100 Matthew P. Romaniello

Astrakhan on the north shore of the Caspian Sea, importing both raw cotton and silk from the Middle East that was then produced as finished cloth for domestic sales.[35] Both the mines and the textile mills remained under foreign control. The state sold licences to allow these merchants and craftsman to establish their businesses and employ a Russian workforce, but did not control the businesses themselves.

Foreign merchants also became involved in projects outside of commerce. Peter the Great's first embassy to China in 1692 was led Eberhard Isbrand Ides, a Danish merchant who had operated in Russia for a few years before the embassy. Adam Brand from Lubeck, another merchant, acted as the embassy's secretary.[36] Ides and Brand led a cosmopolitan assemblage of more than two hundred and fifty men, including nobles and merchants, to negotiate new terms between Russia and China following the earlier Treaty of Nerchinsk (1689). Ides and Brand were part of a wave of men recruited from the West to live and work in Peter's Russia, becoming part of a large community of foreigners living in one of Moscow's neighbourhoods, the Nemetskaia sloboda ('German district'), with Dutch, Danish, English, German, and Italian residents.[37] Peter's recruits included not only scientific and technical specialists but also artists, musicians, architects, and craftsman from a broad spectrum of trades. In his own household, Peter employed a master cook from Denmark, John Felton, an Italian weaver, and relied on two English merchants to advise him on commercial matters.[38] The tsar was personally involved in many of these decisions. Shortly after Whitworth arrived in Moscow, the tsar wrote to express his concern that three of the five recently-arrived British carpenters were not sufficiently well-trained to work in his shipyards and requested the assistance in immediately hiring five more.[39]

Relations between England and Russia undoubtedly cooled following the workhouses' destruction, even as Peter the Great continued to hire English and Scottish specialists for his service. Whitworth attempted to repair the relationship, but struggled with Russia's expectation of concessions on the part of the English. Some of these were minor. For example, in March 1706, the Ambassadorial Chancellery prepared a list of the thirty best graduates for the Moscow School of Navigation to be sent to London for advanced study in navigation or mathematics.[40] By the summer, the tsar officially requested the English crown to fund the education of twenty of these pupils. Initially Whitworth declined, as 'Gentlemen of Quality' should be able to pay for themselves, but Peter held firm with his assertion that these men were all 'gentlemen, yet their parents were but in a mean condition'. Whitworth arranged for the men's transportation to London less than a month after the original meeting.[41] In addition to this type of concession to repair the relationship, there were no restrictions placed Russia's interest in recruiting more men or in purchasing new materials from England. In May 1706, for example, the tsar instructed an agent to purchase new lathes and navigation equipment in England and arrange for the shipment to be sent to Russia, which proceeded without any interference from the English crown.[42]

These small improvements in the relationship between the two countries did not restore Whitworth's faith in future negotiating success. Early in 1707, Whitworth suggested to the foreign secretary that the relationship might not be salvageable. 'Tho' I know by former Experience how disagreeable any proposition would be in behalf of the Merchants, especially those of the Tobacco Company, yet I little imagin'd to have met with so very cold a reception, and such unequal returns to her Majesty's Terms of Friendship and affection, which confirms me in the opinion... that all my solicitations would be in vain for the present, and I could be of no further use to them here'.[43] Despite Whitworth's expectations, English merchants continued to purchase new licences for Russians exports, including one by Dodd and Crisp to export 'masts, bowsprits, spars, sawn plans, yards, clapboards, and other ship's timbers, wherever they are able to find them, and freely purchase them, collect and deliver them to Riga along the river Dvina'.[44] Dodd and Crisp's purchased the licence only one month after Whitworth's dire predictions, suggesting that while diplomatic relations may have cooled, the merchants' themselves continued to prosper.

Therefore, considering the breadth and depth of foreigners working in Russia, the English tobacco workhouses were hardly unusual. Whitworth's actions on behalf of the English government, however, were, and the consequences of those actions were not easily resolved. Two English merchants importing tobacco, and then establishing the workhouses to finish the leaf as rolled tobacco fit neatly into this well-established pattern. The mines, the textile mills, and the workhouses all employed local Russians working under the supervision of foreign specialists. The English government's destruction of its own merchants' enterprise was an unprecedented event in Russia. It is no wonder rumours immediately spread the English government planned to remove all of its specialists in Russia's service, despite new recruits arriving regularly. After all, there was no explanation offered why the tobacco workhouse was a valuable English enterprise at a time when Englishmen were building ships for Russia or working on the new canal system.[45]

Resolving the dispute

By the end of 1705, the tobacco contract theoretically was resolved when the tsar and the merchants agreed to have all the remaining tobacco purchased by Russians, removing the continuing problem from English hands.[46] On 12 December 1705, Whitworth wrote to the foreign secretary of his successful proposal to the tsar, but he could not 'settle the rate nor other particulars' until he consulted with the contractors.[47] In order to complete the contract, the merchants compiled a list of the total volume of tobacco remaining in Moscow, Vologda, and Arkhangel'sk, which comprised approximately 2,300 hogsheads of leaf tobacco to be sold for 187,724 rubles, 7 kopeks, and

102   Matthew P. Romaniello

10 dengi, payable in instalments.[48] The final transfer of tobacco from English to Russian hands was a slow process lasting several months, but by the end of 1706 the sale of imported tobacco was finally no longer an English problem.[49]

While the tobacco sale theoretically resolved the issue among the English merchants operating in Russia, it had revealed some of the explicit tensions among this group, particularly between those residing in Moscow like Martin and Spilman and those in London. The London group, perhaps surprisingly, wrote to the Board of Trade and Plantations in defence of their Moscow colleagues, assuring the government that 'any Mismanagements done by the Company' were unfounded allegations, as 'Wee are not sensible of the least failure on their part, Butt have punctually complied with every thing, required of Them'. In fact, the contractors argued that all the recent issues in Moscow were the fault of the English consul, Charles Goodfellow, who had inspired the conflict because he failed 'to secure an Interest' in the trade, which 'was purely his fault, and not ours'.[50] To be fair, it was Goodfellow's former servant that led the Russians to discover the destruction of the workhouses so quickly. However, there is no evidence that Goodfellow had any role in the decision to establish the tobacco workhouses, in which he had no investment, as even the contractors noted. Moreover, Whitworth remained a firm advocate for Goodfellow after the tobacco workhouses, praising his service when he departed Russia to return to England in 1707. Whitworth explicitly rebuked the contractors in a letter to the foreign secretary, mentioning that Goodfellow 'had never any salary from Her Majesty, nor from the Russian Company, Yet he had been a reputation to his Country by his handsome way of living and prudent carriage, and has done many service to the rest of the Factory, by virtue of his Commission, and the credit it gave him in this government'.[51]

Whitworth's tense relationship with the tobacco contractors did not alter his commitment to advocating for their interests in Russia. Whitworth's last act as the envoy was a lengthy negotiation with the Russian government in 1712 in hopes of signing a commercial treaty before his departure from office. His proposal focused on two outstanding issues: first, reclaiming the tobacco monopoly, hoping complaints about the contractors' poor treatment by Russian authorities would produce a better result; and second, lowering customs duties at Arkhangel'sk, or at least the cost of the commodities themselves.[52] His proposals failed to receive any positive response from Russia's ministers. When he departed from Russia in the summer of 1712, his time as England's envoy to Russia accomplished very little beyond destroying the tobacco workhouses and selling the remaining leaf in 1705.[53]

Whitworth's two goals in 1712 ignored the ongoing conditions of Russia in the midst of a two-decade long war, which produced substantial debt from constructing a new navy, establishing a new capital, as well as incorporating new territory and population along the Baltic coast. Peter the Great's government tended to make most of its decisions on the basis of its

'This whole business' 103

ability to generate much needed revenue for the state for these massive projects. There was no incentive to lower the cost of commodities for export, adjust customs duties, or even to offer certain products to open market rather than selling them as monopolies. Monopoly licences guaranteed upfront cash; open sales could fluctuate with the market. The tobacco contract opened a new market for English merchants. However, the English failed to turn a profit, regularly protested their treatment in Russia, and, finally, committed a very public, potentially illegal, action under the express orders of the English government. If merchants from Holland or Hamburg were willing to pay in advance for Russian goods, why endorse English merchants in light of their questionable history?

The destruction of the tobacco workhouses was just one act during decades of cooperation between the two countries. It certainly was not the end of English specialists working in Russian service, nor was it the end of English craftsmen supervising Russian employees. Furthermore, a decade later, the same event produced a far different outcome. On 21 October 1716, King Frederick William I of Prussia issued a royal charter to allow two British merchants to establish a tobacco workhouse in Elbingen, with the right to sell their products throughout his kingdom. The business would be built by David Barclay and William Ellins, who offered 'the Secret of their Liquors... for Preserving Rolle-Tobacco', and the services of 'one Mr. Evans, a Considerable Roller & Manufacturer of Tobacco' from London. Barclay and Ellins had convinced the Frederick William that 'the Climate & Ground in our Kingdom of Prussia, has the Quality to bring forth Better tobacco, than it has done hitherto: & that by their Science in Spinning & preparing of Tobacco, this Branch of trade might be improv'd & render'd more profitable to our Subjects'. The British merchants received a monopoly for fifteen years, with the exclusive right to purchase all the tobacco produced in Prussia. Everything manufactured in their new facility could be exported through Königsberg into the Baltic Sea tax free, but anything transported along river to Dantzig or Elbing would pay regular custom.[54] This was an attempt to improve the current domestic production, as villages around Königsberg had been curing and rolling approximately 30,000 pounds per annum of Spanish tobacco, which could now be replaced by domestic production. In addition, the king's grant expected that the new facility could seize part of the Dutch tobacco sales to the Baltic, which was estimated between 40 and 50,000 hogsheads, or more than 1.5 million pounds per year.[55]

In 1705, the potential loss of the English techniques to prepare tobacco and liquors to flavour the product was forcibly prevented by the English government. In 1716, Barclay and Ellins did exactly that in Prussia. Coincidentally, Charles Whitworth was the envoy to Russia in 1705 and the envoy to Prussia in 1716. No one could have been more prepared to prevent the new workhouses' construction. However, Britain was no longer the same country. The Elector of Hanover became King George I of Great Britain in

104 *Matthew P. Romaniello*

1714. During his reign, the security of Hanover was a priority, leading him to pursue a new alliance with Prussia to protect his exposed homelands. This new interest may have provided a reason for allowing the Prussians to gain the production processes to prepare Ukrainian tobacco that the Queen Anne's government had been unwilling to share with Russia. The existing tensions between Russia and Prussia ultimately led to even more difficulties between Britain and Russia over the new Anglo-Prussian alliance, but George I's concerns were clearly not his predecessors'.

Conclusion

In 1714, Friedrich Christian Weber, the Hannoverian envoy to Russia on behalf of George I, reflected a new attitude towards Anglo-Russian relations. Unlike Whitworth's apprehensions about the relationship with Russia during his decade of service in the country, Weber positively reacted to the cosmopolitan culture of the new Russian capital of St. Petersburg. A French craftsman had arrived from Berlin 'to establish a Stocking Manufacture', and had recently completed a large workhouse for his business. The tsar's breweries were run by 'English and Dutch brewers, ... who make good Beer of divers sorts after the way of their Countries'. 'Twenty Shepherds from Silesia' established a new wool manufacturing business in the city of Kazan' on the Volga River, teaching new shearing and spinning techniques to the local workers. A Dutch master supervised Russia's flax production in St. Petersburg with the assistance of 'twenty odd Journeymen, who are Germans'. The flax was spun under the direction of 'an old Dutch-woman, who is set over eighty odd loose Women, to teach them with the Whip how to handle the Spinning-wheel, the Use of which was unknown in Russia before'.[56] From Weber's assessment, it was clear that foreign masters supervising a Russian workforce to produce finishing products was hardly atypical in Russia's cities, not only in the capitals of Moscow and St. Petersburg but also across the empire. British subjects occupied leadership roles in Russian industries, alongside a cosmopolitan community. The only break in this tradition in the destruction of the tobacco workhouses, which reinforces how surprising the foreign secretary's instructions to Charles Whitworth were.

The tobacco contractors and their workhouses reveal an unusual moment for both England and Russia. Tobacco struggled to find willing consumers in Russia following decades of legal restrictions on the importation of the product. When tobacco leaves smoked in pipes proved undesirable, English merchants remarketed the product as a luxury – rolled tobacco – prepared with specialist techniques and foreign flavours. Though the new product seemed more successful than plain leaf, the English government acted against the interest of its merchants to maintain control over its production secrets. In Prussia, Britain was willing to allow the loss of its production processes, because it served its diplomatic interests. Therefore, the

'This whole business' 105

destruction of Moscow's tobacco workhouses was not only about the loss of an industrial 'mystery' but also a public acknowledgement that Russia was not as important to England's long-term interests. Products in the global economy did not only have to find willing consumers likely unfamiliar with a new taste or style but also align with state interests. Russia's embrace of a cosmopolitan culture in its cities as a way of importing new skills and knowledge, including men and material from England, was not sufficient to persuade English authorities of the value of this relationship. Later in the eighteenth century, Enlightenment figures would argue for Russian 'backwardness' in light of Western advances, yet in 1705 it was Russia, but not England, that was open to new opportunities.

Notes

1 An earlier version of this article was presented at *Objects and Possession: Material Goods in a Changing World, 1200–1800*, University of Southampton, in April 2017.TNA, SP 91/4, part 1, ff. 22–25r., 'Whitworth to Harley', 18 February 1705.
2 Richard Hellie, trans. and ed., *The Muscovite Law Code (Ulozhenie) of 1649: Part I, Text and Translation* (Irvine, CA: Charles Schlacks, 1988), ch. 25, article 11, 228.
3 The National Archives (TNA), CO 389/15, ff. 185–89, 'Whitehall to the Lords Commission, August 10th 1697, of the state of Trade between Russia and England'.
4 On Russia's ban and the British contract, see Matthew P. Romaniello, 'Muscovy's Extraordinary Ban on Tobacco', in *Tobacco in Russian History and Culture: From the Seventeenth Century to the Present*, eds. Matthew P. Romaniello and Tricia Starks (New York: Routledge, 2009), 9–25.
5 Among the studies on this topic, see Anthony Cross, *By the Banks of the Neva: Chapters from the Lives and Careers of the British in Eighteenth-Century Russia* (Cambridge: Cambridge University Press, 1997).
6 A. V. Demkin, *Britanskoe kupechestvo v Rossii XVIII veka* (Moscow: Institut rossiiskoi istorii RAN, 1998), 107–14.
7 W. F. Ryan, "Peter the Great's English Yacht: Admiral Lord Carmarthen and the Russian Tobacco Monopoly," *Mariner's Mirror*, 69 (1983): 65–87; Igor' Bogdanov, *Dym otechestva, ili kratkaia istoriia tabakokureniia* (Moscow: Novoe literaturnoe obozrenie, 2007), 35–42.
8 TNA, CO 388/6, A12, 'Copy of an Extract of the outward Cargos of Ten England and Ten Foreign Ships to the Dominions of the Northern Crowns, 10 Aug 1696', and TNA, CO 389/19, ff. 181–297, 'Report to the House of Commons, 1707', here f. 245.
9 On England's smuggling, see Matthew P. Romaniello, "Through the Filter of Tobacco: The Limits of Global Trade in the Early Modern World," *Comparative Studies in Society and History* 49, no. 4 (2007): 916–26.
10 'Some considerations relating to the enlarging the Russia trade, and the contract for importing tobacco into that countrey', Goldsmiths'-Kress Library of Economic Literature, no. 3675.8.
11 British Library (BL), Add MS 37,354, ff. 63–68, "Whitworth to Harley," 11 March/ 28 February 1705, here 66r.
12 BL, Add MS 37,354, ff. 77–78, 'A State of the Tobacco Company Case in Russia', here 77 v.

106   *Matthew P. Romaniello*

13 On Siberia's legal status, see Erika Monahan, *The Merchants of Siberia: Trade in Early Modern Eurasia* (Ithaca: Cornell University Press, 2016), ch. 2.

14 *Pis'ma i bumagi imperatora Petra Velikago*, 12 vols. (St. Petersburg: Gosudarstvennaia tipografiia, 1887) vol. I, #369, 443.

15 Polnoe sobranie zakonov Rossiiskoi Imperii (PSZ), Series 1 (St. Petersburg: Tipografiia otdeleniia sobstevnnoi ego Imperatorskago Velichestva Kantseliarii, 1830), vol. VII, #5164, 26 September 1727, 865–8.

16 BL, Add MS 37,354, ff. 71–74, "Whitworth to Harley," 7/18 March 1705; here 74r.

17 BL, Add MS 37,354, ff. 144–55, "Whitworth to Harley," 9/20 May 1705, here 150v–151r.

18 'A State of the Trade to Russia', reprinted in "Tobacco Trade in Russia, 1705," *William and Mary College Quarterly Historical Magazine*, 2nd series, 3, no. 4 (1923): 253.

19 TNA, SP 104/120, ff. 54v–56r, "Report from the Lord's Commission for Trade and Plantation," 31 May 1705, here 55r-v.

20 TNA, SP 104/120, ff. 56r/v, "John Povey to Harley," 26 May 1705.

21 TNA, SP 104/120, ff. 53r–54r., "Whitworth from C. Hedges," 1 June 1705.

22 TNA, SP 104/120, ff. 56v–57v., "Whitworth from Harley," 23 July 1705.

23 BL, Add MS. 37,354, ff. 271–3, "Whitworth to Harley," 1 July/20 June 1705.

24 TNA, SP 91/4, part 2, ff. 2–8, "Whitworth to Harley," 18/29 July 1705.

25 TNA, SP 91/4, part 2, ff. 1r.–1Av., "Copy of my Letter to Mr Marshall and Mr Peacock," 15 July 1705.

26 TNA, SP 91/4, part 2, ff. 2–8, "Whitworth to Harley," 18/29 July 1705; here 5r-v.

27 TNA, SP 91/4, part 2, ff. 2–8, "Whitworth to Harley," 18/29 July 1705; here 7v-8r.

28 TNA, SP 91/4, part 2, ff. 11r–12r., "Whitworth to Harley," 5 August 1705.

29 TNA, SP 91/4, part 2, ff. 16–18, "Whitworth to Harley," 22 August/2 September 1705; here 16 v.

30 TNA, SP 91/4, part 2, ff. 16r–18r, "Whitworth to Harley," 22 August 1705, recounts the rumors and Whitworth's recent meeting with the tsarist ministers. The first explanation was not readily accepted. Whitworth instructed London of another meeting in which he explained that the Queen's laws banned English subjects from entering into contracts with foreign princes without the monarch's approval, but the Queen still approved of the English shipwrights in the tsar's government. TNA, SP 91/4, Part 2, ff. 32r–34v., "Whitworth to Harley," 7 October 1705.

31 TNA, SP 91/4, part 2, ff. 2–8, "Whitworth to Harley," 18 July 1705, here f. 6 v.

32 Samuel Collins, *The Present State of Russia* (London: John Winter, 1671).

33 Parts of Patrick Gordon's memoirs have been published since the eighteenth century, but recently a complete edition has appeared: Patrick Gordon, *Diary of General Patrick Gordon of Auchleuchries*, 6 vols., ed. Dmitry Fedosov (Aberdeen: AHRC Centre for Irish and Scottish Studies, 2009–2016).

34 For example, an iron mine in Kazan' was run by Peter Muller. Russian State Archive of Ancient Acts, Moscow, f. 159, op. 2, d. 1361, 9 May 1675.

35 Whitworth mentioned this trade in his early notes from Russia but believed the domestic production to be supervised by Persians rather than Indians. TNA, SP 91/4, part 2, ff. 77r–82v, 'Short view of this Commerce in general', 29 July 1705. For a later assessment of Astrakhan's production, see PSZ, vol. XI, #8242, 259–63, 17 September 1740.

36 Both men wrote narratives that were translated into English. Brand, *Journal of the Embassy*; and Ides, *Three Years Travels*.

37 For one example, see Maria di Salvo, 'The "Italian" Nemetskaia Sloboda', in

'This whole business' 107

Personality and place in Russian culture, ed.Simon Dixon (London: UCL School of Slavonic and East European Studies, 2010), 96–109.

38 National Library of Scotland, Carmichael and Gordon Papers, MS 189, John Bell, "Sundry Anecdotes of Peter the First", ff. 12–15.

39 Simon Dixon, trans. and ed., et al., *Britain and Russia in the Age of Peter the Great: Historical Documents* (London: School of Slavonic and East European Studies, 1998), #58, 'Peter I to Andrew Stiles', 11 March 1705, 49.

40 Dixon, *Britain and Russia,* #66, "A list compiled by the Ambassadorial Chancellery," March 1706, 58.

41 TNA, SP 91/4, part 3, ff. 32–55, "Harley to Whitworth," 31 July/11 August 1706, here 33 v.

42 Dixon, *Britain and Russia,* #67, "Peter to Andew Stiles," 14 May 1706, 59; and #71, "Peter to Andrew Stiles," 20 May 1707, 61.

43 BL, Add. MS 37,356, ff. 10–11, "Whitworth to Harley," 7/18 January 1707, here 11r..

44 Dixon, *Britain and Russia,* #70, "Permit issued to the British merchants," 11 February 1707, 61.

45 Perhaps the most famous of these men is John Perry, hired in 1698, wholater published an account of his career in Russian service, *The State of Russia under the Present Czar* (London: Benjamin Tooke, 1716).

46 TNA, SP 91/4, part 3, ff. 5r–10v., "Whitworth to Harley," 29 April 1706.

47 TNA, SP 91/4, part 3, ff. 50r–51v., "Whitworth to Harley," 12 December 1705.

48 TNA, SP 91/4, part 2, f. 106r., "An Account of the Tobacco the Company Have Lying Unsold in Russia," 26 January 1706.

49 TNA, SP 91/4, part 3, ff. 23r–24v., "Whitworth to Harley," 7 July 1706; and TNA, SP 91/4, Part 3, ff. 39r–40v., "Whitworth to Harley," 18 August 1706.

50 BL, Add. MS 37,355, ff. 5–6, "Haistwell, Heathcote, Dawson, and Gold to Whitworth," January 1706.

51 TNA, SP 91/5, part 1, ff. 125–126, "Whitworth to Harley," 12/23 November 1707.

52 TNA, SP 91/7, ff. 297–304 v, "Memoire donné à Monsr. Le Grand Chancelier Golloffkin à Petersbourg le 8e de Mars 1712".

53 TNA, SP 91/7, ff. 275r–281v, "Whitworth to St. John," 8/19 June 1712.

54 TNA, CO 388/20, P53, "Translation and Copy of the King of Prussia's Grant to Barclay and Ellens for manufacturing Tobacco, 1716", received 24 June 1718.

55 TNA, CO 388/20, P53, f. 2r.

56 Friedrich Christian Weber, *The Present State of Russia,* 2 vols. (London: W. Taylor, 1723), 43, 180–81.

6   Goods from the sea countries
Material cosmopolitanism in Atlantic West Africa

Bronwen Everill

On attending an audience and dinner at King Naimbana's home, traveller Anna Maria Falconbridge commented on the fashions of the Temne people: '[The Queen] was dressed in the [Temne] country manner, but in a dignified stile, having several yards of striped taffety wrapped round her waist, which served as a petticoat; another piece of the same was carelessly thrown over her shoulders in form of a scarf; her head was decorated with two silk handkerchiefs; her ears with rich gold ear-rings, and her neck with gaudy necklaces; but she had neither shoes nor stockings on.'[1] Despite the different uses made of fashionable cloth, there were commonalities in the ways they were incorporated into households in this period. Again, Anna Maria Falconbridge noted that, 'we returned to the Queens house to dinner, which was shortly after put on a table covered with a plain calico cloth.' In this era when imported cloths were increasingly being used to decorate the house as well as the body, the use of a calico tablecloth echoed developments else-where in the Atlantic.[2] In fact, the decoration of the home was at least as important as the decoration of the body in adhering to Atlantic trends. In her visit to the Bullom shore, Falconbridge noted that, 'the people appear more inclined to industry ... which a stranger may readily discern, by a superior way their houses are furnished in.'[3]

In the eighteenth century, the port cities of West Africa experienced the development of a newly Atlantic-inflected material cosmopolitanism. While trade had linked Western Africa for centuries, it was only during the eighteenth century that the Atlantic World developed a unique, cosmopolitan material culture. This chapter will explore the development of new 'consumption clusters' (or assemblages) in urban West Africa. The expansion of new forms of global trade, and the incorporation of new goods into existing quotidian and ceremonial rituals – mealtimes, personal display, household decoration, state dinners, annual tariff negotiations – highlights the power of localized value systems in shaping use, and the power of 'the cosmopolitan' in eighteenth century ideas of fashion and 'modernity.'

If cosmopolitanism is going to be reconsidered in the age of resurgent nationalism, then perhaps it is worthwhile to consider the subtle ways that non-cosmopolitan actors' lives were shaped by the presence of trading

Goods from the sea countries 109

diasporas, immigrants, refugees, enslaved communities, and other non-native, or itinerant, inhabitants of their visual and material landscapes. Material cosmopolitanism – defined by Beverly Lemire as 'a wider habitual involvement in diverse material media resulting from global commerce ... plus the new situational activities arising from global trade' – can help to shift the focus from elite internationalism to something grounded in the everyday experiences of less peripatetic actors.[4]

Looking at Western Africa, generally, and Sierra Leone, specifically, will show how material cosmopolitanism was shaped over the eighteenth century, and suggest different ways of interpreting the region's commercial engagement with the Atlantic World towards the end of the period of the legal Atlantic slave trade. Sierra Leone provides an interesting lens to examine this phenomenon because it was settled at the end of the eighteenth century by a group of black loyalist families displaced by the American revolution, was explicitly excluded by charter from the slave trade, and therefore provides a good window of observations on the state of trade and consumption patterns, in what ways they could change it, and what was customary by the end of the eighteenth century, before the widespread legal abolition of slave trading.

Global material cosmopolitanism

As other essays in this volume have highlighted, globalized trade expanded dramatically in the early modern period. But it was also distinctive from the kind of modern globalization described by Christopher Bayly.[5] This was not yet a period of convergence in tastes, but by the mid-eighteenth century, it was close. Fashions, as well as goods, were crossing the Atlantic in multiple directions. But equally important to the circulation of goods, was the impact of consumption changes on production changes. People became not only cosmopolitan consumers, but also producers for distant others, and producers for local consumers with cosmopolitan tastes.

A focus on West Africa can help with this for several reasons. First, there has been a longstanding bias towards understanding African history as *removed* from these cosmopolitan currents in the early modern world. A large historiography has developed to debate the extent of African dependence on global goods. In *How Europe Underdeveloped Africa*, Walter Rodney laid out an important and influential argument about the slave trade's devastating effects on Africa's population and economic potential, and its history of dependency on imported manufactured goods. He argued that 'The lines of economic activity attached to foreign trade were either destructive, as slavery was, or at best purely extractive' and pointed to the demographic effects and the draining of African resources in exchange for European and global goods.[6] Eltis and Jennings, by contrast, have argued that African economies were never dependent on Atlantic goods, and go so far as to argue for the marginal role of the Atlantic in African life.[7] Looking at

110   *Bronwen Everill*

material *cosmopolitanism* highlights the ways that Atlantic goods were incorporated into existing material assemblages, rather than arguing about the centrality or marginality of these goods to African life.

Secondly, 'West Africa' broadly is being treated because sources for the pre-colonial period in any one city are limited in their ability to give deeply textured accounts of these trends. British, French and Portuguese trade statistics to West African ports are almost always generalized to the whole of Africa. Merchant and Company records are more detailed, when it comes to certain aspects of commercial life, but are fragmentary in discussions of African life. An attempt to think about how cosmopolitan fashions in food, clothing, and lifestyles were adapted into existing patterns requires mining both the commercial accounts, and the narrative accounts of travellers – who arrived in droves on the West African coast from the eighteenth century – as well as archaeological investigations.

Material cosmopolitanism in the African Atlantic

The Upper Guinea Coast was a marginal slave trading region, populated by resident European and Eurafrican 'factors', as well as settlers, itinerant European and African merchants and traders, and local populations. Rapidly expanding demand for consumer goods in the cities and their hinterlands, plus changing social relations in the urban areas gave rise to experimentation in debt relationships, financing the slave trade and the gum trade from the perspective of the European merchants, and more importantly, financing the West African consumer revolution.

The growing demand for global goods in Africa over the period has been well-demonstrated by the vast quantities of Indian, New World, and European goods imported in exchange for slaves, ivory, gold, and other African exports. Walter Rodney's *History of the Upper Guinea Coast* outlines the complex trading patterns and the role of consumer demand within Africa: metal, cloth, alcohol, weapons, and the beads and bangles that made up smaller currencies were all integral to Afro-European commerce from the seventeenth century.[8] As Rodney notes, 'being knowledgeable about local requirements, the lançados [resident Portuguese coastal traders] and Afro-Portuguese were aware of what areas needed cloth, and what kind sold best in given districts.'[9] British customs records reveal some 70 categories of goods exported from Britain to Africa in 1787, with cloth of various kinds and for various uses by far the dominant article of trade. For those living in the desert areas of West Africa, blue bafts were particularly in demand.[10]

Archaeological and historical research in the West African slave trade regions has revealed the extent of economic expansion, the development of 'Atlantic taste' and the penetration of Atlantic luxury into the interior.[11] Although locally produced goods far outnumbered imported goods in the archaeological assemblages from Upper Senegal, for instance, the proliferation of the goods, and their impact on the quality and styles of locally-

Goods from the sea countries 111

produced goods, has been noted.[12] Similarly, the decline in Saharan trade goods in local assemblages attests to the shift in commercial focus toward the Atlantic.[13] Closer to the coast, in the Siin region of Senegal, 'the same objects – beads, glass, and tobacco pipes – largely turn up on sites across the region, and no major disparities in wealth emerge in the regional settlement system', suggesting that for the Serer farmers and fishermen, selling their additional produce to the French traders was a means of participating in Atlantic consumer culture.[14] People in the Sierra Leone estuary combined locally produced tools and furniture (like gourd containers and locally-produced earthenware) with imports (like iron and pewter dishes).[15] Indeed, even a brief review of Falconbridge's first trip to Sierra Leone indicates that de Vries's 'consumption clusters' were certainly an important aspect of elite culture on the coast: King Naimbana did not serve coffee or tea to his English guests 'for want of sugar'.[16]

The specificity of certain bundles of trade goods required at various West African ports highlights the indigenous 'consumption clusters' demanded by Africa's consumers. Philip Misevich writes that in the region around Sierra Leone, 'Cargos were carefully sorted based on buyer preferences, which differed from one port to the next and might unexpectedly change within the same port. Failure to account for such preferences was one quick way to guarantee an unprofitable voyage'.[17] Different trading ports required specific assemblages of imports. In 1793, the *Domingo* left the Sierra Leone Colony for Gambia with 'an assortment of goods adapted for the purchase of wax and ivory, as well as cattle'. The *Lapwing* is recorded as leaving for Rio Nunez with 'goods for the purchase of Rice and Ivory amounting to £350'. The *Ocean* went out to Bissau on August 12 with 'goods ordered by two Portuguese merchants of that place, consisting of rum, Tobacco and cloth' and returned on November 1 with one ton of ivory, one ton of wax, 'hogs and St Jago Cloths, and a considerable remainder of goods'.[18] But African consumers, like consumers around the Atlantic World, had tastes that changed over time as well as place. Rhode Island rum, for instance, displaced madeira and brandy as the alcohol of choice in the late eighteenth century.[19] Equally, a glut of certain kinds of consumer goods used in both customary payments and as payment for labour led to the inflation of the 'basket' of goods that made up the trading 'bar'.[20]

As historians have been keen to note, these were reciprocal trading relationships that relied on a European negotiation of local African (and, as time went on, Eurafrican) power structures. The customary payments due to local and regional authorities ensured that trade would stay open, but negotiation and observance of political customs was also part of the process. This meant that those customary payments could change, expand, or contract to reflect changing political dynamics, as well as changing fashions. On a voyage in the 1790s, Joseph Hawkins reported that the king

112 *Bronwen Everill*

informed me that he had been made acquainted with the object of my journey, that he was pleased at my preferring him to his neighbours; that he was willing to trade with me in gold, ivory, or prisoners; that he should wish to trade constantly, and to be furnished with goods from the sea countries, as he called them, in abundance, for which he would pay largely. Having stated my satisfaction at his kindness, and my thanks for the attention bestowed by his favour on me then and while on the road, I told him it was my wish to put his proposals into practice by keeping the trade open constantly and supplying it abundantly.[21]

French customary payment records show that, in order to trade in Galam (Gajaaga) alone in 1797, a list of over four pages of specific consumer items was required to be paid to various members of the elite.[22] This annual customary payment remained exactly the same for the next twenty years, with the same king and princes receiving the exact same assortment year in and year out.[23] For the more powerful state of Futa Toro, which controlled trade on the middle Senegal, customary payments were received for each boat in transit. The Alimami of Fouta received a safe and lock, twenty-eight pieces of guinea cloth, one measure of scarlet cloth, three trade guns, fifty piasters, five hundred lead balls, five hundred gunflints, yellow cambrics, coral, seven trade guns, and sixty pounds of powder. Additionally, he received annually as presents, two trade guns, six guinea cloths, two more guns, fourteen pounds of gunpowder, five hundred gunflints, five hundred lead balls, eight pieces of paper, some scarlet cloth, a mirror, a padlock, and a pair of scissors, amongst other odds and ends.[24] These customary payments, negotiated in 1785, allowed the French to trade up the River Senegal. In good years, when there were no European or African wars preventing trade, they were redistributed to the supporters of the Alimami, and thus made their way into the wider culture, either as consumable items, or as further items of currency for trade or payment.

The ability to respond to African consumer demand was crucial for giving the French a competitive edge in the region. Similar customary payments in the Gambia, Sierra Leone, the Gold Coast, and in the Bights of Benin and Biafra allowed the British to trade along the Upper Guinea Coast. Goods were also used as payment for labor (either to the laborers themselves, or to their owners if they were enslaved and rented out). Contracts written in French and in Arabic script from Saint Louis also show that beef and millet were paid for with guinea cloths.[25] However, attempts to create a perfect market by importing exactly the right assemblages of goods were always hampered by changing tastes, temporary gluts and absences of trade goods, and closed borders as a result of European or African wars. European and American sellers sometimes 'dumped' their cargos for below invoice cost to avoid sickness on the coast or get a cargo back to the Americas.[26] Rising prices for slaves in the second half of the eighteenth century also expanded the range and penetration of consumer goods in the region.

Cosmopolitan fashion

Traditional readings of this growing consumer revolution in Africa build on the evangelical, abolitionist narrative that the luxuriousness of eighteenth century global consumption was deleterious to the work ethic, and had created the worst excesses of the period – namely the slave trade. In Western Africa, the historiography has been tied up with arguments about dependency theory and underdevelopment, and the popular conception of the slave trade as an economic transaction sees slave traders tricking Africans into selling their countrymen for valueless trinkets.

However, Colleen Kriger and others have argued that this was not a matter of Indian and other cloths displacing locally produced clothing, or imported ceramics undermining local industry. As Colleen Kriger notes, within West Africa, 'higher levels of textile output were achieved mainly by expanding the workforce and by exploiting the labour of slaves and family members.'[27] Additionally, 'Imported cloth was also a vehicle for creating new "local" textile products' like the Asante *kente* cloth: weaving bark and bast fibre 'was then harnessed in the eighteenth century to develop a distinctive new textile, *kente*'.[28] Likewise, Thiaw's archaeological survey of Gorée and another of Fort Saint Joseph both point to the continued production of local ceramics.[29] Instead, this period should be understood as one of global economic integration that sees some attempts at mercantilist export specialization – a phenomenon that political economists noted at the end of the century – but also one in which, as de Vries and others have argued, imported luxury goods were increasingly integrated with locally or regionally produced goods to create new consumption clusters. And so you have, in Senegambia, women dressing in Indian and Cape Verde cloths sewed together by their tailor-slaves, wearing Venetian glass bead jewelry, with Moroccan shoes, and French parasols.[30]

A list of exports from Britain to Africa in 1787 shows that nearly £112,000 of cotton goods, nearly £17,000 of linen goods, nearly £3,000 of silk, and over £138,000 of woolen goods were exported to that continent. For a sense of the scale of those values, the cotton goods alone were nearly 350,000 lbs in weight.[31] These cloth imports were always supplemental to domestic cotton production, which provided the fundamental fabrics of African consumption. In the cities themselves, the productions of the immediate hinterland, of networked cities (regional and global), and of *their* hinterlands, were all available. As in Portuguese Africa, 'the propensity to import on the part of Africans was not simply a measure of their need or inefficiency, but instead, it was a measure of the extent of their domestic market'.[32] In the Gambia, south of Gorée, 'Niuminkas also grew cotton seed and carved wood with an iron rod for removing the seed from the fiber. If they had a lot to spend on their families and if any spares were left before begging for food, they would sell those spares to people who had been too busy to grow cotton'.[33] Equally, regional cloth production was a vital part

114 *Bronwen Everill*

of the fashion in Sierra Leone. The Papels living on Bolama island off Bissau, 'manufacture[d] a coarse cotton cloth, about a quarter of a yard wide, which passes currently for money; twenty stripes of a yard long being reckoned at a bar'.[34] The use of cloth as a currency was not exclusive to the complex exchanges of the Atlantic, but was in fact a long-standing part of the Saharan trade currency mix.[35] In Futa Toro, the Fula state along the Senegal River, 'Cloth production in rural economies was usually conducted by weavers linked to one or more village patron who would require their clients to weave whatever cotton thread had been produced by the house-hold's women folk'.[36] These weavers were not paid outright for their work – they demanded favors or things for their families' needs in return when they were required, establishing a permanent relationship of credit and debt within the larger community.

As Kriger notes, 'it was the strip cloths that were intended to be used for making items of clothing that served as money in Muslim trade' and it was important for European and American merchants trading on the coast to assort their imported materials intended for interior currency use into the appropriate strips that reflected the trends in local cotton production – sometimes altering them on arrival at specific ports.[37] Martin Benson, oc-casional captain for vessels sent to Sierra Leone by the Rhode Island firm Brown, Benson & Ives, wrote in 1794 that, 'I will stop at the Cape D Verd Islands and purchase a Quantitiy of St. Jago Cloths as many as I can lay my hands on. This article is of the greatest consequence on the Coast, and is what our Countrymen never meddle with being unacquainted with the patterns in demand'. In Benson's opinion, it was worth the hassle to ensure that the correct cloth was selected and in the right 'patterns': 'It is my in-tention (with God's Blessing) to trade as much as possible with the Natives, there being a difference of at least 40 per cent in favor of the Person who buys of them in preference to the Factors on the Coast'.[38] Dealing directly between St Jago and the Guinea coast, rather than bringing a purely India goods assortment meant that Benson and others could trade with groups like the Papels, whose clothing 'consists of different kinds of St. Jago cloths, tied round their middle, some of which sell for 60 bars'.[39]

Knowing and appreciating the regional as well as the global trade (the same voyage saw Benson 'easily dispose of 5 or 6000 dollars more in India Goods') gave Atlantic traders an edge over their competitors. But what they were seeking on the coast were cash, bills of exchange, or goods that were 'as good as' cash in the New England market. These were not journeys pri-marily to secure specific trade goods (extracted exports) from Africa, but to sell to a thriving market of African consumers, fuelled in large part by in-creasingly available credit, made possible in part by an expansion of the urban port economies and the household assets that it contributed toward building. When ships arrived with goods for sale, the eagerness with which clothing and other Atlantic consumer goods were purchased was noted by ships' captains, suggesting a ready market, but also that demand often

Goods from the sea countries 115

outstripped supply in the early colony of Sierra Leone.[40] The Sierra Leone Company, Brown, Benson & Ives, Brown & Ives, the Compagnie du Senegal, all wrote regularly about the nature of African consumer culture. The contribution to Atlantic fashionable consumption also reveals to what extent West Africans were being imagined in the political economy of the Atlantic world as *consumers*. And ship invoices reveal the variety of goods that were demanded by consumers in Senegal and Sierra Leone: the Schooner *Olive Branch* recorded a separate invoice of the cotton goods it took to Gorée and Sierra Leone, which made up sixty per cent of its cargo by value.[41] This cargo included twenty-one different types of Indian imported cotton cloths and was valued at over $12,000, suggesting that the Rhode Island merchants who fitted her out anticipated a significant market, and significant purchasing power, in the region. Some of these goods were purchased by traders - both 'legitimate' and slave traders - for their annual customs payments to the local African governments. Others were purchased for local transactions in the smaller trading forts in the region. Some were purchased by the Sierra Leone Company for their store, and by Gorée and Saint-Louis's mercantile class for local sales. And some were sold retail direct from the ship. As Searing notes, 'Cotton cloth and iron, common in most transactions conducted by European merchants, were particularly important in purchases of agricultural products like millet and gum.'[42] Indian cottons made up an average of 65.6 percent of the foreign products exported from England to West Africa in the second half of the eighteenth century.[43]

In this way, African trends were not dissimilar to the luxury fashions in other Atlantic port cities where locally produced cotton, linen, or woolen cloth could provide the basic materials for clothing families.[44] The demand for certain types of cloth in certain places, and their change over time reveals the extent to which urban demand drove trade into these port cities, for both men and women. In 1791, Anna Maria Falconbridge described King Naimbana 'dressed in a purple embroidered coat, white sattin waistcoat and breeches, *thread stockings*, and his left side emblazoned with a flaming star; his legs to be sure were *harliquined*, by a number of holes in the stockings, through which his black skin appeared.'[45] This outfit was traded for a 'suit of black velvet' sometime later that day, except for the stockings. Although Falconbridge presents this in a somewhat mocking tone to question the equivalency of British and Temne royalty, Naimbana's use of Atlantic fashions does not differ drastically from those of settlers in Jamaica, Saint-Domingue, or Bahia, for example, where basic and often old and re-fashioned clothing was complemented by one or two pieces of luxury fabric.[46]

As in Temne country, the basics of cutting edge Atlantic fashion were followed with interest by local elites, but incorporated within a local style that took account of climate, access to the different materials, and metropolitan differences (be they based in London, Paris, Lisbon, or

116 *Bronwen Everill*

Futa Jallon). Zachary Macaulay, as governor of the Sierra Leone Colony, visited a trader in Rokel, upriver from the colony, and commented that although he lived in a house built of mud, it was 'finished in a very handsome stile for himself and furnished with Beds Bed hangings, tables and Chairs quite in the European stile [sic]. The house was divided into three comfortable and airy apartments.' Macaulay noted that the trader he dealt with 'always dresses in the European Style and tho we came upon him by surprize we found him in a cloth coat, and shoes'.[47] Atlantic fashions were thus not exclusively the preserve of the port cities, or of the particular *metis* culture of the Senegalese islands' female populations. However, they could act in conjunction with local fashions to mark out access to and participation in the Atlantic trade, as Macaulay's merchant contact suggests. Mungo Park's assessment of local fashion in Senegambia and Mali was that locally manufactured cotton was used to make trousers, loose shirts, and robes, which were the standard dress of men in the interior polities.[48] This was then added to, adorned, and tailored in the cities and their immediate hinterlands to reflect the hybridity of styles, and to reflect social distinctions.

Hybrid credit for cosmopolitan consumption

While it can be tempting to project back onto the slave trade the type of economic relationships that emerged in the second half of the nineteenth century, in fact, many traders, merchants, and government officials engaging with the commercial zones of Western Africa were thinking about them as locations for the consumption of trade goods and manufactures, and about West Africans as consumers, rather than producers. The slave trade was important, obviously, but in varying degrees at various ports. In some places, slaves were rarely sold (comparatively), and other products were accepted in exchange – gold, ivory, gum, wax, dye woods, rice, cloths, palm oil, bills of exchange, and credit.

In the context of this consumer revolution in the Atlantic world, cosmopolitan traders and local merchants faced new challenges in dealing with the cash and credit mechanisms required to do business. Long-distance trade had of course existed in all of the societies involved in the global exchange of the eighteenth century. The use of trading diasporas continued to be the major continuity. The landlord-stranger relationship allowed resident European merchants to trade in a given locality, provided they made a regular customary payment to a 'landlord' who would act as their local representative in any disputes. Marriage 'à la mode du pays' also functioned as a means of integrating the European trading diaspora into local political arrangements, while simultaneously expanding the reach of Atlantic fashion and consumables within African society.

But for diasporas to function, long-distance trade had to be accompanied by adaptable forms of long-distance (and long-term) credit. Hopkins notes that within West Africa, 'at the inter-regional level, it is clear that

Goods from the sea countries 117

professional traders often needed to finance their activities by securing credit, because their initial investment was high and returns were long delayed. Commercial capital was obtained from fellow merchants and from specialized bankers and money lenders'.[49] Trans-saharan trade already made use of the Islamic finance equivalent: suftaja.[50] David Richardson and Robin Pearson have identified the role that Atlantic commerce played in shaping organizational innovations and expanding the commercial networks that both European and African actors were willing to engage with. They identify 'more sophisticated forms of internal regulation in domestic stock companies ... material forms of guarantee' and a changing legal and political framework.[51]

As a result of the shift from fort-based to ship-based trade that accompanied the transition from chartered companies to independent traders (basically, conducting trade from the ship, with maybe a resident factor) institutional, impersonal forms of guarantee gradually replaced the informal, personal credit relationships that had dominated British overseas commerce in the previous century. The rise of mortgage lending, for instance, was an example of how the expanding African Atlantic commerce required new instruments in place of the diasporic or family networks that came before.[52] One trader described the process, which lasted well into the nineteenth century: 'When a ship is going down the coast, they leave the goods on shore: and when she comes back, they are paid in palm oil; and sometimes, of late, when the ship has a small quantity of goods remaining, they have left it with the natives to be paid the next voyage'.[53]

As described by Richardson and Pearson: 'Bonny, which emerged as the largest single port servicing British slave ships in Africa from 1730, credit protection became associated with still other – more impersonal – mechanisms .... notably the use of letters of recommendation inscribed on ivory bracelets or disks ... with the more impersonalised, state-regulated systems of Bonny apparently being associated with faster loading rates and much higher levels of slave exports than those tied to other more personalised and decentralised ones linked to kinship'.[54] In Ouidah, credit and debt worked both ways. Europeans landed goods for African slave traders – sometimes amounting to the value of 70 slaves. Africans, meanwhile, accepted promissory notes to be settled for the goods that made up the trading currency of the coast when the European ships were set to leave at the end of the season.[55] In Senegal, African consumers became creditors to the commercial companies based in Saint-Louis throughout the eighteenth century, as the resident European and Eurafrican merchants came to rely on the local agricultural economy to supply them with food and water.[56]

But the Sierra Leone Company store in Freetown and its factory in Freeport attempted to move towards currency as a means of controlling the trade to ensure a closed system, which would prevent the slave trade from sneaking into the exchange. This made the operation of this diaspora settlement different in terms of the relationship between material and credit

118 *Bronwen Everill*

cosmopolitanism from the rest of the coast. Wage labor would allow African consumers to access these global goods with cash, rather than having to bring slaves to market. Macaulay ensured that the trade 'is entirely transacted by the intervention in every case of a Money Medium. If a Stranger brings Ivory or Gold, he sells it at the current price and receives his money, which he again lays out to his taste. In the same way do all the Natives whether Timmanies, Bullams or Mandigoes manage their trade, and no objection is now heard made against the innovation'. And the Company store ensured it had even more customers by tying Company wages (in cash) to purchases of goods from the Company store as well.[57] Even visiting ships who wanted contracted services in the port had to pay in Sierra Leone currency, as well as buy provisions through the Company store.[58] In this way, the Company store began operating, at the very end of the eighteenth century, as the mediator of credit in a way that further adapted the trading fort mechanism.

The variety of forms of credit and currency and the willingness of European actors to respond to local African political and economic needs in formulating the accepted exchange reflects the flexible and negotiated nature of commercial cosmopolitanism on the Upper Guinea Coast. It also highlights the varied nature of African trade in the regions that were less involved in slave exportation. Although slaves were exported from the Upper Guinea Coast, and increasingly over the eighteenth century, these sites of exchange were as much about developing African consumer markets as they were about extracting resources and labourers from Africa. The consumers in the port cities of Saint-Louis, Gorée, Freetown, and the smaller settlements along the coast, as well as the interior polities like Futa Toro, were an important part of the global consumer revolution, shaping fashions, trade, and exchange practices.

Conclusion

Although it has been historiographically common to think about early modern trade with Africa as an extractive, resource-oriented trade, in which Europeans were seeking to monopolize exports – largely of labor – for the New World, the innovations of consumer credit and the discussions of consumers and the consumer and commercial revolutions as they penetrated Atlantic African societies suggests that in fact the driving force of commercial interaction in these contact zones was, until the end of the eighteenth century at least, the African consumer.

Fashion – including the highly lucrative and consumer-driven trade in cloth – helped to define the economies of the commercial zones of Senegambia and Sierra Leone. Material cosmopolitanism was produced through the consumption of 'goods from the sea countries' as well as the mixture of local and global products. Cosmopolitanism, therefore, presents a good paradigm for thinking about the impact of the Atlantic on African

Goods from the sea countries 119

life in the eighteenth century. Rather than arguing over whether African societies and economies remained 'pure' or were made 'underdeveloped' by reliance on material culture from elsewhere, material cosmopolitanism allows us to think about how the local and global interacted in daily use, alongside the broader changes in credit relationships, personal relationships, and politics that were taking place in the wider Atlantic world. The ability of these places to participate in the consumer revolution and adapt the products of the global commercial revolution to their specific economies and political and social needs shaped innovations in credit in the Atlantic world. Local fashion, local industries, and local politics shaped the types and quantities of goods that formed Atlantic West Africa's engagement with the consumer revolution.

Notes

1 Anna Maria Falconbridge, *Two Voyages to Sierra Leone during the years 1791-2-3* (London, 1794), Letter III, Bance Island, 10 February 1791.
2 Christina J. Hodge, "Widow Pratt's World of Goods: Implications of Consumer Choice in Colonial Newport, Rhode Island," *Early American Studies* 8, no. 2 (2010): 232; Chloe Wigston Smith, "'Callico Madams': Servants, Consumption, and the Calico Crisis," *Eighteenth-Century Life* 32, no. 2 (2007): 29–55; Laurel Thatcher Ulrich, *The Age of Homespun* (New York: Vintage, 2009), 220–21.
3 Falconbridge, *Two Voyages*, 8 June 1791.
4 Beverly Lemire, *Global Trade and the Transformation of Consumer Cultures: The Material World Remade, c. 1500-1820* (Cambridge: Cambridge University Press, 2018), 7.
5 Christopher Bayly, *The Birth of the Modern World* (Oxford: Oxford University Press, 2004).
6 Walter Rodney, *How Europe Underdeveloped Africa* (London: Bogle-L'Ouverture Publications, 1972), 5.
7 David Eltis and Lawrence Jennings, "Trade between Western Africa and the Atlantic World in the Pre-Colonial Era," *American Historical Review* 93, no. 4 (1988): 936–59.
8 Walter Rodney, *A History of the Upper Guinea Coast, 1545-1800* (Oxford: Oxford University Press, 1970), 171–2. See also A.G. Hopkins, *An Economic History of West Africa* (London: Longman, 1973), chapter three; Philip Curtin, *Economic Change in Precolonial Africa: Senegambia in the Era of the Slave Trade* (Madison: University of Wisconsin Press, 1975); Toby Green, ed. *Brokers of Change: Atlantic Commerce and Cultures in Pre-Colonial Western Africa* (Oxford: Oxford University Press, 2012).
9 Rodney, *History of the Upper Guinea Coast*, 181.
10 British National Archives (BNA) CUST 17/10
11 Ann Brower Stahl, "Colonial Entanglements and the Practices of Taste: An Alternative to Logocentric Approaches," *American Anthropologist*, New Series, 104, no. 3 (2002): 827–45; Stahl and Adria LaViolette, "Introduction: Current Trends in the Archaeology of African History," *Journal of African History*, 42, no. 3 (2009): 354.
12 Ibrahima Thiaw, "Atlantic Impacts on Inland Senegambia: French Penetration and African Initiatives in Eighteenth- and Nineteenth-Century Gajaago and Bundu (Upper Senegal River)" in *Power and Landscape in Atlantic West Africa:*

120 Bronwen Everill

Archaeological Perspectives, eds. J. Cameron Monroe and Akinwumi Ogundiran (Cambridge: Cambridge University Press, 2012), 57.

13 Susan Keech Mcintosh and Ibrahima Thiaw, "Tools for Understanding Transformation and Continuity in Senegambian Society, 1500–1900," in *West Africa during the Atlantic Slave Trade: Archaeological Perspectives,* ed. Christopher DeCorse (London: Leicester University Press, 2001), 30–31.

14 Francois Richard, "Political Transformations and Cultural Landscapes in Senegambia during the Atlantic Era: An Alternative View from the Siin (Senegal)?" in *Power and Landscape in Atlantic West Africa,* eds. Monroe and Akinwumi Ogundiran, 100. Bronwen Everill, "All the Baubles That They Needed: 'Industriousness' and Slavery in Saint-Louis and Gorée," *Early American Studies,* 15, no. 4 (2017): 714-739; Bronwen Everill, *Not Made By Slaves: Ethical Capitalism in the Age of Abolition* (Cambridge, MA: Harvard University Press, 2020).

15 Joshua Montefiore, *An Authentic Account of the Late expedition to Bulam on the Coast of Africa* (London, 1794), 42–43.

16 Falconbridge, *Two Voyages,* 10 February 1791.

17 Philip Misevich, "The Sierra Leone Hinterland and the Provisioning of Early Freetown, 1792-1803" *Journal of Colonialism and Colonial History,* vol. 9, no. 3 (2008).

18 Huntington Library, MSS MY 418, Macaulay's Journal.

19 Ty Reese, "Liberty, Insolence, Rum: Cape Coast and the American Revolution," *Itinerario* 28, no. 3 (2004): 18–38; Brooks, *Yankee Traders,* 7; Jay Coughtry, *The Notorious Triangle: Rhode Island and the African Slave Trade, 1700-1807* (Philadelphia: Temple University Press, 1981), 6–7.

20 Reese, "'Eating' Luxury: Fante Middlemen, British Goods, and Changing Dependencies on the Gold Coast, 1750-1821," *The William and Mary Quarterly* 66, no. 4 (2009): 851–872.

21 Joseph Hawkins, *A History of a Voyage to the Coast of Africa, and Travels into the Interior of that Country; Containing Particular Descriptions of the Climate and Inhabitants and Interesting Particulars Concerning the Slave Trade* (Philadelphia: S.Custick & Co, 1797), 67–68.

22 Archives Nationales du Senegal, Dakar. Coutumes, 1797, AOF G 13G14. See also David Richardson, "West African Consumption Patterns and Their Influence on the Eighteenth-Century English Slave Trade," in *The Uncommon Market: Essays in the Economic History of the Atlantic Slave Trade,* eds. Henry A. Gemery and Jan S. Hogendorn (Academic Press Inc, New York, 1979), 308. For more on African consumerism, see Jeremy Prestholdt, "On the Global Repercussions of East African Consumerism," *American Historical Review* 109, no. 3 (2004): 755–81; Ty Reese, "'Eating' Luxury," 851–72; George Metcalf, "A Microcosm of Why Africans Sold Slaves: Akan Consumption Patterns in the 1770s," *Journal of African History,* 28, 3 (1987): 377–94; Basil Davidson, *The African Slave Trade* (Oxford: James Curry, 1960; 1996), 108; Stanley B. Alpern, "What Africans Got for their Slaves: A Master List of European Goods," *History in Africa* 22 (1995): 5–43.

23 Archives Nationales du Senegal, Dakar. Coutumes, 13G16 1817.

24 Archives Nationales du Senegal, Dakar. Coutumes, AOF 13G15, 1807.

25 Archives Nationales du Senegal, Dakar. Coutumes, AOF 13G1, 26 August 1782.

26 John Carter Brown Library BFBR B.523 F.4 Providence 2 October 1816 Brown & Ives to Young. Instructions for Capt Gideon Young, Master of the Ship Charlotte, for a voyage to the Coast of Africa.

27 Colleen E. Kriger, "'Guinea Cloth' Production and Consumption of Cotton Textiles in West Africa before and during the Atlantic Slave Trade," in *The*

Goods from the sea countries 121

Spinning World: A Global History of Cotton Textiles, 1200-1850, eds. Giorgio Riello and Prasannan Parthasarathi (Oxford: Oxford University Press, 2009), 106–26.

28 Kriger, "Guinea Cloth", 124–25.

29 Thiaw, "Slaves Without Shackles: An Archaeology of Everyday Life on Gorée Island (Senegal)" in *Slavery in Africa: Archaeology and Memory,* ed. Paul Lane and Kevin MacDonald (Oxford: Oxford University Press, 2011); Thiaw, "Atlantic Impacts on Inland Senegambia," 57.

30 Bronwen Everill, "'All the Baubles that They Needed': 'Industriousness' and Slavery in Saint-Louis and Gorée," *Early American Studies* 15, no. 4 (2017): 714–39.

31 BNA CUST 17/10 Exports from Britain to Africa 1787.

32 John Thornton, *Africa and Africans in the Making of the Atlantic World* (Cambridge, Cambridge University Press,1998), 45.

33 NCAC Fajara Oral Archive, the Gambia, 306 A 15/9/74; Alhaji Kemo Kuyate; Niumi History...slave trade; Banjul; BK Sidibe and D. Wright; Date and place: 15 September 1974. Banjul, the apartment of Donald Wright. Recorded by Donald Wright, Interpreter BK Sidibe. Translated by Binta Janneh.

34 Joshua Montefiore, *An Authentic Account of the late Expedition to Bulam on the Coast of Africa* (London, 1794), 25.

35 Colleen Kriger, *Cloth in West African History* (Oxford: AltaMira Press, 2006), 80–81.

36 Roy Dilley, "The Visibility and Invisibility of Production Among Senegalese Craftsmen," in *Commodification: Things, Agency and Identities,* eds.Wim van Binsbergen and Peter Geschiere *(The Social Life of Things Revisited)* (Munster: Lit, 2005), 231.

37 Kriger, *Cloth in West African History,* 82.

38 John Carter Brown Library BFBR B.513 F.6 Newport 11 September 1794 Martin Benson to BB&I

39 Montefiore, *An Authentic Account of the late Expedition to Bulam,* 25.

40 John Carter Brown Library BFBR B.513 F.7 Ship Charlotte 30 Jan 1795 Captain Martin Benson; TNA CO 270/3 26 Jan 1795, Council Meeting. Trading timing and the vagaries of ships' arrivals did not always benefit merchant captains, however. For example, in 1800, when a combination of factors glutted the colony with cheap goods, Brown and Ives suffered as a result. George E. Brooks, *Yankee Traders, Old Coasters and African Middlemen* (Boston: Boston University Press, 1970), 56–57.

41 John Carter Brown Library BFBR B.611 F.7 Cotton Goods Shipped on Olive Branch included: Jannah Mamody, Burboon Gurrahs, Aliabad Emerties, Mow Sannas, Mugga Sannas, Sannah Emerties, Chadpore Cossaks, Mow Sannas, Salalpore Mamoody, Beerboon Baftas, Oud Cossaks, Manahpore Gurrahs, Judgea Baftas, Suchipore Baftas, Chittabully Baftas, Chittabully Fine Baftas, Kyrabad Lawns, Moharage Gungy Sauns, Blue Gelly Handkerchiefs, Fine Check, Double Custas, Musteo Pieces, Bandano Handkerchiefs, Lungee Handkerchiefs.

42 James Searing, *West African Slavery and Atlantic Commerce* (Cambridge: Cambridge University Press, 1993), 69.

43 Joseph Inikori, *Africans and the Industrial Revolution* (Cambridge: Cambridge University Press, 2002), Appendix 9.5; Maxine Berg, "In Pursuit of Luxury," *Past and Present* 182 (2004): 110–12; David Richardson, "West African Consumption Patterns and Their Influence on the Eighteenth-Century English Slave Trade," in *The Uncommon Market: Essays in the Economic History of the Atlantic Slave Trade,* eds. Henry A. Gemery and Jan S. Hogendorn (New York:

122 *Bronwen Everill*

Academic Press, 1979), 312–15; Kazuo Kobayashi, *Indian Cotton Textiles in West Africa: African Agency, Consumer Demand and the Making of the Global Economy*, 1750-1850 (Basingstoke: Palgrave Macmillan, 2019); Jody Benjamin, The Texture of Change: Cloth, Commerce and History in Western Africa, 1700-1850. Doctoral Dissertation, Harvard University, 2016.

44 For instance, in Boston: Ulrich, *Age of Homespun*, 218–19.

45 Falconbridge, *Two Voyages to Sierra Leone*, Letter 3, 10 February 1791. Falconbridge herself later commented that she would have offered to darn the stockings but worried about accidentally stabbing the king.

46 Robert S. DuPlessis, *The Material Atlantic: Clothing, Commerce, and Colonization in the Atlantic World, 1650-1800* (Cambridge: Cambridge University Press, 2015), 168–69; 174; 179. Falconbridge regularly attempts to mock the 'backward' African inhabitants she meets; for instance, she also points out condescendingly that Naimbana's queen was 'about forty-five or six, at which age women are considered old here.' Average life expectancy in Britain at the same time was just over 38 years.

47 Huntington, MY 418 Macaulay's Journal, Folder 22 June 1–17 January 1797–1798, 30 Nov 1797.

48 Kriger, *Cloth in West African History,* 96.

49 Hopkins, *An Economic History of West Africa*, 71.

50 John Hunwick, "Islamic Financial Institutions: Theoretical structures and aspects of their application in Sub-Saharan Africa," in *Credit, Currencies, and Culture: African Financial Institutions,* eds. Endre Stiansen, Jane I. Guyer (Uppsala: Nordik Africa Institute, 2000), 72–96.

51 Robin Pearson and David Richardson, "Social Capital, institutional innovation and Atlantic Trade before 1800," *Business History* 50, no. 6 (2008): 767.

52 Pearson and Richardson, "Social Capital and Atlantic Trade," 773.

53 G.C. Redman, 1842 as cited in C.W. Newbury, "Credit in Early Nineteenth Century West African Trade," *Journal of African History* 13, no. 1 (1972): 84.

54 Pearson and Richardson, "Social Capital and Atlantic Trade," 770.

55 Robin Law, *Ouidah: The Social History of a West African Slaving Port, 1727-1892* (Athens, OH: Ohio University Press, 2004), 133–35.

56 Everill, "All the baubles that they needed," 734–36.

57 Huntington Library, MSS 418 Box 20 Folder 21, 7 June 1797: Remarks on the Health, Trade, Cultivation, and Civilization of Sierra Leone.

58 John Carter Brown Library, BFBR B.611 *Olive Branch.*

7 From the Indian Ocean to the Atlantic

The commercial ventures of Oman–Zanzibar

Jeremy Prestholdt

In the spring of 1840, the Sultan of Oman and Zanzibar's flagship, the *Sultana*, arrived in New York City. The vessel had sailed from Zanzibar, the emergent entrepôt of East Africa, on a commercial venture. Thus, it carried Indian Ocean products highly valued in the United States, including Zanzibari cloves, East African ivory, Omani dates, Yemeni coffee, Persian carpets, and even a gift of Persian Gulf pearls for President Martin van Buren. The *Sultana* was under the command of an Arab emissary with African and Persian officers, an English captain, and a South Asian and East African crew. The *Sultana*'s crew and cargo thus represented a microcosm of the cosmopolitan Western Indian Ocean world, and it evidenced the Sultan of Oman–Zanzibar's direct engagement with distant world regions.[1]

American ships frequented Zanzibar and Muscat in the first decades of the nineteenth century. Indeed, they made up the majority of Atlantic-based vessels visiting Zanzibar in the late 1830s. Yet, the *Sultana* was the first ship of the sultanate to reach America's burgeoning metropolis. New Yorkers had seen nothing like the *Sultana*, and the ship and its crew quickly became a spectacle. In New York and across the United States, the sultan's flagship would make headlines. Crowds amassed to see the vessel, and a brass band even visited the docks to serenade the ship.[2] More than a week after its arrival, New York's *Morning Herald* reported that the crew was 'still the curiosity of the city.'[3] Though the *Sultana* did not visit Washington, DC, its journey bolstered diplomatic relations between Oman–Zanzibar and the United States. President Martin van Buren wrote to the Sultan of Oman–Zanzibar, Sayyid Saʿīd, that the arrival of the *Sultana* was 'a source of lively satisfaction for me, in my desire that frequent and beneficial intercourse should be established between our respective countries.'[4]

The *Sultana*'s journey to the US was extraordinary, but it also represented the extension of a long history of the sultanate's efforts to strengthen economic ties with other world regions—a history that dated to at least the seventeenth century. These efforts expanded dramatically in the eighteenth century in the context of increasing Omani economic and political influence in Eastern Africa, as we will see. By the early nineteenth century, the Sultanate of Oman–Zanzibar operated a small fleet of interoceanic trading

124 *Jeremy Prestholdt*

vessels that traversed the globe and projected the sultanate's interests not only in the US but also Europe, Southern Africa, South Asia, and as far as East Asia. Most of the sultanate's ships were converted men-of-war manufactured in Bombay, Cochin, and New England. Several of these vessels regularly traveled from Zanzibar to Bombay and Calcutta to procure cotton goods, rice, sugar, and metal ware.[5] They also sailed south to Mauritius and Réunion. But in the 1830s and 1840s Sayyid Sa'īd dramatically expanded the scope of these ventures. In 1838 the sultan sent an emissary to London, followed three years later by a merchant vessel from Zanzibar. In the interim, Sayyid Sa'īd ordered the 1840 trade mission to New York City, the first trade mission from an Indian Ocean, Arab, or African state to travel nearly the entire length of the Atlantic.

The 1840 voyage of the *Sultana* to New York, an itinerary that included St. Helena, would be the most significant Omani–Zanzibari attempt to solidify ties with North America's financial and commercial center. Sayyid Sa'īd reasoned that he could reverse Zanzibar's economic relationship with the North Atlantic by delivering African and other Western Indian Ocean goods directly to the United States. More precisely, he aspired to exert greater control over trade with the Atlantic world and turn a greater profit both for Zanzibari-based merchants and his own government.[6] Accordingly, the objective of the *Sultana*'s mission was to determine the feasibility of direct trade with New York carried out by Omani–Zanzibari vessels. The *Sultana*'s journey to the US would be followed by a great number of missions stretching across several decades and traversing multiple oceans. These would include Omani and Zanzibari trading ventures to Canton, Istanbul, Marseilles, and Hamburg. Each of these sojourns evidenced Omani–Zanzibari desires to exert greater control over East Africa's global relationships. More precisely, the *Sultana*'s 1840 mission and similar voyages demonstrated the critical importance of overseas commerce to Muscat, Zanzibar, and the wider eastern African region in nineteenth century. Just as important, they evidenced long-term Omani–Zanzibari efforts to address the asymmetry of their economic relationships with the North Atlantic.

Elsewhere I have argued that pre-colonial East African consumer interests, informed by local social logics of demand, shaped relationships with merchants and manufacturers in United States, Western Europe, Southern Arabia, Western India, and elsewhere.[7] This essay explores another critical dimension of Eastern Africa's relationships with distant world regions before European colonial rule: the capacity of the Sultanate of Oman–Zanzibar to send its own commercial ventures to Atlantic ports as well as across the Indian Ocean region. These ventures, I suggest, highlight global economic networks shaped not only by Western states and empires but also by the enterprise of many other important actors. To exemplify this point, I will begin by outlining the rationales and strategy that undergirded Omani–Zanzibari commercial voyages. Thereafter, I will offer greater detail of the mission to New York City in 1840, a voyage that generated more records than any other in Omani or Zanzibari history.

The Indian Ocean world and the Sultanate of Oman and Zanzibar

The early nineteenth century was a period of rapid global integration. In the Western Indian Ocean region, this was an era of economic growth and Omani expansionism. By the late 1830s, the Sultanate of Oman and Zanzibar controlled all of the major ports of the Swahili and Makran coasts. The subsequent period of political stability and dramatic economic growth would only be interrupted by the colonization of the Eastern African region by Britain, France, Germany, and Italy. Economic growth was a result of rapidly increasing regional exchange alongside the expansion of plantation slavery both in Oman and along the East African coast. The world was becoming more completely integrated, and in no small part this was a consequence of expanding networks of trade and economies of industrialization and slavery.[8]

Given emergent global economic asymmetries and the expansion of European empires in the early nineteenth century, unidirectional models of contemporaneous global relations—those that emphasize how wealth flowed to industrializing states and European empires projected military power across the world—have a clear logic. Yet, such unidirectional understandings of global relations can also obscure the way in which less powerful entities affected global relations. Similarly, they ignore the myriad interests, strategies, and actions of these less powerful actors. The failure to recognize multidirectional global relationships may even unwittingly project contemporary inequalities back in time in ways that hinder a more nuanced understanding of how relationships between world regions have changed across time.

Oman–Zanzibar offers an instructive example of the multidirectionality of global relationships in the early nineteenth century. Zanzibaris attempted to develop alternative modes of engagement with the wider world, commercial relationships that could better advantage the sultan and his elite subjects. To this end the sultan proclaimed Zanzibar a free port of trade, invited firms from diverse nations to do business there, and encouraged new forms of plantation agriculture on Zanzibar and Pemba Islands dependent on enslaved laborers. The sultan also recognized that traveling directly to distant ports and searching for new commercial partners in nations with which Oman–Zanzibar already had relations offered a key means of gaining greater wealth.

From the 1790s, Zanzibar's emergent position as a Western Indian Ocean entrepôt dramatically redefined the town. It also led to the relocation of the capital of Oman–Zanzibar from Muscat to the East African coast. The focus of regional commercial activity at Zanzibar in the early decades of the nineteenth century made it the region's unrivalled entrepôt and cemented Zanzibar Town's position as regional hub unlike any other since the decline of the Sultanate of Kilwa in the early sixteenth century. Commerce and an

126   *Jeremy Prestholdt*

increasingly diverse population made Zanzibar a cosmopolitan hub. If cosmopolitanism implies an ability to think and act beyond the local, Zanzibari networks and creole esthetics grew out of impressions and first-hand experiences of the world through trade, travel, and access to diverse information flows.

Zanzibaris evidenced a form of cosmopolitanism typified by what Homi Bhabha, Carol Breckenridge, and Dipesh Chakrabarty summarize as the ability to see, 'the larger picture [of the world] stereoscopically with the smaller.'[9] Seeing the world stereoscopically, Zanzibaris interpreted and re-combined esthetic motifs from Southern Arabia, the Mediterranean, and the Atlantic world in ways that addressed local social and political interests. A cosmopolitan vision also fostered a desire to exert greater control over global networks. This was perhaps nowhere more evident that the sulta-nate's commercial missions abroad, which would be central to Sultan Sayyid Sa'īd's vision for the sultanate in the early nineteenth century. Recognizing the potential of such missions, his successors in Zanzibar, Majid bin Sa'īd and Barghash bin Sa'īd, elaborated these initiatives over much of the fol-lowing century, a point to which I will return.

There was nothing new about the Sultanate of Oman and Zanzibar's ef-forts to exert greater control over global networks of exchange in the early nineteenth century. Controlling commerce had long been a primary interest of regional powers, from medieval Swahili city-states to sixteenth century Portuguese colonists and Omani governors of the East African coast in the eighteenth century.[10] Specifically, after regaining Muscat from the Portuguese in 1650, the Sultanate of Oman became a significant maritime force and economic power in the Western Indian Ocean region. This would have long-term repercussions for the Swahili Coast and Makran. In the second half of the seventeenth century, Oman built a considerable naval fleet and several Swahili polities requested Omani assistance to remove the Portuguese. Thus, the Swahili Coast became a focus of Omani overseas efforts. Swahili–Omani forces slowly regained much of the coast, culmi-nating in the fall Mombasa, the last Portuguese stronghold north of Mozambique.[11]

The end of Portuguese rule offered Omani strategists an entrée into the wider East African coastal region. Like earlier Portuguese administrators, Omanis sought both political power and economic access in East Africa. Accordingly, the Omani sultanate placed garrisons in Pate, Mombasa, Zanzibar, and Kilwa. In the early eighteenth century Oman was wracked by civil war between the Ya'rubi and Busa'īdi lineages, and this factional struggle extended to the Swahili Coast. Nevertheless, local Omani admin-istrators gained unprecedented control over the all-important trade in Gujarati cloth to Eastern Africa and ivory to South Asia.[12] With the con-solidation of Busa'īdi power and the end of the Omani civil war in 1749, the sultanate's interests turned to the Swahili Coast once again. Ultimately, the Busa'īdis would make their greatest investments in the small island of

Zanzibar, and its position as a regional entrepôt would allow the island to produce far greater wealth than Oman.[13]

At the end of the eighteenth century, the Sultanate of Oman–Zanzibar was a trans-Indian Ocean state that spanned from the Arabian Desert and the Omani coast to Baluchistan and the southern Swahili Coast (modern Tanzania). And in the early nineteenth century the fortunes of the sultanate rose significantly. Indian capital and commercial relations with Western India stimulated the regional economy, encouraged greater migration, and cemented Busaʿīdi rule.[14] Indian capital underpinned Busaʿīdi commercial interests, and in the early decades of the nineteenth century the Busaʿīdi Sultan of Oman–Zanzibar began to more fully exploit economic opportunities in Eastern Africa, attracting merchants from across the globe.[15]

Following Sayyid Saʿīd's 1837 conquest of Mombasa, Zanzibar's greatest rival state on the East African coast, the Sultanate of Oman–Zanzibar exerted influence over nearly the entire Swahili Coast.[16] Thereafter, the sultan began to make Zanzibar his effective capital, ruling the transoceanic sultanate, including its Persian Gulf tributaries and the interior of Oman, from East Africa. The political pivot from Muscat to Zanzibar signaled a symbolic shift in the history of Zanzibar, East Africa, and indeed the wider Western Indian Ocean region. Never had a Southern Arabian state made its capital on the East African coast. Never had East Africa enjoyed direct commercial relations with so many world regions. And no subsequent external power would become as deeply integrated into or affected by the social landscape of the Swahili world as the Busaʿīdīs.[17] For the following half century, Zanzibar, the sultan's seat of power, dominated East Africa's oceanic interface. Zanzibar became the economic and political nucleus of the Swahili Coast, the largest city in the East African region, and a cosmopolitan Indian Ocean cultural node.

Zanzibar and the world

The concentration of economic activity at Zanzibar reoriented the Swahili world, facilitating or strengthening ties with the East African interior, Southern Arabia, South Asia, Europe, and the Americas while drawing diverse residents, migrants, enslaved people, and travelers. As the Busaʿīdis consolidated their control of Swahili cities, the sultan banned many foreign merchants from direct trade with mainland ports. At the same time, he made Zanzibar a free port and attracted regional trade and investment. As a result, few ports in the world have commanded an unrivalled relationship with such a vast hinterland as nineteenth century Zanzibar. The island capital functioned as an intermediary between the greater East African region, stretching from Lake Malawi to the Eastern Congo and Southern Somalia, and ports as distant as Boston, Istanbul, Calcutta, and Canton. Much like Bombay and Singapore, Zanzibar acted as a hub of significant economic

128   Jeremy Prestholdt

and social activity that shaped and was shaped by its regional environs and transoceanic linkages.

Zanzibar-based firms, most of which were subsidiaries of Western Indian financial houses, began offering generous lines of credit, which brought more cash into circulation, fueled coastal trading ventures to the interior, and stimulated agricultural production for export. This increased commercial activity transformed the East African region.[18] Notably, in an effort to expand clove production on Zanzibar and Pemba, in the early decades of the nineteenth century Zanzibaris imported unprecedented numbers of enslaved people from the mainland. In 1837, the sultan's plantations alone had roughly 200,000 clove trees and experimented with both nutmeg and coffee cultivation.[19] Both the number of slaves and amount of land cultivated would increase significantly in the coming decades.[20] By the time the *Sultana* sailed for New York in 1840, Zanzibar had become the primary regional supplier of diverse imported goods and the most important regional market for East African exports. Zanzibar was exporting cloves to Bombay, and Zanzibaris were more dependent on slave labor than ever before.[21]

Zanzibar's economic vitality similarly attracted seasonal and permanent migrants from other Swahili cities, the Comoros, Madagascar, Southern Arabia, Kutch, Gujarat, Bombay, and elsewhere. While Swahili would act as the island's lingua franca, many Western Indian Ocean languages were spoken in Zanzibar Town. These included Makua, Yao, Zaramo, Oromo, Amharic, Malagasy, and multiple Arabic dialects as well as multiple South Asian and European languages such as Gujarati and English. South Asian, Southern Arabian, and East African merchants dominated the Zanzibari market, but in the early decades of the nineteenth century Americans also found an economic niche.

US demand for East African ivory, Yemeni coffee, Persian rugs, and Sumatran pepper, among other commodities, fueled a wider American trade in the Indian Ocean region. The East African market was particularly attractive to merchants of Salem, Massachusetts because they could operate largely free of competition from larger Boston and New York firms. Additionally, the market supplied two commodities essential to New England industries: hides for regional leatherworks and high quality gum copal, a resin necessary for the varnishes used in the local furniture industry. As a result, Salemites came to dominate the American trade with Zanzibar and they fiercely defended this niche. By end of the 1830s, most of the Atlantic vessels visiting Zanzibar hailed from Salem.[22]

East Africans consumed a great variety of American manufactured products. American cargoes bound for Zanzibar frequently included cloth, beads, and brass wire as well as gunpowder, guns, sugar, wheat flour, shoes, furniture, and clocks. Much of the cloth, beads, and brass wire was consigned to those heading up caravans for the interior. American furniture, clocks, and agricultural goods, on the other hand, appealed to consumers on the coast and islands.[23] Among these items cloth stood out. Cotton cloth

From the Indian Ocean to the Atlantic 129

was the single largest category of imports in East Africa, and therefore regional interest in American cloth was a boon to Salem's merchants. Industrially produced, unbleached calicos from Massachusetts' Lowell Mills, called *merekani* (American) in Swahili, were particularly popular.

Merekani, later manufactured in multiple US mills, would be the mainstay of America's economic relationship with East Africa for much of the nineteenth century. The ascent of *merekani* in the East African market is evident in the early decades of the century. By the 1830s, the popularity of American unbleached cottons in East Africa began to challenge that of the *kaniki,* the Western Indian indigo cotton textile with the longest history in regional markets.[24] *Merekani* became so successful in the 1830s that British manufacturers, in an effort to capture additional market share, produced imitations stamped with American trademarks.[25] A few years after the *Sultana*'s 1840 mission to New York, the British Consul at Zanzibar noted that *merekani* had come into 'universal use' in both East Africa and Southern Arabia. By the end of the 1840s, East Africans consumed more *merekani* than any other variety of cloth.[26]

US–Zanzibar trade was of growing import for both states in the 1830s, and this precipitated an official treaty of free trade in 1833. When the commercial treaty went into effect the following year, the US granted the Sultanate of Oman–Zanzibar 'most-favored nation' status. The sultan's relationship with American merchants would deepen considerably thereafter. For instance, in the 1840s Sayyid Saʿīd chartered American ships to carry cloves and ivory to Bombay and Calcutta.[27] As Thomas McDow has shown, the sultan also wished to leverage relations with the US to acquire a steamship, which would allow for greater ease of mobility across his far-flung realm.[28] Moreover, the sultan sought to take full advantage of the tariff allowances enshrined in the 1833 treaty, which exempted the sultan from import duties in US ports. Under such favorable terms, sending his own vessels to America, Sayyid Saʿīd reasoned, could greatly benefit Zanzibari merchants and the royal family. Thus, the Sultan of Oman–Zanzibar attempted to exert greater control over global economic linkages and raise the sultanate's international profile. In an early example of this dual enterprise, the sultan sent Ali bin Nasser, the Governor of Mombasa, to London in 1838 both to attend the coronation of Queen Victoria and investigate the prospects of direct trade with England.[29]

Sayyid Saʿīd's vision for exerting greater control over maritime commercial networks was contingent on the sultanate's maritime capabilities. The sultan had built up a substantial navy in the early decades of the century, and this had been critical to Omani influence in the Persian Gulf and expansion on the Eastern African seaboard. The majority of the vessels in his fleet were dhows of various build and tonnage, some of which had been outfitted for war. Though the tonnage of these vessels was usually less than that of European-style ships, they had great range. Indeed, Omani-based dhows traversed the breadth of the Indian Ocean. In the 1830s, Omani dhows traded as far as Madagascar and Java.[30]

130 *Jeremy Prestholdt*

The sultanate's fleet likewise included a number of European-style ships such as barks, brigs, frigates, and schooners, which the sultan employed for military, commercial, and diplomatic purposes. After the defeat of Mombasa in 1837, however, the sultan's need for a substantial fleet of warships lessened considerably. From this point forward, many of his vessels of war were converted into ships of trade and diplomacy.[31] For instance, in early 1824 Sayyid Sa'īd used his Bombay-made, seventy-four-gun warship the *Liverpool* to travel to Jeddah to perform the hajj. In a diplomatic gesture, the sultan later gifted the *Liverpool* to the English East India Company.[32]

In the latter 1830s, the sultan's fleet included the sloop of war *Sultana*, a corvette, brigs, and six frigates, the most impressive of which was the 1100-ton *Shah Allum*.[33] In 1839 the sultan commissioned another vessel, a schooner named *Nasiri*, which was constructed in Zanzibar, and the *Salihi*, a bark of the same size as the *Sultana*, built in the United States in 1840.[34] Unlike the *Nasiri* and *Salihi*, most of the large vessels in the sultan's fleet, including the *Sultana*, were commissioned in Bombay or Cochin. By the early 1850s, the sultanate's fleet boasted about twenty European-style vessels, a number large enough that an American merchant in Zanzibar remarked that it nearly equaled the size of the US naval fleet.[35]

The Indian Ocean in the Atlantic

In early 1840, Sayyid Sa'īd began preparing the *Sultana* for its voyage to the United States. Like many other vessels of Sayyid Sa'īd's navy, the *Sultana* was a creole product of a cosmopolitan Western Indian Ocean world. Described by Richard F. Burton as 'strong and handsome', the *Sultana* was a European-style three-mast, 300-ton sloop of war built of teak in 1833 at Bombay's Mazagaon docks.[36] In its early years the *Sultana* traveled between Western Indian Ocean ports such as Zanzibar, Muscat, and Bombay. In 1835, the *Sultana*, at that time still outfitted with a full complement of cannon, rescued the crew of the USS *Peacock*. The American vessel had been attacked by pirates after foundering on a reef near Masirah Island south of Muscat.[37]

The *Sultana* likewise sailed to Calcutta and Mauritius, and its voyage to the United States was an extension of these earlier missions. Specifically, the New York venture was an attempt to forge new economic relations with the US and strengthen diplomatic ties with Washington. As outlined above, among the Americans in Zanzibar in the 1830s, Salemites dominated the market. However, in 1839 representatives from New York firms seeking to break Salem's hold on the Zanzibari market approached the sultan to propose direct trade with New York City.[38] This offered an opportunity to expand trade with the US significantly, and the sultan shrewdly decided to explore the possibility. As a result, the sultan dispatched the *Sultana* to New York on orders to avoid Salem and Boston entirely. Sayyid Sa'īd not only wished to take advantage of free trade with the United States but also to impress upon New Yorkers the

From the Indian Ocean to the Atlantic 131

diversity and quality of trade goods available in his East African, Southern Arabian, and Persian Gulf domains. Therefore, the *Sultana* delivered to New York nearly twelve tons of Mochan coffee, about sixteen tons of copal from the East African coast opposite Zanzibar, nine tons of Zanzibari cloves, over a hundred East African ivory tusks, Omani dates, leather (likely from Barawa), and Persian rugs.[39]

The chief envoy for the mission to America and the crew of the *Sultana* were also emblematic of Indian Ocean cosmopolitanism. The sultan chose his chief secretary, Ahmad bin Na'aman, to lead the mission. Born in the Persian Gulf, Na'aman studied in Bombay, gained fluency in English, and served as secretary to Sultan Sayyid Sa'īd as well as his successor, Sultan Majid. Na'aman lived much of his life in Zanzibar and acted as the sultan's envoy to England, Egypt, and China as well as to the US.[40] Muhammad Abdullah, who was Persian by birth, served as his first lieutenant. Muhammad Juma, who was Swahili from Zanzibar, served as Na'aman's second lieutenant. Juma was the most important mariner on board and would effectively take over the position of the first lieutenant on the *Sultana*'s homeward journey. The majority of the crew were experienced Malabari sailors who Na'aman recruited in Bombay. In Zanzibar, Na'aman augmented the crew with enslaved East Africans owned by him and his lieutenants.[41] Finally, the sultan commissioned an English captain, William Sleeman, who was familiar with the course for North America.[42]

The *Sultana* arrived in New York at the end of April 1840. For the next several months the vessel captivated New York and gained national headlines. As word spread of the extraordinary ship, New Yorkers flocked to the quay to get a glimpse of the ship and crew. To placate the crowd at the docks, Na'aman gave a speech, which only intensified popular interest. Indeed, the pier at which the *Sultana* was moored became so overcrowded that the sailors were 'almost killed by the pushing, and pressing, and squeezing of the mobs.' Crowds would follow the crew far beyond the docks as well.[43]

Na'aman consigned the *Sultana*'s cargo to representatives of the firm Barclay and Livingston, and within three days much of it had found buyers.[44] For the return voyage Na'aman requested a range of American products. On the advice of Jairam Sewji, the custom's collector and likely Zanzibar's wealthiest merchant, Na'aman purchased nearly 90,000 yards of *merekani* cloth as well as beads, guns, gunpowder, china, and paper.[45] He also purchased mirrors, sugar, music boxes, glassware, chandeliers, crockery, looking glasses, and miscellaneous items for the sultan and other elites.[46] The *Sultana*'s mission had an important diplomatic dimension as well. The practice of sending gifts of great value to foreign leaders was long established protocol amongst political elites in the Western Indian Ocean and Eastern Africa. Thus, in an effort to cement diplomatic relations with the United States, Na'aman presented President Martin Van Buren with a number of gifts. The most valuable of these were two Najd studs from the

132 Jeremy Prestholdt

prized breed of Arabian horses. In addition, the sultan forwarded a gold bar, a string of pearls, two large pear-shaped pearls, two silk Persian carpets, six cashmere shawls, rose essence, and a gold mounted sword.[47]

The Board of Aldermen of New York and the city's Common Council were particularly keen to host and entertain Ahmad bin Na'aman during his sojourn.[48] The envoys were treated as honored guests. But as the *Sultana*'s departure date drew near, disaster struck the ship. In early August a fierce storm swept through the city and lightning struck one of the *Sultana*'s masts, shattering it.[49] Damages were extensive. Yet, the Navy received orders from Washington, DC to refit the *Sultana* at the government's expense. The *Sultana* was therefore towed to the Brooklyn Navy Yard and its crew became official guests of the US Navy. The US government spent a considerable sum to refit the *Sultana*, including giving it a new mast.[50] With the completion of repairs in early August 1840 the 'celebrated Arab ship' departed New York for Cape Town en route to Zanzibar.[51]

Legacies of the *Sultana*'s Voyage

Oman-Zanzibar would not send another ship to the United States, but the *Sultana*'s journey represented a significant extension of the sultanate's efforts to cultivate trade and diplomacy with distant states. In the years that followed, Sayyid Sa'īd's efforts and those of his descendants would be just as vigorous. For example, in 1842, when the sultan was under pressure from Britain to prohibit the export slave trade, he sent the *Sultana* to London in an attempt to negotiate for its continuance. This time, the *Sultana* carried an envoy and gifts for Queen Victoria.[52] The mission had little effect on Britain's demands. As diplomatic relations with Britain frayed in the debate over the export slave trade from East Africa, Zanzibari relations with the United States strengthened.

Ahmed bin Na'aman became a key supporter of closer economic and diplomatic relations with the United States. In the years after his return from New York he would be a central figure in the 'American faction' (or 'American party') of the sultan's advisors. In 1842 the British Consul Atkins Hamerton claimed that Na'aman was working to convince Zanzibar's elites, and the sultan in particular, that the British were 'very inferior people to the Americans.'[53] Hamerton further claimed that, 'all correspondence and matters which the Imaum [sultan] deems of consequence he submits it for the approval of the American party.' Moreover, according to Hamerton, the American Consul acted as a conduit for all of the sultan's foreign letters.[54] The sultan, his advisors, and Zanzibar's commercial elites saw the Americans as valuable economic partners. They also appreciated the utility of America as diplomatic leverage against Britain, particularly in the context of negotiations regarding the export slave trade. Nevertheless, US influence would be short lived. While Na'aman remained chief secretary until the sultan's death, Sayyid Sa'īd's relationship with Britain remained paramount.

From the Indian Ocean to the Atlantic 133

Figure 7.1 The *Sultana* in London. Image from *The Illustrated London News* of 18 June 1842 entitled "Landing of the Queen's Presents." Courtesy of John Weedy, iln.org.uk

In conversation with the US Consul in 1847, the sultan emphasized that the British, not the Americans, were his 'best friends'.[55]

While the Americans and the British vied for influence in Zanzibar, both harbored deep concerns about the sultan's economic missions. Although ships from many US ports, including Providence and Boston as well as Salem, frequented Zanzibar, American merchants were concerned that the sultan's ventures would flood East Africa with American goods. More precisely, they believed that Zanzibari importation of *merekani* cloth—that 'great staple article of trade'—and other American-made items would ruin US commercial interests in East Africa. Moreover, duty-free trade with the US meant that the sultan could export East African ivory at savings of twenty to twenty-five percent over the American merchants, thus giving Sayyid Sa'īd a distinct trade advantage in exports to the US.[56]

American merchants were concerned about the sultan's other ventures as well, including those to Britain. One merchant theorized that the sultan might begin to import not only cloth but also guns and gunpowder of the same quality as the American varieties and, simultaneously, force Indian firms in Zanzibar to sell exports to him. This, the Americans theorized,

134 Jeremy Prestholdt

might push them out of the market altogether.[57] British merchants harbored similar concerns, notably because the sultan did not pay import duties in Britain or Zanzibar. In 1847, these fears deepened when the sultan sent two of his merchant vessels to Europe, one to London and the other to Marseilles.[58] Soon thereafter, British merchants in Zanzibar wrote to the sultan in protest. They curtly asked that trade with European states 'continue untouched and uninfluenced by your highness.'[59]

Sayyid Sa'īd continued to send missions abroad, including the famous vessel *Sultana*. In fact, the *Sultana* would remain in commission until it was wrecked off the Kenyan coast on its return from India, likely in the early 1850s.[60] In 1856, Sultan Sayyid Sa'īd would die onboard his frigate, the *Queen Victoria,* en route to Zanzibar from Oman.[61] Soon thereafter, the Government of British India forced a separation of the administrations of Oman and Zanzibar, effectively dividing the two states. But Sayyid Sa'īd's successor in Zanzibar, his son Majid, continued to buy ships for use in trade. Among these was the infamous *Shenandoah*, a Confederate Navy commerce raider, which he refitted and redubbed *El Majidi,* and the *Africa*, a merchant vessel purchased from the German firm Oswald & Co.[62] Sultan Majid dispatched these and other vessels to London, Marseilles, and Bombay as well as to Hamburg and Istanbul.[63] Sultan Majid's successor, Sultan Barghash, went even further, visiting Britain himself in 1875.

Much like earlier envoys, Barghash capitalized on the attention his visit received to raise the profile of the East African sultanate and promote investment in and trade with Zanzibar. Perhaps most importantly, Sultan Barghash expanded his father's commercial vision by using state funds to promote regular, direct trade with Bombay, the Western Indian Ocean's emerging industrial center. Specifically, in the 1870s he purchased six steamships from Germany and Scotland. With this fleet he initiated his own steamship service between Zanzibar and Bombay as well as to Madagascar.[64] This service offered stiff competition to the British steamers that dominated the Western Indian Ocean routes, particularly as Barghash offered cargo space at bargain rates.[65] Barghash's steamers regularized transoceanic traffic and significantly increased trade and travel between Zanzibar and Bombay. Alongside British steamers, Barghash's fleet freed merchants from the seasonal rhythms of the monsoon, reduced travel time, and integrated Zanzibar more completely into a network of steamship services linking Indian Ocean ports from Aden to Singapore.[66] With direct and reliable service to Zanzibar, Bombay firms substantially increased exports to East Africa, delivering more revenue to the Sultanate of Zanzibar's coffers.

Conclusion

The nineteenth century was an era of substantial growth for Oman and Zanzibar and a period of global integration on the Swahili coast generally. Though a minor player on the global stage, the Sultanate of Oman and

From the Indian Ocean to the Atlantic   135

Zanzibar (and later the Sultanate of Zanzibar) attempted to exert greater control over transoceanic exchanges. By financing commercial ventures aboard, the sultanate aimed to shape emergent transoceanic relationships in an era of increasing global connectivity. The *Sultana*'s mission to the United States and many similar ventures evidenced the ability of Oman–Zanzibar to benefit from new global engagements. Perhaps more than any single vessel, the *Sultana*, in its journey to the United States, evidenced the sultanate's initiative and investments in charting its own economic course in a period of increasing interdependence and imperial expansion.

The *Sultana* and other Omani–Zanzibari vessels explored the possibility of multidirectional trade wherein Omani–Zanzibari ships delivered African, Arabian, and Asian products to distant shores. In this way, each mission was part of a wider, ambitious strategy to expand economic relationships with states well beyond the Indian Ocean region while bolstering diplomatic ties with those distant nations. The Atlantic ventures also reflected the new material and political interests that bound Oman, Zanzibar, and the wider East African region with distant ports and oceans. Each ship, mission, cargo, and crew were emblematic of the historical changes affecting the Swahili coast and the socioeconomic trends that were remaking the nineteenth century world through the interface of oceanic basins.

Omani–Zanzibari commercial ventures did not fundamentally change global economic relationships. Yet, they evidenced the multidirectional networks that existed alongside imperial projects. In an age of increasing Western dominance, Omani–Zanzibari overseas ventures demonstrated that more equal economic relationships with Atlantic states and other Indian Ocean ports were possible. Zanzibaris delivered Western Indian Ocean goods to the United States as well as to Mauritius and India and thus realized greater profits from regional trade. They also developed relationships with merchants that did not frequent Zanzibar. In short, though the nineteenth century voyages discussed in this chapter are now largely forgotten, they demonstrate that Omanis and Zanzibaris were able to affect and in some instances even reorient trade in substantive ways. And while the long-term dividends of this practice were minimal, Oman–Zanzibar's outward projection through its many commercial ventures reveals an important history of multidirectional global relationships. Omani–Zanzibari commercial ventures highlight global economic networks shaped not only by European empires and other powerful states but also by the interests and enterprise of much smaller, often less powerful actors.

Notes

1 Hermann F. Eilts, "Ahmad bin Na'aman's Mission to the United States in 1840, The Voyage of Al-Sultanah to New York City," *Essex Institute Historical Collections* 98, no. 4 (1962): 219–77; Jeremy Prestholdt, "The *Sultana* in New York: A Zanzibari Vessel Between Two Worlds," in *World on the Horizon:*

136 *Jeremy Prestholdt*

Swahili Arts Across the Indian Ocean, eds. Prita Meier and Allyson Purpura (Champaign, IL: Krannert Art Museum and Kinkead Pavilion, 2018), 114–29.

2 "Ahamet Ben Aman," *Niles National Register* May 23, 1840.

3 "The Arabs," *Morning Herald* May 9, 1840.

4 "To His Highness Seyd bin Sultan, Imaum of Muscat, Martin Van Buren, president of the United States of America," *New York Spectator* June 4, 1840.

5 Historical Society of Philadelphia, Henry Drinker Papers, "A Private Journal of Events and Scenes at Sea, at the Cape and in Zanzibar by Sandwith Drinker, Commencing August 9th. 1840. Sultanee, New York to Zanzibar," 88.

6 The sultan's vessels traded on behalf of the sultan himself as well as his family and leading merchants of Zanzibar. For instance, included in the cargo of the *Sultana* in 1840 were consignments from five prominent Zanzibar-based merchants.

7 Jeremy Prestholdt, *Domesticating the World: African Consumerism and the Genealogies of Globalization* (Berkeley: University of California Press, 2008).

8 Sven Beckert, *Empire of Cotton: A Global History* (New York: Vintage, 2015); Jürgen Osterhammel, *The Transformation of the World: A History of the Nineteenth Century* (Princeton: Princeton University Press, 2014); Christopher Bayly, *The Birth of the Modern World, 1780–1914: Global Connections and Comparisons* (Malden, MA: Blackwell, 2004).

9 Carol A. Breckenridge, Sheldon Pollock, Homi K. Bhabha, and Dipesh Chakrabarty, "Cosmopolitanisms," in *Cosmopolitanism*, ed. Carol A. Breckenridge, Sheldon Pollock, Homi K. Bhabha, and Dipesh Chakrabarty (Durham, NC: Duke University Press, 2002), 11.

10 Thomas Vernet, "Les cités-états Swahili de l'archipel de Lamu, 1585–1810. Dynamiques endogènes, dynamiques exogènes," (PhD diss., Centre de Recherches Africaines, Université Paris 1 Panthéon-Sorbonne, 2005).

11 Tonio Andrade, "Beyond Guns, Germs, and Steel: European Expansion and Maritime Asia, 1400-1750," *Journal of Early Modern History* 14 (2010): 176–7; Jeremy Prestholdt, "Navigating the Early Modern World: Swahili Polities and the Continental-Oceanic Interface," in *The Swahili World,* eds. Adria LaViolette and Stephanie Wynne-Jones (New York: Routledge, 2017), 517–28.

12 Thomas Vernet, "Les cités-états Swahili et la puissance omanaise, 1650–1720," *Journal des africanistes* 72, no. 2 (2002): 102–8; Justus Strandes, *The Portuguese Period in East Africa* (Nairobi: East Africa Publishing House, 1961), 242–3.

13 M. Reda Bhacker, *Trade and Empire in Muscat and Zanzibar: Roots of British Domination* (New York: Routledge, 1992); Beatrice Nicolini, "Oman's maritime activities throughout the Indian Ocean, 1650-1856 CE," in Oman: A Maritime History, eds. Abdulrahman Al Salimi and Eric Staples (New York: Georg Olms Verlag, 2016), 141-59.

14 Fahad Bishara, *A Sea of Debt: Law and Economic Life in the Western Indian Ocean, 1780–1950* (Cambridge: Cambridge University Press, 2017).

15 Abdul Sheriff, *Slaves, Spices & Ivory in Zanzibar: Integration of an East African Commercial Empire into the World Economy, 1770–1873* (London: James Currey, 1987).

16 Randall Pouwels, "The Battle of Shela: The Climax of an Era and a Point of Departure in the Modern History of the Kenya Coast," *Cahiers d'Études Africaines* 31, no. 123 (1991): 363–89; Beatrice Nicolini, "The Myth of the Sultans in the Western Indian Ocean during the Nineteenth Century: A New Hypothesis," *African and Asian Studies* 8, no. 3 (2009): 239–67.

17 Erik Gilbert, "Oman and Zanzibar: The Historical Roots of a Global Community," in Cross Currents and *Community Networks: The History of the Indian Ocean World*, eds. Himanshu Prabha Ray and Edward A. Alpers (New Delhi: Oxford University Press, 2007), 163–78; Bhacker, *Trade and Empire.*

From the Indian Ocean to the Atlantic 137

18 Sheriff, *Slaves, Spices, and Ivory*; Bhacker, *Trade and Empire*.
19 Peabody-Essex Museum Library (hereafter PEM) MH-14 Richard P. Waters Papers, Personal Papers, Journals (1836-1839), Folder 1, August 3, 1837. See also Sarah K. Croucher, *Capitalism and Cloves: An Archaeology of Plantation Life on Nineteenth-Century Zanzibar* (New York: Springer, 2015).
20 Frederick Cooper, *Plantation Slavery on the East Coast of Africa* (New Haven: Yale University Press, 1977); Jonathon Glassman, *Feasts and Riot: Revelry, Rebellion, and Popular Consciousness on the Swahili Coast, 1856–1888* (Portsmouth, NH: Heinemann, 1995).
21 Sheriff, *Slaves, Spices, and Ivory*; Cooper, *Plantation Slavery*; Prestholdt, *Domesticating the World*.
22 Jeremy Prestholdt, "On the Global Repercussions of East African Consumerism," *American Historical Review* 109, no. 3 (2004): 755–81; Anna Arabindan-Kesson, "From Salem to Zanzibar: Cotton and Cultures of Commerce, 1820–1861," in *Global Trade and Visual Arts in Federal New England*, eds. Patricia Johnson and Caroline Frank (Durham, NH: University of New Hampshire Press, 2014), 288–303; P.L. Simmonds, "The Gums and Resins of Commerce," *American Journal of Pharmacy* (March 1857): 80, 134; H. Northway, "Salem and the Zanzibar-East African Trade, 1825–1845," *Essex Institute Historical Collections* 90 (1954): 123–53, 261–73, 361–88; and Cyrus Brady, *Commerce and Conquest in East Africa* (Salem: Essex Institute, 1950).
23 Prestholdt, *Domesticating the World*.
24 Prestholdt, "On the Global Repercussions"; Arabindan-Kesson, "From Salem to Zanzibar"; Pedro Machado, *Ocean of Trade: South Asian Merchants, Africa and the Indian Ocean, c. 1750–1850* (Cambridge: Cambridge University Press, 2014); Edward Alpers, "Gujarat and the Trade of East Africa, 1500–1800," *International Journal of African Historical Studies* 9, no. 1 (1976): 22–44.
25 W.S.W. Ruschenberger, *A Voyage Round the World; Including an Embassy to Muscat and Siam, in 1835, 1836, and 1837* (Philadelphia: Carey, Lea & Blanchard, 1839), 47.
26 Zanzibar National Archives (hereafter ZNA) AA1/3 Hamerton to [obscure], March 26, 1847.
27 Prestholdt, "The *Sultana* in New York."
28 Thomas F. McDow, *Buying Time: Debt and Mobility in the Western Indian Ocean* (Athens, OH: Ohio University Press, 2018), 66–67.
29 "Her Majesty," *Morning Post*, August 25, 1838; Kauleshwar Rai, *Indians and British Colonialsm in East Africa, 1883-1939* (Patna: Associated Books, 1979), 5.
30 "Letter from Edmund Roberts to Louis McLane, May 14, 1834," in *New England Merchants in Africa: A History Through Documents, 1802–1865*, eds. Norman Bennett and George E. Brooks, Jr. (Boston: Boston University Press, 1965), 156–63.
31 Abdurrahim Mohamed Jiddawi, "Extracts from an Arab Account Book, 1840–1854," *Tanganyika Notes and Records* 31 (1951): 26.
32 Bhacker, *Trade and Empire*, 98; Joseph B.F. Osgood, *Notes of Travel; or, Recollections of Majunga, Zanzibar, Muscat, Aden, Mocha, and other Eastern Ports* (Salem: George Creamer, 1854), 59; Ruschenberger, *Voyage*, 85.
33 James Kirkman, "The Zanzibar Diaries of John Studdy Leigh, Part I," *International Journal of African Historical Studies* 13, no. 2 (1980): 287–88; British Library, India Office Records (hereafter IOR) R/15/1/89 Atkins Hamerton to L.R. Reid, Bombay, June 7, 1840.
34 Kirkman, "The Zanzibar Diaries," 287–88; Richard F. Burton, *Zanzibar: City, Island, and Coast. Vol. 1* (London: Tinsley Brothers, 1872), 268.
35 Osgood, *Notes of Travel*, 66-7; Burton, *Zanzibar*, 268; US Consulate, Zanzibar,

138 *Jeremy Prestholdt*

National Archives, Washington, DC (microfilm, hereafter USCZ), Roll 1, Vol. 1-3, Abbott to Webster, March 12, 1851.

36 Burton, *Zanzibar,* 267; *Bombay Gazette* September 4, 1833; "Edmund Roberts to John Forsyth, Bombay, October 23, 1835," in *New England Merchants* 160–61.

37 Ibid.; "The Arabian Corvette Sultani," *New York Spectator* May 14, 1840.

38 Eilts, "Ahmad bin Na'aman's Mission."

39 PEM MSS 1624 "Ahmad bin Na'aman Account Book, 1839-1840"; Eilts, "Ahmad bin Na'aman's Mission," 250. On the popularity of Barawan leather in the US see, PEM MH 94 Fabens Papers, Box 4, fol.4, M. Shepard to F. Fabens, January 7, 1847.

40 USCZ Roll 2, Vol. 4–5, Speer, "Report on Zanzibar, 1862."

41 "A Private Journal," 106.

42 Ibid., 30.

43 "Arrival of an Arabian Ship—Trade Between the United States and Muscat," *Morning Herald,* May 5, 1840; Jiddawi, "Extracts," 30.

44 "Ahmet ben Haman to Sec. of State John Forsyth, 14 May 1840," in *Public Documents Printed by Order of the Senate of the United States, during the First Session of the Twenty-Sixth Congress, Vol. 7* (Washington: Blair and Rives, 1840), Document 488, 5.

45 "Ahmad bin Na'aman Account Book"; Jiddawi, "Extracts," 29.

46 "Trade with Muscat," *Morning Herald,* August 10, 1840; Eilts, "Ahmad bin Na'aman's Mission," 252; "Ahmad bin Na'aman Account Book."

47 Eilts, "Ahmad bin Na'aman's Mission," 255.

48 "Arrival from Arabia," *The North American and Daily Advertiser,* May 7, 1840; *Morning Herald* May 15, 1840.

49 "Additional Damage done by the Terrible Storm on Monday," *Morning Herald* August 5, 1840.

50 "News from England," *Morning Herald* August 1, 1840.

51 "Additional Damage."

52 Jiddawi, "Extracts," 30; "Presents for Her Majesty," *Illustrated London News* June 18, 1842; Robert Nunez Lyne, *Zanzibar in Contemporary times: A short history of the southern east in the nineteenth century* (London: Hurst and Blackett, 1905), 39-40; John Milner Gray, *History of Zanzibar from the Middle Ages to 1856* (London: Oxford University Press, 1962), 209.

53 "Sub-Enclosure 1 in Twentieth Enclosure in No. 269. Captain [Atkins] Hamerton to the Honourable the Secret Committee of the Honourable the Court of Directors, Feburary 9, 1842," in *Correspondence with the British Commissioners at Sierra Leone, Havana, Rio de Janeiro, Surinam, the Cape of Good Hope, Jamaica, St. Paul de Loanda, and Boa Vista, Relating to the Slave Trade. Vol. 2. Class A* (London: William Clowes and Son, 1844), 415–6.

54 British Consul Atkins Hamerton claimed that Ahmad bin Na'aman even remarked to fellow Zanzibaris that, "if the Americans would be their friends," they need not fear God, the Governor-General of India, or the British Foreign Secretary Lord Palmerston. "Sub-Enclosure 7 in Nineteenth Enclosure in No. 269. Captain [Atkins] Hamerton to the Private Secretary of the Governor of Mauritius, October 4, 1841," in *Correspondence with the British Commissioners at Sierra Leone, Havana, Rio de Janeiro, Surinam, the Cape of Good Hope, Jamaica, St. Paul de Loanda, and Boa Vista, Relating to the Slave Trade. Vol. 2. Class A* (London: William Clowes and Son, 1844), 408.

55 USCZ, Roll 2, vol. 4, S. Speer, US Consul, "Report on Zanzibar," 1862; USCZ, Roll 1, Despatches, Vol. 1–3, Despatches from the US Consuls in Zanzibar, 1836–1908, Consul Ward to Buchanan [Secretary of State], March 13, 1847.

56 PEM Michael Shepard Papers, MH 23 Shipping Papers, Correspondence

From the Indian Ocean to the Atlantic 139

(1843–46) Box 12, folder 3, Ward to Shepard, Zanzibar June 13, 1846; Consul Ward to Buchanan [Secretary of State], March 13, 1847.
57 PEM Michael Shepard Papers, MH 23 Shipping Papers, Correspondence (1843–46) Box 12, folder 3, Fabens to Shepard, June 13, 1846.
58 Consul Ward to Buchanan [Secretary of State], March 13, 1847; ZNA AA1/3 Atkins Hamerton, January 3, 1847.
59 ZNA AA1/3 F.R. Peters and J. Pollock to Sultan Sayyid Sa'īd, February 20, 1847.
60 Burton, *Zanzibar*, 267–8.
61 Emily Ruete [Sayyida Salme bint Sa'īd], *Memoirs of an Arabian Princess* in ed. E. Van Donzel, *An Arabian Princess between Two Worlds: Memoirs, Letters Home, Sequels to the Memoirs, Syrian Customs and Usages* (New York: E.J. Brill, 1993): 231; ZNA AA1/3 Hamerton to Clarendon, November 10, 1856.
62 Oxford, Bodleian Libraries, Papers of Richard Thornton, Journals, MSS. Afr. s. 49, May 14, 1861.
63 IOR L/P&S/9/49 Kirk to Wedderburn, March 9, 1871.
64 USCZ Roll 3, vols. 6-7, Consul Cheney, "Trade in Zanzibar for the Year, 1883-4."
65 Edward D. Ropes, Jr., *The Zanzibar Letters of Edward D. Ropes, Jr., 1882-1892*, ed. Norman Bennett (Boston: Boston University Press, 1973), 34, fn. 113; School of Oriental and African Studies Library, University of London. MacKinnon Papers PPMS1/Corr 1, Box 22/Fol. 88, Holmans to MacKinnon, June 1, 1879; Prestholdt, "On the Global Repercussions."
66 Anne K. Bang, *Sufis and Scholars of the Sea: Family Networks in East Africa, 1860–1925* (London: Routledge Curzon, 2003), 58.

Part II

Institutions, practices, and agents

8 Hats, furs and Indigenous traders in a global trade[1]

Ann M. Carlos

Introduction

'He threw his bonnet ... and bought himself a good felt hat.'[2] For men, hats were an essential part of everyday dress for men for centuries. The shape and structure of the hat changed with fashion trends with wider or narrower brims and higher or lower crowns.[3] In fact, men's hats were so ubiquitous that we pay them little attention. Yet in the seventeenth and eighteenth century, that good felt hat was the end result of a global trade that spanned continents.

A good felt hat was one made from beaver wool felt. Felt is a nonwoven fabric of wool, fur or hair that is matted together. Beaver wool felt is light, waterproof, easy to shape, maintained it shape in the rain, and not easily torn and so is the best of materials for men's hats then and today. The quality of the hat depended crucially on the amount of beaver wool in the matted fabric. Less expensive and lower quality hats would have very small amounts of beaver wool or, indeed, none. In the seventeenth century, the highest quality hats perhaps made exclusively of beaver wool could cost between £3 or £4 or two to three months wages of a low-skilled worker; in the eighteenth century, the price had fallen and ranged from 9 to 27 shillings.[4]

Hats may have been a required item of dress but hats were also durable. As in so many areas, the work of Gregory King, who was a pioneer in political arithmetic or the economic structure of early modern England can be used to provide an estimate of the number of hats in England at the end of the seventeenth century. In his table titled 'Annual Consumption of Apparell, anno 1688,' King estimates that there were about 3.3 million hats purchased each year, which is close to one for every person over the age of fourteen.[5] A proposal to Parliament in 1690 for a hat tax also had the annual consumption at roughly three million, although it could have been using King's numbers. The high end of that market would be small but with incomes rising over the eighteenth century, so too would the purchases of higher quality hats.

Hats were not only sold on the domestic market but also exported and because exports were taxed, we have an enumeration of the number of hats

144   *Ann M. Carlos*

leaving the country. Based on Elizabeth Schumpeter's *English Overseas Trade Statistics*, she estimated that just over 100,000 hats were exported in 1710, a number which tripled to 300,000 a year by 1730.[6] A record 600,000 hats were exported in 1750 with exports declining in the subsequent twenty years. Millions of hats left England in the first half of the eighteenth century. Most were shipped to Spain and Portugal and from there to the Iberian American colonies, predominantly Brazil.

If hats were part of a global trade, at the heart of this expanding industry lay the primary raw material, beaver wool. All felting furs have a double coating of hair. The outside layer is comprised of long stiff hairs and an underfur which consists of shorter hairs next to the pelt. This undercoat can be felted because each hair has barbed ends that, when open, can be compressed into the material we call felt.[7] As its name suggests, beaver wool comes from the pelt of the beaver. The transformation of a beaver pelt into a felt hat was a highly skilled occupation in which the first step was to remove the wool layer. Unfortunately for felters, these hairs were naturally covered in keratin which essentially kept the barbs closed and thus made the wool difficult to felt. Stripping the keratin from the wool was difficult and each felter had his own procedure. However, on pelts worn or used as clothing, the keratin broke down over time which made such pelt valuable to felters and hatters. Felt was therefore made from a combination of older worn pelts and the pelts of more recently trapped animals.[8]

The discovery and then the subsequent wide-spread use of a process known as carroting after the 1720s relaxed the constraint on the number of worn pelts because it turned fresh pelts into a facsimile of worn pelts. In this process the beaver wool was brushed with a solution, based on nitric acid but which included diluted salts of mercury, which broke down the keratin. This carroting process also improved the felting qualities of wool from rabbit and hare and encouraged an expansion of output across the quality spectrum. Unfortunately, the process had serious health consequences for the workers. As the wool felt was shaped it had to be heated and as a result the felt released mercury vapour which attacks the nervous system. Mad hatters were all too real.

By the mid seventeenth century, the European beaver, *Castor fiber*, which had been widespread throughout Europe, had been hunted to near-extinction. Fortunately for the felting industry, furs and pelts began to arrive from the North American colonies. Although the North American beaver, *Castor canadensis*, was widespread in North American, there were at this time few well-developed trading links between the two continents; and what the hatting industry required was a steady and reliable supply of raw materials. Dutch, French, and English merchants sought to provide the necessary commercial structures.

One such set of merchants came to form the Hudson's Bay Company (HBC). Based on information and vision from two French Canadian voyageurs, Médart Chouart, Sieur des Groseilliers, and Pierre Esprit

Radisson, they were able to acquire a royal charter in 1670 for a 'Company of Adventurers' to trade into Hudson Bay.[9] The HBC was a joint-stock company with shares of £100 face value and limited liability for investors; the company was run by shareholders elected from those shareholders with the requisite number of shares.[10] Because of its northerly position the region was poised to be a source of prime beaver pelts.[11] The area covered by the charter stretch from the Rocky Mountains through present-day Alberta, Saskatchewan, and Manitoba in the west and to the height of land of the St Lawrence in Ontario and Quebec to the south and east. These are the ancestral lands of the Algonquian-speaking peoples, the Cree, Assiniboin, Dakota and many others, as well as the more northerly Athapaskan-speaking Chipewyan. How these various agents, Indigenous and European traders organised the sale, purchase and transportation of pelts in the focus of this chapter.

The Hudson's Bay Company located its trading posts strategically at or near the major rivers flowing into Hudson Bay: Moose Factory, Fort Albany, York Factory, and Fort Churchill, thus accessing the hinterlands of the Missinaibi and Abitibi, Albany, Nelson, and Churchill Rivers. The drainage basins of the Nelson and Churchill rivers stretch deep through the great Plains of Canada to the Rocky Mountains. E.E Rich described this strategy as sleeping by a frozen sea. But as I argue below, and in Carlos and Lewis, *Commerce by a Frozen Sea,* the Company actively pursued the trade but within the limitations created by the environment; physical, cultural, and linguistic. While much focus has been given to the English company, trade could only occur if Indigenous groups made a decision to carry pelts and furs to these Bayside posts. Only Indigenouss trapped and traded beaver and other fur bearing animals in the eighteenth century. Thus the decision to trade was a conscious decision as it required a large investment of time, both in trapping and preparing pelts and in paddling down river to the Bay and the return journey up river all of which could take many weeks.

If Rich saw the HBC as sleeping, building off the work of Polanyi, Rotstein has described these posts as administrative centers run by English merchants.[12] As I discuss extensively below, trade at these posts was not administered by London but was driven by and responded to market forces operating in England, Europe, and the Canadian hinterland. Rather than see this trade as a quintessential administered trade, I argue that Polanyi's focus on political, social, cultural, and administrative factors rather than being an alterIndigenous to market trade actually provides the framework within which the market operated but that many have not seen past the structure. I first begin by describing the agency issues that faced the HBC as a business organization in managing this trade. The following section describes how Indigenous cultural and social practices structured the operation of the trade and were made manifest in the actual trade environment. I argue that those often considered subaltern Indigenous actors were actively determining relative prices, quantities supplied and quality of trade goods.

146 *Ann M. Carlos*

Market power by Indigenous traders was purposefully used to affect the quality and types of trade goods brought to Hudson's Bay for trade and in the degree to which Indigenous groups used competition to bargain over the available surplus.

Creating a new trade

The furs and pelts from eastern North America in the second half of the seventeenth century arriving to Holland, France, and England was pursued by independent traders who sold their furs to merchants and merchant houses for export to Europe. In contrast to this atomistic trading structure, the Hudson's Bay Company, founded in 1670, was a joint-stock, hierarchical company with a head office in London and posts around Hudson Bay operated by salaried employees. Decisions concerning hiring, purchase of trade goods, renting of ships and sale of furs were initially intended to be made solely by the head office, while the factors in the Bay factories conducted the actual trading of European commodities for furs, and packing of the furs for shipment back to London. Ultimately, the actual decisions about trade were determined by the tastes and preferences of the supposed subaltern agents and by market conditions both in Europe and in Canada.

The great distance between London and Hudson Bay, made very real in the single ship a year that arrived and departed the posts in late summer, left the company open to problems of information and control of its managers and employees. The Governor and board of directors, known as the Court of Assistants, faced a classic agency problem of managerial opportunism. How would it or could it manage its managers? How could it ensure that its managers worked in the best interest of the company and not in their individual best interest? For long-distance trading companies being able to minimise agent opportunism determined long-run success. As I have shown in a series of papers, depending on the trading environment, long-distance trading companies chose strategies along a spectrum from punitive (severely punishing bad conduct) to reward (for good conduct).[13] Yet overseas managers had better information than the head offices about the many aspects of the trade under their supervision because it was they who conducted trade with Indigenous traders. At the same time, the head office had to be able to determine (at some level) if what it was being told represented the lived reality at the posts. The solution to this tension between allowing the post factors some degree of autonomy while at the same time ensuring the arrival of information that would allow the head office to discern between those working in the company's best interest and those acting opportunistically would lead, in the case of the Hudson's Bay Company, to continuous incremental changes to Company policies and to an extensive archive of journals, letter books and accounting ledgers which form the source material for this analysis.[14]

Trade relations

Joint-stock trading companies obtain capital by selling shares to the public who can then trade them on the secondary market. Historically, owners of these shares have rights as specified in the company's charter. In the case of the Hudson's Bay Company, individual shareholders with the requisite number of shares could run for Governor, Deputy Governor and Court of Assistants with all shareholders voting on these positions at the annual general meeting. Thus the Company was run by a subset of its shareholders directly but with all shareholders having voting power and an expectation of dividends.[15] Profitability or not of the company would be reflected in the market price of the shares on the secondary market. For these reasons, the head office was very attentive to trade conditions in Hudson Bay both in ensuring that company factors actually worked in the company's interest and not on their own behalf in private trade and that the type and price of trade goods met Indigenous tastes and preferences.

Prices and trade goods

As the equivalent of owners of a general store, the company directors had to supply its posts with commodities that would encourage Indigenous traders to trade their furs and to return the following year to trade again. Although the original investors in the Hudson's Bay Company had little experience in the fur trade having been attracted into the industry given a strong demand for pelts from felters and hatters and the need for a supply of high quality English felting furs, the pre-existing English, French, Dutch colonial trades ensured that information was available both on output market demand and also on the types of commodities in most demand by local traders: iron wares, guns, ammunition, knives, tobacco, cloth, and blankets being among the essentials. As is discussed below, this list of trade goods expanded from pedestrian to luxury by the mid-eighteenth century.

In setting up the company, the head office had to decide whether they would send goods and allow the post factors to decide on the price in trade or whether the directors would set a bench mark price for each good. The former would cede decision making authority to the post factors who might or might not act opportunistically. It would also leave open the possibility of competition over prices across the Bay side posts. Given such issues, the decision was to send out a benchmark price list. In creating this price list, the Company had to consider the cost/purchase price of European goods to be offered in trade; to cover the wages of its employees, head office expenses, transportation costs and any tariffs or taxes; and to take into account the expected future market price of furs, especially beaver pelts.

The Court of Assistants thus created a price list both for European trade goods in terms of furs and for furs in terms of European trade goods. The list, known as the *Official Standard,* set a price for each type of fur and each

148   *Ann M. Carlos*

type of trade good in the unit of account. Because Indigenous communities worked in a specie-less economy, the Company created a unit of account that would make sense in the local economy. It was called the *made beaver (mb)* which was the value assigned to a prime beaver skin (in essence, a prime beaver skin was the benchmark). For example, in 1700 at Fort Albany, the price of cloth was 2 mb a yard meaning that an Indian trader trading at Fort Albany at the *official standard* would exchange two prime beaver pelts for a yard of cloth. Those same two prime beaver skin would also buy four ice chisels, while fourteen prime beaver pelts were needed to buy a gun. But traders brought more than beaver pelts to the post: a marten was valued at one quarter *made beaver*, a red fox at a half and a moose skin at six *made beaver*. Because all furs and goods were assigned a *made beaver* price, in accounting terms this implied an exact equivalency between the furs received and the goods expended. If the post received 200 prime beaver skins in trade, it exchanged the equivalent in trade goods of 200 *mb*.

The existence of this *official standard* has been used as evidence to argue that this was an administered trade dictated by Europeans. Many, working from E.E. Rich and Abraham Rotstein, have argued that this list which changed only infrequently is the very antithesis of market forces. Indeed, Rich wrote that 'there was no escaping the conclusion that in trade with Indians the price mechanism did not work' because 'Indian habits of trade ... were quite alien to a European trade system.'[16] Although given credence in subsequent literature, Rich's statement was false. Trade was a ubiquitous component of the Indigenous economy and with it an understanding of the relative value of various commodities. What differed were the cultural norms surrounding the act of trading. Indeed, as all European traders quickly learned if they were to be successful, actual trade interactions had also to follow Indian custom. That the *Official Standard* changed infrequently is correct, but what is missing from this discussion is an understanding of the actual prices at which goods exchanged for furs. For all parties, the *official standard* represented a focal point.

The head office in London set up the *Official Standard* with the expectation that each of its post factors would adhere rigidly to the specified rates. However, it quickly became clear to the post managers and more slowly to the head office that such a policy was not in the Company's best interests. Indigenous traders came to the posts with certain expectations about the structure and form of trade exchange. Central was an opening gift-giving ceremony in which each side exchanged gifts with the other prior to a more formal negotiation on the prices at which furs would be exchange for trade goods (on the part of Indigenous traders) or trade goods exchanged for furs (on the part of the post factors). However, the *Official Standard* left no room for gifts or negotiation. It was, in effect, a take-it-or-leave-it price set by the head office but without gift exchange there would be no continuing trade. The question was how to incorporate gift exchange which from the head office perspective were additional costs in a manner that minimised opportunism by its post factors. By the end of the seventeenth century, post factors were allowed to trade away from the *Official Standard* but the flexibility remained underpinned by the *Official Standard*. For example, the *Official Standard* price of a pound of Brazilian tobacco was 1 mb at Fort Albany in 1716 but the chief factor noted in his letter to the head office that he had, in that actual trade, traded below the official price at half a pound per mb.[17] It must be remembered that the actual price received by Indigenous traders was the value of the gifts and the goods received in actual exchange.

Due to the distances involved and the isolation of the Hudson's Bay Company posts, the head office had to put into place systems that would allow it both to understand the nature of the trade at the posts and to turn that information into useful knowledge that would allow it to monitor and control its overseas agents to maintain the profitability of the trade for its shareholders.[18] The information available to the head office came in the form of letter books, post journals, inventory of goods remaining (with copies kept at the posts), and the account books carried along with the furs purchased in the summer trading season on the annual ship to London. Additionally, the head office had a record of the goods that it shipped to the posts to the posts and the sale prices of the furs it received.

To ensure maximal information from these documents, the head office required it post managers to organise the letters and account books in a very specific manner. Kitty Locker has argued that by 1700 the East India Company created rhetorical structures such as fixed headings or topics.[19] The HBC required similar structures, in particular requiring that its factors respond to each paragraph by number as given in the letter from London. Indeed, James Isham in response to criticism on this issue, wrote that he had 'taken care to correct my fault according to your honour's desire in this paragraph.'[20] Although factors might answer by paragraph number, the content might not meet satisfaction as seen in the London response Richard Norton at Churchill in 1739. The head office scolded him saying: 'In our last letter to you we desired you would give us a particular account of the quantity of water you mix with the brandy you dispose of to the Indians ... you have only thought fit to tell us that this is a point of management peculiar to yourself and ... that you cannot think of revealing to us a thing that will be so prejudicial to yourself, surely this is one of the most unreasonable answers that was wont send from a servant to his masters.'[21] Richard Norton was demoted from chief at Churchill to assistant at York to gain more experience.[22]

As important as were the letter books, the account books were vital to the directors' ability systematically to dissect its trade. As with the letter books, the head office sent out specific instructions on how the books were to be maintained. They specified the exact account titles, what they expected to see appear on the debit and the credit side and how the accounts were appear on the page. Each post was required to follow the same conventions and

150   *Ann M. Carlos*

provide the same information. This allowed the head office not only to follow the trade within one post across time but also to make comparisons across posts and factors. Within the accounts, perhaps the two most important were those relating to inventories and to the *overplus*. The *overplus* was a synthetically created measure that told the head office about the correspondence of expenditures and purchases by both Indigenous traders and the company officials. As in the example given above, the *overplus* was a number that could increase or decrease depending on how close or not to *Official Standard* trade occurred.

The *Official Standard* provided an exact accounting equivalence of trade goods exchanged for furs. But as factors traded away from that standard, either below or above, there had to be an accounting of the goods remaining or expended and of the trade goods given as gifts. Again to use an example for Fort Albany, in 1716, Richard Staunton, the governor at the post, took in furs valued at 20,583 mb. If Richard Staunton had been trading at the *Official Standard*, he would have paid 20,583 mb in European trade goods for those furs. However, in that year, he paid out 13,810 mb in trade goods. He also expended 928 mb in gifts. So in total he purchased 20,583 mb of furs for 14,734 mb of European trade goods. The *overplus* in this year at Fort Albany was 5,745 mb. The company tracked the *overplus* very carefully in assessing the effectiveness of its post factors and governors. It is very important to understand that the *overplus* is not a measure of exploitation but rather it was the outcome of negotiation between two independent parties, as I discuss later in this chapter. Indigenous traders were not forced to trade and neither were they dependent on company products. Indeed, the fur trade was a small component of the Indigenous economy.[23] Those who were not satisfied could decide not to return in subsequent years. However, for the company, as a joint-stock infinitely-lived entity, trade into the future was essential.

Because the company wanted to ensure that its managers worked in the company's best interest and not on their own private trade, the head office needed to keep track of the goods being sent out to the posts. Every year, the head office scrutinised the lists of goods sent to the posts with the lists of inventories said to be remaining from the goods sent out in the previous year along with the trade good request submitted by the chief factor for the following year. One example comes from the general letter to Governor Isham at Churchill in 1744 which read 'we are surprised you should indent for any guns as you have a large quantity by you and dispose of so few in a year.' In its letter to Fort Albany the following year, the directors wrote that 'we perceive you have a great many scrapers remaining in your factory and you trade very few.' The same level of scrutiny was paid to the furs shipped and the accompanying invoices. For example, in the general letter to Fort Albany in 1739, London officials wrote of discrepancies between the number of furs shipped and the invoice: cask 2 had 900 martens more than the invoice; cask 7 had 70 otters more; cask 19 had one cat more and one woodchuck less, while cask 26 had listed one beaver coat more rather than 2 cub and one parchment.[24]

Perhaps one indication that the London office was able to maintain control over its post factors is that the Hudson's Bay Company has been in continual existence for the 350 years from its inception in 1670. Despite the various admonishments written to post factors over the years, the Company was equally willing to commend and to issue those same managers with gratuities for a job well done. As a result, many of the managerial staff worked at these distant and isolated posts for their whole working careers, only returning to England or Scotland when they retired.[25]

The role of Indigenous traders

To the extent that one views the fur trade through an administered trade lens, there can be no role for Indigenous traders other than to bring pelts and furs to the posts to be exchanged for trade goods supplied by European companies at pre-determined prices. However, the HBC records provide a unique window onto Indigenous trading patterns and power and allow us to assess the extent to which fur prices responded to market forces and competition. Due to head office insistence on a complete accounting record of all activities at its Bay-side posts, it is possible to recreate (to some small degree) the complexity and importance of Indigenous trading patterns.[26] The fur trade brought two very different cultures into contact: the one literate with the then most advanced technology; the other still in a world of stone and bone and wood.[27] These differences obscure the fact that both societies had a long tradition of trade and commerce. Archaeological evidence is very clear on the existence of long-distance trade in North America north of urban Mexico. So trade, trading and negotiating was not a new concept.

The impact of Indigenous culture on trade with Europeans has already been alluded to. Trade had to conform to Indigenous practices or there would be no future trade. Thus the gift-giving ceremony was a very important part of the negotiations. Despite the fact that the trading season for the Hudson's Bay Company posts took place over six hectic weeks in summer, each group that came down to the post to trade had to be treated to a gift exchange ceremony with each side sitting and exchanging gifts to cement their friendship. In addition to smoking a pipe, drinking some alcohol, varied trade goods would be presented. Those designated as trading captains might receive a suit of clothing or other goods. Indigenous traders would gift some pelts. These gift exchanges were not of equal value in that the value of the furs received was less than the European trade goods received, which can again be ascertained from the expenses accounts kept by the post factors.

Very telling of the nature of the relationship is the language of the Canadian fur trade, whether at the Hudson's Bay Company posts or for the French voyageurs. Clearly the fur trade epitomised a cross-cultural world

152   *Ann M. Carlos*

with each side supplying commodities the other side wanted. But how those needs and wants were expressed give some insight into the power relationships. The language of the trade was a mixture of Cree dialects. Indeed, given that the HBC anticipated being in the fur trade for decades but the traders coming to the post might change, investment on the part of the traders to learn the language helped reduce cross-cultural barriers. The head office encouraged its post factors to learn the language and sought to send out apprentice managers with a language facility. Indeed, James Isham, sent to York Factory in 1732 and served at the Bay almost continuously until he died in 1758. During his time at the Bay, among other observations, he wrote up a Cree/English vocabulary dictionary and a phrase book for traders. The head office in London had this printed and sent back to their posts.[28] While these elements speak to consideration towards the Indigenous traders, at issue is whether those traders were able to influence the fundamental nature of the trade either in terms of the type or quality of trade goods or prices.

Trade goods

The fur trade brought iron technology to Indigenous societies in North America. Iron pots, awls, knives were superior to the stone, bone and wood tools being used but not all European technologies were superior and despite access to guns, powder and shot, Indigenouss groups continued to use traditional hunting methods. Trade would also allow groups access to a range of non-essential items such as lace, cloth, mirrors or hawk bells. In all, the HBC records tell us that Indigenous traders had access to between sixty and seventy different goods, some of which came in a range of sizes and colors. From the outset, the London directors were aware that the company's very existence depended on providing commodities that the traders would find pleasing and that would attract them down to the Bay-side posts in subsequent years. Indeed, the company letters document a search for commodities that would entice more Indians to trade. There was a continuous demand in the annual letters from the head office wanting to know what goods the Indians found satisfying. An example can be found in the letter to York Factory in 1680 when the Governor there was told: 'Send us home by every return of our Ships all such goods as are either defective or not acceptable to the Natives and inform us wherein they are deficient. And also to direct us exactly as you can of what form, quality & condition every sort of good is demanded there for the best satisfaction of the Indians, And wee will do our utmost that you shall be supplied with every species of Commodity in perfection.'[29]

Understanding what goods would sell and what goods were more likely to bring more people to trade made better business sense than buying and shipping goods that would not sell and have to be transported back to England. But it also tells us that the HBC was aware of agency on the part of Indigenous traders. There were two issues in the preceding statement. The

Hats, furs and Indigenous traders   153

first related to goods that were deficient or defective. The second referred to Indigenous tastes and preferences.

Defective goods were not merely goods that were defective upon inspection at the Bay post but also those that turned out to be defective in the sub-arctic climate which was something that could only be learned with time. In particular, climate played a large role in the performance of iron products.[30] It transpired that any iron product – hatchet, ice chisel or gun – with a small defect such as an air pocket could have severe consequences in the harsh northern winter. Water in these small cracks would expand when frozen and cause frost wedging leading to structural weaknesses such that the hatchet could shatter when used or a gun explode when fired. These blemishes in no way affected performance in a temperate climate but Indigenous traders quickly deduced that these blemishes were problematic and they examined all metal products very careful refusing to purchase any with blemishes. Thus what emerges in the letters from post to headquarters and head-quarters to Bayside is a learning process in which the London office and the manufacturers has to come to an understanding of what is happening. The following statements show both the time it took and the solutions the company sought:

> 1697 – let us know of 'any failure in any of the guns and whose they were and any other commodity...'

> 1699 – 'And hope these guns will prove good, or which pray advice, and note the name and make of those that proves otherwise.'

> 1717 – 'We take notice what you write as to the guns sent last year that they were not so good as those you carried with you ... but hope those we now send you will prove otherwise for we have taken particular care therein and to encourage the gunsmiths have advanced the price with them 3/- a gun more than we paid them for those you carried with you...'[31]

Statements to this effect continued through the period to the 1740s with the Company sending better quality metal products, English producers grappling with the impact of severe climate on their products, and the head office sending out armourers to each of its posts to examine, fix and repair. The company also sent out iron bar so that some of the metal products could be made at the post.

In its annual letter of 1738, the Directors asked the post managers to explain the 'Indians dislike of particular goods, their refusal and reason for the same...' In response, in 1739, James Isham at York Factory sent an itemised list of roughly twenty entries explaining that some of the beads were too large and heavy and the colour was not right; the kettles were too small for their weight, the handles fell too far over the side and the ears were too

154   *Ann M. Carlos*

weak; cloth was too narrow and thin; combs too weak; button shanks too weak and break; fire steels faulty; rings too large for female hands.[32] As a result, product quality and characteristics were crafted directly by Indigenous traders, presumably on the basis of much discussion back in the home community.[33]

This short list of product problems not only illustrates the Company's determination to provide commodities that met the consumers tastes and preferences but this short list also shows the wide variety of goods shipped to the posts for trade. In *Commerce by the Frozen Sea,* we fully described the range of commodities. Conceptually, we begin by grouping the products. One such group relates to producer goods that reduced the time needed in hunting and gathering, such as fishhooks, flints, ice chisels, hatchets, twine, scrappers, guns and powder Then there were household goods such as kettles, awls, blankets and fire steels which improved household work such as cooking or making clothes. We then grouped Brazilian roll tobacco and alcohol into one category and then all other luxury goods which included many similar items to those found on household inventories in colonial America and England: baize, beads, cloth, combs, gartering, handkerchiefs, hats, lace, scissors, shirts, thimbles.[34]

An examination of the relative purchases by grouping shows quite dramatic shifts over the eighteenth century. The proportion of producer and consumer goods purchased from 1716 to 1770 at York factory falls from over 70% of purchases for producer goods to roughly 10% each. Alcohol and tobacco rise to roughly 15% of purchases but it is the thirty or more luxury items that expand to almost 30% of purchases. In 1740, for examples, Indigenous traders at York Factory purchased 26 pistols, 189 blankets, 56 scissors, 987 yards of cloth and 346 combs.[35] It would appear that male Indigenous traders were coming to the post as they would to any store with a shopping list. There was alcohol available for trade but most traders (Indigenous and European) consumed alcohol during the gift-giving ceremony but interestingly when given the opportunity to trade furs for alcohol, Indigenous traders chose to buy other items. Indeed, the beauty of the *made beaver* unit of account is that we get the amount of each item purchased in each year in each post denominated in the same way. Again by way of example for York Factory in 1740: 6,418 *made beaver* worth of luxury items were purchased; 4,543 mb of tobacco was purchased and only 3,510 mb of alcohol.[36]

Fur price index

The *made beaver* unit of account allows one to add together apples and oranges or guns and lace to appreciate the relative demands for different types of commodities. It gives us a window into an environment that to this point was opaque at best. Clearly decisions were being made within Indigenous communities, just as in the head office in London, about what

Hats, furs and Indigenous traders 155

types of goods were needed for the coming year. Indeed, we also know that there was a strong second-hand market for the durable goods, with awls, hatchets, guns being traded further west to those communities to distant to travel to the Bay Posts over the course of a summer. However, the *made beaver* unit of account also allows me to say more than this. It also allows a discussion of market conditions and the relative bargaining power of Indigenouss versus Europeans.

All accounts had to be kept in the *made beaver* unit which valued items in terms of the *Official Standard*. Using these accounts, the directors were able to ascertain how far or how near to that standard trade took place. The numerical measure of distance from the *Official Standard* is, as discussed earlier, the *overplus*. The *overplus* can be conceived of also in index form. If we let 100 represent the *Official Standard*, a fur price index is the *made beaver* value of trade goods and gifts expended/purchased in trade divided by the *made beaver* value of furs taken in trade expressed as a percentage. So to use the same example from Fort Albany in 1716, the official value of goods and gifts received by Indigenous traders was 13,810 mb plus 928 mb in the gift exchange divided by the official value of furs which was 20,583 multiplied by 100. This gives a fur price index of 71.6. This index is not a measure of exploitation rather a measure of what each side accepted in trade. It is an indication of the relative distribution of gains at any point in time.

In Carlos and Lewis we calculated such a fur price index for each of the three main trading posts, Fort Albany, York Factory, and Fort Churchill for each year of the trade from 1715 to 1770.[37] The essential pattern for each post is the same. The fur price index lies around 70 in the 1720s and 1730s but then starts to increases over the next three decades to around 120 in the early 1760s. This is a substantial change and it tells us that by the end of the period, Indigenous consumers were receiving 20% more goods in trade valued at the *Official Standard* for the furs they were selling rather than 30% less as in the 1720s. In other words the price of a pelt at the Hudson's Bay Company trading posts was rising in that each pelt or fur garnered more in European goods. A rise in the price of pelts and furs is equivalent to an increase in the value of the labour used to trap and prepare those pelts.

To the extent that this was an administered trade, there should have been little variation in the prices paid for pelts and furs. To the extent that the Hudson's Bay Company is viewed as a monopsonist or the sole buyer of pelts and furs, changes of this magnitude in prices must be explained. Price changes of this magnitude imply both that the trade was not administered and that the HBC was not immune from market forces.

The fur price index gives us information on the relative distribution of gains between the parties. Increases in the price index tell us that Indigenous traders were extracting relatively more of the gains over the eighteenth century. Their ability to do so comes from changes in underlying market conditions; with changes in market conditions in Europe and in Canada flowing into the market for furs. In the late 1720s, the new technology for

156 *Ann M. Carlos*

removing keratin from fresh pelts became more available. Although this carrot of mercury led to severe neurological symptoms over time for hatters and felters, it also changed the mix of parchment and coat beaver, reducing the amount needed of the latter. Prices in the European fur markets reflect this rising from around 7/- per prime beaver pelt in the 1720s to over 16/- per pelt for a time in the early 1750s. As a joint-stock company, the directors had no reason to pass any of this price increase on to its customers. However, the price increases in the European market induced independent French voyageurs to increase their fur purchases in Canada both by travelling further into the interior and by offering higher prices to Indigenous traders.[38]

Ray and Freeman were the first to document the ways in which Indigenous traders played off the French voyageurs and Hudson's Bay Company traders.[39] This is also well documented in the post letters to headquarters. Essentially, Indigenous traders told each side that unless they increased the prices paid (in European goods) for their furs and pelts, they were going to the opposition, which was a credible threat. It did not have to be going to the opposition in the current year but in subsequent years. As a result, both French and Hudson's Bay Company traders complied and as a consequence increases in the output market price of pelts in Europe were passed through to the Indigenous trappers and traders, as we document in the dramatic changes in the fur price index. How changes in supply and demand play out depends very much on the market environment in which it is taking place.[40]

Conclusions

In this chapter, I examine the ramifications stemming from a global trade in wool felt hats. This often ignored object, a man's hat, was, in fact a cosmopolitan object which traded in cosmopolitan spaces. These hats were shipped not just to consumers in Europe but also back to the American Colonies and the Caribbean islands. From Portugal and Spain, these hats had major markets in South America. Yet in the context of global cosmopolitans, it is not the hats themselves which are the primary interest, but rather the raw material from which they were constructed. Beaver wool felt was made from the inner layer of wool from beaver pelts whose supply by the end of the seventeenth century came from North America and, in particular, from the region now known as Canada. While beaver roamed throughout the whole of North America, premier pelts came from regions where the winter was colder and longer, and so the further north the source, the more prized the pelt.

Of particular interest for this volume are the commercial practices involved in exchanging goods for furs and furs for goods. The North American fur trade brought together two very different societies, one Indigenous and one not. The trade provided Indigenous communities access to previously

Hats, furs and Indigenous traders 157

unknown iron technologies and a range of manufactured goods from the mundane to the luxury. Discussion of this trade is not recent. The work of Harold Innis and E.E. Rich in the middle of the twentieth century provided detailed and insightful discussions of that trade. But it was a discussion steeped in a world view that saw one side as superior and the other with little or no agency; a world view encapsulated in the work of Karl Polayni in general and Abraham Rotstein for Canada who argued that the fur trade was an administered trade, themes that percolate through much of the subsequent literature.

Beginning with the work of Arthur Ray and extended by Ann Carlos and Frank Lewis, we argued that Indigenous traders rather than being subaltern actors, had, in fact, significant and consequential agency. Clearly, Indigenous traders were subaltern in the sense that they were socially, politically and geographically outside English and French power structures, although Indigenous communities were able and willing to use that power structure to further their own ends. As I discuss in this chapter, the fur trade, as it developed through the decades after the chartering of the Hudson's Bay Company in 1670, was the product not of solely an English (or French) design but rather the result of cross-cultural interactions that allowed Indigenous traders to meld and mold both the actual trading practice and the actual goods traded to meet Indigenous tastes, preferences and demands. Indigenous cultural practice of gift-exchange very quickly became a vitally important part of trade negotiations. The language of the trade was Cree, or some dialect of Cree. The importance of language to the Hudson's Bay Company is found in the letters of the head office stating that they hoped to send apprentices with a facility for language; in the fact at least one of its post factors, James Isham, created an English-Cree phonetic dictionary and more importantly, the company had this printed and shipped back to its Bay-side posts.

As an infinitely-lived joint-stock company, the Hudson's Bay Company navigated its side of the trade relation by requiring meticulous and detailed letters and accounts from it post managers. These records allow a window into Indigenous agency that is un-paralleled. The letters from head office to the posts and from the post managers to London document with the ways in which Indigenous traders pushed back on the quality and types of goods sent. As I discussed above, the letters document how Indigenouss quickly discerned what to European were trivial blemishes but potentially fatal in the sub-arctic winter and through their refusal to purchase such products pushed English and European gun and metal product manufacturers to understand the impact of sub-arctic winters on metal.

The detailed account books required of every post and factory in each year generated not just a very large quantity of data on the types and quantity of trade goods purchased with furs and pelts in each year, these accounts also allowed Carlos and Lewis to create a fur price index that measured the relative distribution of gains between the Hudson's Bay

158   *Ann M. Carlos*

Company and Indigenous traders. Over the course of the century to 1770, the Hudson's Bay Company and Indigenous traders responded to market forces of supply and demand such that the price that Indigenous traders received for their pelts and furs rose substantially - with the fur price index rising from 70 to 120 on a benchmark of 100.

The eighteenth century Canadian fur trade is often seen as a trade between sophisticated and more powerful European powers and Indigenous communities without written language or access to iron technology. Despite these difference, the evidentiary record for the eighteenth century Canadian trade tells us that Indigenous communities were equal and active partners in this global trade.

Notes

1 This chapter is heavily drawn from many years of work on the impact of a commercial fur trade on Indigenous communities and on the Hudson's Bay Company. Much of his work was conducted with Frank Lewis whose insights will be sorely missed by economic historians and by me. Frank D. Lewis died March 2018.

2 Daniel Defoe, *the Complete English Tradesman* (New York: Guinn Co, 1966).

3 E.E. Rich, "Pro Pelle Cutem," *The Beaver* (Spring 1958).

4 £3 in 1700 would be £405 or $544 in 2017 (measuring Worth www.http://eh.net/howmuchisthat/) The price of the Mad Hatter's hat at Alice's tea party was 10/6 and so at the lower end of the quality range. Fiona Clark, *Hats* (London: Anchor Press, 1982); John F. Crean, "Hats and the Fur Trade." *Canadian Journal of Economics and Political Science* 28, no. 3 (1962): 373–86; Michael Harrison, *The History of the Hat* (London: Herbert Jenkins, 1960).

5 See chapter 1 in Ann M. Carlos and Frank D. Lewis, *Commerce by a Frozen Sea: Native Americans and The European Fur Trade* (Philadelphia: University of Pennsylvania Press, 2010) for a more extensive discussion. Population figures come from E. A. Wrigley and R. S Schofield, *The Population History of England 1541–1871* (Cambridge: Cambridge University Press 1989), 529.

6 Elizabeth Schumpeter, *English Overseas Trade Statistics, 1697–1808* (Oxford: Oxford University Press, 1960), 66.

7 Other animals whose hair can be used for felting are, for example, alpaca, rabbit or hare. Men's hats predominantly use beaver, rabbit or hare.

8 The number of worn pelts available would be bounded by the number of people wearing or using such pelts and willing to trade them.

9 The canonical history is E.E. Rich, *Hudson's Bay Company 1670–1870*, 2 Vols. (London: Hudson's Bay Record Society, 1958).

10 See William Robert Scott, *The Constitution and Finance of English, Scottish and Irish Joint-Stock Companies to 1720*, 3 Vols. (New York: Peter Smith, 1951).

11 The winter coats tend to be thicker in more northerly locations due to the colder weather.

12 E.E. Rich, "Trade Habits and Economic Motivation Among the Indians of North America," *The Canadian Journal of Economics and Political Science*, 26, no. 1 (1960): 35–53. Abraham Rotstein, "Karl Polanyi's Concept of Non-Market Trade," *Journal of Economic History* 1 (1970): 117–26

13 Ann M. Carlos and Stephen Nicholas, "Agency Problems in Early Chartered Companies: The Case of the Hudson's Bay Company." *Journal of Economic History*, 50, no. 4 (1990): 853–75 and Ann M. Carlos and Stephen Nicholas,

Hats, furs and Indigenous traders 159

"Managing the Manager: An Application of the Principal Agent Problem to the Hudson's Bay Company" *Oxford Economic Papers*, 45, no. 2 (1993): 243–56.

14 See www.gov.mb.ca/chc/archives/hbca/

15 Scott, *Constitution and Finance*.

16 Rich, "Trade Habits and Economic Motivation," 49 and 42. Rotstein, "Karl Polanyi's Concept of Non-Market Trade."

17 For a complete discussion see Arthur J. Ray and Donald Freeman, *"Give Us Good Measure": An Economic Analysis of Relations Between the Indians and the Hudson's Bay Company before 1763* (Toronto: University of Toronto Press, 1978).

18 For more detailed discussion of this issue see Ann M. Carlos and Santhi Hejeebu, "The Timing and Quality of Information: The Case of the Long-Distance Trading Companies, 1650–1750," in *Information Flows: New Approaches in the Historical Study of Business Information*, eds Jari Ojala and John McCusker (Finland: Studia Historica, 2007), 137–68.

19 Locker Kitty. 1994. *"Creating Formula: The Emergence of Common Solutions to Recurring Rhetorical Problems in the Correspondence of the British East India Company, 1600–1800."* Paper presented to the Conference on College Composition and Communication.

20 Davies, K. G., ed. *Letters from Hudson Bay* (London: Hudson's Bay Record Society, 1965), 31

21 Hudson's Bay Company Archives. *London Correspondence Outward - Official, 1670-1770*, MG 20 A6/1 -11. Ottawa: Library and Archives Canada.

22 He was subsequently promoted after a few years more experience.

23 Carlos and Lewis, *Commerce by a Frozen Sea*, chapters 3 and 5.

24 Hudson's Bay Company Archives. *Correspondence Outward - Official* [from London], 1679–1770, MG 20 A6/1-11. Ottawa: National Archives of Canada.

25 Dating to a later period, George Simpson gives the length of service of chief factors and chief traders in 1832. Many of the older men had worked thirty or forty years in Canada. Glyndwr Williams, *Hudson's Bay Company Miscellany* 1670–1870 (Winnipeg: Hudson's Bay Record Society, 1975 vol XXX).

26 Carlos and Lewis in *Commerce by a Frozen Sea*, ch 3, and Ann M. Carlos and Frank D. Lewis, "Marketing in the Land of Hudson Bay: Indian Consumers and the Hudson's Bay Company, 1670–1770," *Enterprise and Society* 3, no. 2 (2002): 285–317.

27 Kathryn E. Holland Braund, *Deerskins and Duffels: The Creek Indian Trade with Anglo America, 1685–1815* (Lincoln: University of Nebraska, 1993).

28 The dictionary and phrase book were written phonetically. A formal written Cree syllabary would be created in the 1840s. See Carlos and Lewis, *Commerce by a Frozen Sea*, chapter 3 and E.E. Rich, ed., *James Isham's Observations and Notes 1743-1749*, (London: Champlain Society 1949) which has reprinted Isham's dictionary.

29 Carlos and Lewis, *Commerce by a Frozen Sea*, 96.

30 Arthur J. Ray, "Indians as Consumers in the Eighteenth Century," in *Old Trails and New Directions: Papers of the Third North American Fur Trade Conference*, eds Carol M. Judd and Arthur J. Ray (Toronto: University of Toronto Press, 1980), 255-71 was perhaps the first to document this issue and the role of Indigenous consumers in pushing the boundaries of European iron technology.

31 Hudson's Bay Company Archives. London Correspondence Outward - Official, 1670–1770, MG 20 A6/1 -11. Ottawa: Library and Archives Canada.

32 Carlos and Lewis, Commerce by a Frozen Sea, (pp. 96–100).

33 Women were generally not part of the trading parties yet many of the concerns

160 *Ann M. Carlos*

expressed in Isham's list pertain to products that women would use such as pots, beads, buttons, cloth, combs, as they do to guns, fire steels, or powder.

34 Carole Shammas "Changes in English and Anglo-American Consumption from 1550–1800," in *Consumption and the World of Goods*, ed. John Brewer and Roy Porter (London: Routledge, 1993), 177–205.

35 Carlos and Lewis, *Commerce by a Frozen Sea*, Table 6 (pp. 81–86).

36 This translates into about eight two-ounce drinks per person per year among the Indigenous population in the York Factory hinterland. English and Colonials were imbibing much more. John J. McCusker, "The Business of Distilling in the Old World and the New World during the Seventeenth and Eighteenth Centuries: The Rise of a New Enterprise and its Connection with Colonial America," in *The Early Modern Atlantic Economy*, ed. John J. McCusker and Kenneth Morgan (Cambridge: Cambridge University Press, 2000), 186–226.

37 Carlos and Lewis, *Commerce by a Frozen Sea;* "Marketing in the Land of Hudson Bay."

38 Ann M. Carlos and Frank D. Lewis, "Property Rights, Competition and Depletion in the Eighteenth-Century Canadian Fur Trade: The Role of the European Market," *Canadian Journal of Economics* 32, no. 3 (1999): 705–28.

39 Arthur J. Ray and Donald B. Freeman, *"Give Us Good Measure": An Economic Analysis of Relations between the Indians and the Hudson's Bay Company before 1763* (Toronto: University of Toronto Press, 1978)

40 The impact of market organization is also discussed in Pim de Zwart, "Globalization in the Early Modern Era: New Evidence from the Dutch-Asiatic Trade," *Journal of Economic History* 3 (2016): 520–58.

9 The social networks of Cosmopolitan Fraudsters

The Prussian Bengal Company as a transnational corporation[1]

Felicia Gottmann

> Whatever they claimed in their official letters, the employees of the East India Companies had unofficial (and often underhand) dealings with one another, as well as with a number of Asian traders and brokers. Historians who read Company documents at their face value were making a grave error, and were also demonstrating an inability to penetrate the complex webs of sociability that eventually enabled Phoonsen [a Dutch East India Company Employee] to flee Surat for English protection in Bombay.[2]

In August 1756 a European ship, known variously as *Prince Henry of Prussia* and *Le Prince Henri de Prusse*, foundered in the Ganges mouth. As the name implied, this was a Prussian ship, the first to be sent by the newly-founded Prussian India Company trading to Bengal. Overseeing a multi-national European crew, the supercargo onboard was French and the Captain Flemish. Neither of them turned out to be very good company servants. Captain Clinkaert, drunk and physically abusive not only to his lieutenant and son-in-law but also to several members of the crew, had managed to alienate their original French river pilot who now refused to work for them again. The Captain moreover, getting drunk in his cabin, neither emerged when they neared the difficult sandy parts of the river nor had a boat sent ahead. Instead, when the ship finally ran aground, he continued to ignore the new pilot's requests, contradicted his orders, and abandoned the still perfectly safe ship, commandeering part of his crew to wrap up and disembark his own possessions and very substantial private cargo. How and why had this voyage failed so miserably? This chapter investigates this case study which in turn sheds light on the functioning and specific challenges of transnational enterprise in the eighteenth-century.

Historians of European imperial expansion, especially those focusing on the various East India Companies, have for many decades preferred to study their subjects from a national perspective, concentrating on only one of the various individual East India Company, those vast state-sponsored and shareholder-financed enterprises which held national monopolies over the

162   *Felicia Gottmann*

trade between their European home country and the regions east of the Cape of Good Hope.[3] Scholars of the Indian Ocean World on the other hand have long been aware of the cosmopolitan nature of the commercial networks spanning its shores, and that these connections withstood – and incorporated – various European East India Company traders whose joint private trading operations crossed religious, ethnic, and linguistic boundaries and spanned the Indian Ocean and South China Sea.[4] These days many European economic and imperial historians take the point that Sanjay Subrahmanyam has been making for decades: these various Eurasian histories were not nationally discrete but inextricably connected.[5] Thus, in line with new research that has emphasized the multinational and pan-European character of western imperial expansion in the early modern period more broadly, scholars have also begun to illuminate the multinational nature of the European East India Companies, not only in their clandestine private-trading activities on the ground in India and China, but now also as an integral part of their institutional make up back in Europe.[6] Like other institutions of imperial expansion these companies profited from incorporating wider European expertise and capital, especially at the outset, when experienced personnel was not yet available in sufficient numbers in the home country, but also during the companies' maturity, when other Europeans who, despite stringent legislation against this, had made successful careers in the employ of a foreign company were nevertheless often permitted to join or rejoin their national enterprise bringing home with them valuable experience, contacts, and capital.[7]

However, if all East India Companies were to some extent multinational, some companies and certain stages of their development were clearly more so than others. All companies relied on foreign expertise in their early years and continued to engage a number of foreign company servants, sailors, or military and religious personnel; but the many smaller companies, such as the Ostend, Swedish, Danish, and Prussian enterprises, often referred to as 'interloping companies', were to a much greater extent made up of multinational, multilingual, and often even multi-confessional groups of Europeans. Following this volume's definition of 'practical cosmopolitanism' as the ability to adopt, adapt, and operate across two or more different cultural codes or 'vernaculars' simultaneously, these are cosmopolitan commercial enterprises. To clarify this distinction a differentiation borrowed from business and management studies is helpful. Certain economists and business historians differentiate between 'national', 'multinational', and 'transnational' enterprises. 'Multinationals' are defined in the literature as 'firms that operate in more than one country', 'are owned in their *home* economy and invest in *host* economies'.[8] 'Multinational trading networks' then are 'firms that engage in trade intermediation between countries, and own assets in more than one country', which makes the East India Companies archetypal 'proto-multinationals'.[9] Many simply leave it at that; the UN for instance uses the terms 'multinational' and 'transnational'

The social networks of Cosmopolitan Fraudsters   163

interchangeably.[10] However, following the differentiation introduced by Peter F Drucker writing in *Foreign Affairs* over 20 years ago, some work in management studies has sought to distinguish between multinational and transnational companies, characterizing the latter as attempting to operate globally without any national character or bias.[11] This distinction is particularly useful for our purposes. In our context this would mean a trading enterprise counts as 'multinational' if it traded beyond its own national network. An enterprise or trader would only be 'transnational' if there is no strong evidence of national preference even within this multinational trading network. The Prussian East India Companies of the 1750s were such enterprises.

Transnational enterprise: the Prussian Bengal Company

All East India Companies were by definition multinational, being based in their respective European metropolis and trading with at least one, but usually several, localities abroad. The smaller, 'interloping' companies however, were more than this: they were proto-transnational enterprises. Whilst officially domiciled and registered in one single European country, Sweden, the Austrian Low Countries, or Prussia for instance, their shareholders, directors, merchants, and sailing personnel were transnational: in the Prussian Companies, set up in the 1750s to trade to India and China, non-Germans outnumbered Germans – not even Prussians alone – 20 to eight amongst the directors and main shareholders or board-members, and 26 to twelve amongst those of the ship's officers and merchants whose nationality, residency, and sometimes even partial biographies it has been possible to reconstruct on the basis of the surviving documentation.[12] As institutions moreover, both companies were deliberately set up to minimize national character. Frederick II of Prussia promised to exempt them from seizures during wartime, guaranteed the rights of foreign investors, and declared Emden a *Porto franco,* or international free port.[13] The legal framework adopted by the Bengal company copied practices in use internationally, relying for instance on the French *Code Maritime* as the basis for regulating the relationship with sailing personnel.[14] Official documents, such as the companies' statutes, passports, and the contracts and instructions it issued to its agents, employees, and partners were all drawn up in several languages at once.

If the transnational character of these companies as institutions is thus clear, the question remains whether the individual merchants involved in the companies can also be classed as transnational or cosmopolitan agents, and what in turn this entailed for their operations and for their principals back at home. In reconstructing the first Bengal voyage this chapter uses a particularly well-documented case study that allows us to trace the activities of a multinational group of European private traders in India, acting both in concert and for their individual accounts. This makes it possible to establish

164   *Felicia Gottmann*

whether this already multinational makeup facilitated or hindered cosmo-politan commercial exchanges on the ground in India. Investigating in how far their commercial interactions were 'cosmopolitan', that is genuinely transnational, or whether they remained culturally and nationally-bounded, the chapter will then conclude as to what this entailed for a smaller cosmopolitan commercial enterprise such as the Prussian East India Company, which had neither access to its own imperial institutions abroad nor to any international market control or policing mechanisms.

Thanks to a protracted legal case that compiled as evidence multiple sources of commercial paperwork, letters, other forms of written documentation, and the testimony of several sworn witnesses, we can reconstruct a detailed map of the commercial interactions of the four agents in charge of the first and last voyage of the Prussian Bengal Company.

The Royal Prussian Bengal Company was founded in 1753, and, like its sister company, the 1751 Royal Prussian China Company with whom it shared a director and several investors, it was based in the newly-acquired Prussian port of Emden, near the Dutch boarder in East Frisia. Also like its sister company it was resolutely transnational in its make-up: its original founder was British, and only one of its directors, David Splitgerber who also co-directed the China Company, was Prussian, the other three were prominent Flemish merchants based in Antwerp and Ghent respectively, with two French directors having to withdraw shortly after their nomination due to pressure from their local chamber of commerce.[15] Those whom these directors chose to put in charge of the first ship they fitted out for the return voyage to Bengal were just as international: the captain and the third supercargo were Flemish, the first supercargo Scottish, and the second supercargo French. Unfortunately for the investors these four turned out to be so untrustworthy that the result was less of a principal-agent problem and more of a principal-agent disaster.

As an important part of their benefits and often far outweighing the value of their wages, all officers and merchants on East India Company ships were permitted a certain amount of private trade, classed as *pacotille* or *port-permis,* which, depending on company conventions, was stipulated either in storage volume or monetary value. It was, if not expected, then at least tolerated, that the company employees would vastly exceed their allowance. Most companies also tolerated that their own agents on the ground, most usually in concert with other resident merchants from their own nation, from various other East India Companies, or from India themselves, conducted their own private trade on chartered or privately-own ships across the Indian Ocean region. Variously known as 'country trade' or 'voyage d'Inde en Inde', this was a highly profitable business.[16] Although often theoretically illegal or at best semi-legal, recent scholarship has demonstrated that both these forms of private trade could have distinct advantages not only for the individual traders but also their companies back in Europe: from opening up new trading posts and routes, to supplementing the

The social networks of Cosmopolitan Fraudsters 165

company's limited purchasing money in Asia, private trading enterprises by company servants served as trial runs for new products, brought the companies extra profits via the commissions imposed at company auctions, filled niches in high-quality, specialist and custom-made supplies that the company could not provide, and was a lucrative way of remitting large fortunes back to the metropolis.[17] Such practices were thus often tolerated, rarely prosecuted, and sometimes actively encouraged. What was certainly not encouraged however, was blatant barratry and theft, such as the abduction of a company-owned ship for private trading voyages using the company's own funds as capital. And that was exactly what the Prussian Bengal Company supercargoes and captain did, rather shamelessly so.

The Bengal Voyage

We can reconstruct the journey and actions of the officers and merchants in great detail thanks to the documentation amassed in the subsequent court case against the captain and supercargoes, the proceedings against the insurers, and the observations of Dutch and English East India Company officials and the letters they intercepted.[18] In December 1754 the ship, *Henry Prince of Prussia,* sailed from Emden under the command of the Flemish Captain Mathias Clinkaert, who had previously served with the Swedish East India Company, one of the many links between the Ostend and the Swedish Company.[19] The three supercargoes similarly had prior experience in the East India trade. They consisted of another Flemming, Johan or Jean Broutaert, as third supercargo; of the second supercargo, the Frenchman Nicolas-Joseph Thirion de Chanlay, who had spent 10 years on the Coromandel Coast as a French East India Company servant; and of the first supercargo, a Scot, John Young, who, also having served in the Swedish East India Company, maintained loose ties with the Scoto-Swedish East India trading network surrounding Charles Irvine.[20] Extensive previous experience should have been a boon: the Bengal Company's sister organization trading to China had had great success in their first voyages employing captains and supercargoes with previous experience in the Ostend and Swedish companies. Thanks to these experienced captains the first expeditions to Canton had been quick and efficient undertakings; and, being able to draw both on their familiarity with the trade and its merchandise and on their good personal relationships with agents of other companies, the supercargoes had managed to acquire a good selection of profitable merchandise despite the difficult economic climate both in Canton and on the oversaturated market back in Europe.[21] In the case of the Bengal Company however, their agents' previous experience of the trade and their extensive private-trading contacts – and ambitions – proved a bane rather than a boon for the principals back in Europe.

The outward journey to India already did not bode well. As the directors later explained in their memorandum, a new trading company, especially

166   *Felicia Gottmann*

one that operated in the sphere of the established East India Companies who had in the past demonstrated that they were prepared to be quite ruthless when it came to squashing such new enterprises, had to make its first journey as swiftly as possible to outrun its competitors and potential opponents.[22] Instead, the supercargoes thought to convince the captain to make several unplanned stops *en route* to trade for their personal account, quite possibly with the bullion the company was shipping to pay for Bengali trade goods and which the supercargoes had had signed over to them barely two months into their journey. The captain denied them the stops they demanded in Madeira, the Canary Islands, the Cape of Good Hope, and Ceylon which the ship reached in excellent time in May 1755.[23]

However, by the time they reached San Thome and Madras (Chennai) on the Coromandel Coast, the supercargoes had convinced the captain to see their point, their point presumably being the immense profit that could be made through private trading. Hence, instead of sailing straight to Bengal as they had been instructed, the supercargoes spent two and a half months in the French factory of Masulipatam (Machilipatam), since, as British records reveal, they had found at an earlier stop in Madras that the EIC there held firm to their instructions not to trade with them.[24] In Masulipatam they sold almost the entirety of the cargo of precious metals which the company had intended to pay for fine Bengali textiles. Part of it they used to order Coromandel cottons and to be converted to Rupees, but a good deal of it they appear to have employed to acquire a large cargo of salt and pepper which they shipped to Bengal where they finally arrived in August that same year. There they suffered a further delay, as their attempts to evade the taxes they were supposed to pay on their salt and pepper cargo led the Indian authorities to impound it until the dispute was resolved in December 1755. At this point they abandoned all pretense of trading for the company's account and engaged in what contemporaries as well as a number of the unhappy sailors and crew recognized was barratry: having spent 4 months in Bengal, they invented a fake charterer and under his name, but really for their own private gain, they had the ship sail back to the Coromandel Coast. With Young staying in Bengal to continue his rather shady operations there, Chanlay travelled with the ship and spent a whole 8 months on this expedition. From Bengal Chanlay, the Captain, and their associates took passengers to Madras and stopped in different locations along the Coromandel Coast to sell a cargo of rice and precious manufactured goods which they had acquired after the sale of their salt and pepper cargo in Bengal. Arriving back in Madras in mid-March 1756, Chanlay then spent another 4 months travelling the Coromandel Coast to trade with his private network, before charging another cargo predominantly of salt, but also of alum, tutenague, and cottons to be shipped back to Bengal in July 1756 where the ship fell victim to the Captain's alcoholism and irascible temper and foundered. The *Prince Henry*, which had only run aground but was not substantially damaged, remained largely water-free and accessible for a few

The social networks of Cosmopolitan Fraudsters   167

days, which later-on made the supercargoes' claims that all their paperwork had been sadly lost in the wreck rather unconvincing.

The loss of the ship finally brought home to the supercargoes that they found themselves in a rather awkward situation. They forged paperwork to cover-up their private trading voyages, trying to make them appear chartered voyages undertaken to generate profits for the company, but the result was profoundly unconvincing. The captain took ill and died whilst the supercargoes were still trying to agree how to draw up the required journals and paperwork post-facto to give credence to their stewardship. As it turned out, this and did not stand up in the ensuing court case the company directors started against the three survivors and the captain's widow and heirs.

All of this is interesting to us for two reasons. As part of the court case, the directors amassed a large amount of detailed evidence on the entire expedition and on the company's attempts at redress. This permits us firstly to analyse how a transnational (as opposed to the more traditional multi-national) enterprise dealt with the typical challenges of cross-cultural long distance trade, that is above all with principal-agent problems. Secondly, this allows us to map the captain and supercargoes' trading contacts and preferences, to investigate the development of their network over time in order to establish whether their already multinational makeup facilitated or hindered cosmopolitan commercial exchanges on the ground in India, i.e. whether or not they revealed national preferences in their dealings and if that changed over time.

Commercial Cosmopolitans? A study in network development

Quantitatively their trading network is easily summarized. Taking together their joint undertakings and their individual commercial dealings, the captain and the three supercargoes had commercial interactions with a total of 38 identifiable individuals or groups of whom three pulled out of contracts. The remaining 35 identifiable trading contacts include: thirteen Frenchmen, six individuals and one ship from the British Isles, seven Indians, two Dutchmen, the Danish Company's local director, one Armenian, one Persian, and three individuals whose national background remains unclear.[25] The actual number was significantly higher, including for instance an unknown number of Mughal merchants travelling as passengers on the journey from Bengal to the Coromandel Coast and an even higher number of Frenchmen with whom Chanlay had personal and financial dealings; but as no details as to their exact numbers and identities have been preserved they are not included here. This consequently entails a particular bias against Indian merchants who have a greater tendency to remain unnamed in the Prussian documents, which make several mentions of a 'marchand maure', a 'gentil' or 'un noir' ('a Moorish merchant', a 'gentile', or 'a black') who appear to have had dealings with the Prussian employees - often to their cost.[26]

168   *Felicia Gottmann*

Unless an individual can be clearly identifiable from the records they have not been included here.

Such a lack of precise numbers is not as much of a problem as it would first seem however, because mere numbers tell us comparatively little. To make sense of their network we need to study it both diachronically and qualitatively. For there is a distinct expansive pattern to their commercial interactions. At the beginning of their illicit trade, that is from their arrival on the Coromandel Coast in June 1755 onwards until their arrival and installation in Bengal, when they were still operating jointly, their main contacts were French and British company employees and private traders. This was due not only to the fact that the Flemish presence in India was negligible by comparison, but also that Young and Chanlay appear to have been the driving forces behind these private trade activities. Their previous experience as employees of the French and Swedish Company was decisive at this early stage, so much so that for a time they also seem to have considered sailing the ship under Swedish flag.[27] All in all in this first stage the network remains homophilic, that is marked by the tendency of individuals to associate and bond with similar others.

Through intermediation of co-nationals resident in India and acting as bridges or brokers in a second stage of network development, the supercargoes began to trade with those who were not their co-nationals, first indirectly and, in a third stage, eventually also directly. The social and commercial network of the Europeans living in India was much more cosmopolitan than that of our four new arrivals. As Elisabeth Heijmans' chapter in this volume illustrates, company officials stationed in the various trading posts regularly socialized and traded with their equivalents from the other European companies. They were therefore the first to help bridge the gap to non-British and French trading partners for the supercargoes. Thus the French governor of Masulipatam helped them broker a deal with a Dutch merchant, de Metteren, who sold them the initial salt and pepper cargo which they shipped from there to Bengal in the summer of 1755. The European and Christian communities in India were, despite all rivalries and conflicts, closely interlinked and the Prussian private traders managed to tap into this network: Renault, or Renaud, the head of the French factory at Chandernagore, took out a personal loan on the Armenian Minas Elias who stood in as a strawman for Young. Since Young kept the requisite paperwork and receipts however, Renaud was unable pay back Elias. Wishful of ridding himself of his obligation, Renaud finally had a Chandernagore notary certify that he handed over the remaining sum to Ziegenbalg, director and treasurer of Danish East India Company in Frederiknagore (today's Serampore in West Bengal) to be given to Elias and others to whom it belonged. This demonstrates not only the interconnectedness of the international Euro-Christian trading networks in India, but also our supercargoes' increasing ability to tap into these. More cosmopolitan even than the resident company employees were some of the private traders who had settled

The social networks of Cosmopolitan Fraudsters 169

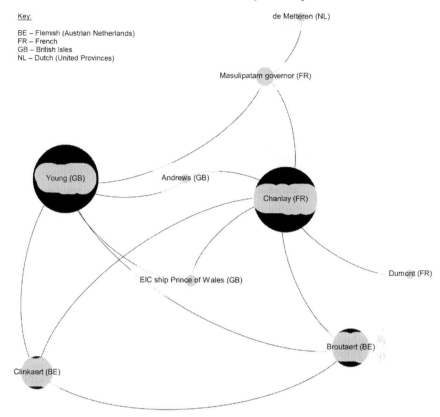

Figure 9.1 The Prussian Company employees' interactions upon arrival on the Coromandel Coast (spring & summer 1755).[28]

in India. These were equally important in helping the Prussian employees expand their contacts. The Armenian Minas Elias is one such example. Robert Pasley is another: a Lisbon-based Scottish private merchant who stayed in the Dutch settlement in Chinsura in Bengal, Pasley played a key-role in connecting the supercargoes to the Bengali mercantile community, recommending the services of his banyan merchant-broker who subsequently helped them in their purchases.[29] During this second stage then, the supercargoes expanded their network via Christian and European private traders and resident company employees who acted as connectors.

Engaging the services of local brokers finally meant that the Prussian employees began to have direct commercial interactions outside of European and Christian circles. It was customary practice for international traders in India to employ local merchant-brokers, banyas or banias in Bengal.[30] By relying on European brokerage during the first stages of their network development, the supercargoes' purchases would thus have been

170 *Felicia Gottmann*

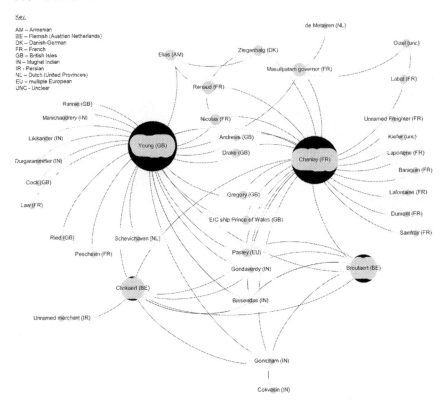

Figure 9.2 The Prussian Company employees' commercial network in India: synchronic overview.

doubly intermediated: first through a banya brokering the sale between producer and the European intermediary, and the latter then re-selling to the Prussians. In this second stage of their network development, the Prussians finally cut out some of the European intermediation. During their first stay in Bengal they worked with several Indian merchants and brokers. Some of these, such as Bissendas, they employed permanently whilst other acted as intermediaries only on a case-by-case basis: Gonicham for instance helped them sell their salt and pepper cargo and buy a return cargo to the Coromandel Coast. Agents acting officially for the Prussians *qua* Prussians therefore connected to all four, Bissendas or Merza Gondaverdy who acted as their official representative or *vakil* in their tax dispute. It would also have been an Indian intermediary who arranged for the paying passengers, all Indian merchants with their servants, who travelled on the Prussian ship from Bengal to the Coromandel Coast. In this final stage our private traders' network became more cosmopolitan: next to their continuing contacts with various European agents, Chanlay sailed in the company of Indian merchants, the Captain freighted cargo for a Persian trader, and Young engaged

The social networks of Cosmopolitan Fraudsters 171

in a series of rather shady loans and financial transactions with Bengali merchants and bankers.

However, even taking the temporal dimension into account, a description of their network that relies only on enumerating the different nodes themselves remains somewhat misleading. Their commercial network must be studied, not only quantitatively and diachronically, but most importantly qualitatively, investigating the relative strength of the ties. And once we take into account the relative importance of each interaction we notice that despite the expansion of the number of nodes over time, the primacy of the homophilic connection persists: the strongest ties are predominantly between members of the same national or linguistic group. The third visualization of their network (Figure 9.3) takes into account both the financial and commercial importance of transactions and their frequency: where connections were sustained over time, made up of more than a single

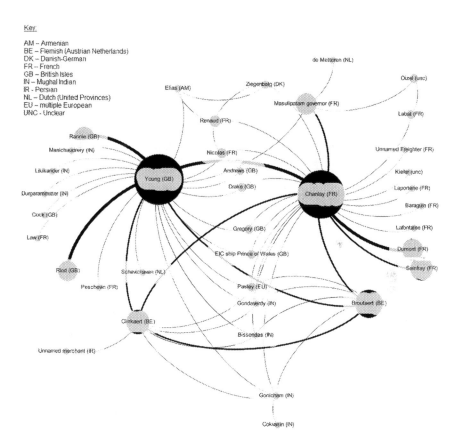

Figure 9.3 Network adjusted to relative tie strength, indicating the frequency, duration, and relative importance of interactions.

172   *Felicia Gottmann*

transaction, and financially particularly significant, both edges and nodes have been enlarged.

Young, whilst he maintained a cosmopolitan network overall, had the strongest ties to a co-national, the Scot David Rannie. After leaving India, he left his servant, Ried, in charge of his affairs.[31] In Chanlay's case, perhaps because he had spent many of his formative younger years amongst the French in India and thus had a pre-existing local network of co-nationals, this national preference is even more marked. On his return to Coromandel Coast from Bengal, he not only spent most of his time in French posts, he also acquired most of the return cargo from French intermediaries, both local merchants and ship captains. His network on the Coromandel Coast was mainly national, at best European: he did spend time in British posts and freighted cargo for a Dutch merchant, but unlike Young in Bengal, he had little interaction with local Indian merchants and bankers, and the relative strength of his ties with fellow Frenchmen far exceeded those with other Europeans.

The persistence of national preference was more than just an unconscious cultural bias. In unstable or precarious situations it was a rational choice as it mirrored our private traders' relative ability to mobilize social and political capital which was greatest in their national inner-circle. Consequently the national preference was strongest the more marginalized and vulnerable the supercargoes' situation. Their first arrival on the Coromandel Coast was one such situation. Given the hostile Franco-British take-over of the first ever Swedish East India Company ship to sail there 20 years earlier, and the warnings which the Dutch and British East India Companies did indeed send out to their Indian servants to inform them of the Prussians' arrival, the supercargoes were right to be wary of what reception they would face.[32] By the same token all three supercargoes reverted to their national network when under pressure, notably once it became clear, after the loss of their ship, that their malfeasance could not be concealed. The supercargoes then tried to maximize their social capital. Broutaert and Young, returning to their respective mother countries, did so quite effectively. Young, after quarrelling with the other two supercargoes, used his EIC contacts to charter, travel on, and transport his substantial cargo on two British vessels. Back in Britain he carefully shored up his network and reputation, spreading through the British East India circles that he was an innocent victim, very ill-used and unfairly treated by the directors of the Prussian Company.[33] He settled in a country house near Richmond, at an easy travelling distance from London and continued to travel in later years, albeit cautiously so: having failed to have him extradited from London, the Prussian Company directors made another attempted to have him arrested when he was in Denmark in the late 1760s. This was again unsuccessful and Copenhagen even refused to confiscate his possessions after his death there in 1769.[34]

Broutaert also opted for the offence as the best defense. Having returned to the Austrian Low Countries, he employed his connections in, and knowledge of, the Flemish legal system to counter the directors' legal case

The social networks of Cosmopolitan Fraudsters 173

against him with one of his own, demanding compensation for the financial losses he had suffered in their service due to the loss of the ship. His ploy was successful. He won the case in Ghent and again on appeal in the Malines court, and more than ten years later the company directors were still engaged in a legal battle over the question of jurisdiction.[35]

Chanlay however seemed to have put his faith in his existing network, in his forged paperwork, and in his well-known disagreement with Young. He therefore appears to have decided to focus on rescuing his literal, rather than his social capital. He stayed with the saved cargo in Bengal, using the time to recoup the company's remaining assets and to make up for his personal losses by then investing these. He thereby amassed a tidy fortune, some of which he remitted back to his wife in France, mainly, albeit not exclusively, through French channels. It is not clear why Chanlay thought he would be found innocent, but he did accompany the rest of the goods they had acquired for the company back to Emden when a retrieval mission was sent in the 1760s. Unlike him, Broutaert and Young wisely avoided setting foot onto Prussian territory ever again. Hence Chanlay was the only one who was convicted in person for barratry and he spent the rest of his life in a rather uncomfortable Prussian prison. Chanlay's failure to invest in the right kind of capital thus costs him dearly but his final attempt to use his network to shore up his reputation in the ongoing trial gives a last snapshot of his social and commercial network which confirms both his very limited cosmopolitanism and the persistence of national bias we have found so far. In response to the memorandum the directors had drawn up against him and the other accused in Paris, Chanlay produced 17 certified documents testifying to his 'honnour, morals, and behaviour'.[36] The vast majority of the signatories were French, none were British or indeed Indian: eleven of the 17 certificates came from Frenchmen or groups of Frenchmen employed or formerly employed in India totaling 22 individuals. Another three statements were signed by French officials and from metropolitan France. Only three came from non-French individuals: two employees of the Danish Company, including the above-mentioned Ziegenbald, in Frederiknagore (Serampore) in India, and one from the Dutch captain of the Prussian retrieval ship.

The institutional challenges of transnationalism: globalization and its discontents

As individuals all four private traders were thus very limited in their cosmopolitanism. If they were companies we would class them as multinational rather than transnational, with a clearly identifiable home base and the persistence of national and cultural bias. Acting as individuals however, they would not have been important. It is only as a group that they managed to take over the ship and thereby finally lose it together with most of its cargo. One deviant individual amongst the quartet in charge of the voyage would

174   *Felicia Gottmann*

not have posed a problem, but as a group they made up the entire management of the expedition - and as a group they operated transnationally. Their combined ability to draw on several different national networks, institutions, and forms of social and political capital, utilizing what from company's perspective were entirely foreign, third-country resources meant that when seen from the company's perspective they constituted what Drucker would call 'transnational top management'.[37]

Their transnational top management is one of the aspects that distinguished the small, 'interloping' European East India Companies whose supercargoes and ships' officers were in their majority foreign (such as the Prussian, early Swedish and Ostend Companies), from the large national ones where the majority of employees in leadership positions were nationals (like the EIC or VOC). All companies had greater control over national employees due to their ability to more effectively enforce punishments for eventual malfeasance for instance by seizing their employees' local assets. Only in the larger and more established companies however did these more easily-coerced individuals constitute a majority in the management consortia of captains and supercargoes who controlled the expeditions. Large national companies were thus able to restrict particularly blatant forms of deviancy, such as barratry, more effectively. A second aspect which enabled them to do so, and which similarly set them apart from the smaller 'interloping' companies was empire: companies who combined trade with imperial expansion had yet another way of policing their employees abroad and enforcing eventual punishments outside of the metropole. Without international institutions or supranational legal frameworks and extradition agreements, cosmopolitan enterprises such as Prussian East India Companies which did not have or seek colonial control, were at a distinct disadvantage.

The larger and more established East India Companies had institutional mechanisms to deal with the inevitable problems of long-distance trade. Three solutions were the most common and all relied on the peculiar intertwining of corporate and state sovereignties that defined early modern Europe and its imperial and economic expansion: company-collaborations or 'cartels'; official diplomatic pressure and state intervention; and tightening colonial control.[38] Inter-company collaboration, what the VOC themselves called 'cartels', could be very effective. The VOC had not only purchasing agreements with other companies, for instance with the French in 1750s Bengal and on the Coromandel coast, but since 1740 had also arranged for a 'cartel met de Fransche natie' ('a cartel with the French nation') in Pondicherry to exchange deserters and were keen to set up a similar agreement with the British.[39] Those agreements however, were decidedly not open to newcomers, perceived 'interlopers' such as the Prussians: as the boards of directors of both the VOC and EIC made very clear, their agents in Asia were not to help the new arrivals.[40] An alternative mechanism open also to the small 'interloping' companies was to lobby for official diplomatic

The social networks of Cosmopolitan Fraudsters   175

intervention, which, thanks to the tight community of interests between early modern governments and commercial corporations, often took place. However, this could only mitigate inter-company hostilities to a certain extent. It eventually succeeded gaining recognition and some compensation for the Swedish Company and, in the Prussian Bengal Company case, Frederick II's intervention with his staff in Lisbon allowed the Company to get hold of a legal deposition by Robert Pasley to use in their case against Chanlay.[41] However, without further international agreements, most notably extradition agreements, this could do little to bring to justice Chanlay's Flemish and Scottish associates. Together with extradition agreements, it was thus the third mechanism of corporate-state collaboration, namely colonial control, that provided the most effective answer to the challenges of cosmopolitan capitalism in the eighteenth-century. Paired with the development of the nation state at home, imperial expansion abroad permitted the tighter policing of long-distance trading expeditions thereby limiting the opportunities for transgressive transnational commercial behaviours that could harm economic interests in the metropole.

For a while at least smaller companies, such as the Scandinavian, Ostend, and Prussian East India Companies, provided an alternative to the imperial model, relying instead on collaboration both with local powers and agents and with other foreign, mostly European traders. Ultimately however, those companies that survived also became beneficiaries of, and contributors to, European imperialism. The Scandinavian Companies for instance played a major role in channeling private British fortunes, notably made from the opium trade.[42] The 1750s Prussian Bengal Company did not last long enough to even reach that stage. The infidelity of its transnational management combined with the onset of the Seven Years' War spelt the end of the company.

The story of the Prussian Bengal Company thus presents a double failure of commercial cosmopolitanism. On an individual level its agents on the ground in India retained marked national preferences in their dealings, which increased the more tenuous their personal situation became. On an institutional level the Prussian company, with its transnational directorship, merchants and sailing personnel, was an example of commercial cosmopolitanism - but as an institution it was a failure. In the early modern world the mechanisms of successfully containing or prosecuting 'transnational top management' gone bad were simply too limited.

The challenges of commercial cosmopolitanism in the early modern era are thus remarkably similar to those of transnational capitalism in the modern one. As Drucker argued, since 'basic economic decisions are made in and by the global economy rather than the nation-state', 'a central challenge, therefore, is the development of international law and supranational organizations that can make and enforce rules for the global economy'. Consequently the Prussians' double failure of cosmopolitanism two and a half centuries ago is mirrored by a similar but much broader

176 *Felicia Gottmann*

double failure today. The lack of transnational institutions capable of setting and enforcing rules for the global economy, was according to Drucker, 'largely to blame for the precipitate decline in confidence in and respect for government that has been a conspicuous and disturbing trend in almost every country'. The consequence is a vicious circle. The institutional failure of commercial cosmopolitan collaborations to set and enforce strict rules ultimately results in – and is then again reinforced by – the rise of anti-cosmopolitanism on a national and individual level. Over 250 years after the events in Bengal, more than 20 years after the publication of Drucker's article, over a decade after the 2008 crash, and even amidst a truly global pandemic, the worrying trend towards nationalist and authoritarianism populism continues across the world.

Notes

1 Research for this article was funded by the Leverhulme Trust (Early Career Research Fellowship 2014-396). I am deeply grateful for their support. A note on the use of 'nation' and 'transnational' in this chapter: The modern usage of 'nation' as synonymous with the nation-state is not applicable in this period. Both 'nations' and 'states' existed in this period, but very rarely coincided. Some modern nation states were developing at precisely this time (Britain and France are prime examples) but they were exceptions. Moreover, while states and their institutions are indeed crucial to the argument of this chapter, Prussia, the state in question, was a composite and territorially-fragmented monarchy, not a modern nation-state. 'Nation' is nevertheless a very useful term. Just as important as state institutions in this essay is the cultural sense of community that did not – and still often does not – overlap with state boundaries. While the term works in the case of the French protagonist, some of the chapters' main actors, the Scottish and Flemish for instance, do not have their own 'nation state' to this day, but still have a very strong sense of national identity. 'Nation' in that sense is not at all an anachronistic concept. It was a commonly-used contemporary expression referring to a shared linguistic and cultural identity which at the same time had some kind of legal and institutional framework: take 'The Holy Roman Empire of the German Nation'. The term moreover had a strong link in-ternational trade: 'nations' in the early modern usage as a an incorporated 'community of provenance' had been established as civic, legal, and commercial institutions in foreign trading entrepôts for centuries even where they did not have a clearly corresponding 'nation state' back at home: take for instance the Flemish 'nation' in Spain or Portugal (Daviken Studnicki-Gizbert, *A Nation upon the Ocean Sea: Portugal's Atlantic Diaspora and the Crisis of the Spanish Empire, 1492–1640* (Oxford University Press, 2007), 18–19.). On the etymology in the German context in particular, see Joachim Whaley, ""Reich, Nation, Volk": Early Modern Perspectives," *The Modern Language Review* 101, no. 2 (2006). Since it denotes a transcendence of both state and cultural, i.e. national boundaries, the term 'trans-national' is thus particularly useful here, especially as its application to business history also allows us to define a particular type of multinational trading enterprise and consequently lets us draw useful parallels with the contemporary world.
2 Sanjay Subrahmanyam, "Introduction: The Indian Ocean World and Ashin Das Gupta", in *The World of the Indian Ocean Merchant 1500–1800. Collected Essays of Ashin Das Gupta*, ed. Uma Das Gupta (New Delhi: Oxford University Press, 2001), 1–22 (2).

The social networks of Cosmopolitan Fraudsters   177

3 For two notable exceptions see: Louis Dermigny, *La Chine et l'Occident: le commerce à Canton au XVIIIe siècle, 1719–1833*, 4 vols. (Paris: S.E.V.P.E.N, 1964). Holden Furber, *Rival empires of trade in the Orient, 1600–1800* (Minneapolis: University of Minnesota Press, 1976). And more recently Philippe Haudrère, *Les compagnies des Indes orientales: trois siècles de rencontre entre Orientaux et Occidentaux, 1600–1858* (Paris: Éditions Desjonquères, 2006).

4 See for instance Ashin Das Gupta above.

5 Sanjay Subrahmanyam, "Connected Histories: Notes towards a Reconfiguration of Early Modern Eurasia 1," *Modern Asian Studies* 31, no. 3 (1997); Sanjay Subrahmanyam, *From the Tagus to the Ganges: Explorations in Connected History* (New Delhi; Oxford: Oxford University Press, 2005); Sanjay Subrahmanyam, *Mughals and Franks: Explorations in Connected History* (New Delhi; Oxford: Oxford University Press, 2005).

6 See Felicia Gottmann and Philip Stern, eds., *Crossing Companies,* special issue of *The Journal of World History* 31 no. 3 (2020). Cf. note 7 below.

7 The best-known case is undoubtedly that of the Hume brothers, who, after having been linchpins of the Ostend Company and involved in the Swedish Company, returned to Britain and joined the English East India Company. The members of the network around Charles Irvine had similar experience in crossing company lines, these are particularly well documented thanks to the surviving correspondence held in the John Ford Bell Library (JFB) in Minnesota. On these see Meike von Brescius, "Private enterprise and the China trade: British interlopers and their informal networks in Europe, c.1720–1750" (unpublished PhD thesis, University of Warwick, 2016); Hanna Hodacs, *Silk and Tea in the North. Scandinavian Trade and the Market for Asian Goods in Eighteenth-Century Europe* (London and Basingstoke: Palgrave Macmillan: 2016); Andrew MacKillop, "Accessing Empire: Scotland, Europe, Britain, and the Asia trade, 1695- c.1750," *Itinerario*, 29 no. 3 (2005): 7–25; and Douglas Catterall, "At Home Abroad: Ethnicity and Enclave in the World of Scots Traders in Northern Europe, c. 1600–1800," *Journal of Early Modern History* 8 no. 4 (2005): 319–57. In the eighteenth century many of such company-crossers were at some stage in their career linked to either or both the Ostend Company and the Swedish East India Company. On the Ostend connection see Jan Parmentier, "The Sweets of Commerce: The Hennessys of Ostend and their Network in the Eighteenth Century," in *Irish and Scottish Mercantile Networks in Europe and Overseas in the Seventeenth and Eighteenth Century,* eds. David Dickson, Jan Parmentier, and Jane Ohlmeyer (Gent: Academia Press, 2007), 67–91; "In the Eye of the Storm: The Influence of Maritime and Trade Networks on the Development of Ostend and *Vice Versa* during the Eighteenth Century," in *Trade, Migration and Urban Networks in Port Cities, c. 1640–1940,* ed. Adrian Jarvis and Robert Lee (St, John's Newfoundland: Research in Maritime History No. 38, 2008): 67–80; "A touch of Ireland: Migrants and migrations in and to Ostend, Bruges and Dunkirk in the seventeenth and eighteenth centuries," *International Journal of Martime History* 27 no. 3 (2015): 662-79. On the Swedish connection see also Christian Koninckx, *The first and second charters of the Swedish East India Company (1731–1766)* (Kortrijk: Van Ghemmert, 1980); Leos Müller, "Scottish and Irish Entrepreneurs in Eighteenth-Century Sweden," in *Irish and Scottish Mercantile Networks,* 147–74; and, more generally, Steve Murdoch, *Network North: Scottish Kin, Commercial and Covert Associations in Northern Europe, 1603–1746* (Leiden: Brill, 2006).

8 Geoffrey Jones, *Multinationals and Global Capitalism: From the Nineteenth to the Twenty First Century* (Oxford: Oxford University Press, 2004), 3 [emphasis in original]. Cf. Robert Fitzgerald, *The Rise of the Global Company* (Cambridge: Cambridge University Press, 2016).

178 Felicia Gottmann

9 Geoffrey Jones, *Merchants to Multinationals: British Trading Companies in the nineteenth and Twentieth Centuries* (Oxford: Oxford University Press, 2002), 1 and idem, *Multinationals and Global Capitalism,* 17. Cf. Mira Wilkins, "Multinational Corporations: An Historical Account," in *Transnational Corporations and the Global Economy*, eds. Richard Kuzul-Wright and Robert Rowthorn (Basingstoke: Macmillan, 1998), 95–133; Nick Robins, *The corporation that changed the world: how the East India Company shaped the modern multinational* (London: Pluto Press, 2012); and Stewart Clegg, "The East India Company: The First Modern Multinational?," in *Multinational Corporations and Organization Theory: Post Millennium Perspectives* (*Research in the Sociology of Organizations, Volume 49*), ed. Christoph Dörrenbächer, Mike Geppert (Bingley: Emerald, 2017), 43–67.

10 Cf. Kuzul-Wright and Rowthorn, eds., *Transnational Corporations;* and Jones, *Multinationals,* 5–6

11 Peter F. Drucker, "The Global Economy and the Nation-State," *Foreign Affairs*, vol. 76 (September/ October 1997): 159–71. Available on www.foreignaffairs. com/articles/1997-09-01/global-economy-and-nation-state [last consulted 7 May 2020]. See for instance John R. Schermerhorn Jr, *Exploring Management* 3rd edition (Hoboken: John Wiley, 2012), 162, 412.

12 Geheimes Staatsarchiv Preussischer Kulturbesitz (GStaPK) in Berlin (I. HA Rep 96 Nr. 423 A-H and I. HA Rep 68 Nr. 434–439), and the Municipal Archives (MA) and Johannes-a-Lasco-Bibliothek (JLB) in Emden (II 57, 58, 64 in the MA and Kunst MS 37 and 404 in the JLB).

13 The guarantees were set out in the respective charters and octroys accorded by Frederick see Emden MA II 57 and 58, and GStaPK I. HA Rep 68 Nr. 438 fols 11–14. On the Porto Franco see: GStaPK I. HA Rep 68 Nr.68 Nr 435 fols 64, 79–80, 81–84 and 95–96.

14 On this see especially GStaPK, I. HA Rep 68 Nr. 439: *Mémoire de déduction des preuves et conclusions à fins civiles sur crimes de baraterie* (Paris: Knapen, 1763), 174ff.

15 GStaPK, I. HA Rep 96 Nr. 423 F and Rep 68 Nr. 438.

16 For overview of all of these forms of private trade across the different companies see Maxine Berg, Timothy Davies, Meike Fellinger, Felicia Gottmann, Hanna Hodacs, and Chris Nierstrasz, "Private Trade and Monopoly Structures: The East India Companies and the Commodity Trade to Europe in the Eighteenth Century," in *Chartering Capitalism: Organizing Markets, States, and Publics,* ed. Emily Erikson (*Political Power and Social Theory*, Volume 29, 2015): 123–45.

17 See Emily Erikson, *Between Monopoly and Free Trade: The English East India Company* (Princeton: Princeton University Press, 2014); Berg et al., "Private Trade and Monopoly Structures"; Chris Nierstrasz, *In the Shadow of the Company: The Dutch East India Company and its Servants in the Period of its Decline (1740–1796)* (Leiden: Brill, 2012); and idem, *Rivalry for Trade in Tea and Textiles. The English and Dutch East India companies (1700–1800)* (Basingstoke: Palgrave Macmillan, 2015); Ole Feldbæk, *India Trade under the Danish Flag, 1772–1808: European Enterprise and Anglo-Indian Remittance and Trade* (Copenhagen: Studentlitteratur, 1969), and Hodacs and von Brescius above.

18 GStaPK, I. HA Rep 68 Nr. 438 and 439. British Library, London (BL): IOR/H/94,39–40; IOR/H/95,623-39; IOR/E/4/861, pp 683–684; IOR/E/1/41 ff. 13–14v; IOR/E/4/862,246; and IOR/D/149 ff 49–50. Dutch National Archives (DNA), The Hague: VOC, 2850.

19 GStaPK, I. HA Rep 68 Nr. 439 (no folio numbers) on the ship's journey. On Clinkaert's previous involvement with the Swedish and Ostenders see Rijkuniversiteit, Gent: Fonds Hye-Hoys, 1922 and 1852. Cf Koninckx, *The Swedish East India Company,* 281 n. 361.

The social networks of Cosmopolitan Fraudsters 179

20 GStaPK, I. HA Rep 68 Nr. 439. On Young's involvement in the Swedish Company, see Koninckx, *Swedish East India Company*, 344. On the Irvin network's relationship to Young see JFB: (Charles Irvine Correspondence - CIC), especially I series a: Abercromby, 7 April 1752 and idem, London, 10 June 1758.

21 See Felicia Gottmann, "Prussia all at sea? The Emden-based East India Companies and the challenges of transnational enterprise in the eighteenth century," *The Journal of World History* 31, no. 3 (2020).

22 GStaPK, I. HA Rep 68 Nr. 439: *Mémoire de déduction des preuves*, 19. Instances in which the established Companies had acted to destroy competition from new enterprises include their actions against the Ostend Company and its successor enterprises, as well as against the Swedish Company, most notably at Porto Novo. On these see: Conrad Gill, "The Affair of Porto Novo: An Incident in Anglo-Swedish Relations," *The English Historical Review* 73, no. 286 (1958): 47–65; more generally: Koninckx, *The Swedish Company*; and on the Ostend Company: Michel Huisman, *La Belgique commerciale sous L'Empereur Charles VI: La Compagnie d'Ostende* (Brussels and Paris: Henri Lamertin and Picard & Fils, 1902); Norbert Laude, *La compagnie d'Ostende et son activité coloniale au Bengale, 1725–1730* (Bruxelles: M. Hayez, 1944); Jan Parmentier, *De Holle Compagnie. Smokkel en legale handel onder Zuidnederlandse vlag in Bengalen ca 1720–1744* (Hilversum: Verloren, 1992).

23 Unless indicated otherwise all details on the expedition are taken from the *Mémoire de déduction des preuves*, which draws on the sworn testimony of two of the officers, over 500 letters and other documents. The evidence collected in this a 284-page document is confirmed by other documentation in the German and British Archives, as well as by the outcome of the court case itself. On the court case in particular see GStaPK, I. HA Rep 68 Nr. 438 to 439.

24 BL: IOR/H/94 (East Indies Series 2), 39–40.While this held true in Madras this was by no means universally so: Both Chanlay and Young very quickly established a long-term trading relationship with Andrews, another local head of the EIC's operations on the Coromandel Coast: GStaPK, I. HA Rep 68 Nr. 439: *Mémoire.*

25 Given both the limited information on, and the high degree of mobility by some of the individuals involved, some of these classifications may easily be contested. On Reid and Pasley for instance see below. Also note that the 'British' here include an EIC ship with whose officers the supercargoes negotiated but did not name, which is why the ship is given its own node in the below graphs.

26 'A Moorish merchant', i.e. a Muslim merchant; 'a gentile', i.e. a Hindu; and 'a black', which in the European mind-set of the time could refer to any South Asian person.

27 Note that the Swedish Company did not at this time officially trade on India's eastern coasts, which would be frequented by the Swedish only in a private capacity. Out of the 39 ships that the Swedish Company sent east during its second charter (1746-66), only 3 were sent to India and then to Surat via the Arabian Sea, not to the Coromandel Coast and the Bay of Bengal. See Koninckx, *The Swedish Company*, 64.

28 A note on the network graphs: They are based on data collected from GStaPK, I. HA Rep 68 Nr. 439, relating to the trial, in particular, but not exclusively, the *Mémoire de déduction des preuves*.The visualisations in this chapter are modified versions of undirected one-degree or one-step ego networks. That means that instead of depicting a complete network- which is hardly ever possible in the case of historic networks and their fragmentary data sources - they show all connections between the egos (the four supercargoes) and their alters, but not between the alters themselves. The one-degree or one-step limit allows for an easier grasp of the main characters' connections, but should not mislead us: in reality this was much denser network since many of the alters had dealings with each

180   *Felicia Gottmann*

other (which would be depicted in a 1.5-degree ego network) and with a host of other actors (which would be included in a 2-degree ego network). In the visualisations for this chapter exceptions to the one-degree limit have been made in cases of brokerage: when a certain alter was instrumental in establishing the connection of another alter to the ego, as in the case of Elias below, a 1.5 degree connection is included; and intermediation: when an alter acted as bridge to another who remained in indirect contact with the egos but still thereby entered into a transaction with them, as in the case of the Masulipatam governor and the Dutch merchant de Metteren above, a 2.0-degree is included.

29 Pasley's name was also the cover the supercargoes and captain adopted to conceal their own private trading activities, by forging paperwork to make him out as having chartered the return voyage from Bengal to the Coromandel Coast: a fraud that the Company directors were able to discover thanks to Pasley's legal deposition and letter from Lisbon in answer to their enquiries. See GStaPK, I. HA Rep 68 Nr 438 fols 175-6 and *Mémoire de deduction,* 212–14. On the Scottish Pasley family and their connections to India and Lisbon see John Bernard Burke, *A Genealogical and Heraldic Dictionary of the Peerage and Baronetage of the British Empire* (8th edition. London: Colburn, 1845), 778; and the family history John Malcolm, *Malcolm: Soldier, Diplomat, Ideologue of British India* (Edinburgh: Birlinn, 2014).

30 On the role of banyas see Irfan Habib, "Merchant communities in precolonial India," in *The Rise of merchant empires: long-distance trade in the early modern world, 1350–1750,* ed. James D. Tracy (Cambridge: CUP, 1990), 371–99; and, on Bengal in particular, J. Marshal, "Masters and Banias in Eighteenth-Century Calcutta," in *The Age of Partnership: Europeans in Asia before Dominion,* eds. Blair B. Kling and M. N. Pearson (Honolulu: University of Hawaii Press, 1979), 191–213.

31 We have no further information as to Ried's background and nationality, which is inferred as British on the basis of his connections and name, taking 'Ried' to be a German-French transliteration of the more common 'Reed'.

32 BL: IOR/E/4/616,85; and IOR/E/4/861,126. DNA: VOC, 332 (Letter to Governor General and Council in Batavia dated 8 October 1753). On the Swedish incident see Gill, "The Affair of Porto Novo". On the first voyages and the hostile reception of the Swedish Company more generally see Koninckx, *Swedish East India Company,* 69–108.

33 JFB: CIC: series Ia: Abercromby, 10 June 1758.

34 GStaPK, I. HA Rep 68 Nr 438 fol 200.

35 GStaPK, I. HA Rep 68 Nr 438 fols 183-84 & fol 190, 193–7.

36 GStaPK, I. HA Rep 68 Nr 439 (folios unnumbered). The memorandum in question is the *Mémoire de déduction des preuves.*

37 Drucker, "The Global Economy and the Nation-State".

38 On this see Philip J. Stern, *The Company-State: Corporate Sovereignty and the Early Modern Foundation of the British Empire in India* (New York; Oxford: Oxford University Press, 2011); and Stern, "The Ideology of the Imperial Corporation: "Informal" Empire Revisited," in *Chartering Capitalism: Organizing Markets, States, and Publics,* ed. by Erikson, 15–43.

39 'A Cartel with the French nation': DNA: VOC, 332 (Letter to Governor General and Council in Batavia dated 27 Sept 1751 and idem dated 8 October 1753).

40 See BL: IOR/H/94 (East Indies Series 2),39–40 and DNA: VOC, 332 (Letter to Governor General and Council in Batavia dated 8 October 1753) amongst others.

41 See note 29 above.

42 On the Scandinavian-EIC link see: Leos Müller, "Scandinavian trade in Canton and 'borrowed Bengal Money' – the global role of minor European companies trading in Asia 1760–1786," *Journal of World History* 31 no. 3 (2020).

10 Quasi-cosmopolitanism

French directors in Ouidah and Pondicherry (1674–1746)[1]

Elisabeth Heijmans

> The governor of Madras offered us his services and good correspondence; he pressed me again to send my wife in Madras where she would be safe; he told me that that the Dutch were determined to attack the Company in Pondicherry. The [English] governor has always been good to us. However, he may have some personal interests in this behavior; he has ships of his own for his private trade on the sea [...] maybe he is pressing me to send my wife in Madras to be assured that we will not attack them.[2]

The director of the French East India Company in Pondicherry (Coromandel Coast), François Martin wrote these words in his dairy in September 1689, when the Nine Years' War opposing England to France had broken out in Europe. Early modern European companies were created to operate intercontinental trade efficiently. However, trading companies still relied on their agents overseas to enter in the local commercial systems. This necessity generated relations across religious or imperial boundaries independently from the situation in Europe just as the above mentioned relation between the English governor of Madras and the French director of Pondicherry.

Since the foundational work of Curtin on cross-cultural trade, scholars have established that commercial relations were not necessarily confined to specific communities but rather crossed religious, ethnic, language or cultural boundaries in the early modern period.[3] Various mechanisms to enforce trust in intergroup commercial relations have been put forward such as the maintenance of regular correspondence, recommendations and reputation based previously fulfilled commitments.[4] In line with this historiography, this article explores the impact of local power relations on the creation and maintenance of inter-group commercial connections through the cases of French company directors based overseas like the above mentioned director of Pondicherry. What did it mean for French directors' 'commercial cosmopolitanism' or their ability to bridge commercial cultures?

The analysis focuses on inter-group connections of French directors of Ouidah in the Bight of Benin (west coast of Africa) and the settlement of

182 *Elisabeth Heijmans*

Pondicherry on the Coromandel Coast (India). Despite major political, commercial and cultural differences of the two contexts, a comparative perspective between case-studies situated in to the Indian and Atlantic Oceans enables the finding of common mechanisms in both factories. Furthermore, it reproduces the contemporary link between the two Indies.[5] The chronology covering the first decades of the French presence in Ouidah (1703–1746) and Pondicherry (1674–1719), before French territorial expansion on the west coast of Africa or the development of strong French commercial and military power in the Indian Ocean, is a relevant testing ground to study French directors' inter-group connections in a context of power which was not in the advantage of the French.

It is worth mentioning that the present analysis is based on and limited to sources coming from European institutions. Additionally, and perhaps as a consequence of the nature of the sources, a great majority of inter-group commercial relations reported consist of connections with other European representatives in both regions of analysis.[6] Although the sources describe other commercial connections, details are often absent. The article is therefore widely focused on inter-imperial relations (i.e. interactions between European empires) while integrating relations with local merchants and rulers when available. Despite these limitations, it remains possible to demonstrate how connections to individuals belonging to specific groups (mainly other Europeans) took on a central role in French directors' efforts to create other inter-group connections locally.

Directors could develop connections across (mostly) European empires for different goals; firstly, in the name and for the interest of the chartered company they represented and, secondly, in their personal name and for their private trade. While the two were frequently interrelated they are analysed distinctly to observe whether local power relations could impact them differently. Indeed, inter-group relations referred to in the official correspondence of directors to their superior in France could be affected differently by the context than private trade connections informal by nature and found in other European sources. After a brief outline of the context of Pondicherry and Ouidah, the article presents inter-group commercial connections made for the interest of the company in Pondicherry and in Ouidah. It then moves to cases of private trade and inter-group connections for the personal interest of directors.

Local power dynamics in Pondicherry and Ouidah

When the French East India Company (1664–1719) settled in Pondicherry on the Coromandel Coast in 1674, the surrounding region was the scene of frequent political changes particularly since the decline of the Vijayanagara in Southern India a century earlier.[7] Despite a political fragmentation, the region was commercially connected through the various ports along the Coromandel Coast.[8] For the French in Pondicherry this also meant good connections with other European settlements on the coast: the English East

India Company in Fort St. George in Madras and Fort St. David near Cuddalore, the Portuguese in Portonovo, the Danes in Tranquebar and the Dutch in Neguepatnam and Ceylon, among others. In terms of commodities coveted by Europeans, the hinterland of the Southern Coromandel Coast produced cotton but also indigo and saltpeter. Pondicherry became a major provider painted textiles for the French East India Company. This company remained officially in charge of the administration of Pondicherry until the Company of the Indies (1719–1769) took over its settlements and trading factories in 1719. The company placed its agents as directors of settlements to ensure smooth trading operations overseas. The roles of directors overseas were however far from limited to commercial activities.

To ensure the resilience of trading factories and their connections to the production in the hinterland, directors also had a political role. Relations between French directors with rulers were not on an equal basis. Under the sultan of Bijapur, the Marathas and the Mughals the directors were maintained in a subordinate position. The Mughal emperors gradually lost their authority in practice on the region of the Southern Coromandel Coast during the first decades of the eighteenth century but that did not translate in an increase of independence for the French in Pondicherry right away. Local Mughal governors' aspirations for independence strengthened their need to assert authority on the French settlement. As a result, the majority of French directors' interactions with Indian rulers consisted of sessions where they offered presents or paid tributes to gain the ruler's protection.[9] Because of this subordinate position in the first decades of the eighteenth century, negotiations undertaken by French directors with local rulers often required the mediation of a well-connected intermediary.[10]

Regarding the political situation in the region of the French trading fort of Ouidah, in the Bight of Benin, the beginning of the eighteenth century was marked by recurrent conflicts between the kingdom of Hueda and the neighbouring kingdom of Allada until the interior kingdom of Dahomey conquered the kingdom of Hueda (1727–1733). Even after the Dahomean conquest, the political situation remained unstable because of confrontations with the interior kingdom of Oyo.[11] For the French, and other Europeans, the main purpose of their presence in Ouidah was the slave trade to the Americas and the West Indies.[12] The French factory was administrated by the French company benefitting from a trade monopoly in the Bight of Benin called the Guinea/Asiento Company until 1713, when the factory came under the administration of the French navy. In 1720 the factory came back in the trading monopoly of the above mentioned Company of the Indies.

Europeans in Ouidah did not acquire any rights to the land on which their forts were built during the eighteenth century. Just as on the neighbouring 'Gold Coast', African sovereigns granted them concession to build a fort for which they had to pay a tribute.[13] Therefore, in Ouidah agents appointed as directors of the factory entered in hierarchical relationship with rulers.

184   *Elisabeth Heijmans*

Interactions with African sovereigns, both under Hueda kings and later, Dahomey kings, consisted mainly of tribute payments and diplomatic gifts. The directors had rarely direct contacts with the sovereigns as an official intermediary was in charge of mediating between European agents and the African administration.[14] Aside from the French fort, there was an English fort and after 1721 a Portuguese one in Ouidah. Additionally, the Dutch had a fort in Jakin in the neighbouring kingdom of Allada and other European forts were present on the 'Gold Coast'.

Just as on the Coromandel Coast, the close presence of multiple Europeans increased commercial competition among them to the benefit of the local sovereigns and merchants. Furthermore, to avoid conflicts among Europeans and increase control, sovereigns imposed neutrality among Europeans in both places. Under the Hueda kings, it took the form of a treaty that was signed by European agents under King Amar (1703–1708).[15] In the case of Pondicherry, the Maratha leader Shivaji and the Mughal emperor after him forbade conflicts among Europeans on their territory, at least in theory.[16] The combination of hierarchical relations with local rulers and close presence of other Europeans led to a context of power relations in Pondicherry and in Ouidah relevant for the study of French directros' 'commercial cosmopolitanism'. In this special environment, what types of interactions did the French foster, with whom and for what purpose?

In the changing political environment of the Bight of Benin, European agents acknowledged the necessity to create a united front to compensate for the vulnerability of their position. Particularly during the period of high insecurity of the Dahomean conquest, the weak military position of Europeans in Ouidah was most visible. During the war, Huffon (King of Hueda 1708–1727) repeated attempts at reconquering Ouidah provoking political instability around European forts and creating a sense of solidarity among European factors. It was clear for actors who were familiar with the environment either because they experienced it or because they were well informed, that European 'nations' were individually too weak and the only way they could exercise pressure was in a communal effort. It is important to state that it was fear rather than genuine solidarity that led Europeans to state openly the need for a common front.[17] The same fear and awareness of individual weakness motivated the support of the Portuguese Vice Roy of Brazil to a 'common resistance'.[18] Europeans also tried to communicate their demands to the King of Dahomey together to have more weight in the negotiations.[19] However, this was not a constant phenomenon and it was tied to the circumstances of vulnerability in which the French, English and Portuguese were in Ouidah at that precise moment in time. As such this solidarity tells us more about the strength of the Hueda and Dahomey kings than the ability of French directors to bridge commercial cultures.

The case of Ouidah might seem exceptional, or at best similar to other places where multiple European trading lodges were confined into a controlled space such as for instance, Surat in Gujarat. However, even in regions where European appeared to have a higher degree of control over their settlements as was the case in Pondicherry, the asymmetrical relationship with rulers coupled with a weak military position led to a form of common front. The threat of a blockade of Madras by the Mughal general Da'ud Khan Panni in 1702 led the English governor of Madras to on the support of the French and Danish agents on the Coromandel Coast against the Mughals.[20] While the French director was in favour of such a coalition, it never materialised because the French were not in a position to oppose the Mughal general. The attempt to play on the solidarity of Europeans demonstrates the weak position not only of the French but also of the English in the early eighteenth century. In sum these inter-group connections were related to the situation of vulnerability of the actors which is an important characteristic of the 'commercial cosmopolitan'.

Demonstrating the need for different European agents to support each other deconstructs the tendency to study one specific European state and thereby overestimate its power. However, framing the local power dynamics exclusively in terms of Indian or African rulers against an allegedly united European front also runs the risk of opposing two homogenic sides. As shown in the opening quote, the 'solidarity' between the English and the French company could also be provoked by the Dutch threat. The letter reveals different power relations overseas than on the European continent, not only in reaction to Indian rulers but also among European actors. This is worth noting as it nuances the simplistic opposition between Indian sovereigns on the one side and all Europeans on the other.

European power relations

Coromandel Coast

In the Indian Ocean and on the west coast of Africa, power relations among Europeans had local specificities and were no projection of the power dynamics in Europe. When the French East India Company settled permanently in Pondicherry in the early 1670s, the Dutch East India Company (VOC), which had gained power over the course of the seventeenth century, was slowly declining in India.[21] While the English East India Company's position in the region increasingly strengthened at the end of the seventeenth and early eighteenth century. The activities of the French East India Company in Pondicherry (1674–1719) coincide with the height of the competition between the Dutch and English companies on the Indian subcontinent. Aside from the strong presence of these European companies, Danish and Portuguese actors played a part in the power dynamics.

The French were no major actor in the Asian context and in order to keep their commercial foothold in India, they attempted to navigate the transition in power relations among Europeans in the region. Particularly after the conquest of Pondicherry by the VOC in 1693 until 1699, the French were

186   *Elisabeth Heijmans*

aware of the vulnerability of their position. They indiscriminately tried to maintain good relations with other European powers on the Coromandel Coast. These attempts were most successful with the Danish governor of Tranquebar and the English governor of Madras with whom the French communicated regularly and exchanged services such as the transport of commodities and provisions.[22] While good relations with the Dutch were rarer, the French director negotiated with the Mughal authorities jointly with the Dutch on at least one occasion.[23] However, after the declaration of War of the Spanish Succession (1701–1713) in Europe opposing the English and Dutch to the French, communication with the Dutch stopped while it remained frequent with the English. This phenomenon is the sign of a discrepancy between European power dynamics in Europe and in Asia.

This discrepancy was stated explicitly by the French director of Pondicherry, François Martin at the early stage of the War of Spanish Succession. The English governor of Madras, Thomas Pitt, offered to protect French merchandise and some inhabitants against an attack of the Dutch Company, and Martin accepted. However, Martin felt the need to justify the contradictory choice of placing the Company's goods under the protection of their enemies in Europe. He explained to the directors in Paris that power relations in India were to be distinguished from Europe: while the English and the Dutch were formally allied in Europe, the English and the French were informally allied in India.[24] One of the most illustrative examples of the informal Anglo-French persisting during the War of Spanish Succession was the fact that the French director of Pondicherry, Pierre Dulivier, lent gunpowder to the English governor of Madras, Edward Harrison.[25] The French were clearly not afraid that this gunpowder would be used against them. Furthermore, during the same period Dulivier borrowed money from the Spanish governor of Manila but also the governor of Madras in the name of the French Company.[26] The trust between the two informally allied companies was nevertheless not blind, they kept an eye on each other's movements. The French director sent spies to both the English and Dutch settlements and the English governor sent multiple spies to Pondicherry to cross check information.[27] The alliance was based on a fragile balance of power and if signs appeared that one or the other would gain more power in the region the informal alliance was at stake.

The commercial cosmopolitanism of the French directors was based on interdependent relations with the English East India Company. While the English needed the French as allies to increase their power against the Dutch company, the French developed a strong dependency on the English company for the transport of goods between settlements in India. This dependency on English logistics made the French particularly vulnerable in negotiations. When the French took an English ship as prize in 1709, although it was a legitimate prize considering the war context in Europe and it was estimated to 40,000 *livres* which would have been welcome in the context of war and limited support from France, the director of Pondicherry of the time, Hébert and his council decided to return the prized ship to the English company.[28] The English governor had threatened to attack the only French ship left in Asia, but most effectively, he also warned the French director that he would simply keep 20,000 *livres* worth of goods it had been assigned to transport from Bengal to the Coromandel Coast on two of the English company boats. The French director was not in a position to negotiate with the English. The transport between Bengal, where an increasing quantity of commodities destined to France were coming from, and Pondicherry were at stake, not only this time but also any future transport until the Company would send new ships in Asia. To the directors in Paris, Hébert explained that the Mughal emperor would not suffer any breach of the neutrality among Europeans.

While the Mughal emperor was probably part of the reason, the decisive factor was the English threat to stop transporting goods and keeping the current French merchandise from Bengal. In contrast, a few years earlier, still during the war of Spanish succession, the director of Pondicherry had behaved quite differently with a Dutch ship made prize. In 1705, when a Dutch ship was captured by the French company, not only did the director of Pondicherry decide to keep the ship and its commodities but also to take members of the crew hostage. In an attempt to force a ceasefire on the Dutch on the whole Coromandel Coast, the French director imprisoned the Dutch commissary, Phoonsen, and made him sign a local truce. However, the truce was never recognised by the VOC and Phoonsen was fired. The VOC was not in the same interdependent relations that characterised the EIC and the French company, it still enjoyed a stronger position than the English and did not need to compromise with the French company. The fact that the French director nevertheless tried shows how European power relations in India were shaped by local and regional factors rather than European based priorities.

Bight of Benin

In the Bight of Benin, European power relations also shifted throughout the seventeenth and early eighteenth century. The Dutch West India Company (WIC) had increased its control over many Portuguese trading factories over the course of the seventeenth century and imposed a tax on Portuguese merchants trading in the region. However, by the last quarter of the century the WIC's presence started declining and in the beginning of the eighteenth century both Portuguese merchants from Brazil and the English Royal Africa Company (RAC) created in 1672 took on a more important role.[29] The RAC engaged in commerce with Portuguese traders bypassing the WIC tax.[30] When the French Asiento Company arrived in Ouidah in the early years of the eighteenth century, they increased the already competitive environment in the region to the dismay of the Dutch. The records of the WIC testify to the efforts of the Dutch to drive the French Asiento Company out

188   *Elisabeth Heijmans*

of the Bight of Benin in its early beginnings. Multiple resolutions were taken in Elmina to impede the French development in Ouidah, in 1704, Dutch envoys were sent to the Hueda King to convince him to expel the French out of Ouidah and, a year later, measures were taken to attempt to decrease the French influence on the slave trade without real success.[31]

Despite the intense competition on the Bight of Benin, Europeans in Ouidah itself maintained good relations, willingly or not. In the 1730s, the French director offered presents such as wine from Bordeaux to the two other European representatives in Ouidah: the English and the Portuguese.[32] The good relations between the French directors and their competitors appear limited to the very specific context of Ouidah and the presence of multiple European trading factory under the authority of the Hueda and later Dahomey kings. In the early 1740s, during the war of Austrian Succession (1740–1748) opposing the English and later the Dutch to the French, the French director of Ouidah visited the English governor of Cape Coast Castle and the Dutch governor of Elmina and reported tensions with the English governor to the directors in Paris.[33] While, it the cause of these tensions might seem obvious considering the conflict opposing the two kingdoms, the animosity of the English was triggered by the context of local power relations between the English and the French. The French company had attempted to create a new trading post in Anamabo on the 'Gold Coast' near an English factory, coming thereby in direct competition with the increasing presence of the English in the region. Compared with their situation in Ouidah, the English were in a much stronger position on the 'Gold Coast' and had therefore no need to cooperate with the French whose presence there was very limited.

In contrast, relations with the Dutch in Elmina evolved positively for the French director during the first half of the eighteenth century.[34] The drastic drop in French ships coming to the Bight of Benin in 1746–1748 led the French director to instruct directors in Paris to send commodities and supplies through the Dutch governor of Elmina who had already showed his good will by delivering letters to the French in Ouidah.[35] Alternatively, the Parisian directors could send the supplies to the Netherlands were they would be loaded on a Dutch ship and secretly delivered to the director in Ouidah.[36]

By far the most used communication and supply network was the Portuguese channel through Brazil. The commercial connection with Bahia dos Santos constituted an important part of the European trade in the Bight of Benin.[37] It was based on the high African demand in Ouidah for a specific tobacco produced in Bahia.[38] Additionally voyages between Ouidah and Bahia were much more frequent than with Europe, more or less every three months according to the director. Aside from engaging in slave trade for their own 'nation', the different European representatives in Ouidah increasingly tried to become intermediaries between Portuguese merchants from Bahia and their tobacco on the one hand, and the slave trading routes in Ouidah.[39] During the War of Austrian Succession, Portuguese merchants from Brazil constituted therefore an important channel for medical and food supply for the French in Ouidah and relations with Portuguese traders and the Vice Roy of Brazil were paramount for their survival.[40] When in 1743, the Dahomean king imprisoned the Portuguese director in Ouidah for siding with his enemies, the French negotiated to save his life successfully.[41] The help offered by the French to the Portuguese director in Ouidah should be placed in this regional power and commercial dynamics. Indeed, the difficult negotiation was not exclusively based on the necessity to create a united front mentioned above and, the French director stated explicitly that this successful negotiation would ensure the much-needed support of Portuguese authorities and merchants from Brazil for commercial and survival purposes.[42]

Beside their connections with other European governors and representatives on the Coromandel Coast and in the Bight of Benin, another way for French directors to access Dutch and English support for communication, supplies and loans despite European wars were Huguenots merchants. The French East India Company for instance accessed English trading channels through the Huguenot merchant Chardin based in Madras who enabled the sale of French laces in Manila and corals in China on the company's behalf.[43] In 1712, towards the end of the War of Spanish succession, when the director of Pondicherry had exhausted all possibilities of credit he turned to the widow of Chardin for a loan.[44] In Ouidah, by the end of the war of Austrian Succession, the director sent multiple letters via Dutch ship to the address of the Huguenot firm Testas and Son in Amsterdam.[45] Through its connections to the French directors in Paris and its access to Dutch shipping, the Testas and Son firm was an important intermediary between the directors in Paris and the factory of Ouidah.

European governors and representatives on the Coromandel Coast and in the Bight of Benin did not form a homogenous group. When and who the French directors managed to build good relations depended on the stage of expansion and relations of interdependence. The commercial cosmopolitanism that linked different European governors to the French directors was thereby not only related to commercial gain but was imbedded in local power dynamics among Europeans distinct from the context of conflict in Europe. French directors developed ties across imperial boundaries out of vulnerability and their partnerships with other Europeans was based on a specific power balance. If that balance changed the agreements between companies were at risk.

Private trading inter-group connections

Private trade was widespread among French employees in Ouidah and Pondicherry. Although private activities were officially illegal, they were to a certain extend tolerated.[46] Company servants understood early on that

190   *Elisabeth Heijmans*

chances of personal profit lay in the local and regional trading connections and implied crossing imperial and cultural boundaries. While cooperation between European companies was meant to support French expansion and the companies' commerce, it was not disconnected from private trade interests. As seen in the introduction, the English governor Elihu Yale had offered multiple times to Martin to protect his wife and his employees. Martin suspected the real motivations of the English governor were not genuine help but the protection of his ships and his private trade. Indeed, the English governor was deeply engaged in private trade, as most of his colleagues in the EIC.[47] English Company servants strove for good relations with the French not only to develop the English East India Company's trade, but also to protect their own investments and wealth.

Private trade connections were less bounded to local power dynamics with local rulers and other Europeans but official good relations nevertheless facilitated the creation and maintenance of private trade connections across imperial boundaries. Martin for instance had personal contacts with a Portuguese administrator of the *Estado da Índia*, Manuel de Sousa de Meneses (in office from 1681–1715) that were likely to involve private trade.[48] Close cooperation between the English and the French companies also created opportunities for the private trade of company servants. In 1709, the former director of Pondicherry, Dulivier, invested in a partnership with the governor of Madras and the director of Pondicherry, Hébert.[49] An English ship would pass by Pondicherry to sail to China and the South Sea with half of its crew provided by the English and the other half by the French Company and, both English and French passports.[50] Since the EIC had allowed private trade for its servants who developed a local commercial network with Indian merchants,[51] partnerships with English company servants enabled French directors to indirectly integrate country trade routes they would otherwise not have access to.

In Ouidah, close contacts with other European representatives in Ouidah itself and in the Bight of Benin also facilitated private trade. In 1721, the director of Ouidah had a private trading partnership with Portuguese and Euro-African traders in Savi (the capital of the Hueda Kingdom) and in Jakin (in the neighbouring kingdom of Allada).[52] His partners enabled him to integrate slave trading routes while he traded enslaved Africans to Portuguese merchants from Brazil. Good relations with the Portuguese from Brazil had a double aim: solidarity in an environment that could be difficult to navigate and personal enrichment for the director. Private trade was not exclusively for directors as, for instance, in 1728, the priest of the French fort and two employees engaged in private trade of gold and enslaved Africans.[53] They were acting in partnership with members of the crew of the French ship *Le Mars* of Marseille, the Dutch factor in Jakin and the English governor in Ouidah.[54] Just like in Pondicherry, private trade connections were tied to the state relationships among Europeans in Ouidah and the Dutch in the Bight of Benin.

French directors used the good relations they maintained with other European representatives in both regions to develop private trading connections. Because private trade connections of French company servants lacked formal mechanisms to avoid cheating, they relied on already proven good will and exchange of services. While private trading partnership were not necessarily tied to local power dynamics and could have theoretically crossed more cultural and national boundaries, private connections of the French company servants followed the context of local alliances and competition in India and on the west coast of Africa. Cross-cultural connections of the French directors being limited they used local formal and informal alliances with other Europeans to integrate local trading routes they had not been able to access directly.

Conclusion

Connections of French directors in Pondicherry and Ouidah were geared mostly towards their nearby European counterparts. While it is certain that directors had important cross-cultural connections beyond those with Indian and African sovereigns and their designated brokers, the archive available does not allow us to investigate these relationships. The analysis was therefore limited to a fragment of the directors' commercial cosmopolitanism: their connections with other European commercial partners. Trans-imperial commercial partnerships and exchanges of services in the name of the French company followed local power relations in two ways. Firstly, it was based on the relative political and commercial weakness of some European, among which the French, towards local rulers on the Coromandel Coast and in the Bight of Benin. This meant in practice a circumstantial cooperation among European representatives based on the vulnerability of their positions with Africans and Indians rather than a genuine solidarity. Secondly, good relations and commercial exchanges took place along the lines Europeans power dynamics in both regions and these dynamics were distinct from the European context. The close relations between the English governors of Madras and the French directors of Pondicherry continued despite the war opposing the two countries while cooperation with the Dutch was unreachable despite some attempts. In the Bight of Benin, a distinction existed between European relations in Ouidah itself where local rulers impacted greatly the necessity to 'unite' and the larger Guinea Coast where relations with the growing English power was proven more difficult than with the Dutch.

In theory, illegal private trade connections of directors were less tied to local power dynamics, in practice however these private contacts followed already existing cooperative relations between the companies. On the Coromandel Coast, illegal private trading activities of French directors mostly involved the English governor of Madras with whom they maintained good relations throughout the early eighteenth century. In Ouidah,

192 *Elisabeth Heijmans*

illegal private trade partnerships involved mostly the Portuguese and the connection to Brazil but also the English and the Dutch. Existing good relations among European representatives generated opportunities and trust for private trade relations. The two were intertwined which meant that private trade practices also affected the incentives for exchanges of services and local power relations indirectly impacted private trade partnerships in the early years of the French expansion.

In the course of the eighteenth century, power relations with local rulers and among Europeans in the Bight of Benin and on the Coromandel Coast evolved. The French East India Company grew stronger in India and came to be perceived as a competitor to the EIC in the region. French directors took advantage of the fragmentation of Mughal power and the legalization of private trade in Asia for French company servants to increase their territorial ambitions. The French director failed to negotiate a local truce with the English governor during the Seven Years War (1756–1763) and conflicts between the two companies in India could not be avoided.[55] Interestingly, however, private trade partnerships with the English company servants continued. A change in the power relations could affect cooperation but it did not necessarily stop the existing private trade relations. With regards to the VOC, the economic power of the Dutch in the Indian Ocean decreased during the eighteenth century and was paralleled with an increase in private trade partnerships with French company servants. More importantly, as shown by Catherine Manning, private trade partnerships of the French after 1719 involved many Indian merchants.[56] In Ouidah, the main evolution in power relations during the second half of the eighteenth century was the increase of presence and political and economic power of the Portuguese community from Brazil strengthening the already important connection to Brazil. Private trade of French company employees was legalised after 1767 and private trade connections French directors unsurprisingly included Portuguese from Brazil, Euro-African and African merchants.[57]

Throughout the eighteenth century, commercial cosmopolitanism of French directors remained affected by local power relations however, the first decades of their presence in Pondicherry and Ouidah highlight the vulnerability of their position locally. It shows how their inter-group connections were limited, not only to Europeans but to a specific group of European partners according to evolving local power dynamics. Connections across imperial boundaries, even if they involve representatives of different European states can hardly be considered bridging different commercial cultures. Nevertheless, trans-imperial commercial partnerships gave French directors access to otherwise unreachable cross-cultural trading connections. While a comparative research on personal commercial connections of French company servants over the course of the long eighteenth century is still lacking, the "quasi-cosmopolitanism" of French directors appears to be symptomatic of the early phase of expansion.

Notes

1 This article has been written as part of the ERC-2012-StG-312657-FIGHT project.

2 François Martin, *Mémoires de François Martin, fondateur de Pondichéry (1665–1696)* (Paris: Société d'éditions géographiques, maritimes et coloniales, 1931), 3: 48.

3 Philip D. Curtin, *Cross-Cultural Trade in World History* (Cambridge: Cambridge University Press, 1984) and Francesca Trivellato, Leor Halevi, and Catia Antunes, eds., *Religion and Trade: Cross-Cultural Exchanges in World History, 1000–1900* (Oxford, New York: Oxford University Press, 2014).

4 Francesca Trivellato, *The Familiarity of Strangers: The Sephardic Diaspora, Livorno, and Cross-Cultural Trade in the Early Modern Period,* Reprint edition (New Haven, Conn.; London: Yale University Press, 2012), 226 and Peter Matthias, 'Risk, Credit and Kinship', in *The Early Modern Atlantic Economy*, ed. John J. McCusker and Kenneth O. Morgan (Cambridge: Cambridge University Press, 2000), 29.

5 Abbé Raynal, *Histoire philosophique et politique des établissemens et du commerce des Européens dans les deux Indes* (Amsterdam, 1770).

6 For more information on other political and commercial inter-group relations see Elisabeth Heijmans, *The Agency of Empire: Connections and Strategies in French Overseas Expansion (1686–1746)* (Leiden-Boston, 2020).

7 John F. Richards, *The Mughal Empire*, The New Cambridge History of India. 1, *The Mughals and Their Contemporaries;* 5 (Cambridge: Cambridge University Press, 1993), 240.

8 Radhika Seshan, *Trade and Politics on the Coromandel Coast: Seventeenth and Early Eighteenth Centuries* (Delhi: Primus Books, 2012), 8.

9 For more information on gift giving in Pondicherry and Ouidah see, Heijmans, *The Agency of Empire*, 104-140.

10 Archives nationales d'Outre-mer [Hereafter ANOM] C2 69 f.152, letter of Dulivier, 26 February 1715 and Niccolao Manucci, *Storia Do Mogor, or, Mogul India, 1653–1708*, trans. William Irvine (Calcutta: Indian Editions, 1965), 3: 375.

11 Robin Law, *The Slave Coast of West Africa, 1550–1750: The Impact of the Atlantic Slave Trade on an African Society* (Oxford: Oxford University Press, 1991), 231.

12 The region was a major slave trading hub in at the close of the seventeenth and eighteenth centuries. Estimates based on the Trans-Atlantic Slave Trade Database show that between 1700 and 1750 around 580 572 enslaved Africans were taken from the Bight of Benin on a total of 2 229 European ships. See www. slavevoyages.org.

13 Kwame Yeboah Daaku, *Trade and Politics on the Gold Coast, 1600–1720: A Study of the African Reaction to European Trade* (Oxford: Clarendon Press, 1970), 51.

14 Law, *The Slave Coast of West Africa, 1550–1750*, 206–7.

15 Reference to the treaty in Dutch archives date it from 1703 in HaNA WIC 484 f°230: Brief W. DE LA PALMA aan bewindhebbers, 10 October 1703. The renewed version of the treaty is given in Jean-Baptiste Labat, *Voyage du chevalier Desmarchais en Guinée et isles voisines et a Cayenne. Fait en 1725, 1726 et 1727* (Paris, 1730), 29–30.

16 ANOM C2 68 f.265, letter of Hébert, 12 February 1709 and V.G. Hatalkar, *Relations between the French and the Marathas (1668–1815)* (Bombay: T.V. Chidambaran Register University of Bombay, 1958), 16.

17 William Snelgrave, *A New Account of Some Parts of Guinea and the Slave-Trade* (London, 1734), 118.

194   *Elisabeth Heijmans*

18 Arquivo Público da Bahia [hereafter APB] 23 f°90, letter Vice Roy of Brazil to Lisbon, 30 July 1728. Cited in Pierre Verger, *Flux et reflux de la traite des nègres: entre le golfe de Bénin et Bahia de Todos os Santos du XVIIe au XIXe siècle* (Paris-Den Haag: Mouton, 1968), 146.
19 ANOM C6 25, letter of Levet, 26 August 1733.
20 ANOM C2 66 f.155, diary of Martin, Februray-March 1702.
21 Chris Nierstrasz, *In the Shadow of the Company: The VOC (Dutch East India Company) and Its Servants in the Period of Its Decline (1740–1796)* (Leiden: Brill, 2012), 73–77; Emily Erikson, *Between Monopoly and Free Trade: The English East India Company 1600–1757* (Princeton, NJ: Princeton University Press, 2016), 14.
22 ANOM C2 63 f. 56, letter of Deltor, 7 April 1686; ANOM C2 66 f.33, diary of Martin, August-September 1701 and C2 66 f.39, diary of Martin, November 1701ANOM C2 65 f. 33, letter of Martin and Chalonge, 14 September 1699 and Martin, *Mémoires de François Martin*, 3: 321.
23 Indian Office Records [Hereafter IOR] G/19/35 f. 32, Public Proceedings Fort Madras, from fort St David to Madras, 14 March 1702/3 (old calendar).
24 ANOM C2 67 f.10, letter of Martin, 15 February 1703.
25 IOR/P/ 239/ 85 f.190 (1708–1709) Public Proceedings Fort Madras and Council meeting minute, 19 November 1713 in *Procès-verbaux des délibérations du Conseil Souverain de Pondichéry* (Pondichéry: Société de l'Histoire de l'Inde Française, 1913), 128.
26 Council meeting minute, 19 June 1708 in *Procès-verbaux des délibérations*, 39–40.
27 ANOM C2 66 f.39, diary of Martin, November 1701; IOR/G/19/35 (1703–1704) f° 138 letter from fort David to Madras, 9 November 1703.
28 ANOM C2 68 f.304, letter of Hébert, 12 February 1709.
29 Roquinaldo Ferreira, "From Brazil to West Africa: Dutch Portuguese Rivalry, Gold Smuggling, and African Politics in the Bight of Benin," in *The Legacy of Dutch Brazil*, ed. Michiel Van Groesen (Cambridge: Cambridge University Press, 2014), 82; Henk den Heijer, *Goud, ivoor en slaven: scheepvaart en handel van de Tweede Westindische Compagnie op Afrika, 1674–1740* (Zutphen: Walburg Pers, 1997), 194.
30 Heijer, *Goud, ivoor en slaven*, 168–69.
31 Nationaal Archief [Hereafter HaNA] NBKG 1, Resolutie, 3 October 1704 and HaNA NBKG 1; NBKG 6; NBKG 70 no. 6; Resolutie, 4 February 1705.
32 ANOM C6 25, letter of Du Bellay, 21 November 1733 and 17 January 1734.
33 ANOM C6 25, letter of Levet 14 June 1743.
34 Numbers are from the transatlantic Slave Trade Database. ANOM C6 25, letter of Levet, 13 octobre 1746.
35 ANOM C6 25, letter of Levet 13 October 1746.
36 Archives nationales de la marine [Hereafter AN/MAR] B/3/439, Council of the Navy, 11 September 1745.
37 See Verger, *Flux et reflux de la traite des nègres*.
38 Verger, 28–29.
39 This was the case of the director Bouchel in ANOM COL E 140, Dubor: *Mémoire* to the Council of the Navy, 1721.
40 ANOM C6 25, letter of Levet, 13 October 1746.
41 ANOM C6 25, letter of Levet, 14 June 1743.
42 ANOM C6 25, letter of Levet, between August 1743 and January 1744.
43 ANOM C2 66 f.9, letter from Martin, 22 February 1701.
44 Council meeting minute, 23 February 1712: "*Ne voulant point avoir affaire à la compagnie*" in *Procès-verbaux des délibérations*, 109.

Quasi-cosmopolitanism 195

45 ANOM C6 25, letters of Levet, 25 February 1744; 12 October 1746 and 13 October 1746.
46 Private trade of employees in India was legalised in 1719 and 1767 for Ouidah.Catherine Manning, *Fortunes à faire: The French In Asian Trade, 1719-48* (Aldershot: Variorum, 1996); Simone Berbain, *Études sur la traite des Noirs au golfe de Guinée. Le comptoir français de Juda au XVIIIe siècle* (Paris: Larose, 1942).
47 Søren Mentz, *The English Gentleman Merchant at Work: Madras and the City of London 1660–1740* (Copenhagen: Museum Tusculanum Press, University of Copenhagen, 2005), 224.
48 Souza, "Portuguese Colonial Administrators and Inter-Asian Maritime Trade," 39.
49 ANOM C2 68 f.311–312, letter of Hébert, 12 February 1709.
50 NL-HaNA 1.04.02. inv. no. 8373 Coromandel 1 208–216, account given to Johanens van Steelant, director general of the Coromandel Coast and gouverneur of Nagapattinam, 1 July 1709.
51 Mentz, *The English Gentleman Merchant at Work*, 10.
52 ANOM E 140, personnel file of Dubord: Mémoire to the navy council, 1721.
53 ANOM C6 25, Dupetitval "Affaire du Vaisseau le Mars de Marseille", 1728 and Berbain, *Études sur la traite des Noirs*, 65.
54 ANOM C6 25, Lettre de Dayrie (Jakin), 12 August 1728.
55 Watson, *Foundation for Empire*, 152.
56 Catherine Manning, *Fortunes a faire : the French in Asian trade, 1719-48* (Alderschot, 1996).
57 For example see ANOM C6 25, *Interrogatoire du nommé Joseph le Beau*, 8 September 1787.

11 Commercial Cosmopolitanism? The case of the firm De Bruijn & Cloots (Lisbon) in the eighteenth century

Cátia Antunes, Susana Münch Miranda, and João Paulo Salvado

Introduction

The Portuguese maritime expansion and consequent empire building is often perceived as the first moment in Early Modern globalization. One would intuitively expect Portugal and its empire then to continue at least actively participating in the globalization wave of the seventeenth and eighteenth centuries, albeit not necessarily at the forefront.[1] When looking at the outreach, outputs and geographical extent of the Portuguese empire, it can certainly be said to have been a global phenomenon, with that 'globality' also being reflected in the international participants involved in exploiting the empire and in redistributing products and rents across differentiated economic and social systems.

It is only, however, when zooming in on the business behaviour of foreign firms operating in Lisbon that we are forced to account for the deviances, asymmetries and resistances that came about with these firms' participation in the exploitation of Portuguese colonial business.[2] Although these firms were certainly participating in a globalized system of exchanges, the commercial system (as in the set of rules, including, but not exclusively, the state institutions and the Portuguese merchant community itself) in which they operated was far from global. On the contrary, as a commercial market place and while embodying the extreme trends of eighteenth-century globalization, Lisbon remained a localized system that resisted change.

This chapter uses eighteenth-century sources for Northern European merchant firms (mostly Dutch) established in Lisbon as a stepping stone for analysing how their mercantile knowledge and ways of conducting business adapted to the workings of the Lisbon market. It is in their capacity to adapt to and find solutions for challenges arising from operating in a system with a specific, albeit radically different, socio-economic logic from that of their place of origin that we will problematize and analyze the cosmopolitan nature of these firms and the cosmopolitan solutions they devised.

Cosmopolitanism and the world of trade

In 2006, Margaret Jacob defined cosmopolitanism as 'the ability to experience people of different nations, creeds and colours with pleasure, curiosity and interest, and not with suspicion, disdain, or simply a disinterest that could occasionally turn into loathing'.[3] This definition is partly rooted in the work by Karen O'Brien, who emphasized the connection between intellectuals participating in the Enlightenment and the development of a concept of cosmopolitan history.[4] Jacob, however, moved beyond O'Brien's framework by emphasizing the personal character of the cosmopolitans and their attitudes towards the outside world, rather than their role in a specific intellectual development that can be classified as cosmopolitan. In this sense, Jacob's work has deeply influenced the conceptualization of cosmopolitanism as being rooted in the transnationality of (multiple) exchanges.[5]

The idea, rather than well-defined concept, of cosmopolitanism has also been widely adopted by Early Modern historians interested in merchants, trading communities and commercial settings. Ashin Das Gupta, for example, introduced the environment in which merchants in the Indian Ocean operated in a cosmopolitan space, where cross-culturalism, transnationality, cooperation, but also competition and violence were all co-existing categories to be reckoned with by those seeking to be successful in trading in and around the Indian Ocean.[6] A similar opinion was voiced by Bernard Bailyn about the Atlantic. When considering the major themes surrounding the concept of Atlantic history, he made the case for the importance of 'Atlantic cosmopolitanism' as a key to understanding commercial and intellectual exchanges in the Atlantic basin.[7] Other historians have simultaneously classified specific ports as places where cosmopolitan merchant communities settled as essential elements of economic exchanges and intellectual progress.[8] Collectively, these works reflect Jean-Jacques Rosseau's impression of merchants who, he claimed, *'ne réside plus que dans quelques grandes âmes cosmopolites, qui franchissent les barrières imaginaires qui séparent les peuples, et qui, à l'exemple de l'être souverain qui les a créées, embrassent tout le genre humain dans leur bienveillance'.*[9]

Even, however, if there would appear to be a consensus that merchant cosmopolitanism existed and that its analysis is concomitant to the thoughts and actions of individuals and communities, few voices have questioned the role that a concept such as cosmopolitanism may play in explaining the success, placement and development of specific merchant firms, networks and communities, and the extent to which cosmopolitanism is used as a concept for translating knowledge transference, adaptability and hybridity of professional and economic behaviour.[10] This chapter looks at the firm De Bruijn & Cloots, a Dutch firm in Lisbon in the early eighteenth century, in order to examine the needs and utility of the concept of cosmopolitanism as applied to the study of Early Modern firms.

198 *Cátia Antunes et al.*

The Cloots: a Pan-European Enterprise

Willem de Bruijn and Paulo Cloots arrived in Lisbon from Amsterdam shortly after Christmas 1712 and, in the weeks that followed, went on to establish a business of their own.[11] Although they set up an autonomous trading house, all the indications suggest that their establishment in Lisbon was part of the strategy of the Amsterdam merchant banking firm Jean-Baptiste & Paulo Jacomo Cloots to extend its business operations to Portugal.

The rise of the Cloots family dates back to Paulo Cloots (1633–1705), a Catholic burgher, originally from Maastricht, who married Catherina de Pret, from a wealthy Antwerp family, in 1662. Among their offspring, Jean-Baptiste (1670–1747) and Paulo Jacomo (1672–1725) fared particularly well and managed to extend the family's economic and social rise. Their success as large-scale merchant bankers rested on their wide, international network of business partners and agents, encompassing connections in the 1710s to Hamburg, London, Antwerp, Paris, Nantes, Madrid, Cadiz, Genoa and Venice.[12] Their continuing good fortune in business marked their social ascension and was mirrored in Jean-Baptiste's decision to establish his residence on Herengracht, one of Amsterdam's noblest neighbourhoods.[13] His brother Paulo Jacomo moved to Antwerp in 1717 upon marrying his cousin, Jeanne de Pret. In this way, the Cloots family's ties to the De Prets deepened, with Paulo Jacomo becoming the brother-in-law of Jacomo de Pret, one of Antwerp's leading merchant bankers.[14] In 1719, Paulo Jacomo was made a baron as a sign of appreciation for the financial services he provided to Emperor Charles VI and later became one of the first investors in the Ostend Company, founded in 1722.[15] A third brother, Egidio Cloots, took up residence in Cadiz, probably in the early 1700s, thus extending the family's network to the Iberian Peninsula. Egidio played a significant role in handling the logistics of shipbuilding materials sent from Amsterdam during the years that Paulo Jacomo held the contract to supply the *Intendencia de Marina*.[16]

In the case of Lisbon, the family connections of this merchant banker firm were ensured by a nephew, Paulo Cloots, who arrived in the Portuguese capital at the age of twenty-two.[17] As he had not yet completed his training, he became De Bruijn's junior partner in Lisbon, with his uncles' blessings. Willem de Bruijn, in turn, was also born into a family of merchants in Amsterdam, probably in 1687.[18] Before moving to Lisbon, he had worked as a business clerk at the *comptoir* of the Cloots in Amsterdam.[19] While there, he not only acquired experience in trading, but also developed extended networks, which he later used in Lisbon to operate autonomously.

De Bruijn & Cloots and the Lisbon office

The branching-out of the Cloots family to Lisbon could hardly have been more timely. Owing to the discovery of Brazilian gold in the late 1690s, the Portuguese capital was by then developing into a leading port city, pushed by a thriving colonial market that paid in gold. Lisbon's rising importance in European and global trade also owed much to the city's status as the staple port of Portuguese colonial trade, a position dating back to 1649, when trade flows with the three major Brazilian ports (Bahia, Rio de Janeiro and Recife) were placed under a compulsory convoy system of protection.[20] Hence, for foreign merchants, establishing in Lisbon at this particular juncture entailed expectations of obtaining Brazilian gold in exchange for supplying foodstuffs and all sorts of manufactured goods that were in high demand in the colonial market. Like many other foreign merchants (English, Dutch, Italian, French and German) who settled in Lisbon in the early decades of the 1700s, De Bruijn and Cloots were also aiming to take advantage of the opportunities presented by the vitality of the Portuguese colonial trade and make use of the extensive European network of the Cloots' Amsterdam firm.[21]

Upon their arrival, De Bruijn and Cloots were immediately confronted with two problems. Firstly, they struggled to find suitable accommodation as Lisbon lacked proper merchant houses. Were it not for the welcoming support of the Dutch community and the opportunity to rent a room in one of the better established Dutch merchant houses in the city, they would have been homeless. Luckily, an additional opportunity presented itself as their landlord announced that he wanted to repatriate to the Netherlands, thus leaving them with a one-storey house where they could also accommodate their business operations. Secondly, they soon discovered that trade information was hard to come by in Lisbon as nowhere in the city were commodity brokers to be found, and payments in the market place were delayed, leading to slow turnover. Moreover, they regarded the local merchants as behaving like shopkeepers rather than businessmen.[22]

These first impressions of Lisbon as a market place in the first quarter of the eighteenth century are remarkable in many ways. We will address three specific topics in the local market that somehow shocked the newcomers; these are telling of the asymmetries and resistances provoked by commercial systems within a globalization process and that thus locked out the merchant cosmopolitanism inherent to these type of firms operating across multiple borders. These specific topics are the infrastructures of commerce (warehousing), human capital (skills, knowledge and merchant practices) and access to information (the quantity, quality and means of gathering information).

When Willem de Bruijn and Paulo Cloots settled in Lisbon, they inserted themselves into a commercial system whose main features had been defined as early as the sixteenth century. Trade with colonial offshoots in Asia or the

200   Cátia Antunes et al.

South Atlantic went through Lisbon, the staple port for colonial merchandise, and which, under a restriction dating back to the 1590s, was considered open exclusively to Portuguese subjects. Hence, foreign merchant communities in Lisbon were theoretically confined to the role of intermediaries in importing European goods and re-exporting domestic and colonial goods.[23] By the time De Bruijn and Cloots arrived, Lisbon was undergoing a period of rapid growth against the background of the Brazilian gold cycle and the accompanying rise in the volume and value of Portuguese colonial trade. By 1700, its 140,000 inhabitants were crowded into a restricted urban environment still marked by a strong medieval legacy. This was mirrored in high rental costs for housing, as experienced by De Bruijn and Cloots.[24] Throughout the early decades of the 1700s, continual waves of foreigners and immigrants flowed to the capital, thus increasing the pressure not only on housing, but also on the infrastructures of commerce. Warehouse facilities, mainly located on the riverside close to the customshouse, were insufficient and increasingly inadequate for accommodating the expansion of the *entrepôt* trade flowing through the harbour. Like many other foreign trading houses, De Bruijn and Cloots resolved the problem by converting their home into their *comptoir*. They did this, as early as January 1713, by turning their largest room into an office for storing petty goods, while transforming the ground floor into a stockroom for bulky commodities.[25]

The stimuli brought about by the spectacular growth in trade impacted on the Portuguese mercantile community operating in Lisbon, with the arrival of newcomers boosting the numbers of colonial traders throughout the early decades of the eighteenth century. Aside from low entry barriers, this expansion was attributable to the rising demand from the Brazilian market, which in turn attracted increasing numbers of players. This development denotes the role of private trade in the Portuguese commercial system, especially in the Atlantic. Indeed, within the legal framework set up by the monarchy, colonial commerce was carried out by merchants operating in free competition.[26] During the Brazilian gold cycle, exclusive access to an expanding colonial market provided Portuguese wholesalers with a range of new business opportunities. Not surprisingly, this reinforced their specialization in the colonial flows and their inclination to forego other activities such as shipping to Europe and the discounting of bills of exchange, which activities were then taken over by foreign merchants settled in Lisbon.[27] As a group, Portuguese Atlantic traders largely comprised individuals of humble origins, mostly immigrants from rural areas such as Portugal's north-western region, with subsequently low levels of literacy. Moreover, merchant training was poor, and this problem was further compounded by the group's high level of volatility and consequently very limited intergenerational transmission of skills. Indeed, trading houses extending further than one generation were very rare. And although increased competition prompted a few efforts to modernize education and training, the incentives for

Commercial Cosmopolitanism? 201

merchants to raise their profile were still low for reasons related to the protected environment within which they operated.[28]

In contrast to most Portuguese businessmen, De Bruijn and Cloots had undergone intensive training at the firm of Jean-Baptiste & Paulo Jacomo Cloots in Amsterdam and were skilled merchants. Given the Amsterdam firm's focus on international trade and finance, the two men were both proficient in foreign languages, including French and Portuguese.[29] They certainly also had mathematical knowledge and had gained expertise in the geography of markets, relative freight costs, standards of weights and measures in different countries, exchange rates of coins, the prices of a wide range of commodities, and in double-entry bookkeeping. These skills were mirrored in the way the firm recorded transactions and correspondence in the close to sixty books of accounts now held in the Portuguese National Archive. Far from being exceptional, the care De Bruijn and Cloots took in compiling these accounts is exemplary of eighteenth-century Dutch merchants' attitude towards their bookkeeping.[30]

As perhaps could be expected, these business skills reflected the unprecedented levels of sophistication that had been attained by the Dutch commercial and financial organization by the early seventeenth century. As Europe's primary commodity exchange market, Amsterdam had developed a large community of brokerage traders, whose business was to buy and sell ship cargos for various Dutch and foreign merchants; that is, to bring together buyers and sellers.[31] Eventually, these specialized brokerage houses also began advancing credit both to buyers and sellers, thus arranging for immediate financing of their transactions and allowing for a rapid turnover of cargos and returns, with resultant savings on interest charges. This contrasted with Lisbon's commercial and financial life, where Portuguese merchants concentrated on colonial trade circuits. This choice had implications for Lisbon's role as a hub for colonial goods, and in turn retarded the development of institutions such as a stock exchange for commodities and a banking system, while also hampering the emergence of brokerage trading houses.[32] Price information and actual transactions hinged on direct and personal contacts between buyers and sellers, and specifically between Portuguese and foreign trading houses, especially for the Atlantic trade. The only exception regarded access to Asian commodities, which were mediated by the House of India (*Casa da Índia*), the Crown's agency, and which also distributed monopolized goods such as Brazilian dyewood. Slower turnover of stocks were the inevitable outcome of this commercial organization, and this resulted in higher interest and warehousing charges.

De Bruijn and Cloots deployed various tactics as a means to counteract these higher costs of doing business in Lisbon. Although engaging in wholesale trade may have been their major goal, they ended up carrying out various activities, ranging from shipping to financial services and tax farming. As wholesalers, they participated in importing European goods and re-exporting domestic and colonial goods, handling a wide range of

202 *Cátia Antunes et al.*

commodities such as wool, olive oil, sugar, tobacco, tea, grain, naval fittings (sailcloth and ropes), linen and woollen fabrics. As was usual in the eighteenth century, they traded not only for their own account, but also engaged in commission business for a wide network of business partners. By the 1720s, their international network extended to Archangel, Hamburg, London, Bristol, Amsterdam, Antwerp, Paris, Nantes, La Rochelle, Bayonne, Lyon, Bilbao, Madrid, Badajoz, Seville, Cadiz, Turin, Genoa and Livorno. In the domestic market, meanwhile, they had dealings with merchants in Porto, the second largest city in Portugal, as well as in Beja, Elvas and Estremoz (in the southern province of Alentejo).

Their attention was also attracted by the thriving colonial market, as evidenced by their early efforts to establish contacts with well-connected Portuguese individuals able to broker business arrangements and facilitate contacts with the royal authorities. Indeed, as early as January 1714, they had an agent in the royal court who promised them access to the protected colonial markets.[33] Meanwhile they also reached out to Portuguese businessmen, through whom they could circumvent the laws excluding them from trading directly with Portuguese America or Asia. While exchanging European manufactures and intermediate goods (textiles, nautical fittings and gunpowder) for gold or tropical commodities was the major enticement for interloping the Brazilian market, in the case of trade with Asia De Bruijn and Cloots were looking for access to the tea supply markets, given that demand for tea in Northern Europe was rapidly increasing in the first two decades of the 1700s and far exceeded the quantities able to be supplied by the Dutch and English East India companies (VOC and EIC respectively).[34] Recognizing this trend, the firm made efforts to buy tea in the Lisbon market in the early days of their presence there, albeit with little success owing to the small quantities available and the low quality.[35] The high price this commodity fetched in the Amsterdam market entailed the promise of profit margins of 200 to 300 per cent on cargos of tea (green and black). This stood in sharp contrast to the Brazilian trade, where margins in the late eighteenth century hovered around twenty per cent.[36] However, operating in these two geographical areas posed different challenges, given the distinct rules and differing financial requirements associated with the specific patterns of trade.

To interlope the Portuguese Atlantic trade, De Bruijn and Cloots resorted to two types of agency. In the first of these, itinerant traders (*comissários volantes*) travelled back and forth in the Brazilian fleets, carrying mainly fabrics and haberdashery, which they dispatched as their own in the Lisbon customshouse, and bringing back trade earnings in the form of gold and colonial goods.[37] In the second type of agency, trading houses in Rio de Janeiro, Bahia and Recife worked as commissioning agents redistributing textiles, as well as commodities with a slower turnover (such as gunpowder, guns and pistols), in the colonial market in exchange for commission of three to four per cent.[38]

Commercial Cosmopolitanism? 203

Neither of these forms of agency, however, could be used to interlope the Portuguese Asian trade, not only because of the latter's stricter legal framework, but also because its specific trading pattern required higher levels of capital investment. In this case, entering into a partnership with a Portuguese businessman was paramount since only a Portuguese subject could request a licence (or passport) for a ship to navigate outside the *Carreira da Índia* (Cape Route) and to call on ports under Portuguese jurisdiction, whether in the South Atlantic, the Indian Ocean or the South China Sea.[39] Between 1715 and 1721, De Bruijn and Cloots organized two commercial voyages to Asia under the name of Manuel de Castro Guimarães, son of a Lisbon wholesale trader with well-established connections to the royal household and the household of Prince Francisco, the king's elder brother.[40] Navigating under Portuguese pavilion not only provided access to port cities under Portuguese rule, but also to those under the jurisdiction of the EIC and VOC.

The first voyage (1715–1719) called at Mozambique before setting sail for Madras and Calcutta, where ivory, slaves and gold were exchanged for tea, textiles and porcelain. During the inbound voyage, the ship called at Rio de Janeiro, where, after selling part of its cargo, it was confiscated by the local authorities, acting on a complaint that both the ship and its cargo belonged to foreigners. During the enquiries, however, Manuel de Castro Guimarães was able to produce papers to substantiate that he was the sole owner of the ship and cargo; as a result, the ship was allowed to return to Lisbon several months later.[41] While using a strawman was undoubtedly a way to circumvent the restrictions of the Portuguese commercial system, the strategy was not devoid of risks. Indeed, the Portuguese mercantile communities (both metropolitan and non-metropolitan) were well aware of these tactics deployed by foreigners and did not refrain from protesting whenever they felt their exclusive rights to have been infringed, as on this occasion. These protests then caused delays in turnover. And so while the ship eventually arrived in Lisbon in January 1719, with a cargo composed of green tea, pepper, porcelain and gold, the distribution of returns was a protracted process and remained uncompleted as late as 1727.[42]

Nevertheless, and despite these hindrances, the profits were high enough to justify investing in a second voyage, which took place between 1719 and 1721. On this occasion, De Bruijn and Cloots obtained permission through Manuel de Castro Guimarães for their ship to call at Macao, although the passport expressly forbade calling at any Portuguese ports in India, Brazil or Angola.[43] Information gathered to date on this second journey reveals that the capital invested in this voyage amounted to 86.4 million *réis*, which De Bruijn and Cloots raised through two partnerships: one for outfitting the ship (eleven investors) and another for the cargo (seventeen investors). Not surprisingly, almost fifty per cent of the shares in the first of these two partnerships were held by Dutch merchants (established in Lisbon and Amsterdam), followed by French, English and German businessmen. In the

204   Cátia Antunes et al.

partnership for the cargo, by contrast, the capital contributed by Dutch investors came only third, after Portuguese and English capital, with the remainder comprising contributions from German and French investors. When the ship anchored at Lisbon in October 1721, three quarters of her cargo was composed of black (bohea) and green tea, with porcelains, raw silk and drugs making up the rest, and the voyage was considered a success.[44]

Zooming out of the Lisbon market, it is hardly surprising that De Bruijn & Cloots decided to invest in imports of bohea tea, which was classified by the VOC and EIC as unmarketable in Europe and thus left unsold in the Canton market. This opportunity prompted private traders in the Southern Netherlands to invest in fitting out fleets to sail to China, where they bought up as much tea in Canton as possible. Two of the men behind this bold move were none other than Paulo Jacomo Cloots and Daniel de Bruijn, uncle and brother of Paulo Cloots and Willem de Bruijn of Lisbon respectively, and two of the main driving forces behind the chartering of the Ostend East India Company (1722), the main trade of which comprised massive imports of bohea tea into the European markets.[45] After this company had been established, and despite the success of their China voyage, De Bruijn and Cloots ceased organizing voyages to Asia. Shortly after the Ostend Company's charter was suspended in 1727, however, they revived their plans to interlope the Portuguese Asian trade. This time, they partnered with Rodrigo Sande de Vasconcelos, a wholesaler with long-standing connections to Macao and with whom they planned to establish a company for which they tried, albeit unsuccessfully, to obtain a charter that would guarantee them exclusivity in trading with that territory.[46]

De Bruijn & Cloots also successfully engaged in the business of issuing and discounting bills of exchange. Using both their network of agents and the parent firm's connections in Amsterdam, they took advantage of the opportunities presented by an expanding market economy, where demand for financial services was high. Against the background of expanding commercial ties between Portugal and Europe in the Atlantic and Asian trades, financial operations to fuel overseas trade were in high demand in the early 1700s, and De Bruijn & Cloots were in the best position to satisfy these demands. They cleared bills not only for Portuguese merchants, but also for other foreign trading houses with businesses in Lisbon.

Ten years after emerging on the Lisbon business scene, De Bruijn & Cloots extended their activities to tax farming. By then, they were already running a successful business and had well-established connections within the Dutch merchant colony, as mirrored in Paulo Cloots' marriage to Maria Luísa van Zeller (1705–1777), a daughter of Jan van Zeller, the most prominent and influential Dutch businessman in Lisbon.[47] On 16 November 1721, De Bruijn & Cloots, together with Arnaldo van Zeller, Paulo's brother-in law, were granted the Portuguese tobacco monopoly, for which they agreed to pay an exorbitant annual fee of 720 million *réis* in return for

Commercial Cosmopolitanism? 205

the exclusive right to process and sell Brazilian tobacco in the domestic market (including the Atlantic islands of Azores and Madeira) for a three-year period from 1722 to 1724. As stated in a letter sent to Amsterdam, this step was taken after careful consideration and on the assumption that this business would enable them to amass a substantial fortune. Indeed, they hoped that operating as tax farmers would enable them to 'repatriate blessed'.[48] In addition to expecting the rents extracted to far exceed the annual fee and the operating costs, the Dutch merchants also assumed they would be able to benefit from other sources of profit derived from privileges usually granted to the tobacco monopoly holders. These comprised firstly the exclusive right to supply the Spanish tobacco monopoly and secondly, and more importantly, the prerogative to dispatch an annual ship to Brazil outside the convoy system. This prerogative represented an opportunity for De Bruijn & Cloots to openly participate in the Brazilian trade, while also entailing expectations of better prices, owing to the lack of competition, both when selling domestic and European commodities and buying colonial goods.

De Bruijn, Cloots and Van Zeller held the Portuguese tobacco monopoly between 1722 and 1727, having been granted a second period of three years in 1724. During this period they put in place an innovative business plan that reflected their integrated view of the tobacco monopoly and their goal to fully exploit its interconnected businesses. On the one hand, they became large-scale importers of tobacco, aiming to supply this raw material not only to the domestic monopoly, but also to the European markets. On the other hand, they expanded their participation in Brazilian colonial trade by way of the annual ship that they were allowed to dispatch outside the convoy system. As a result, the firm supplied seventy per cent of the raw material processed for the Portuguese domestic market between 1722 and 1727, while also re-exporting 3.1 million pounds of tobacco to other European markets. However, profits derived from these activities may have fallen short of the partners' expectations because, firstly, their importing and exporting activities were affected by unfavourable market conditions that impacted both on producer prices, which experienced an upward trend until the 1730s, and on wholesale prices in the European markets. Secondly, exploiting the annual licensed ship to Brazil proved to be more difficult than they had anticipated. Despite the firm's efforts to obtain information about market conditions in Salvador (Brazil), where tobacco was procured, matching supply to demand was difficult and, more often than not, the market was overstocked by the time the ship arrived back in Lisbon shortly after the annual fleet. As a result, turnover was slow, while opportunistic behaviour from agents based in Salvador brought added risks.[49]

While their exploiting of the tobacco-related businesses may have fallen short of De Bruijn & Cloots' expectations, it was the tobacco monopoly itself that caused the firm's downfall. By the end of the second tax farm in 1727, the Dutch partners' outstanding debts to the royal treasury amounted

206   *Cátia Antunes et al.*

to over 140 million *réis*, an exorbitant amount for any business. Despite making efforts to repay their debts to the state and to fellow merchants, Willem de Bruijn and Paulo Cloots decided in 1741 to flee the country. Their failure lay largely in the financial losses incurred in the first tax farm, which were attributable to the decline in tobacco consumption that followed after a royal decree increased retail prices by twenty per cent a few months before their contract started. Although aware of this increase, De Bruijn, Cloots and Van Zeller underestimated the risks of operating the monopoly in an environment of higher retail prices and consequently offered a contract fee of an economically dangerous level, probably because they were confident that they could generate additional earnings from organizational innovations and from exploiting the interconnected businesses. However, the scale of their business model demanded high levels of investment and, although this aspect still needs to be further investigated, earnings from the Portuguese Atlantic trade may have been lower than they had anticipated. After the financial losses incurred under the first contract, and despite a better sales performance under the second contract, the partners faced liquidity problems and difficulties in raising short-term credit, especially as the second contract drew to a close.[50]

Integrating locals, cosmopolitans and global shakers: a conclusion

With the exception of the tobacco monopoly, De Bruijn & Cloots proved highly successful in adapting to a different commercial system. Not only did they make use of their parent firm's extensive international network, but they were also able to quickly build a new network in Lisbon, composed of Portuguese businessmen and influential individuals at the royal court. Their ability to pool capital and to supply European commodities to the ever-growing Brazilian market allowed them to reap rents from the Portuguese colonial business and thus to exploit asymmetries between distinct commercial systems.

In the eighteenth century, Amsterdam and Lisbon were commercial market places moving at different rhythms, in accordance with the diverse roles they played in the world trading system, and which in turn also impacted on the major features of their respective mercantile groups. Individualization and anonymity in business, professionalization and specialization were characteristics of the Dutch, a globalized mercantile group operating in a 'modern institutional setting'.[51] By contrast, the Portuguese merchants were characterized by personalized business and a high level of fluidity. It is questionable whether the interplay between these two models of doing business in Lisbon resulted in significant transference of merchant knowledge. Keen to cling to their skills and to use them to obtain competitive advantages, it is doubtful whether the Dutch were willing to pass on the way they conducted business to people outside their community. In turn, the incentives for them to innovate and adopt new business

Commercial Cosmopolitanism?   207

techniques from the Portuguese remained low because of the limited competition they faced in the protected environment offered by colonial trade which remained a central feature of the Portuguese commercial system until 1810. Leading members of the group were aware of the low educational profile of the majority of people in this commercial system, and in the mid-1700s this began to be perceived as a problem by the central authorities, too. As part of a broader set of educational reforms, it was consequently decided in 1759 to establish a Portuguese School of Commerce to provide commercial training for merchants, clerks and accountants. This represented a singular case of state intervention in commercial education.[52]

Three elements stand out in the case of De Bruijn & Cloots and are indicative of the firm's cosmopolitan behaviour. Firstly, its capacity to overcome the systemic limitations imposed by institutional and mercantile practices in the Lisbon market. Overcoming these limitations meant dealing with personal frictions and investing in better information circuits, besides those promoted by foreign brokerage, in search for practices overlapping with those of their parent and sister firms in Amsterdam, Antwerp and Cadiz. Secondly, overcoming the systemic limitations opened the door to adapting mercantile practices, to mechanisms for circulating capital and information, and to understanding the regimes for obtaining access to standing institutions (such as that of the fiscal contracts). Thirdly, the firm's ability to adapt resulted into two different ways of working the system: one that was a hybrid and involved techniques and frameworks learned within the Amsterdam market, combined with the opportunities offered in the Lisbon environment, and another that can be seen as a 'commonality of best practices', in which functioning within the Lusophone world nexus became accessible. Rather than having cosmopolitan ideas, De Bruijn and Cloots behaved as cosmopolitans who, instead of *thinking about* the world, *adapted to* it magisterially.

Notes

1 Francisco Bethencourt and Diogo Ramada Curto, eds. *Portuguese Oceanic Expansion, 1400–1800* (Cambridge: Cambridge University Press, 2007).
2 Here we follow the definition of firms used by business historians and based on the concept of ownership structure. For the Early Modern period, this definition comprises family firms, partnerships and corporations. See Andrea Colli and Paloma Fernández, 'Business History and Family Firms', in *Sage Handbook of Family Business,* eds. Leif Melin, Mattias Nordqvist and Pramodita Sharma (London: Sage, 2013), 269–92; Andrea Colli and Mary Rose, 'Family Business' in *The Oxford Handbook of Business History,* eds. Geoffrey G. Jones and Jonathan Zeitlin (Oxford: Oxford University Press, 2007), 194–217.
3 Margaret C. Jacob, *Strangers Nowhere in the World: The Rise of Cosmopolitanism in Early Modern Europe* (Philadelphia: University of Pennsylvania Press, 2006), 1.
4 Karen O'Brien, *Narratives of Enlightenment: Cosmopolitan History from Voltaire to Gibbon* (Cambridge: Cambridge University Press, 1997).

208 *Cátia Antunes et al.*

5 Jeroen Duindam, Tülay Artan and Metin Kunt, eds., *Royal Courts in Dynastic States and Empires. A Global Perspective* (Leiden: Brill, 2011).

6 Ashin Das Gupta, *The World of the Indian Ocean Merchant, 1500–1800* (New Delhi: Oxford University Press, 2002).

7 Bernard Bailyn, "Introduction: Reflections on Some Major Themes", in *Soundings in Atlantic History: Latent Structures and Intellectual Currents, 1500–1830,* eds. Bernard Bailyn and Patricia L. Denault (Cambridge MA: Harvard University Press, 2009), 31.

8 Benjamin Schmidt, *Innocence Abroad. The Dutch Imagination and the New World, 1570–1670* (Cambridge: Cambridge University Press, 2001), 7; Jos Gommans, "South Asian Cosmopolitanism and the Dutch Microcosms in Seventeenth-Century Cochin (Kerala)," in *Exploring the Dutch Empire: Agents, Networks and Institutions, 1600–1800,* eds. Cátia Antunes and Jos Gommans (London, Bloomsbury, 2015), 3–27.

9 'only still resides in a few great cosmopolitan souls, who overcome the imaginary barriers that separate peoples and who, following the example of the sovereign being who created them, embrace the entire human race in their benevolence'. Jean-Jacques Rousseau, "Discours sur l'origine et les fondements de l'inégalité parmi les hommes," in *Œuvres Complètes de J.J. Rousseau* (Paris 1790), VII, 147.

10 Daniel Swetschinski, *Reluctant Cosmopolitans: The Portuguese Jews of Seventeenth-Century Amsterdam* (New York: Littman Library of Jewish Civilization, 2004); Michael N. Pearson, *Cosmopolitanism in Indian Ocean Port Cities: A Historical Perspective and Contradiction* (New Delhi: Noorish Publishers, 2012). Cátia Antunes, "On Cosmopolitanism and Cross-Culturalism: An Enquiry into the Business Practices and Multiple Identities of the Portuguese Merchants of Amsterdam," in *Cosmopolitanism in the Portuguese-speaking World,* ed. Francisco Bethencourt (Leiden: Brill, 2017), 24–39.

11 This firm's business archive is currently held in the Portuguese National Archive of Torre do Tombo. It comprises merchant accounting books, correspondence and diaries covering the period from 1713 to 1741. In-depth research on this archive is currently underway.

12 On this merchant banker family, see I. de Stein d'Altenstein, *Annuaire de la noblesse de Belgique,* vol. 16 (Brussels, 1862): 278–82 and François Labbe, *Anacharsis Cloots, Le Prussien Francophile: Un Philosophe au service de la Révolution Française et Universelle* (Paris: Editions l'Harmattan, 1999), 29–30.

13 For Herengracht, see Cornelia Fanslau, "'Wohl dem der's sehen kann'. Private Amsterdam Art Collections, 1770–1860", in *Luxury in the Low Countries: Miscellaneous Reflections on Netherlandish Material Culture, 1500 to the Present,* ed. Rengenier C. Rittersma (Brussels: Pharo Publishing, 2010), 162–63.

14 On the De Prets, see Karel Degryse, *De Antwerpse Fortuinen: Kapitaalsaccumulatie, -investering en -rendement te Antwerpen in de 18de Eeuw* (Antwerp: Genootschap voor Antwerpse Geschiedenis, Universiteit van Antwerpen, Centrum voor Stadsgeschiedenis, 2006), 334–37. See also Mary Lindemann, *The Merchant Republics: Amsterdam, Antwerp and Hamburg, 1648–1790* (Cambridge: Cambridge University Press, 2015), 298.

15 See Jan Parmentier, *De holle compagnie: Smokkel en legale handel onder Zuidnederlandse vlag in Bengalen, ca. 1722–1744* (Hilversum: Verloren, 1992), 11 and Ruud Paesie, *Voor zilver en Zeeuws belang: De rampzalige Zuidzee-expeditie van de Middelburgse Commercie Compagnie, 1724–1727* (Zutphen: Walburg, 2012), 22.

16 See Ana Crespo Solana, *El comércio marítimo entre Amsterdam y Cádiz, 1713–1778* (Madrid, 2000), 38.

Commercial Cosmopolitanism? 209

17 Paulo Cloots, born on 24 November 1690, was the second son of Thomas Cloots (1663–1699) and his wife Maria Anna Clock. Following the early death of his father, Paulo was taken under the wing of his uncles.

18 His parents were Jan de Bruijn and Anna Clark. He had an older brother, Daniel de Bruijn (baptized in 1680), who was also a businessman. See "Netherlands, Births and Baptisms, 1564–1910," database, *Family Search* (https://familysearch. org/ark:/61903/1:1:XB5J-YYC: accessed on 10 July 2015).

19 Lisbon, Arquivo Nacional da Torre do Tombo ('ANTT'), Junta da Administração do Tabaco ('JAT'), bk. 193, fol. 7 and 12.

20 See Leonor Freire Costa, Pedro Lains and Susana Münch Miranda, *An Economic History of Portugal, 1143–2010* (Cambridge: Cambridge University Press, 2016), 125–26, 194–95; and H.E.S. Fisher, "Lisbon as a port town in the eighteenth century," in *I Porti come impresa económica. Atti della Diciannovesima Settimana di Studi, 2–6 maggio 1987,* ed. Simonetta Cavaciocchi (Neuilly sur Seine 1988) 703–29.

21 Lisbon's pivotal role in European and global trade from the 1690s was mirrored in the vitality of its foreign merchants' communities. On the Dutch see Cátia Antunes, *Globalization in the Early Modern Period. The Economic Relationship between Amsterdam and Lisbon, 1640–1705* (Amsterdam: Aksant, 2004); on the English see Richard Lodge, "The English Factory at Lisbon: Some Chapters in Its History," *Transactions of the Royal Historical Society* 16 (1933): 211–47 and H.E.S. Fisher, *The Portugal Trade: A Study of Anglo-Portuguese Commerce, 1700–1770* (London: Methuen, 1971); on the French, see Jean-François Labourdette, *La nation française a Lisbonne de 1669 a 1790: entre colbertisme et libéralisme* (Paris: Fondation Calouste Gulbenkian, 1988).

22 ANTT, JAT, bk. 193, fol. 1, letter to Jean-Baptiste and Paulo Jacomo Cloots, 3 January 1713.

23 L. Freire Costa, P. Lains and S. Münch Miranda, *An Economic History of Portugal, 1143–2010.*

24 Teresa Ferreira Rodrigues, ed., *História da População Portuguesa. Das longas permanências à conquista da modernidade* (Porto, Edições Afrontamento, 2008), 196.

25 ANTT, JAT, bk. 193, fol. 14, letter to Jean-Baptiste and Paul Jacomo Cloots, 17 January 1713.

26 Unlike the Spanish *Carrera de Indias,* where trade was an exclusive right of the merchants belonging to the merchant guilds of Seville, Mexico and Lima, Portuguese colonial trade was open to any Portuguese merchant.

27 Jorge Pedreira, "Os Homens de Negócio da Praça de Lisboa de Pombal ao Vintismo, 1755–1822. Diferenciação, Reprodução e Identificação de um Grupo Social" (Unpublished PhD diss., University of Lisbon, 1995), 119.

28 João Paulo Salvado, "Os grandes negociantes de Lisboa da primeira metade do século XVIII: origens geográficas e perfil social," paper presented at XXXIV Encontro da Associação Portuguesa de História Económica e Social, Lisbon, 2014.

29 ANTT, JAT, bk. 203, pp. 225–6, letter to José da Cruz da Silveira, 14 May 1715 ('si vous n'entendez pas trop bien la langue française je vous écrirai en portugais, comme vous pouvez faire a moi, car j'entends le portugais très bien e en contraire je vois que le français vous est difficile').

30 B.S. Yamey, "Scientific Bookkeeping and the Rise of Capitalism," *Economic History Review* 1, no. 2–3 (1949): 102.

31 W.D. Smith, "The Function of Commercial Centers in the Modernization of European Capitalism: Amsterdam as an Information Exchange in the Seventeenth Century," *Journal of Economic History* 44, no. 4 (1984): 985–1005. In 1720, there were 395 licensed brokers operating in Amsterdam, to which a

210 *Cátia Antunes et al.*

further 800 unlicensed brokers could be added. See Milja van Tielhof, *The 'Mother of All Trades': The Baltic Grain Trade in Amsterdam from the Late 16th century to the early 19th century* (Brill: Leiden, 2002), 154.

32 Jaime Reis, *O Banco de Portugal das Origens a 1914: Antecedentes, Fundação e Consolidação, 1821–1857*. vol. 1 (Lisbon: Banco de Portugal, 1996).

33 ANTT, JAT, bk. 193, fol. 257, letter to Jean-Baptiste and Paul Jacomo Cloots, 16 January 1714.

34 The rise in demand for tea began in the early decades of the eighteenth century. See Ronald Findlay and Kevin O'Rourke, *Power and Plenty. Trade, War and the World Economy in the Second Millennium* (Princeton NJ: Princeton University Press, 2007), 291–92. See also Chris Nierstrasz, *Rivalry for Trade in Tea and Textiles: The English and Dutch East India Companies, 1700–1800* (Basingstoke and New York: Palgrave Macmillan, 2015).

35 ANTT, JAT, bk. 193, fol. 33, 6 February 1713; fol. 77, 30 May 1713.

36 ANTT, JAT, bk. 185, fol. 188, 7 March 1719. See Jorge Pedreira, "Tratos e Contratos: actividades, interesses e orientações dos investimentos dos negociantes da praça de Lisboa (1755–1822)," *Análise Social* 31, no. 136–37 (1996): 368.

37 In the Portuguese Atlantic trade, foreign merchant houses regularly used these itinerant traders as commission agents to interlope the Brazilian market. For that reason, they were banned from engaging in colonial trade by a Royal Decree of 6 December 1755. See Pedreira, *Os homens de negócio*, 71.

38 On these forms of agency, see Cátia Antunes, Susana Münch Miranda and João Paulo Salvado, "Between Brazil and Asia: The Global Business of De Bruijn & Cloots of Lisbon, 1713–1737," paper presented at the Economic History Society Annual Conference, University of Cambridge, April 2016.

39 On the *Carreira da Índia*, see C.R. Boxer, *The Portuguese Seaborne Empire, 1415–1825* (Manchester: Carcanet, 1991) 205–27 and Stuart Schwartz, "The Economy of the Portuguese Empire" in *Portuguese Oceanic Expansion, 1400–1800*, ed. Francisco Bethencourt and Diogo Ramada Curto (Cambridge: Cambridge University Press, 2007), 19–48, especially 26–28.

40 A knight of the Order of Christ, Manuel de Castro Guimarães had served as a clerk at the Royal Supreme Court (Desembargo do Paço) since 1705 and was appointed a knight of the royal household in 1710 (ANTT, Chancelaria da Ordem de Cristo, bk. 58, fol. 328; Idem, Chanc. D Pedro, bk. 30, fol. 6; Idem, Registo Geral de Mercês ('RGM'), bk. 4, fol.183). Guimarães was also a minister on the Treasury Board of Prince Francisco's household (*Casa do Infantado*). See Maria Adelaide Pereira Moraes, "Desceram do monte, atravessaram o mar (Castro de Guimarães e seu termo)," *Boletim de Trabalhos Históricos*, Guimarães, 38 (1987): 61–103.

41 Lisbon, Arquivo Histórico Ultramarino ('AHU'), Rio de Janeiro (Castro e Almeida), bx. 17, docs. 3678 and 3682.

42 ANTT, JAT, bk. 190, 4 March 1727.

43 ANTT, RGM, D. João V, bk. 4, fol. 183, 6 May 1719.

44 See Antunes et al., "Between Brazil and Asia."

45 Karel Degryse, *De Antwerpse Fortuinen: kapitaalsaccumulatie, -investering en -rendement te Antwerpen in de 18e eeuw* (Antwerp: Genootschap voor Antwerpse Geschiedenis, 2005).

46 The terms of the business deal proposed to the Crown are unknown (AHU, Conselho Ultramarino, Reino, bx 353). On this plan, see also Tiago C.P. dos Reis Miranda, "A Companhia de Comércio da Ásia de Feliciano Velho Oldemberg, 1753–1760" in *O terramoto de 1755: impactos históricos*, ed. A.C. Araújo et al. (Lisbon: Livros Horizonte, 2007), 199–207.

47 Born in Amsterdam, Jan van Zeller established himself as a businessman in Porto in the late seventeenth century before moving to Lisbon, where he eventually

became Resident Minister of the King of Prussia (1717–1734). See Pedreira, *Os Homens de Negócio*, 227 and Luiz de Mello Vaz de São Payo, "Uma linhagem cosmopolita do Porto," in: *XV Congreso internacional de las ciencias genealógica y heraldica*, vol. 3 (Madrid: Instituto Luis de Salazar y Castro, 1983), 91–127, especially 105–6.

48 ANTT, JAT, bk. 199, fol. 93-93 vᵒ.

49 See Susana Münch Miranda, "Risk and Failure in Tax Farming: De Bruijn & Cloots of Lisbon and the Portuguese Tobacco Monopoly, 1722–1727," *Itinerario: International Journal on the History of European Expansion and Global Interaction* 43, no. 1 (2019): 122–45. On the problems commonly faced by merchants operating in the Portuguese Atlantic trade, see Dauril Alden, "Vicissitudes of Trade in the Portuguese Atlantic Empire during the First Half of the Eighteenth Century," *The Americas* 32, no. 2 (1975): 282–91.

50 Miranda, "Risk and Failure in Tax Farming".

51 Jan de Vries and Ad van der Woude, *The First Modern Economy: Success, Failure and Perseverance of the Dutch Economy, 1500–1815* (Cambridge: Cambridge University Press, 1997).

52 L.L. Rodrigues, R. Craig, and D. Gomes, "State Intervention in Commercial Education: The Case of the Portuguese School of Commerce, 1759," *Accounting History* 12, no. 1 (2007): 55–85; L.L. Rodrigues and R. Craig, "English Mercantilist Influences on the Foundation of the Portuguese School of Commerce in 1759," *Atlantic Economic Journal* 32, no. 4 (2004): 329–45.

12 The limits of cosmopolitanism
Ottoman Algiers in the seventeenth and eighteenth centuries

Michael Talbot[1]

Cosmopolitanism, as Francesca Trivellato argued in her seminal work on *The Familiarity of Strangers*, is often linked with the notion of tolerance, between or of different cultures and religions in a given space.[2] However, Trivellato provided an important caveat, that 'policies of religious toleration, however, cannot be equated with tolerant and cosmopolitan attitudes of mutual respect.'[3] If tolerance necessarily had limits, depending on the context in which it was practiced, then for cosmopolitanism to function there absolutely had to be a degree of reciprocity between the parties that comprise the cosmopolitan environment based on more than just tolerance, but respect for each other's practices *in practice*.[4] There is, therefore, a close link between commercial cosmopolitanism and legal frameworks that must necessarily enshrine not only tolerance but also reciprocal and mutually recognised and defined practices. In exploring the limits of cosmopolitanism, it is important to move from such very broad abstract terms into a more coherent analytical framework, and for that one need look no further than that outlined by Wolfgang Kaiser in his edited volume on *La Loge et le Fondouk*. In his introduction, Kaiser proposes that mercantile practices need to be considered through three spatial categories: *lieux*, 'places', permanent buildings and institutions in which commerce was transacted, such as ports, khans, and market stalls; *places*, which we might translate here as 'zones', a set of *lieux* grouped under a common judicial and institutional practice, such as markets and stock exchanges; and *espaces*, 'spaces', a broader economic sphere defined, to use Kaiser's definition, 'by practices solidified by routine.'[5] *Espace* is the space through which a port links its hinterland and regularly visited destinations overseas. So, the model Kasier proposes sees us zoom in and out, from individual buildings performing specific functions, to groups of buildings operating under a common set of practices, to economic regions that link different zones and places together.

This chapter explores the limits of commercial cosmopolitanism through the example of commercial interactions between the Ottoman Regency of Algiers and its trading partners from Northern and Western Europe in the eighteenth century. That Regency is often lumped together with the other North African states technically subject to the Ottoman sultan (plus

The limits of cosmopolitanism 213

Morocco) as 'the Barbary States'. This term, 'Barbary', is not a neutral term, but instead is part of a continuing legacy of European colonialism in North Africa, a means, if you will, to deflect from the barbarism of French, Italian, British, and Spanish empire.[6] In the eighteenth century, attitudes towards the North African polities, and Algiers in particular, became a coherent discourse on the limits of cosmopolitanism. The notion that Algiers, its rulers and subjects, were demonstrably separate from civilised human commerce became an increasing means of justification to erode the commercial spaces Algiers had established to facilitate trade and peaceful interactions. Algiers, as this paper will argue, provided a particular *espace* that aimed to balance its duty as a frontier state on a perpetual war-footing with its role as a major emporium in the Western Mediterranean. In seeing how Algiers's trading partners attempted to subvert their mutually-agreed commercial treaties, the conclusion emerges that cosmopolitanism was fine – so long as it was on terms acceptable to the Western Europeans.

The common enemy of the human race

In 1750, a detailed and popular book on Algiers by the French diplomat Jacques Philippe Laugier de Tassy, which had already been translated into Dutch and Spanish, was put into English by an anonymous translator who claimed to have lived in North Africa for a number of years.[7] This new and expanded version of Laugier de Tassy's tome was given a new title with a wider appeal than the original *Histoire du Royaume d'Alger*. This was, instead, *A Compleat History of the Piratical States of Barbary, viz. Algiers, Tunis, Tripoli, and Morocco*; Algiers had been downgraded from a kingdom or realm, to a piratical state.[8] Such a label was to stick to Algiers and the other North African Regencies nominally subject to the Ottoman sultans, indeed until this day, with numerous books focusing on 'Barbary' as synonymous with corsairs and pirates. Such a persistent entanglement of North Africa with piracy is in part due to the centrality of North Africa to the construction of the United States of America, in part the *mission civilisatrice* of French colonialism, and in part a legacy of the legal discussions of the eighteenth century.[9] Notable among the former was the call to arms of the Swiss diplomat and lawyer Emer de Vattel (1714–1767). In his highly influential *Le Droit des Gens* of 1758, Vattel envisaged a system in which the 'law of nations' was not a pluralistic system, but one based firmly on the moral values and political interests of Western Europe. He singled out the 'Barbary' states as a key example of polities that lived beyond the pale of what was acceptable:

> Finally, there is another case, where the nation is generally accountable
> for the attacks of its members. This is because, by its customs and by the
> maxims of its government, it accustoms and authorises its citizens to
> pillage and mistreat foreigners indiscriminately, to conduct raids into

214   *Michael Talbot*

neighbouring countries, and so forth [...]. All nations have the right to enter in league against it, to suppress it, to treat it as a common enemy of the human race. The Christian nations would not be unjustified to unite themselves against the Barbary Republics, in order to destroy the shelters of the plunderers of the sea, for whom the love of plunder or the fear of a just punishment are the only rules of peace or war.[1]

The attitude of Vattel, in singling out the North African states as barely human and advocating their collective punishment was at once influential on attitudes towards conflict with those states, but also reflected pre-existing policies of European states towards their North African neighbours. In 1728, the fleet of Étienne Nicolas de Grandpré bombarded the city of Tripoli and threatened Tunis; but it was Algiers that, in the later seventeenth century, had suffered the brunt of this indiscriminate bombing aimed at subduing their naval power and, as Vattel's theory would later articulate, collectively punishing the population of a piratical nation.[11]

One of the many problems with Vattel's view here is that it ignored the fact that European privateers were ever more active in the waters of the Mediterranean. Indeed, during the War of the Austrian Succession, British and French privateers and warships had created so many problems in the Eastern Mediterranean that the Ottoman authorities had brought in strict new legal measures to limit the violence.[12] Moreover, dismissing the activities of Algerian maritime forces as 'piracy' means losing sight of the wider geopolitical importance of Algiers within the Mediterranean. As the most westerly of the nominally Ottoman territories, it was, in many ways, a first line of defence between the Ottoman maritime world and the wider world beyond. Therefore, in order to understand the attitude of Algiers to trade and commercial travel in the seventeenth and eighteenth century, and in particular its practice of cosmopolitanism, it is crucial to examine how the Algerian authorities visualized commercial space beyond its borders.

Peaceful commerce in the Abode of Holy War

The open sea was an area shared by friends and enemies of Algiers, and treaties with foreign powers attempted to regulate encounters between Algerian and foreign ships at sea. I argue that this is in part due to the changing political position of Algiers in the Mediterranean combined with an increase in traffic coming from North and West Europe, the so-called 'Northern Invasion'.[13] On the one hand, as Colin Heywood has demonstrated, Algiers and Ottoman North Africa in general were part of a defensive boundary between the Ottoman and non-Ottoman world, and, indeed, between the Islamic and non-Islamic world.[14] At the same time, this situation was complicated by the growing autonomy of Algiers as a de-facto independent state, going even further than other autonomous Ottoman

The limits of cosmopolitanism   215

provinces in the seventeenth and eighteenth centuries in making its own treaties with foreign powers. So, as well as being a major commercial centre in its own right, Algiers was also a frontier garrison town, and frequently involved in conflicts with other polities, both as a front-line of defence for the wider Ottoman realms beyond, and for its own political interests. This does not make Algiers peripheral, nor militaristic, but the way in which we view Algiers as a commercial space must in part be framed by the fact that managing conflict was a defining feature of the state in its relations with foreign powers. Discerning how the Algerian authorities attempted to regulate peaceful commercial relations with friendly powers – who were often entangled with the enemies of Algiers in one way or another – in a maritime region marked by warfare and violence will in turn help us to understand the limits of cosmopolitanism in the Algerian context.

In translations of treaties and letters, the British often gave Algiers the title, 'the Famous and Warlike City and Kingdoms of Algiers'.[15] 'Warlike' is perhaps a rather unusual way of describing a polity, and the translators arrived at this epithet through an interpretation of one of the titles of the city employed by the Algerian authorities in official correspondence, *dārü'l-cihād*. By translating this phrase as 'warlike', something is certainly lost. The deys of Algiers, in referring to their polity as being in 'the abode of holy war', which is the literal translation of the term, set themselves aside from other peaceful parts of the sultan's 'well-protected domains' (*memālik-i maḥrūse*). Indeed, it was employed by the Ottoman state itself to refer to parts of the Empire in the midst of conflict, for instance in Ottoman chronicles, such as that of İbrahim Peçevi when referring to Erzurum, and Mehmed Raşid when speaking of Belgrade.[16] Indeed, the twentieth-century Ottoman historical and geographical encyclopaedia *Ḳāmūsü'l-'alām* defined *dārü'l-cihād* as historically being cities on the borders, generally hosting garrisons (*tevārīḫ-i 'Osmāniyede ḥudūdda bulunub ekseriyā mu'asker ittiḫāz olunan*), such as Belgrade, Baghdad, and the North African regencies.[17] The use of this term by the authorities in Algiers in the seventeenth and eighteenth century seems to indicate that this was not just a garrison city, but that it occupied a separate legal space to areas not in the *dārü'l-cihād*. That is, being a city in the Abode of Holy War meant that Algiers needed to take being a perpetual warzone into account in its commercial dealings with friends and foe alike, and this meant being clear on who indeed was friendly, and who was not.

The delineation of Algiers as a *dārü'l-cihād* meant that in their treaties with European powers in the seventeenth and eighteenth centuries, the deys were able to modify the usual provisions of freedom of movement at sea to be more in line with the exigencies of operating in a warzone. Freedom of movement to and from Algiers for peaceful commercial purposes was continually emphasised in diplomatic correspondence, but explicitly in terms of reciprocity. Such a desire for smooth traffic is illustrated clearly in the

216   *Michael Talbot*

Algerian treaty with Britain of 1686. The Ottoman Turkish text of article 3 of that agreement states that:

> If the ships of the Emperor of Britain or of his subjects, and likewise the corsair ships or merchant ships of Algiers, encounter one another in the open sea, they are free from being sought out and being harmed. They will respect and assist [each other] and will depart from each other, and no person shall be hindered in their business.[18]

One crucial difference between the Ottoman Turkish and English texts here is the idea of being 'sought out'. The English text says that British and Algerian ships 'shall freely pass the seas and traffic without any search, hindrance or molestation'.[19] The Ottoman text does not say that British ships could pass without any search, but forbids the process of corsairing, that is, seeking out the victim (*aramak*), and harming them (*incitmek*). This not only demonstrates a fundamental misunderstanding between the spirit of the Ottoman Turkish and English texts of the treaty, but also gives us a sense of how disputes could occur between the subjects of the two polities.

This shows, however, how the Algerians and the Europeans attempted to regulate encounters in the open sea in order to allow the Algerians to police their frontier, but also permit the continuation of commerce. One question must have arisen very early on in these encounters, however: how would an Algerian ship know that a ship flying the British flag was indeed a British ship? This would require some sort of up-close interaction with the suspect vessel, and the question of being searched arises in the very next article (number 4) of the treaty. This important provision gave certain rights to Algerian vessels to conduct searches of British ships outside of their territorial waters:

> If [Algerian] corsair ships encounter British merchant ships, whether big or small, and if they encounter them outside of the places ruled by the British emperor, they may go to the ship in a rowboat with two men in addition to the oarsmen; more than two men may not approach the ship. Providing that the captain of the aforementioned ship holds a pass and permission at that time, displaying a passport of the king, or a person being his captain-general, or someone serving in his place as the captain-general of England and Ireland or holding the captain-generalship of Scotland, or for whichever of the three said kingdoms, it is expedient that the rowboat going to the said ship will complete its duties swiftly so that [the ship] may return on its way. Moreover, a merchant ship may not be hindered in its journey if is fit to pass. If one of the British corsair ships encounters an Algerian corsair or merchant ship in any place, if the said ship holds a passport from the ruler of Algiers or the British consul residing nearby, at that time the said ship may not be disturbed by anyone in anyway, and may continue peacefully on its journey.[20]

The limits of cosmopolitanism 217

Thus, the Algerians – and the British – had a right to send a small boarding party to a ship in order to ascertain that it held the correct travel documents, and was what it claimed to be. If the captain could produce a passport from the relevant authorities, the ship would be permitted to continue on its journey, with the implication that those who were not carrying such documents were liable to be attacked as enemies. This agreement for the interruption of free passage over the high seas was a significant matter that meant that even in times of peace between Britain and Algiers, they sent parties to each other's vessels.

One of the earliest formal treaties between Britain and Algiers, dated June 1662, gives a more specific context as to why these searches were so important. The Ottoman Turkish text says specifically says that the Algerians would have the right to search for Genoese, Spanish, and Portuguese subjects and goods.[21] This concern of the Algerians that enemy nations might use friendly or neutral ships as cover morphed into the more general and reciprocal right to search ships at sea. As such, the right for Algerian vessels to board friendly ships to ensure they were indeed friendly was included in all subsequent treaties between Algiers and Western powers, right up to the peace agreement with the United States in 1815 (article 7).[22] The wording of the article that would become the standard one in foreign treaties predates the British treaty of 1686, being found, for instance, in the treaty signed with the Dutch in 1680 (article 4).[23] The language is the same, stipulating that if the Algerians encountered Dutch ships outside of the seas ruled by the Dutch (*in Zee en buyten de Plaetsen van de hoog-gemelde Heeren Staten dependerende sullen ontmoeten / en pleine Mer…n'entant point dans les Places dépendantes desdits Seigneurs Estats Generaux*) they could send a ship to inspect for passports.[24] This is, I believe, a result of the definition of Algiers as being in the *dārü'l-cihād*; as the Algerians were never truly at peace, they maintained belligerent rights to search belligerent and neutral vessels on the open seas. Although such rights can be traced to earlier legal practices, nonetheless, the Algerians were clearly trying to create a distinct commercial space in which the filter of their military frontier would allow friendly and neutral shipping under a common series of practices based on mutual respect and reciprocity.[25] So far, so cosmopolitan; indeed, as Trivellato argued, clear boundaries and distinctions were in part what allowed commercial cosmopolitanism to function within its specific legal setting.[26] However, it is when the agreed rules of the Western Mediterranean *espace* were challenged that we can see the limits of that cosmopolitanism itself.

A letter from Bektaş Muhammad Dey, 1709

The libraries and archives of Western Europe are full of texts in Ottoman Turkish and Arabic that give the perspective of North African rulers and officials on the practices of regulating commercial space of the Western Mediterranean. One example is a rather unassuming letter from the early

218   *Michael Talbot*

eighteenth century held in the British Library. At the beginning of the month of Zilkade 1121 (the end of December 1709), Bektaş Muhammad Dey, the governor of Algiers, dispatched a letter to Queen Anne of Britain.[27] The top of the document bore a calligraphic signature, which read: 'Bektaş Muhammad Dey, Protected Algiers of the West in the Abode of Holy War'.[28] Addressing the queen as 'the model of the Jesuan princes and pillar of the Messian sovereigns', this was, to all intents and purposes, a letter between equal monarchs.[29] Indeed, this greeting was in the same spirit as that employed by the Ottoman sultan – Bektaş Muhammad's nominal overlord – when writing to foreign Christian monarchs. Aside from the usual flattering titles and formalities, the letter itself deals with fundamental questions of freedom of movement and legal jurisdiction affecting both British and Algerian merchants and ships. Bektaş Muhammad mentions several disputes between Algiers and the British in this letter to the queen, which aimed to demonstrate in turn his strict adherence to legal agreements, the unscrupulousness of the Europeans, and his mercy as a ruler in seeking to keep the commercial zone in operation. In doing so, he provides an insight into the legal regime that existed between the Ottoman regencies in North Africa and the Europeans with whom they traded, and sometimes fought, as well as a sense of a lack of reciprocity in the observance of those diplomatic and commercial frameworks.

The first case concerned the freedom of movement for European ships at sea. The letter first emphasised that, in conformity to the requirements of the legal provisions of the capitulations (*'ahdnamemizde şer'-i ahkām muḳteżāsınca*) made between Algiers and Britain, as well as due to 'our well-established friendship' (*rāsih-dem dostluǧumuz*), whenever Algerian ships encountered British merchant vessels on the open sea, they did not commit violence or injury against them.[30] However, the letter went on to give an example of a British ship that had been stopped on its voyage, providing a legal justification. The previous year, an Algerian vessel had encountered a British ship somewhere on the open sea, and because the British did not possess a passport for their journey, the Algerians brought them to Algiers.[31] After an inspection (*teftiş*) the captain produced a British travel document, and the ship was released with all of its merchandise (*gemi cemī mat'ayı ile iṭlāḳ*). This passage presents the legal regime of free movement, as the Algerians saw it, functioning correctly and legitimately. The British ship had freedom of movement that was guaranteed by appropriate documentation in the form of a passport. When this was not produced, the Algerians had the right to search the ship and/or take the ship back to their seat of government, and to inspect it for enemy goods and persons there, releasing it only after this inspection had been completed. The language used is precise and based upon the provisions of diplomatic and commercial treaties. In other words, the search of this particular British ship cannot be seen as arbitrary, but grounded in law and common practice, an expected

The limits of cosmopolitanism 219

and necessary part of policing the commercial space of the Western Mediterranean.

Immediately after this, a rather different case is presented, beginning with the blunt statement that 'one of our ships took a ship of Denmark and brought it here.'[32] As the Algerians had several treaties with the British by 1709 but would not have one with the Danes until 1747, this meant that the Danish ship could be seized as a legitimate prize, and its crew enslaved, both being the property of a technically enemy power. However, the British consul – referred to as a *balyoz* – started legal proceedings (*da'vā eydüb*) to secure its release by claiming that this ship was, in fact, a British ship. The dey's response was clear: 'A large state council and a great council was convened in order to judge the case in accordance with Islamic law and regal law, and on examining the regal law-codes, the said boat was not found to have any vestiges of being British.'[33] In order to ascertain the truth, the ship's captain and crew were brought before the divan to answer the council's questions, which proved decisive. The council learned that on spotting the mysterious vessel, the Algerians had raised a French flag, and in return the other ship raised the banner of Denmark (*Danimarḳa sancaġı diküb*). Moreover, on inspection, the ship was found to contain neither a British flag nor passport, and most of the crew (*ekser-i ṭā'fesi*) were Danes. From this, and more, the letter concluded that 'all the people of the council knew that this was an enemy ship, and that its seizure and captured was lawful'.[34] Here, Bektaş Muhammad demonstrated that the concerns and complains of the British consul were being dealt with in a strictly legal manner, with due process. The description of this case continues, noting that after receiving a letter from the queen in 1709 claiming that British subjects were among the crew, 'for your sake, twelve individuals were released and were given to your servant, the consul'.[35] Thus, even after the case had been closed, the Algerian authorities were still willing to investigate to ensure justice.

These two cases of legal regularity and mercy were a rather long preface to reach the heart of the letter's purpose. The British, in Bektaş Muhammad's eyes, were not acting in the same good faith as his government. The first accusation made against the British was one of treachery. The dey claimed that 'whenever [the consul] asks for wheat, it is given [to him]' (*herbarı buġday ṭaleb eyledikçe verilub*), but the consul then sent the wheat on to Barcelona, 'even though', the dey complained, 'Barcelona is our enemy' (*ḥālbuki Varsolina bizim düşmānımızdır*). Even then, he was willing to permit this, as British soldiers were currently stationed there and assumed the wheat was for their benefit. This, then, was another example of Algerian mercy to contrast with the dey's complaint against the conduct of the British that was at the letter's core:

Some merchants of this place hired a French *saitée* from Alexandria, and on their coming here encountered one of your ships, and were taken, seized,

220 *Michael Talbot*

and captured. We communicated to your servant, the consul, many times in order to save [them]. He said that[36]

> A prize taken under the flag of our enemy cannot be requested because it is a legally valid flag.

The conclusion was that, as the matter was subject to custom ('*ādete*), the case was dropped. With the parting lines of the letter, Bektaş Muhammad wrote that the consul should inform the queen of the security and protection (*hfż ve şiyānetimiz*) he had given to British subjects, presumably in the hope that she would intervene on behalf of the Algerian victims of the British attack on a French ship. Her reply does not indicate that any action was taken on this case.[37]

This letter from the dey of Algiers to the queen of Britain raises three fundamental issues about the place of Algiers in the commercial and legal space of the Mediterranean in the seventeenth and eighteenth centuries. First, from the Algerian perspective, the British were at best bending, and at worst breaking the terms of their treaties. If the entire point of the commercial agreements between London and Algiers was to allow British ships to trade to, from, and around Algiers without being targeted as enemy ships, then British being crewed with enemy subjects, flying enemy flags, and sending staple crops to enemy territory, all whilst refusing to treat Algerian ships in friendly, reciprocal manner, rather strained the underlying foundations of those agreements. This can be explained, at least in part, through a shifting balance of power in the Mediterranean, the Algerian fleet no longer being a match for the British or French navies, with increasing violence against Algiers and Algerian merchants an important part of the story. I would also argue that the lack of reciprocity was also in part due to the lack of official Algerian – or any North African or Ottoman – representation in European capitals. This meant that there was no real way for the authorities in Algiers to ensure that the rights of free trade given to Algerian subjects in their treaties with their Western European partners were actually enforced.

Legal institutions and the limits of commercial cosmopolitanism

In Algiers itself, there were two main legal spaces in which any disputes, and this was set out in the British treaty of 1686: 'If there are any legal proceedings between one of the subjects of the king of Britain and a Muslim, or someone subject to Algerian authority, the said legal proceedings are to be heard by the illustrious [dey] or the divan, [and] not by any other person. If the legal proceedings are among themselves, in that case the British ambassador is the one who hears the case, [and] not any other person.'[38] The same language, and almost precisely the same phrasing, in subsequent treaties between the Algerians and various European states.[39] The real test of this

The limits of cosmopolitanism 221

reciprocal legal and commercial zone, however, is to see what would happen to Algerians involved in litigation abroad. Such cases are quite hard to track down, but there are traces scattered around the Algerian and European archives. In the absence of Algerian consuls with whom to register transactions and disputes, more ad hoc forms of record-keeping took place. For example, in June 1757, an Algerian merchant named Muhammad bin Azourz – recorded in French as Mahmet Zourzé – incurred a number of expenses surrounding a transaction for wheat in Toulon.[40] The record of this transaction is a short note written in French and in Arabic, specifically in the Algerian dialect of Arabic. Muhammad had sold a cargo of wheat in Toulon, and during his stay had incurred a number of expenses relating to his food and board. Without a formal Algerian consul in Toulon to register a receipt of the transaction, this note represents one way in which a formal record could be made to avoid future claims or litigation. The Algerian merchant submitted his account to the local commissioner-general and the naval intendent, who in turn arranged for Alexis de Bourbon, the interpreter for oriental languages, to provide a translation into Arabic, with one copy staying in France, and another going back to Algiers with the merchant.

Regular agreements like freighting arrangements would be registered in the chancery of the relevant consulate in Algiers. A good example of a typical sort of freighting agreement can be found in the registers of the French consulate in Algiers from the end of the seventeenth century, entered into the registers in the presence and under witness of the *chancellier*, Guillame Carrière on 3 June 1686.[41] Noted as an '*obligation*', in essence a legal commitment, the entry recorded that the barque *St Catherine*, captained by François Cauvière, was to freight the goods of 'Amet Marabout' of Tripoli and 'Abdraman Boutallam' of Algiers. A number of terms were laid down, but the basic element was that Cauvière would receive 900 *piastres Mexicanes* for the voyage to Tunis of twenty days' duration. On completing the job, the captain would deliver half of the consignment, following which the factors would have ten days within which to pay him his dues. The transaction was formalised by being 'sworn, done, and published' (*ce quy est juré, faict, et publié*) in the consulate in the presence of the *chancellier* and other officials. On this particular entry, there was also a brief summary of the agreement in Arabic, stating that the voyage of the saitée (*al-ṣaṭiyya*) would be to Tetuan and Tunis, and that the payment of nine hundred *ri'al*s would be made on arrival in Tunis (*ajara 'alā al-waḍa' li-Tūnis bi-tis'a mi'a ri'āl*). This simple process of registering the contract of freight at the French consulate had the same sort of implication as registering documents with a *qadi* to seal their legality. The agreement was registered at the consulate rather than the *qadi* court because it is a French formulation. Other transactions were more formally registered into the Algerian state records, such as a case in 1768 and 1769 of a Jewish merchant whose cargo, freighted on a British ship, had been seized by French privateers, in which the Algerians demanded, and received, compensation for their merchant's losses, with a document being produced in

222 *Michael Talbot*

Ottoman Turkish to be registered in both the French consulate and the Algerian state archive.[42] In these ways, the state and consular authorities, and the merchants themselves, had a clear paper-trail in case of any dispute, and, what is more, the variety of forms of proof accepted here attest to the cosmopolitan nature of commerce within Algiers itself. Far from being a space with arbitrary law, Algiers, because of its deep intercultural connections as a major commercial centre, developed a series of practices designed to secure and encourage commerce, rather than to hinder or disrupt it. This was indeed a form of cosmopolitanism.

However, time and time again, the archival records show that, just like in the cases presented by Bektaş Muhammad Dey at the beginning of the eighteenth century, the standards of legal proof and documentation required were quite different when it came to Algerian merchants trying to make their case in foreign courts. One case that I have explored elsewhere is that of Giovanni Xeno / Yani Ikseno, an Ottoman Greek merchant operating out of Algiers in the mid-eighteenth century.[43] In 1764, Xeno was hired as supercargo on behalf of one of the main merchants of the city, Ali Hoca, to freight a significant quantity of grain from Morocco, via a major merchant, Muhammad Ben-Taleb. As was common for such voyages, Xeno contracted the services of a European freighter, the Livorno-based Lefroy and Charron, who drew up a charter party with a British ship, the *Experience*. So, in true cosmopolitan Mediterranean style, Moroccan wheat destined for Algiers was being freighted on a British ship secured by a contract between an Ottoman Greek and the Algiers-based representative of Livornese agents. The voyage did not go to plan, and after a series of disasters, caused in no small part by the British captain, Xeno found himself and his cargo bound not for Algiers, but for the British port at Gibraltar. The British captain went straight to the Vice-Admiralty Court, demanding payment for his freighting charges through sale of the cargo of grain, arguing that Xeno had delayed the journey and that a significant quantity of the cargo had gone rotten. At this point, Xeno began compiling a truly impressive set of documents, gathered from across the Mediterranean, in Spanish, Italian, English, and Arabic, with witnesses including local European consuls and European and Moroccan merchants, and records of correspondence between himself and the ship's captain. It was a very strong case to show that it was the British captain, rather than Xeno, who was in breach of contract and therefore liable. Yet, the British judge in Gibraltar, Craig Huw, ruled in favour of the British captain, ordering that the grain be sold at public auction for payment of the debt. However, the British captain took the grain instead to Malaga, where he sold the cargo at below market value. Further documents gathered by Xeno proved that the grain was all of a good quality – contrary the captain's initial claim – and that he had sold it contrary to the court's ruling. Yet, once again, the judge ruled in favour of the British captain. In his judgement, he refused to acknowledge that the cargo was the property of the Algerian merchant Ali Hoca, therefore invalidating Xeno's

The limits of cosmopolitanism 223

role as supercargo. He also ruled that any security offered by the Moroccan Ben-Taleb was not sufficient for the following reasons:

> The security of a Moor residing in Barbary (being refused by the plaintiff) was not thought sufficient or responsible to the judge...and the judge most humbly submits that having no instructions as to Moorish cargoes or effects, had he refused a British subject what appeared to him and in the opinion of the merchants of Cadiz and Gibraltar to be his just right, he might not have been found liable to the payment of freight in a British court of justice.[44]

That is, because the security was offered by a Moor – i.e. a Muslim – from Barbary, - i.e. North Africa – it was not valid. In addition, Huw admits that he was concerned about setting a precedent by which a 'Moor' might win a case over a British merchant, going simply on the advice of local merchants rather than the mountain of evidence provided by Xeno. The British consul in Algiers, who had done much to help Xeno during the case, observed in a letter to the British government, 'what can be said of that court, where not the conviction but the imagination and suspicions of the judge are set up against evidence and written regular obligations?'[45]

So, quite contrary to the 'Barbary' narrative, it was in fact the European courts that discarded written evidence, not the other way around. Similarly, by the later eighteenth century, it was the armed ships of the French and British privateers who would frequently plunder Algerian cargo, not Algerian pirates ravaging European shipping. In 1799, the French privateer *Brutus* seized an Algerian ship, recorded variously as the *Rachel* or *Rahhel* in the French records.[46] It was a freighter carrying wheat provided by the notable Algerian Jewish merchant Bacri, ordered by an Algerian merchant based in Lisbon, Abdelkerim Ben-Taleb. The ship left Algiers carrying a passport from the dey, and flying the Algerian flag. En route, it was seized by the French ship *Brutus* and taken to Malaga to be sold, on the basis that it was travelling with provisions to an enemy of France, Portugal. Bacri immediately complained to the French authorities, and the case went before the Conseil des Prises.[47] In deciding the legality of the prize, the court posed the following questions: Is an Algerian ship exempt from being seized if it is carrying enemy cargo or cargo to an enemy territory? Was the ship in question under enemy ownership? Was the crew comprised of enemies? Was the cargo, and its destination, therefore enemy? In order to answer these questions, Bacri, with the help of Ben-Taleb, ensured that interviews were conducted with the crew and other relevant parties to be presented to the court.

In its judgement, the Court des Prises decided that Algerian ships would be exempt from being seized only if the ship were considered Algerian, rather than whether or not the goods were shipped on the account of an Algerian merchant. This was, however in direct contravention to the treaties

224 *Michael Talbot*

between Algiers and France and Britain, which specifically stated that ships of France/Britain and ships of Algiers were to be free from harm and molestation, and specifically that the wares and money on board belonging to any other kind of traveller (i.e. neither French/British nor Algerian) was similarly free from harm and seizure.[48] The judgement of the Court des Prises highlighted in particular Article 2 of the 1719 treaty between Algiers and France, which stated specifically that 'there will be will be peace between the Emperor of France and the Most Illustrious Pasha, Dey, Divan, and Militia of the city and realm of Algiers and their subjects, so that they can reciprocally go about their commerce in the two realms and navigate in complete security, without being able to impede them under any cause or pretext whatsoever.'[49] This article dates back to the later seventeenth century, when the French, British, and Dutch sought to protect their own goods from seizure by Algerian corsairs, but it was quite specifically reciprocal and in still in force at the end of the eighteenth century, and therefore applicable in this case.

That same treaty, in Article 21, permitted the Algerians to establish 'une personne de qualité' in Marseille to protect the interests of Algerian merchants trading there, but, at least in these later cases, the impact of such a figure was minimal. The closest thing there was at the end of the eighteenth century was an individual named Simon Abucaya, who seems to have acted more as an agent for Bacri and his mercantile house than a general Algerian consul. Had there been an effective Algerian consul to enforce their treaty rights, perhaps things might have been different, although by this point I suspect they would have been unable to make much of an impact. However, the court began its judgement on a rather different footing, ignoring the reciprocal rights of Algerians. The statements collected from the crew of the *Rahhel* attested that the ship was the property of Ben-Taleb, described as an Algerian or a 'Moor of Lisbon'. However, the court had to decide whether the ship was under enemy ownership. As Ben-Taleb was an Algerian subject, it should have been considered the ship of an ally. However, the court decided that because Ben-Taleb was 'established and domiciled' in Lisbon, he was Portuguese, and therefore the ship was too. In addition, although there were Algerians as part of the crew, a large part consisted of Portuguese subjects, and as such the court decided that the crew should be considered an enemy crew. This then left only the final question – was the cargo, and its ultimate destination, that of the enemy? A number of witness statements were collected. One confirmed that the wheat was the property of Bacri's company in Algiers, consigned to an associate company in Portugal, and the majority of witnesses concurred that the wheat was consigned to the Maison Bentaleb in Lisbon. However, the court chose to believe another sole witness, who declared that the wheat was ultimately destined for an enemy company and that the captain had thrown the incriminating paperwork overboard. In the judgement, it states that 'it is true that this witness is the only one who speaks of *throwing the papers into the sea*; but it is easy to

The limits of cosmopolitanism 225

conceive of the motive that has shut the mouths of all the other members of the crew, each interested in saving their own wares.'[50] As such, the court ruled that the Algerian flag was becoming a cover for enemy freighting, and therefore questioned the basis of reciprocity in all existing treaties. The privilege of Algerian neutrality, it was claimed 'so far as it exists, to be fixed in forms and rules, is specific to Algiers, and it is solely relative to the persons and goods belonging thereto; once the deceit is recognised, everything must revert to the communal order; the fraud, once proved, causes the privilege to disappear; justice wants it, the interest of France requires it.'[51] Once again, despite evidence and treaties to the contrary, a legitimate shipment was declared lawful prize not on the basis of evidence presented, but on the assumptions and suspicions of the court, and, crucially, a precedent set on the basis of national interest. This was Vattel's theory in action, with tolerance for the Algerians no longer on the table.

Conclusions

Although the documentation on Algerian merchants in European courts is limited – or at least, still emerging – the cases of Xeno and Bacri/Ben-Taleb are indicative of the general pattern in the later eighteenth century. Piles of documents and witness testimonies, that were a commonplace part of the intercultural transactions of Algiers, simply carried no weight in the European prize and admiralty courts. In part, I suspect, this is due to the lack of consular protection for Algerians that the European merchants were able to enjoy in Algiers. If a French merchant had a problem in Algiers, he had treaty rights to be heard before the dey or divan with his consul in attendance. No such provision existed, or at least was exercised, for Algerian merchants abroad, and, with Algiers no longer the military threat it had been earlier in the century, there were few direct repercussions for the actions of the French, British, and Dutch courts. It is here that we might begin to see the limits of cosmopolitanism or intercultural pluralism. The disregard by the French and British courts for the evidence presented by Algerian merchants and merchants of Algiers, which themselves represented the multilingual and multiconfessional nature of the North African commercial and legal systems, in part speaks to the growing European commercial and political hegemony in the Mediterranean. The permeable frontiers of the Western Mediterranean, as Maria Fusaro describes them, were not matched by the solid boundaries of what we can begin to see as clear national interest.[52]

The treaties between Algiers and their European trading partners reveal an attempt to regulate commerce in a difficult political zone. As a *dārü'l-cihād*, Algiers had to ensure that it performed its role as a barrier against enemies, its own and, to some extent, those of the sultans in Istanbul. At the same time, as a major centre of commerce, it had to find a way to ensure the continuity of peaceful trade. The various regulations agreed with France, Britain, and others, including the reciprocal rights of free movement, search,

226 Michael Talbot

and the legal jurisdiction of the consuls and deys, were therefore designed to regulate peaceful commerce, to filter enemy contraband from friendly cargo. It is clear that by the end of the eighteenth century, the French and British authorities had little interest in assuming good faith on the part of the Algerian authorities. No doubt that from the French and British perspective, there were plenty of complaints to be had about the conduct of Algerian corsairs in implementing this policy, especially as growing national pride and power meant growing egos to be bruised. But what is often ignored is the Algerian perspective on these matters. Returning to the letter of Bektaş Muhammad in 1709, his complaints about the conduct of the British, and attempts to illustrate the strict legality of Algerian actions, would have been dismissed in older histories – and indeed would probably still be dismissed in some more recent ones – as window-dressing for the pirate state. However, there is force in his arguments if we start from the position that the Algerians were not inherently beyond the bounds of recognised legal and diplomatic practice. Indeed, in the cases highlighted, the dey had cause to encourage the British to reflect on how far they were themselves operating within the bounds of established commercial practices.

The articles of peace and commerce were there to ensure the interests of both contracting parties were met. It was in the interest of the Algerian authorities that genuine British and French merchant ships should be allowed to pass, and it was not, for example, an unreasonable request that Algerian goods should not be sold on to Algerian enemies. It was also a reasonable expectation of the Algerian state, given the emphasis in their treaties on reciprocity, that its merchants abroad should be treated as Europeans in Algiers were treated. In Algiers, European and Algerian merchants could submit a variety of paperwork to a number of institutions to ensure their deals and transactions were registered, and to help in the event of subsequent litigation. Domestic law was exercised by consuls alongside the regal law of Algiers and Islamic law, each used for difference purposes with distinct boundaries enabling cosmopolitan legal and commercial interactions. The same cannot be said for many of the cases of Algerian merchants in European courts. If cosmopolitanism is, as Trivellato argues, based in part on mutual respect, then across the eighteenth century we find examples of the limits of cosmopolitanism, with Algiers, and Algerian merchants, dismissed as mere Moors, unworthy of reciprocal treatment within the framework of national self-interest and superiority.

Notes

1 The research from which this paper arose was undertaken as part of the European Research Council project 'Mediterranean Reonfigurations' (ConfigMed), ERC Advanced Grant no. 295868, based at Université Paris 1 Panthéon-Sorbonne.
2 Francesca Trivellato, *The Familiarity of Strangers: The Sephardic Diaspora, Livorno, and Cross-Cultural Trade in the Early Modern Period* (New Haven & London: Yale University Press, 2009), 73.

The limits of cosmopolitanism 227

3 Ibid.

4 For discussions of tolerance in the Ottoman context, see: Karen Barkey, "Islam and Toleration: Studying the Ottoman Imperial Model," *International Journal of Politics, Culture, and Society* 19:1–2 (2005), 5–19; Marc Baer, Ussama Makdisi and Andrew Shyrock, 'Tolerance and Conversion in the Ottoman Empire: A Conversation', *Comparative Studies in Society and History* 51, no. 4 (2009): 927–940.

5 Wolfgang Kaiser, "Introduction" in *La loge et le fondouk: Les dimensions spatiales des pratiques marchands en Méditerranée, Moyen Age – Époque moderne*, ed. Wolfgang Kaiser (Aix-en-Provence: Éditions Karthala, 2014), 9–17.

6 Lotfi Ben Rejeb, '"The general belief of the world": Barbary as genre and discourse in Mediterranean history', *European Review of History / Review européenne d'histoire* 19: 1 (2012): 15–31.

7 Jacques Philippe Laugier de Tassy, *Histoire du Royaume d'Alger, Avec L'Etat de Son Gouvernement, de ses Forces de Terre & de mer, de ses Revenus, Police, Justice, Politique & Commerce* (Amsterdam: Chez Henri du Sauzet, 1725); Jacques Philippe Laugier de Tassy, *Beschryving van het Koningryk en de Stadt Algiers, Met den Tegenwoordigen Staat Regeeringe, Landten Zeemagt, Inkomsten, Staatswetten, Werreltlyk Recht en Koophandel* (Amsterdam: Martin Schagen, 1725); Jacques Philippe Laugier de Tassy, *Historia del reyno de Argél, su govierno, fuerzas de mar y tierra, sus rentas, policía, justicia, politica y commercio*, trans. Antonio de Clarinara (Barcelona: Juan Piferrer, 1733).

8 *A Compleat History of the Piratical Sates of Barbary, viz. Algiers, Tunis, Tripoli and Morocco, Containing the Origin, Revolutions, and present State of these Kingdoms, their Forces, Revenues, Policy, and Commerce* (London: For R. Griffiths at the Dunciad in St Paul's Church-Yard, 1750).

9 Frederick C. Leiner, *The End of Barbary Terror: America's 1815 War Against the Pirates of North Africa* (Oxford: Oxford University Press, 2006); Ann Thomson, *Barbary and Enlightenment: European Attitudes towards the Maghreb in the Eighteenth Century* (Leiden: E.J. Brill, 1987); Ben Rejeb, "The general belief of the world"; Lemnouar Merouche, *Recherches sur l'Algérie à l'époque ottoman: II. La Course: mythe et réalité* (Paris: Editions Bouchene, 2007).

10 Emer de Vattel, *Le Droit des Gens ou Principes de la Loi Naturelle Appliqués à la Conduite & aux Affaires des Nations & des Souverains* (Leiden: Aux Depens de la Compagnie, 1758), vol.2, 133. 'Enfin il est un autre cas, où la Nation est coupable en général des attentats de ses membres. C'est lorsque par ses mœurs, par les maximes de son Gouvernement, elle accoutume & autorise les Citoyens à piller & maltraiter indifféremment les étrangeres, à faire des courses dans les païs voisins &c. Toutes les Nations ont droit de se liguer contre elle, de la réprimer, de la traiter en ennemie commune du Genre humain. Les Nations Chrêtiennes ne seroient pas moins fondées à se réünir contre les Républiques Barbaresques, pour détruire ces repaires d'écumeurs de Mer, chez qui l'amour du pillage, ou la crainte d'un juste châtiment, sont les seules règles de la paix ou de la guerre.' [v2.c6.§78]

11 For an in-depth discussion of de Vattel and his attitudes towards the North African Regencies, see: Walter Rech, *Enemies of Mankind: Vattel's Theory of Collective Security* (Leiden: Martinus Nijhoff Publishers, 2013), especially chapters 2 and 3.

12 Michael Talbot, "Protecting the Mediterranean: Ottoman responses to maritime violence, 1718–1770," *Journal of Early Modern History* 21, no. 4 (2017): 283–317.

13 For a discussion of the utility of this term, see: Maria Fusaro, "After Braudel: A reassessment of Mediterranean history between the Northern Invasion and the Caravane Maritime" in *Trade and Cultural Exchange in the Early Modern Mediterranean: Braudel's Maritime Legacy*, ed. Maria Fusaro, Colin Heywood & Mohamed-Salah Omri (London: Bloomsbury, 2010), 1–22.

228　Michael Talbot

14　Colin Heywood, "A frontier without archaeology? The Ottoman maritime frontier in the Western Mediterranean, 1660–1760" in *The Frontiers of the Ottoman World*, ed. A.C.S. Peacock (Oxford: Oxford University Press, 2009), 493–508.

15　For example: British Library [BL], Additional Manuscripts [Add MSS] 61493 f.7.

16　İbrahim Pençevi, *Tārīḫ-i Pençevī* (Istanbul, 1283 [1866]), vol. 2, 108; Mehmed Raşid, *Tārīḫ-i Rāşid* (Istanbul, 1282 [1865]), vol. 1, 27.

17　Şemseddin Sami Bey, *Ḳāmūsü'l-ʿalām*, vol. 3 (Istanbul, 1308 [1892]), 2082.

18　The National Archives, Kew [TNA], State Papers [SP] 108/11 fol.5. İngiltere pādişāhıñ veyḥud reʿayyesiniñ gemileri ve kezānıñ Cezāyīr'iñ ḳorşan gemileri veyaḥud bāzargān gemileri rū-yu deryada birbirine rast gelirse aramaḳtan ve birbirini incetmekten beri olub riʿayyet ve ḥidmet eyleyeler ve birbirinden erilüb ḥidmetlerine bir kimsne māniʿ olmaya.

19　İbid.

20　İbid. fols.5–6. Ḳorşan gemileri İngiliziñ bāzargān gemilerini rast gelirse gerek büyük ve gerek küçük eğer İngiliz pādişāhıñ ḥüküm ettiği yerlerden ṭaşda rast gelirlerise yalñızça bir şandak gönderile ve kürek çaḳandan ġayri ancaḳ iki adam ile gideler ve gemiye vardıḳda iki adamdan ġayri gitmeye meğer ki ẕikir olunan gemi reʾisiñin iẕn ve icāzet ile ola ol vaḳıtta ḳralıñ pasa-porṭası gösterdikte veyaḥud anıñ ḳapuṭan cenral eylediği kimesne veyaḥud ẕikr olunanıñ yerine ḥidmet eden kimesne İngiltere ve Ayrlanda ḳapṭan genralıñ eden veyaḥud İskoṭandaya ḳapuṭan cenrallıḳ eden ẕikr olunan üç ḳrallık herḳanġisi olur ise umarız ki mezkūr gemiye varan şandal ḥidmetini ʿaleʾl-ʿacele kāmil eydüb döne yoluna gide ve daḥi bāazargān gemisi cğlenmiyüb seferine revāna ola ver budurki eğer İngiliziñ ḳorşan gemilerinden Cezāyīr ḳorşanı veyaḥud bāzargānı her nerede rast gelir ise eğer mezkūr gemiyi Cezāyīr ḥākimiñ ṭarafından veyaḥud yanında ḥāẕır olan İngiliz ḳonsolos ṭarafından pasa-porṭa bulunur ise ol vaḳıtta ẕikr olunan gemiyi bir kimesne bir şeyini doḳunmayub selāmet ile yoluna gider.

21　TNA SP108/1/2.

22　J.C. Bancroft Davis (ed)., *Treaties and Conventions Concluded Between the United States of America*, 15.

23　*Tractaet van Vrede en van Commercie* [...], *[...]*(The Hague, 1680), 4; *Traitté de Paix et de Commerce* [...], (La Haye, 1680), 3.

24　Ibid.

25　Travers Twiss, *The Law of Nations, Considered as Independent Political Communities. Part II: On the Rights and Duties of Nations in Time of War* (Oxford: Clarendon Press, 1863), 146–47; Wilhelm G. Grewe, *The Epochs of International Law*, trans. Michael Byers (Berlin: Walter de Gruyter, 2000), 410–11.

26　Trivellato, *Familiarity of Strangers*, 96.

27　BL, Add MSS 61493, f.14. There is similar letter at fol.12.

28　Ibid. "Bektaş Muhammad Dey, Dārüʾl-cihād-ı maḥrūsa-ı Cezāyīr-i Ġarb."

29　Ibid. "ʿamdetüʾl-mulūküʾl-ʾİsāviye ve zīretüʾs-selāṭīnüʾl-Mesiḥiye'. 'Jesuan', and 'Messian' were synonyms for 'Christian'.

30　Ibid. "her ḳaçan rū-yu deryada İngiliz tüccār gemilerine rast geldiklerinde bir ferde ẕalim ve taʿaddī"

31　This appears to be related to *The Mary Gally* of Dublin. For correspondence on this matter, including additional Ottoman Turkish letters from Muhammad Bektaş, see: BL Add MSS 61535 fols.119–36.

32　BL Add MSS 61493. 'bir gemimiz bir Danimarḳ gemisi alub bu ṭarafa duḫūl eylediği'. Colin Heywood has examined the case of this particular vessel, *The Isabella* of Kirkcaldy, in "Ideology and the profit motive in the Algerine *Corso*: The strange case of the *Isabella* of Kirkcaldy, 1709–1714" in *Anglo-Saxons in the*

The limits of cosmopolitanism 229

Mediterranean: Commerce, Politics, and Ideas (XVII-XX Centuries), eds. Carmel Vassallo and Michela D'Angelo (Msida: Malta University Press, 2007), 17–42. An earlier letter of the dey on this subject, dated the middle of Şeval 1120 (end of December 1708), can be found at: BL Add MSS 61535 fol.163.

33 BL Add MSS 61493, f.14. "Da'vāsı şer'an ve ḳānūn faṣl olmaḳ içün büyük dīvān ve 'azīm meşveret vaẓi' olan ḳānūn-nāmelere naẓar olunub vechen mine'l-vücūh meẕkure gemide bir İngiliz 'alāmatı bulunmayub."

34 Ibid. "cemi' ehl-i dīvān düsmān gemisi eydiğini bildiklerinde aḫẕ ve ḳabẓ ḥakkı olunmuştur."

35 Ibid. "ḫaṭırıñız içün derununda bulunan on-iki 'aded-i nefer iṭlāḳ ve balyoz ḳūllarıñıza vermiştir."

36 Ibid. "bu ṭaraḳ tüccārları İskenderiye'den bir Fransız şeyṭiyesi kıra eydüb bu ṭarafa gelirleriken bir gemiñiz rast gelüb alub aḫẕ ve ḳabẓ etmiş ve ḥalāṣ içün bir kaç def'ā balyoz ḳūllarıñıza söyleyüb dediği düsmānımız sançāğı altında alınan şey ṭaleb olunmaz zīrā mu'teber olan sancāḳdır dedikte."

37 BL Add MSS 61493, f.17–18.

38 TNA, SP108/13. "İngiliz ḳralıñ re'ayasından bir kimesne bir müslümān ile veyāḫūd Cezāyir ḥükümünde olan kimsneler ile da'vāları olsa meẕkūrlarıñ da'vāları devletlü veyāḫūd dīvān ṭaraflarından faṣl olunur ġayrı kimesneden olunmaya ve eğer beyninlerinde da'vāları olur ise ol zamānda İngiliz balyoz olan kimesne da'vāları faṣl eyder ġayrı kimesnden olmaya."

39 For example, this from the Tuscan treaty of 1748: 'İmparaṭor-ḳralınıñ re'āyāsından bir kimesne bir müslümān ile veyaḥūd Cezā'ir'iñ ḥükümünde olan kimesneler ile da'vāları olsa meẕkūrlarıñ da'vāları devletlü dāyı ve dīvān-ı muḥterem ḥużūrunda faṣl oluna bir ġayrı kimesne daḥi olmaya ve eğer mābeynlerinde da'vāları olur ise ol zamānda İmparator balyozu olan kimesne da'vālarını faṣl eyleye' / 'If one of the subjects of the emperor-king has legal disputes with a Muslim or a person subject to Algerian authority, the said legal dispute is to be heard by the illustrious dey and honourable divan, [and] not by any other person. If the legal disputes are among themselves, in that case the emperor's ambassador will hear the case'. Archivio di Stato di Firenze [ADF] 712PO/1/327, No.7.

40 Centre des Archives Diplomatiques de Nantes [CADN], 2MI/967 vol. 3, 176–83.

41 Archives Nationales d'Outre Mer, Aix-en-Provence [ANOM] 45MIOM/12, 3 June 1686.

42 ANOM 45MIOM/5, Ottoman Turkish text undated, French note dated 30 January 1769.

43 Michael Talbot, "When proof is not enough: An Ottoman merchant in the Gibraltar Vice-Admiralty Court in the 1760s," *Quaderni Storici* 153, no. 3 (2016): 753–776. This was part of a wider collection of articles on litigation and elements of proof in the Mediterranean, edited by Wolfgang Kaiser and Johann Petitjean.

44 TNA SP71/11, further observations of Hew Craig, undated.

45 TNA SP71/11, James Bruce to the Earl of Halifax, 18 March 1765.

46 The bundle of papers relating to this case can be found in CADN 22PO/1/74, An IX (1800–1801).

47 Ibid., "Au Counseil des Prises. Memoire POUR les capitaine et armateur du corsair français le *Brutus* CONTRE *les capitaine et propriétaires de la cargaison du navire soi-disant le* Rachel."

48 This goes back to the French treaty with Algiers in 1689, subsequently added to in 1719 and 1765, most recently (for this case) renewed in 1790.

49 Archives Diplomatiques, Traités et accords 171900003, Texte de l'accord, 1719. "Il y aura Paix entre l'Empereur de France et les très Illustre Dey, Pacha, Divan et Milice de la Ville et Royaume d'Alger et leurs Sujets, et ils pourront

230 *Michael Talbot*

réciproquement faire leur commerce dans les deux Royaumes et naviguer en tout Sureté, sans en pouvoir être empêché, pour quelque cause et sous quelque Prétexte que ce soit."

50 CADN 22PO/1/74, "Au Conseil des Prises," 20. "Il est vrai que ce témoin est le seul qui parle du *jet des papiers à la mer*; mais il est aisé de concevoir le motif qui a fermé la bouche à tous les autres gens d'équipage, tous intéressés à sauver leurs pacotilles."

51 Ibid., 21–22. "Le privilège, si tant il est vrai qu'il existe, d'être affranchi des formes des réglemens, est personnel à Alger, il est purement relatif aux personnes et aux objets qui les concernent; la simulation une fois reconnue, tout doit rentrer dans l'ordre commun; la fraude un fois prouvée fait disparoître le privilège; la justice le veut, l'intérêt de la France l'exige."

52 Fusaro, "After Braudel," 7.

13 Making Ireland poor

Poverty, trade, and sectarianism in the eighteenth century Atlantic

James Livesey

Issues of poverty, trade, cosmopolitanism, and empire were mutually entangled in eighteenth century political economy. The rich country/poor country debate, and the anxieties around the corrupting effects of commercial civilisation, which have become key themes for historians of political economy, drove politics around the Atlantic littoral.[1] The focus of this scholarship has been on the growth of societies trading within a shared mercantile system but having different costs for labour. A poor country, like Scotland, had greater growth potential and that created anxiety in the co-ordinating centre of the trading system, England. Historians have paid less attention to the entanglement of cosmopolitanism and economic expansion with their antonyms, sectarianism and poverty.

Sectarianism and poverty are obviously particularly important themes in Irish history, which is too often seen as an exception to or an aberration from the general trend of eighteenth-century commercial, imperial, and political histories.[2] More recent work has emphasised the complex interactions of imperial and local contexts in Ireland and aligned Irish experience with that of the provinces, territories, and dependencies of the British North Atlantic.[3] Imperial ambitions for trade shaped different ideas of commercial cosmopolitanism which in turn generated new kinds of identities. However cosmopolitan aspirations, especially when expressed through imperial institutions, did not always align with cosmopolitan identities.

Changes in the nature of empire, particularly the British Empire, in the late eighteenth century, created the conditions for new kinds of political mobilisation in Ireland. The complex and idiosyncratic forms commercial cosmopolitanism took on in eighteenth century Ireland had significant consequences for versions of imperial patriotism. The Volunteer movement was particularly complex; clearly a revolutionary threat but always reminded by their leader, the Earl of Charlemont, that 'the fame of the Volunteers has been that they act within the Constitution.'[4] The Irish response to the Seven Years War was particularly difficult to understand because the contribution of the Irish trading community to British victory had unforeseen consequences that threatened the role that had been played by Irish traders in the Atlantic world. The Irish case illuminates how fragile

232 *James Livesey*

cosmopolitan identities were, and how the unintended consequences of imperial policies promoting commerce could undermine them. Ireland became poor, and in an absolute rather than relative sense, not by withdrawing from a world of commerce, or even through any obvious policy of planned under-development, but through the particular way in which it participated in the world of commerce.

Poverty is not trans-historical. The influential work of Amartya Sen has established an understanding of poverty not as biological destitution, but as restricted entitlement, which is always political and social in nature.[5] Poverty is radically historical and can only be understood in terms of exclusion from the rights and possibilities present in particular historical contexts. This raises the issue of historical metrics for poverty. Robert Allen's 2001 *Explorations* paper is foundational to the historical study of poverty. It looks at the relationship between consumption bundles, priced locally, and wage rates (the welfare ratio) to establish an empirical basis for judgements about poverty.[6] Allen argues that by this measure poverty was substantially alleviated around London in the eighteenth century because the welfare ratio remained consistently low. Wage earners could rely on sustained periods of high wages, calculated against the consumption goods and rents such wages sustained, which in turn meant they were not dominated by fear of destitution. In Paris the wage ratio did not remain consistently low and so many French workers, if not absolutely poor, lived in fear of poverty.

Did this mean that France was a poor country? A historically nuanced understanding of poverty cannot restrict itself to the relative welfare of individuals. Inequality is a ubiquitous feature of every society, so poverty, and wealth, must also be understood as both individual and collective qualities; countries, or regions, are rich and poor as well as individuals. Despite the predictions of David Ricardo, if a country does not attain the right mixture of culture and institutions it can retain comparative advantage in poverty.[7] Wage rates in a poor country can, and often do, rise, but a poor country cannot emulate the behaviour of a rich country, because it does not have the institutions to sustain wealth, the capacity to create new kinds of value through co-ordinated action.[8] France sustained its capacity for innovation, and could explore multiple pathways to flourishing, and though wages did not always rise, years of growth in the eighteenth century outnumbered years of decline.[9] France sustained its rich institutions which were able to direct public spending to useful tasks.[10] The debates on the economy in France therefore turned on which was the better route to prosperity, and in the early days of the French Revolution there was confidence that poverty could be abolished.[11] France did not have the characteristics of a poor country, which can grow spectacularly, but decline just as quickly. Instead France sustained a steady annual rate of growth for the last fifty years of the eighteenth century.[12] From this point of view French workers in Paris and

Making Ireland poor 233

Strasbourg may have been poor, or at least poorer than workers in London, in the eighteenth century, but France was in no way a poor country.[13]

So was Ireland poor in the eighteenth century? Did it become poor, or had it always been poor? And if we accept the Sen view of poverty what were the patterns of exclusion from entitlement that characterised Irish poverty? Finally, how can we account for Irish poverty in the eighteenth century given that its fundamental institutions such as laws, courts, markets and politics were shared with other areas of the British Empire, which were becoming richer?

Poverty and subaltern cosmopolitanism

Of all the questions posed the second is the easiest to answer. There was a seventeenth-century consensus that Ireland was a rich country but housed a poor people, and the reason was under-population. William Petty, in his *Treatise of taxes and contributions*, argued that, 'fewness of people is real poverty,' and that immigration to Ireland was the route to national flourishing.[14] William Temple's 1673 *Observations upon the United Provinces*, and *An Essay upon the Advancement of Trade in Ireland* contrasted the wealth of the 'full-peopled' Netherlands to the relatively poor because thinly populated Ireland. Richard Lawrence extended the same point. The small number of people living off the rich land kept rents too low and took away any incentive to take on risk, 'when a man may purchase a better rent for 1000 pound in Ireland, than he can for two in England, or three in Holland, or proportionally farm, what prudent man will undergo the difficulties and run the hazards of Trade, when he may dispose of his Mony (sic) with much more ease and safety?'[15] This curious anomaly, of riches and poverty commingled, created an anxiety about what the effects might be on England if the Irish population increased. The fear that Ireland might be the occasion of impoverishing England was articulated by Roger Coke when he argued that the perceived depopulation of England in the 1660s was due to the Navigation Acts, the American plantations and the 're-peopling' of Ireland after the rebellion of 1641.[16] The same argument reappeared even in the changed conditions of the 1770s in a pamphlet arguing that 'the Irish peasant is poor from having too much land, more than he can till properly, and having the necessaries of life much below the worth of labour.'[17] An anonymous proposal to set up an Irish Commission of Trade even used the wealth of the Irish environment to argue that a successful development policy would have to be driven by consumption of imported luxury goods, 'Ireland is so plentifull a country, and affords the necessaries of life so cheap, that a man there by 2 days work can gett enough to sustain him 7; and therefore its not to be expected that a man there should upon this principle of necessity work 6 days when by working 2 he can acquire those necessaries. So that the only way to prevail upon the Irish to work more

234   *James Livesey*

constantly is to bait or tempt their appetites with some luxuries which they love more than they do idleness.'[18] Irish poverty was of a very particular sort.

But just why did Ireland become poor and when? Irish political economists involved with the Patriot movement had an explanation for poverty: British self-interest. The iconic Irish patriot, Charles Lucas, argued that his 'poor country and ruined city' had to be rescued from destitution and corruption by political reform.[19] The anonymous *Examinator's Letters* articulated this position with particular clarity, 'the impolitic system which has, during this century, pervaded the British councils until the year 1778, by laying every possible restriction on all manufactures of Ireland, except plain linen, brown or white, has been the means of giving the Levant trade in woollens, and in all its variety to the French, and has enabled the French, Dutch and Germans to divide the African trade with England, and to supply Spain, Portugal and their colonies with various manufactures, that have enriched the natural enemies of the British empire at the expence [sic] of Ireland.'[20] Another pamphlet complained that 'England hath turned every valuable export of Ireland into her own hands, and she hath not permitted her to receive tea, sugar, tobacco, indigo, rice, coffee and a multitude of other weighty articles, but from herself.'[21] Swift's satires on the Irish Whig schemes for banks and improvements are the best known of these kinds of jeremiads.

Yet, however seductive to Irish *amour propre* this analysis may have been, it required a faith in an extraordinarily self-destructive policy on the part of Britain toward Ireland. The criticisms of the perverse effects of trade regulation were not uniquely Irish, but were the core themes of imperial Patriots and American revolutionaries.[22] Moreover, the critique of imperial trade regulation was not the monopoly of oppositional patriots but was a view held by Prime Ministers as well as radicals. The Irish critique of the perverse outcomes of imperial commercial regulation was of a piece with every other critique.[23] The patriot Whig critique of Imperial trade policy was not uniquely Irish; if Ireland's place in the empire was causing a particular kind of poverty, it was doing so in ways that were more subtle.

Jean Louis de Lolme's 1787 *The British Empire in Europe* noticed an odd contradiction in the way Irish politicians wrote about Irish economic affairs in the late eighteenth century.[24] The great complaint was of Irish poverty, caused by restraint of the woollen trade and restrictions on the colonial trade.[25] However political commentators from Arthur Young to the Earl of Orrery agreed that Ireland, and in particular Irish trade, had been transformed since the 1740s 'the restraints on the trade of Ireland, though detrimental, were not of that calamitous nature which was represented by political speakers, even in the British Parliament, at the time we are speaking of, which was no doubt believed by many individuals in Ireland.'[26] De Lolme thought that the rhetoric around Irish poverty was political and so a reflection of the crisis of the British Empire, 'the design which, at the present

Making Ireland poor 235

period, began to be formed and pursued by the people of Ireland and leaders, of rescuing their trade from the detrimental abridgements, and provincial restraints, under which it lay.' The point here is not that Ireland was not really poor, rather that the perception of poverty was less a response to immiseration than to collective constraint that would have disasterous consequences. The data on wages and prices, as fragmentary as they are, supports de Lolme's contention that the problem of Irish poverty in this period was not a simple matter. Wages and prices were rising together in Ireland from the 1770s to the 1790s, despite the interruptions to trade caused by the American revolution, indicating that the economy was expanding.[27] While there is controversy around this topic, turning on the relationship of wages to prices, the Irish cost of living tracked British indices, albeit with lower wages and prices and while displaying higher volatility, up to the famine.[28] Changes in Irish living standards, though different in absolute terms, reflected British patterns, at least until the catastrophe of the 1840s. Living standards fell on both islands in the Revolutionary era and only recovered slowly. De Lolme's insight was that poverty was a political and institutional fact in Ireland. Irish poverty was strangely similar to French wealth. In both cases welfare indices tracked British conditions, and in both wage earners were vulnerable to greater fluctuations in prices and wages. However the French community retained its faith in its capacity to act collectively to create value while the Irish did not. Ireland became poor in the late eighteenth century because it could not sustain or participate in identities or political institutions that sustained collective action.

Varieties of cosmopolitanism

To understand how Ireland became poor in this sense we need to understand its mid-eighteenth century moment of growth and the subsequent challenges to it. In the diplomatic and commercial conditions of the Atlantic before the Seven Years War Ireland's divided elite gave it an unanticipated comparative advantage in international trade. One of the most important features of early eighteenth-century Irish history was the emergence of a Catholic merchant elite.[29] This new elite did not threaten Protestant Ireland but aligned with it. Ireland's separate but intermittently co-operative confessional merchant communities created networks of coordination and communication that were particularly well-adapted to the fragmented world of Atlantic trade in the first half of the eighteenth century.[30] Irish Catholics enjoyed legal rights to trade in Spanish territories, and through them Irish and British commodities and capital found new markets.[31] Jacobite and confessional networks, both Catholic and Dissenting, also sustained Irish trade with France and the French colonies, even during moments of conflict between Britain and France. In a fragmented world the plurality of Irish identities and commitments created distinct advantages.

236   *James Livesey*

The provisions trade, and particularly the extensive salt beef trade from Cork, is a good example of the complex patterns of mutual interdependence. Provisions of salt beef, pork and butter consistently made up more than two-thirds of Irish exports to the Americas.[32] Cork, argues Thomas Truxes, had the most sophisticated provisions industry in the Atlantic economy in the eighteenth century, relying on a complex network of markets in Munster to source foodstuffs as well as an international network of merchants.[33] Salt beef from Cork served multiple markets, but the key outlets were provisioning, both merchant and naval, and supplying both French and British sugar colonies in the West Indies.[34] This trade was relatively impervious to the effects of war. Despite the twenty-four embargoes placed on Irish food exports at various points after 1740 the trade continued to grow. Intermediaries in Dutch and Spanish ports connected supply chains to the French islands when direct export was impossible and French officials issued passports protecting the trade from privateering.[35] Irish provisioning was visibly integrated into a French, as well as a British, imperial economy. Thomas Lowndes was able to describe the trade with accuracy, even as he denounced it; 'France, as a kingdom, with its wines and brandies, has constantly bought the wool of Ireland, at as small an expence (at least) as it cost Ireland. Then, with part of the profit, arising from the advantageous use France made of that wool, she has victualled her fleets with Irish beef and butter and furnished her sugar colonies with provisions, not easily to be procured elsewhere; and the surplus of the gain from Irish wool has greatly assisted France in carrying on her dangerous and ambitious designs.'[36] The exigencies of commerce imposed themselves on French ministers who might have wanted France to monopolise its colonial trade, and British imperial reformers who could find no cost-effective way of regulating Irish trade.

The mutual interdependence of separate confessional communities was not without its challenges. In 1709 Cork Corporation, made anxious by the evident increase in Catholic wealth, petitioned the Parliament to 'debar Papists from foreign trade.'[37] Such a move was economically impossible. The positions of the Protestant export merchants, holders of capital and inhabitants of the medieval city from which Catholics were excluded, and the suburban Catholic dealers, such as the butchers, were entirely interdependent. Catholic integration into a wider commercial world was ineluctable. The Moylan family, butchers from Fair Lane on the north side of Cork, make a good example.[38] John Moylan was a butcher, whose extensive slaughterhouse operations continued to be the base for the family's wealth. However, from that base his brother, sons and grandsons were able to set up as merchants in Lisbon and Cadiz. His grandson Stephen Moylan moved to Philadelphia in 1768 where he founded the Friendly Sons of St Patrick and, exploiting the family's background, became Quartermaster General of Washington's army. Finally, another son, Francis, became Catholic Bishop of Cork, where he built the Catholic Cathedral of St Mary and St Anne in the neighbourhood of Fair Lane. These patterns of social change, rooted in

Making Ireland poor 237

complex patterns of mutual interdependence, did not cite explicit ideals of commercial cosmopolitanism. However they depended on an implicitly cosmopolitan horizon of co-operation that transcended particular identities.

The travels and work of Thomas Amory, the third of the name, lend us a real insight into the room for manoeuvre that Irish merchants exploited in the first six decades of the eighteenth century. Originally from Devon, Amory's family had settled in Ireland after the Restoration, buying land in Kerry. It owned Bunratty Castle in County Clare from 1712 to 1720. In 1711 Thomas Amory established himself in Angra in the Azores as the supercargo to Nicholas Oursel, a London merchant active in the West Indies trade. On arrival in the Azores the first letters that Amory sent were not to London but to merchants in the West of Ireland; Coursey, Cusack, and Gallwey, all Catholic merchants active in Ennis and Limerick, as well as to his contacts among his co-religionists in Dublin, especially his brother-in-law James Ramsay.[39] As Amory explained to Oursel he thought he would do best as correspondent for trade from Liverpool and especially from Dublin and this required that he cultivate his Irish network.[40]

Irish houses, like the Amorys, articulated Southern European and North Atlantic networks of capital and trade. The most significant network of this nature that has been explored is the use of bills of exchange drawn on the Irish brandy houses of the Charente that facilitated trade between France and Britain.[41] Brandy paper was so secure and traded at such a low discount that it was effectively a way of transferring the profits of engagement in the Southern European trade back into London. The Ostend company had played a similar role. The Sarsfield family, Catholic merchants from Cork, articulated several such networks. Robert Black, a member of a Presbyterian family of wine merchants originally from Armagh and trading from Bordeaux, stayed with Sarsfield in Ostend during his travels in the Low Countries and relied on him for commercial contacts.[42] The Sarsfield's account books are full of transactions that moved across various boundaries. Local Cork Protestant merchant families, such as the Woulfes of Bandon, as well as old Catholic merchant houses such as the Goulds, used the Sarsfield connection to settle bills in Ostend, and the Sarsfields used their connections to move money from the continent through Cork to London.[43] Patrick Sarsfield, established in Ostend, expressed his view to his brother that 'the home trade, without that of Indies,' would not be 'worth the labour.'[44] Their hard work only made sense because of the extended network they managed.

Even merchants working from Irish ports that sustained a much lower volume of trade enjoyed access to complex networks that communicated across imperial, religious and ethnic boundaries. The letter book of John Kelly, a merchant from Limerick, reveals an awareness of imperial contexts as acute as any Cork merchant prince. Like many Irish merchants Roche was a client of Jonathan Gurnell's house in London for insurance, using them in 1744 to insure a cargo of rum from Antigua to Cork.[45] Gurnell was

238   *James Livesey*

also employed to resolve invoices and receipts from trades Kelly made in the timber trade from Trondheim, wine from Bordeaux and textiles to Lisbon.[46] But the most telling elements in Kelly's records are not the elements of the network that can be directly observed but the comments that reveal the complex border-crossing strategies that animated those networks. In a letter to Joseph Percival of Chester Kelly offhandedly remarked that if Percival wished to ship goods to the James River and avoid French privateers, he should do so in the smaller vessels that the Irish used in their interloping trade.[47] In other letters to John Archdeacon in Rotterdam he lets him know that he has intelligence from France that no fleet will be sent to the West Indies in that year, so the market for salt beef will be depressed.[48] The complexities of intra-imperial Atlantic politics and trade opened opportunities but also created difficulties for border-crossing Irish merchants. Amory was put in a difficult position by the unforeseen news that a peace had been signed in 1713. With peace came access to English ports for the signatories, 'since the peace is made no one will load in any English ship, which is a great misfortune to us again as we shall not get half a freight, and if the peace had not happened we should have been full yesterday.'[49]

The role of Irish merchants in the Southern trade had a constitutive role in the establishment of American trade networks in the middle of the eighteenth century. Thomas Amory explained to William Rhett, a merchant at Charleston, how he was able to match supply and demand, and evade efforts at regulation, through his position in the Azores,

> Our trade here the securest is goods from Great Britain as baize, crepes, drugetts, serges, hatts, stockings which constantly goes off well and sells at above cost. But when I have it not from the North generally gett it from Lisbon and we could easily naturalize forreign ships as Portuguese to send to Brazil which if we could get a cargoe suitable there is great money to be gott (Provisions including flour the best trade to Brazil). I could send a ship with those goods. I could make her a Portuguese but no English could go in trade for there is a new order from Lisbon to Brazil to the contrary...[50]

Amory was explaining to Rhett how he could use the techniques developed by Irish traders to open up Brazil to American trade.

The trade of the Atlantic colonies, and particularly of Philadelphia, was predominantly with southern Europe and the West Indies, and Truxes reports that Irish merchants were particularly well embedded in this region.[51] In this letter Amory strategized engagement with the slave trade using the same interloping techniques, 'also could send them under Portuguese colours to Guinea or where you please yet they should go to Brazil if could see an advantage but negroes sells as well at Carolinas as Brazil for these never give above 150 per head at most for lusty negroes and Boyes 40, 50 and 60.' Amory himself moved to Boston in 1719 and his descendants became

Making Ireland poor 239

important members of the Boston merchant community. The techniques for the management of trade and politics were not lost to the family. In 1770 John and Jonathan Amory arranged for Irish linen to be sent to Boston, through London, in order to take advantage of the bounty on sales to England, 'the occasion of our conducting in this manner is the whimsical determination of the trade here, who though they do not suffer Irish linens bought in London to be sold here, yet suffer them purchased in Ireland, and only sent to England for the bounty to be sold.'[52]

Plural confessional communities had uses beyond trade. Irish banks in London, particularly the Fitzgeralds and the Nesbitts, were distinct precisely because they did business far beyond their ethnic base, their comparative advantage lay in intermediation. These banks did not exit the Irish trading community in London because, as Louis Cullen argued, there never was one, in the sense of a network that managed trusted trade amongst known members of community or kin (unlike the Scottish and Jewish communities). Craig Bailey argues this was because the Irish were not restricted to trade and had access to other spheres on same basis as English merchants. Bailey argues that the Irish Catholic banking community was particularly complex, simultaneous mobilising ethnic networks while enjoying the same access to resources and institutions as any other London house.[53] Bills drawn on Nesbitts were used by the Sarsfields in their complicated network. A 1725 transaction between Dominic Sarsfield, John Harper and James Morris was settled with bills from Knox and Nesbitt.[54]

The Seven Years War initially created even more opportunities for this enterprising, border-crossing trading community. Irish beef found its way to French armies by being traded in the port of Monte Cristi in Spanish Hispaniola for French sugar from the neighbouring Saint Domingue.[55] The war was initially a boon to the Irish houses in London because their ability to trade across borders made them useful in army contracts. In 1756, Nesbitts moved 6000 barrels of beef and 4000 firkins of butter to Portugal, thus from the outset of the Seven Years War, the Nesbitts demonstrated that they could animate their networks to raise the necessary capital and transport goods to see through large-scale government contracts. They even got contract to supply pay to troops in campaign against the French at Louisbourg, Cape Breton Island, by using French networks. However, the Irish banking houses in London, particularly the Nesbitts and the Fitzgeralds, who had even survived the traumatic effects of the South Sea Bubble on Irish investors, lose their distinctive function, become vulnerable and close by the late 1770s.[56] The hybrid Irish networks were threatened by the changes in imperial structures at the end of the Seven Years War.

International, cosmopolitan, border-crossing networks created interesting identities that extended beyond the trading community. One of the most fascinating characters who exhibited hybrid cosmopolitanism was the Franco-Irish Comte de Kearney, a captain in the French service in India in Lally's Irish regiment. Having been captured near Pondicherry he recounts a

240 *James Livesey*

series of adventures, mostly having to do with his time as a prisoner of war where he seems to have infuriated his captors. In one of his picaresque tales he recounts a shipwreck where because he understood English he understood the British officers were considering taking their chances on their own. His appeal to common humanity shamed them into making an effort to save their French prisoners: 'Hearing these words an English officer called Scott, a furious man prone to the most violent fits of temper, cried: 'what, one single Irish Frenchman, and a prisoner of war wants to lay down the law and dares to call us barbarous!' 'Sir,' I calmly replied, 'that's what an Irish Frenchman is for you: our common misfortunes renders us all equals, and here I am as free as you are.' Later in his travels he again insisted on cosmopolitan plasticity of identity when he demanded that the French officers be treated decently: 'I felt honoured to share with the French all the unpleasantness that the English liked to cause them; that I thought little of any man who could think differently in such circumstances; that the Franco-Irish were doubly French.' Kearney was capable of being Irish, British, Franco-Irish or double French.[57]

This hybrid cosmopolitanism was never entirely unnoticed or uncontested. In the aftermath of the War of Austrian Succession the circumstances that had created the curious situation in which Irish trade was simultaneously highly restricted and unregulated began to be examined more closely. John Perceval, Second Earl of Egmont, explained in a submission to the House of Lords considering a new ban on imports of Irish sailcloth, that the various acts restricting Irish trade only had perverse results.[58] Irish purchases in the Baltic may have been revenue lost to English merchants, but the ease of communication between Ireland and the Baltic as well as the cheapness of Baltic product made it impossible, as well as impolitic, to attempt to regulate. Egmont's conclusions were not reassuring to any Irish sense of distinctiveness however. He argued that in the imperial circumstance 'can any man of an open understanding consider Ireland but in the light of four or five great counties added to England.'[59] On the other hand there were arguments for benefits to the Empire from distinct Irish networks. Irish information gathering from merchant sources was likely to be easier and more effective than British:

> and if a way can be found by this means to get intelligence in matters of state, as well as in matters of trade, it will the more concern and oblige England to have this method for intelligence settled in Ireland, and more especially as this covert of presence of trade may probably get the necessary intelligence form abroad with more secrecy and security than any other way and with little or no charge to England.[60]

Whether approving or disapproving, the importance of Ireland's idiosyncratic trading community to the wealth of the country was widely acknowledged.

Making Ireland poor 241

The ambiguities of imperial patriotism

Commercial cosmopolitanism was the condition for the growth in Irish trade, and so in Irish wealth, in the middle decades of the eighteenth century. However, by the 1780s it was commonly accepted that Ireland was poor, and that institutions of imperial political economy were making it poor. The peculiar cosmopolitan accommodation to a world of fragmented trading empires did not survive, but the story is not simply one of imperial imposition of controls. Ireland achieved free trade, of a sort, in 1779 and legislative independence in 1782. Irish merchant communities did not simply collapse into sectarian identities under the pressure of political adjustment. A complex and highly contingent path led from the collective wealth of the 1750s to the national poverty of the 1780s.

For late-eighteenth-century observers, one of the most striking features of politics was the ability of large territorial monarchies, empires, to mobilise the kind of national sentiment that had been previously characteristic of republics. The Seven Years War amplified this kind of patriotism everywhere. The War, and even more particularly the unstable settlement hammered out at the Peace of Paris, is generally accepted as the pivot around which the trajectories of the French and British Empires turned. Provoked by defeat, France entered into a project of reform that would, ironically, result in the end of the monarchy in the Revolution. Britain confronted the task of co-ordinating an expanded empire, meeting the costs of victory and satisfying the sense of disappointment at limited territorial gains. Padraig Higgins has written a fine analysis of the domestic consequences of the extension of the culture of patriotism to Ireland; what I would like to do is to pay attention to the way external structures shaped the political and cultural possibilities for Irish people acting at home and abroad.[61]

The perception that one of the consequences of the Seven Years War was an intensified form of patriotism was current in the 1760s. To celebrate the end of the hostilities the *Comédie française* put on a new one-act comedy on March 14th 1763. Favart's *L'Anglais a Bordeaux*. This was not a demanding piece; Diderot condemned it in his *Corrrespondence littéraire* precisely because it was a crude mixture of cultural clichés about English identity. The plot concerned the relations between Darmant and his captives Milord Brumton and his daughter Clarice. They had become his prisoners when they had taken passage from Dublin to London and their ship had been taken by Darmant's privateering cruiser. Darmant, of course, falls for Clarice and sees in Brumton a fellow noble. The dramatic action, and the comedy, turns on Brumton, who does not act like a noble, but like a patriot. He plays out the national stereotype of the British patriot. The only music that Brumton can listen to is Handel and when he sees his daughter Clarissa reading a French novel throws it out the window. He is also comically melancholic. This is a comedy turn but is also a powerful image of the

242 *James Livesey*

patriot nation. In possibly the only serious speech in the play Darmant explains to his sister how the culture of patriotism worked.

> Madame, learn to better understand the Englishman. His character leads him to the loftiest goals. A profound politician, busy with projects, he strives for the honour to enlighten his fatherland. The least of the citizens, intent on his rights, regards the public papers, and directs England, counts the votes in Parliament, judges the equity of laws, freely pronounces on war or peace and weighs the interests of kings.[62]

However the performance of independent patriotism depended on a more subtle and compromised networks. Brumton is supported, or at least thinks he is supported, by letters of change drawn by English houses on their Bordeaux correspondents. These would all have been Irish and Scottish, since the English had been deported in 1756 and, if real, would very likely have been negotiated through the Nesbitt banking network which was very active in Bordeaux during the war. The same networks were used by French merchants to support their friends and families in the British Isles during wartime.[63]

The challenge to the complex and hybrid Irish merchant community was to negotiate the emergence of unitary Imperial patriotism. As James Vaughn explains there were two programmes that sought to respond to the crisis of imperial over-extension at the accession of George III: radical Whiggism and New Tories.[64] The Irish Patriot movement, aligned to radical Whiggism, attempted to hammer out a distinctive constitutional settlement largely organised around a vision of free trade.[65] The Patriot vision had to compete with an imperial ideal, of the Tories, that was far less optimistic about the capacity of trade and commerce to transcend problems of identity and resource.[66] The Irish problems were intensified as the Tories largely shaped the imperial response. In the aftermath of the Peace of Paris new trade regulations were enforced more rigorously than the old Navigation Acts had been. The loss of the Isle of Man as a smuggling entrepot in 1765 undermined tea smuggling to America by Irish merchants and by the 1770s customs officers were eliminating Irish manufactured goods from American markets.[67] The imperial centre played much greater attention to uniformity in legal practice across the Atlantic, which had particular consequences for arrangements that had been improvised to manage a more complex world. The accommodations and innovations invented in the colonies came under threat, previously secure legal claims became uncertain, and existing networks were threatened.[68]

Increasing regulation of imperial trade during the war and particularly after 1763 had unforeseen consequences, and not only in America.[69] Closing down those hybrid networks was not an accident but an explicit goal of imperial retrenchment. Rose Fuller, the MP and former Jamaican colonist who was familiar with the Irish trade, wrote a series of proposals on Ireland

Making Ireland poor 243

for Grenville in the early 1760s. He proposed that all boats captured smuggling brandy into Ireland should burned, as should the carriages used to transport the liquor.[70] He suggested that the King be petitioned to issue an embargo on the entire Irish provision trade, and that Ireland only be allowed supply British shipping and colonies.[71] Finally he suggested 'that for a further supply to be granted to his majesty there be paid in the Kingdom of Ireland all and the same stamp duties that are now payable in this kingdom.'[72] Imposing taxation in this way would have amounted to extinguishing the limited scope of legislative action in Ireland. Nothing this draconian was actually attempted, but this was the thinking that animated the enemies of the Patriots.

British commitment to and eventual success in the Seven Years War finally ended whatever hesitation or ambivalence there may have been about Britain's role in the organisation of trade and empire in the Atlantic. Contemporaries, such as Favart, remarked on the intensity of national feeling they now perceived to animate British elites and even contrasted it with a cosmopolitan, European sentiment that they hoped would succeed the war. The necessity for Britain to operate as a hegemon, and set the terms for Atlantic trade, had institutional consequences that were if anything more important than the cultural consequences. The reflections of Josiah Tucker on the optimal set of rules for British trade were stimulated precisely by his perception that establishing the role of Ireland in this new world was crucial to its design. The whole-hearted imposition of trade rules, exemplified in the efforts to eliminate systematic smuggling, considerably narrowed the space within which many Irish merchants had linked up networks in Southern Europe and the Spanish colonies with London. The ability Irish merchants, and in particular Catholic merchants, had enjoyed to move money, men and materials between Cadiz, Bordeaux, Ostend and London ceased to offer a privileged niche in Atlantic trade networks and so the hybrid universalism of figures such as the Comte de Kearney or the Black family was imperilled. The unforeseen consequence of these changes was a renewed and intensified concentration on the trade of Ireland itself.

The 'Grenville programme' of intensified control of imperial trade increasingly closed down the space in which Irish Catholic merchants had operated, threatened the mutually beneficial relationship between Catholic and Protestant merchant houses, and drove both back into competition in the legal trade and, in consequence, to assert themselves in Irish towns. The Catholic Committee began agitation against quarterage fees, payable by non-Guild members for the right to trade. Resistance on the part of guild members of the trading towns, all Protestant, understandably increased as a result and began to use sectarian language. In Cork, the *Council Book*, stopped referring to 'non-freeman' in 1755 and began to refer to 'popish quarterers', significantly upping the sectarian ante.[73] The new clarity about trade could have odd results even for the Protestant elite. In 1759 John Maskell, a Catholic merchant in Cork, successfully sued the Council at the

244   *James Livesey*

King's Bench for having being committed to the Marshalsea for non-payment of quartarage dues. A series of law suits conducted by the corporation of Cork eventually established that the law did not guarantee the monopolies claimed by the guilds and corporations of Ireland, effectively recognising a right to trade. In response the Irish Parliament received petitions for councils in Waterford, Cork, Dublin, Youghal, Clonmel, New Ross, and Wexford all demanding that 'popish tradesmen' either pay or conform. The Youghal petition was particularly incensed by the observation by the 'popish tradesmen' that they had more 'correspondents in popish countries than Protestants.' As corporations mobilised on sectarian grounds so too did quarter brothers. Petitions from 'non-freeman', the non-sectarian language for traders from outside the established church, in Cork and Dublin were presented in 1766, and after Parliament had passed the heads of a bill later that year they successfully blocked it in London at the Privy Council (under Poynings Law heads of bills had to go to London, this only changed in 1782). This early struggle over trade was conducted in sectarian terms and was only ended when it was overtaken by the very different world of the American crisis. It prefigured what would happen in Ireland if, and when, the Patriot reform project did not succeed.

There was no inevitability that as the spaces of intermediation between imperial systems closed that competition between elites for a place in the emerging British imperial system had to be expressed in sectarian terms. Radical Whiggism offered other resources, Catholic intellectuals, as they began to organise the Catholic Committee in the 1750s, were at pains to separate political and religious identities. The correspondence and public writing of some of the most important figures in Catholic politics of the 1750s made every effort to distinguish between religious values and ideals and political goals. Charles O'Conor was particularly emphatic on this point: 'if said of the Dutch Catholics were such sound members of the civil establishment in 30 years after the Great Revolution in the Low Countries, by what unavoidable necessity must it be that our Catholics must be attached to an infinitely less formidable Pretender than the king of Spain, and this not in 30 but at the end of 70 years?'[74]

The same point would be made by Wolfe Tone in 1791 and by the Catholic pamphleteers in favour of the Act of Union. However they were not able to combat the new, Tory, model of Empire.

The same observation that the civil institutions could, ideally, create a space for collective flourishing was made by William Drennan, writing from a very different political tradition. Drennan, however, was writing in 1785 as hopes for parliamentary reform on radical lines were fading. As his sister observed, 'there seems to be a timidity about the times creeping over those whose opinions I once thought well of, some of them are grown old and cold, others have ceased to be Volunteers.'[75] Nevertheless Drennan pleaded for a 'constitutional parliament' that would represent 'artisans and merchants' and so would offer 'adequate protection to our infant manufactures

Making Ireland poor   245

and commerce.'[76] The patriot faith in the capacity of political reform to create the context for commercial flourishing remained intact. However, the optimism was balanced by a new perception that religion, trade, and politics were newly articulated in a particularly dangerous way, 'the alliance between church and state has preserved and sanctified the abuses of both. The same dogmatical spirit which established for all future generations a certain system of religious belief, has transferred to our civil constitution an equal authority over the minds of men.'[77] The alliance of church, state, and trade, in the form of political and commercial privilege, created an alliance that would make Ireland commercial but poor; 'the people of Ireland may trade in order to raise money sufficient for an aristocracy to purchase the corruption which secures their own authority.'[78] In the light of that future Drennan addressed his readers as 'fellow slaves.'

Sectarianism did not make Ireland poor; sectarianism was the consequence of failure of Imperial reformers in the aftermath of the Seven Years War to address Irish poverty. Commercial cosmopolitanism was the horizon under which the ethnically and religiously differentiated Irish merchant communities operated for half a century. That horizon was only finally shattered in the failure of the Patriot movement to reform the empire. As Irish political and economic elites struggled to co-ordinate Irish participation in the commercial, and then industrial world, that failure would have enormous consequence.

Notes

1 Istvan Hont, "The Rich Country- Poor Country Debate in the Scottish Classical Political Economy," in *Wealth and Virtue: The Shaping of Political Economy in the Scottish Enlightenment*, eds. Istvan Hont and Michael Ignatieff (Cambridge: Cambridge University Press, 1983), 271–316; Istvan Hont, "The Rich Country- Poor Country Debate Revisited," in *David Hume's Political* Economy, eds. Margaret Schabas and Carl Wennerlind (London and New York: Routledge, 2008), 243–323; Anoush Terjanian, *Commerce and its Discontents in Eighteenth-Century French Political Thought*, (Cambridge: Cambridge University Press, 2012); Paul Cheney, *Revolutionary Commerce: Globalization and the French Monarchy*, (Cambridge MA: Harvard University Press, 2010); Henry C. Clark, *Compass of Society: Commerce and Absolutism in Old-Regime France* (Lanham MD: Lexington, 2007); Albert O. Hirschman, *The Passions and the Interests: Political Arguments for Capitalism before its Triumph*, (Princeton: Princeton University Press, 1997); Istvan Hont, *Jealousy of Trade: International Competition and the Nation-State in Historical Perspective*, (Cambridge, MA: Harvard University Press, 2005).
2 See in particular Ian McBride, *Eighteenth-Century Ireland: The Isle of Slaves*, (Dublin: Gill and Macmillan, 2009) for an argument that Irish sectarianism was a causal factor in Irish divergence from the trends of Atlantic history. The debate on Irish poverty focuses on the famine, but even here framing political questions are relevant; see Joel Mokyr and Cormac O'Grada, "Poor and getting poorer? Living Standards in Ireland before the Famine," *Economic History Review*, 2nd ser. 41, no. 2 (1988): 209–35.
3 Charles Ivar McGrath, *Ireland and Empire, 1692-1770* (London: Routledge,

246   *James Livesey*

2015); Christine Kinealy, "At Home with the Empire: The Example of Ireland," in *At Home with the Empire: Metropolitan Culture and the Imperial World*, eds. Catherine Hall and Sonya Rose (Cambridge: Cambridge University Press, 2007), 169–92.

4 Royal Irish Academy 12 R 38/3, James Caulfield, First Earl of Charlemont, to Thomas Prentice, Dublin 31 July 1788.

5 Amartya Sen, *Poverty and Famines: An Essay on Entitlement and Deprivation* (Oxford: Oxford University Press, 1981).

6 Robert Allen, "The Great Divergence in European Prices and Wages from the Middle Ages to the First World War," *Explorations in Economic History* 38 (2001): 411–47.

7 Erik S. Reinert, *How Rich Countries got Rich and why Poor Countries stay Poor* (London: Constable, 2007).

8 Sophus A. Reinert, *Translating Empire: Emulation and the Origins of Political Economy*, (Cambridge MA: Harvard University Press, 2011); Michael Jacobs and Mariana Mazzucato eds., *Rethinking Capitalism: Economics and Policy for Sustainable and Inclusive Growth* (Chichester: Wiley-Blackwell, 2016).

9 Jeff Horn, *The Path Not Taken: French Industrialisation in the Age of Revolution, 1750-1820*, (Cambridge Mass.: MIT Press, 2006); Gilles Postel-Vinay, *La terre et l'argent: l'agriculture et le credit en France du XVIIIe au debut du XXe siècle* (Paris: Albin Michel, 1998); Thomas Piketty, Gilles Postel-Vinay, and Jean-Laurent Rosenthal, "Wealth Concentration in a Developing Economy: Paris and France, 1807-1994," *American Economic Review*, 96, no. 1 (March 2006): 236–56.

10 Douglass C. North, John Joseph Wallis and Barry R. Weingast, *Violence and Social Orders: A Conceptual Framework for Interpreting Recorded Human History* (Cambridge: Cambridge University Press, 2009).

11 Gareth Stedman Jones, *An End to Poverty? A Historical Debate* (London: Profile, 2004).

12 Philip Hoffmann, *Growth in a Traditional Society: The French Countryside, 1450-1815* (Princeton NJ: Princeton University Press, 1996).

13 Paul R. Sharp and Jacob L Weisdorf, "French Revolution or Industrial Revolution? A Note on the Contrasting Experiences of England and France up to 1800" *Cliometrica*, 6, no. 1 (2012): 79–88. Vincent Geloso, "Were Wages That Low? Strasbourg Wages and Welfare Ratios before 1775" (January 6, 2017). Available at SSRN: https://ssrn.com/abstract=2895077 or http://dx.doi.org/10.2139/ssrn.2895077 downloaded February 2 2017.

14 William Petty, *A Treatise of Taxes and Contributions* (London: Obadiah Blagrave, 1662), 16.

15 Richard Lawrence, *The Interest of Ireland in its Trade and Wealth Stated in Two Parts* (Dublin: Joseph North, 1682) Part two, 7.

16 Roger Coke, *A Treatise Wherein it Is Demonstrated that the Church and State of England Are in Equal Danger with the Trade of Ireland*, (London, 1671), 1–8, 16–18. Ted McCormick, "Population: Modes of Seventeenth-Century Demographic Thought," in *Mercantalism Reimagined: Political Economy in Early-Modern Britain and its Empire*, eds. Philip J. Stern and Carl Wennerlind (Oxford: Oxford University Press, 2014), 334.

17 Anon, *Remarks Upon a Pamphlet Recommending a National Provision for the Poor of Ireland* (Dublin, 1773), 11.

18 National Library of Ireland MS 662, Some reasons suggested for establishing one or more persons in the peculiar and constant study and consideration of the trade and commerce of Ireland, author unidentified, c. 1700.

19 Charles Lucas, *Seasonable advice to the Electors of Members of Parliament at the ensuing General Election* (Dublin, 1768), 39.

Making Ireland poor 247

20 Anonymous, *The Examinator's Letters, or, a Mirror for British Monopolists and Irish Financiers* (Dublin, 1786).

21 Anon., *A View of the Present State of Ireland* (Dublin, 1780), 10.

22 For similar Patriot arguments articulating poverty and imperial corruption see Henry Flood, *A Letter to the People of Ireland, on the Expediency and Necessity of the present Associations in Ireland in favour of our own Manufactures, with some cursory observations on the effects of an union* (Newry, 1779), 11; Anon., *The Commercial Constraints of Ireland Considered* (Dublin, 1779), 186.

23 An important example was Josiah Tucker, *Essay on the Advantages and Disadvantages which respectively attend France and Great Britain with regard to Trade*, (Dublin, 1753) 3rd ed, which he later applied to Ireland, Josiah Tucker, *Reflections on the present Matters in Dispute between Great Britain and Ireland* (London, 1785).

24 Jean Louis de Lolme, *The British Empire in Europe: Part the First, Containing an Account of the Connections between the Kingdoms of England and Ireland, Previous to the Year 1780* (London, 1787).

25 H.F. Kearney, "The Political Background to English Mercantalism, 1695-1700," *Economic History Review* 11, no. 3 (1959): 484–96. But see Patrick Kelly, "The Irish Woollen Export Prohibition Act of 1699: Kearney Revisited," *Irish Economic and Social History* 7 (1980): 22–44.

26 de Lolme, *The British Empire in Europe*, 124.

27 Liam Kennedy and Martin W. Dowling, "Price and Wages in Ireland, 1700-1850," *Irish Economic and Social History* 24, no. 1 (1997): 62–104.

28 For the "optimistic" view see Frank Geary and Tom Stark, "Trends in Real Wages during the Industrial Revolution: A View from Across the Irish Sea," *Economic History Review* 50, no. 2 (2004): 362–395. The argument that Irish wage rates significantly underperformed British indices is developed in Joel Mokyr and Cormac O'Grada, "Poor and getting poorer? Living standards in Ireland before the Famine," *Economic History Review* 41, no. 2 (1988): 209–35.

29 Thomas Bartlett, *The Fall and Rise of the Irish Nation: The Catholic Question 1690–1830*, (Dublin: Gill and Macmillan, 1992); L.M. Cullen, "Catholics under the Penal Laws," *Eighteenth-Century Ireland: Irís an dá Chultúr* 1 (1986): 23–36; Maureen Wall, "The Penal Laws 1691–1760," in *Catholic Ireland in the Eighteenth Century: Collected Essays of Maureen Wall*, ed. Gerard O'Brien (Dublin: Geography Publications, 1989), 1–60; Kevin Whelan, "An Underground Gentry? Catholic Middlemen in Eighteenth-Century Ireland" in *The Tree of Liberty: Radicalism, Catholicism and the Construction of Irish Identity 1760–1830*, ed. Gerard O'Brien (Cork: Cork University Press, 1996), 3–56.

30 Kevin Whelan, "The regional impact of Irish Catholicism, 1700–1850," in *Common Ground: Essays on the historical geography of Ireland presented to T. Jones Hughes*, eds. W.J. Smyth and Kevin Whelan (Cork: Cork University Press, 1988); David Dickson, "Catholics and trade in eighteenth-century Ireland: An old debate revisited," in *Endurance and Emergence: Catholics in Ireland in the Eighteenth Century*, T.P. Power and Kevin Whelan, eds. (Dublin: Irish Academic Press, 1990), 85–110. On the role of merchant communities Kenneth Morgan, "Shipping Patterns and the Atlantic Trade of Bristol 1749-70," *William and Mary Quarterly*, 3rd series, 46 (1989): 506–38; Jacob M. Price, "What did Merchants Do? Reflections on British Overseas Trade, 1660–1790," *Journal of Economic History* 49, no. 2 (1989): 267–284; David Hancock, *Oceans of Wine: Madeira and the Emergence of Atlantic Trade and Taste*, (New Haven CT: Yale University Press, 2009); Bernard Bailyn, *The New England Merchants in the Seventeenth Century* (Cambridge MA: Harvard University Press, 1959).

31 Ciaran O'Scea, "Special privileges of the Irish in the Kingdom of Castile

248   *James Livesey*

(1601–1680): Modern myth or contemporary reality?" in *British and Irish Emigrants and Exiles in Europe, 1603-1688*, ed. David Worthington (Leiden: Brill, 2010), 107–124.

32 Thomas Truxes, *Irish-American Trade, 1660-1783* (Cambridge: Cambridge University Press, 1988), 149.

33 Truxes, *Irish-American Trade*, 147; David Dickson, "Butter Comes to Market: The Origins of Commercial Dairying in County Cork," in *Cork: History and Society. Interdisciplinary Essays on the History of an Irish County*, eds. Patrick O'Flanagan and Cornelius G. Buttimer (Dublin: Geography Publications, 1992), 167–84.

34 R.C. Nash, "Irish Atlantic Trade in the Seventeenth and Eighteenth Centuries," *William and Mary Quarterly* 42, no. 3 (1985): 329–56.

35 Bertie Mandelblatt, "A Transatlantic Commodity: Irish Salt Beef in the French Atlantic World," *History Workshop Journal* 63, no. 1 (2007): 18–47; Richard Pares, *War and Trade in the West Indies, 1739–1763* (London: Frank Cass, 1963) 2nd ed., 345–46.

36 Thomas Lowndes, *A Method to Prevent, without a register, the running of wool from Ireland to France, and to other foreign parts, in order to re-establish the woollen manufacture of England* (London, 1745).

37 David Dickson, *Old World Colony: Cork and South Munster, 1630-1830* (Cork: Cork University Press, 2005), 166.

38 Dickson, *Old World Colony*, 139.

39 Library of Congress, MMC 3227 Box 3, Thomas Amory Outgoing Letterbook 1711, Adam Cusack 12 January 1711, James Gallwey 14 January 1711, Anthony Peres 24 April 1711. Massachusetts Historical Society, Amory Papers Volume 138, Thomas Amory to James Ramsay, 17 May 1711.

40 Library of Congress, MMC 3227 Box 3, Thomas Amory Outgoing Letterbook 1711, Nicholas Oursel 14 March 1711.

41 Louis M. Cullen, *The Brandy Trade under the Ancien Regime: Regional Specialisation in the Charante*, (Cambridge: Cambridge University Press, 1998); idem., The *Irish Brandy Houses of Eighteenth-Century France* (Dublin: Lilliput, 2000).

42 Public Record Office Northern Ireland T/1073/2 Robert Black's Travels from Cadiz in Spain to Holland thence thro' Germany, Flanders, France and Italy, begun in the year 1727 volume 1.

43 National Library of Ireland D 25476, Bills of Exchange held by Dominic Sarsfield, Cork, for Patrick Sarsfield, Ostend, 6 March 1727, 26 March 1727.

44 NLI MSS 2643, Patrick Sarsfield, Ostend, to Dominic Sarsfield, Cork, 10 April 1715.

45 NLI MSS 827, John Kelly, Limerick, to Jonathan Gurnell, London, December 28 1744.

46 NLI MSS 827, John Kelly, Limerick, to Jonathan Gurnell, London, 19 March 1744/45.

47 NLI MSS 827, John Kelly, Limerick, to Joseph Percival and Co., Chester, 7 December 1744.

48 NLI MSS 827, John Kelly, Limerick, to John Archdeacon, Rotterdam, 8 February 1744/45.

49 Massachusetts Historical Society Amory Papers Volume 138, Thomas Amory, Angra, to Messrs Fisher and White, Amsterdam, 16 April 1713.

50 Library of Congress, MMC 3227 Box 3, Thomas Amory Outgoing Letterbook 1711, William Rhett 30 August 1711.

51 Truxes, *Irish-American Trade*, 5, 37.

Making Ireland poor 249

52 Massachusetts Historical Society, Amory Papers, Volume 140, John and Jonathan Amory to Messrs Leathem and Walker, Boston, 25 May 1770.

53 Craig Bailey, "The Nesbitts of London and their Networks," in *Irish and Scottish Mercantile Networks in Europe and Overseas in the Seventeenth and Eighteenth Centuries*, eds. David Dickson, Jan Parmentier and Jane H. Ohlmeyer (Gent: Academia Press Scientific Publishers, 2007), 231–50.

54 NLI D 25477, Receipt, Cork City September 13, 1725.

55 Thomas M Truxes, "Irish Interloping Trade and Colonial Warfare in the 18th Century," in *Irlanda y el Atlantico Ibérico; moilidad, participacion e intercambio cultural (1580-1823)*, eds. Igor Pérez Tostado and Enrique García Hernán (Valencia, 2010), 59–68.

56 Louis Cullen, "Landlords, Bankers and Merchants: The Early Irish Banking World, 1700–820," *Hermathena*135 (1983): 25–44; Patrick Walsh, *The South Sea Bubble and Ireland: Money, Banking and Investment 1690-1721* (London: Boydell, 2014), 75.

57 "A ces paroles, un officier Anglais nommé Scott, homme furieux et toujours porté aux partis les plus violens, s'écria, "comment, un seul Irlandais Français, et prisonnier de guerre, prétends il nous faire la loi, et ose nous traiter de barbares!" Monsieur, luis dis-je tranquillement, voilà ce que c'est qu'un Irelandais Français; notre malheur commun nous rend tous égaux, je suis libre ici comme vous." And: "je me trouvois honoré de partager avec les François tous les désagréments qu'il plairoit à Messieurs les Anglois de leur donner; que je faisois peu de cas d'un homme qui pouvoit penser autrement dans de pareilles circonstances; que les Irlandois François étoient doublement François." Anne-Gabriel Meusnier de Querlon, *Lettre a m le D'Estaing, Chevalier des Ordres du Roi, Lieutenant-Général de Terre et de mer des armés de sa majesté; contenant un détail du Naufrage dans l'Inde, et du retour en Europe du Comte de Kearney, Colonel ci-devant Aide-Maréchal-Général de Logis de l'Armée du Roi dans l'Inde*, (np, 1763).

58 John Perceval, Earl of Egmont, *A Representation of the State of the Trade of Ireland, laid before the House of Lords of England, on Tuesday the 10th of April 1750*, (Dublin, 1750), 18. Egmont sat (occasionally) in the Irish House of Lords and for various seats in the Westminster House of Commons.

59 Ibid., 20.

60 NLI MSS 662, "Some reasons suggested for establishing one or more persons in the peculiar and constant study and consideration of the trade and commerce of Ireland," author unidentified, c.1700."

61 Padhraig Higgins, *A Nation of Politicians: Gender, Patriotism, and Political Culture in Late Eighteenth-Century Ireland* (Madison WI: University of Wisconsin Press, 2010).

62 "Connoissez mieux l'Anglois, Madame; son génie // Le porte à de plus grands objets. // Politique profond; occupé de projets, // Il prétend à l'honneur d'éclairer sa patrie. // Le moindre Citoyen, attentif à ses droits, // Voit les papiers publics, & régit l'Angleterre; // Du Parlement compte les voix // Juge de l'équité des Loix, // Prononce librement fur la paix ou la guerre, // Pese les intérèts des Rois, // Et du fond d'un caffé, leur mesure la terre." *L'Anglois à Bordeaux. Comédie en un acte en vers libres, par Sr Favart, Représentée pour la première fois par les Comédiens du Roi, le Lundi 14 mars 1763* (Avignon: Louis Chambeau, MDCCLXII).

63 See Janneton Darquier, Caussade, to Monsieur Darquier, Dublin, 1 February 1757, in The Bordeaux-Dublin Letters 1757: Correspondence of an Irish Community Abroad (Oxford, 2013), L.M. Cullen, John Shovlin and Thomas M. Truxes eds., 132–33.

64 James Vaughn, *The Politics of Empire at the Accession of George III: The East*

250 *James Livesey*

India Company and the Crisis and Transformation of Britain's Imperial State (New Haven: Yale University Press, 2019).

65 I have explored this movement in James Livesey, "Free Trade and Empire in the Anglo-Irish Commercial Propositions of 1785," *Journal of British Studies* 52, no. 1 (2013): 1–25.

66 C.A. Bayly, *Imperial Meridian: The British Empire and the World, 1780-1830* (London and New York: Routledge, 1989), 115–16; P.J. Marshall, *The Making and Unmaking of Empires: Britain, India and America c.1750–1783* (Oxford: Oxford University Press, 2005), 352–72.

67 Truxes, *Irish-American Trade*, 43–44.

68 William M. Offutt, "The Atlantic Rules: The Legalistic Turn in Colonial British America," in *The Creation of the British Atlantic World*, eds. Elizabeth Mancke and Carole Shammas (Baltimore, MD: Johns Hopkins University Press, 2005), 160–81.

69 Ian R. Christie, "A Vision of Empire: Thomas Whately and the Regulations Lately Made Concerning the Colonies," *English Historical Review* 113, no. 451 (1998): 300–320; Thomas C. Barrow, "Background to the Grenville Program, 1757-1763," *The William and Mary Quarterly*, 3rd series, 22, no. 1 (1965): 93–104.

70 East Sussex Record Office RF 18/94.

71 ESRO RF 18/97.

72 ESRO RF 18/95.

73 *Council Book of Cork*, 684, 687–90.

74 Huntington Library STO 261, Charles O'Conor to Doctor Curry, November 10, 1761.

75 Martha McTier [Belfast], to William Drennan [Newry], undated [1783], in, *The Drennan-McTier Letters, Volume One1776-1793* (Dublin 1998), 143.

76 [William Drennan], *Letters of an Irish Helot, signed Orellana* (Dublin, 1785), 5

77 Ibid., 10.

78 Ibid., 22.

Index

Abdullah, Muhammad 131
Abucaya, Simon 224
Africa ship 134
agency problem; *see* principal-agent
problem
Ahmad bin Na'aman 131–32
alcohol 52, 110, 111, 151, 154, 166;
see also beer, brandy, madeira,
rum, wine
Algiers (city and regency), Algerian
14–5, 212–26
Algonquian languages 145
Ali bin Nasser 129
Alimami 112
Allada kingdom 183–84, 90
alum 166
Amar, king of Hueda 184
ambergris 75
America, Americas 2, 8, 10, 13, 32, 72,
80, 83, 110, 112, 114, 118, 127, 128,
131, 132, 133, 156, 183, 202, 233, 236,
238, 242, 244; North America 4, 10,
11, 12, 15, 131, 144, 146, 151, 156;
South America 13, 144, 156; Spanish
America 9, 72–4, 78–83, 86
Amharic 128
Amory, Thomas 237–39
Amsterdam 47, 189, 198–99, 201–7
Anamabo 188
Andes 78
Ang Sngoun, King of Cambodia 64
Ang Ton, King of Cambodia 64
Angola 203
Anne, Queen of England 96, 104, 218–20
Antigua 237
Antunes, Cátia 1, 33
Antwerp 164, 198, 202, 207

Arabella, ship 86
Arabia, Arabian, Arabic 44, 78, 80, 112,
123, 124, 126, 127, 128, 129, 131, 132,
135, 221, 222
Archdeacon, John 238
Arica 78
Arkhangel'sk 98, 99, 101, 102, 202
Armagh 237
Armenian 9, 27, 167–69
Armory, John and Jonathan 239
Asante 113
Asia, Asian 2, 4, 9, 10, 11, 14, 24, 27, 29,
33, 41, 45, 47, 51, 67, 72, 74, 75, 78, 83,
84, 135, 165, 185–87, 192, 199, 202–4;
East Asia 9, 10, 23, 26, 33, 34, 41, 43,
56, 57, 66, 67, 68, 74, 80, 124, 174;
South Asia 27, 42, 59, 78, 80, 123, 124,
126, 127, 128; South-East Asia 40, 42,
45, 50, 56–68, 74, 76
Asiento Company, Guinea Company
(French) 183, 187–88
Assiniboin 145
Astrakhan 100
Athapaskan languages 145
Atlantic 2, 13, 33, 72, 78, 87, 108–11,
114–9, 123–4, 126, 128, 130, 135, 182,
197, 200–6
Austria 83
Ayutthaya (city) 7, 40–8, 63, 64
Ayutthaya, Dynasty 65
Azores 205, 237–38

Bacri (merchant) 223–25
Badajoz 202
bafts (textiles) 110
Baghdad 215

252 *Index*

Bahia 115, 188, 189, 199, 202
Baltic 80, 92, 102, 103, 240
Bandon 237
Bangka 59
Bangkok 57, 66
bangles 110
Bania, banya 79, 169, 170
Bank of San Giorgio 84
bank, banking, banker 10, 25, 82–4, 86,
  117, 171, 198, 201, 234, 239, 242
Bantam 77
Banteay Meas Province 60
Barawa 131
Barbary 15, 87, 213–14, 223
Barcelona 219
Barclay and Livingston, firm 131
Barclay, David 103
Barghash bin Saʿīd, sultan of Zanzibar
  126, 134
barks; *see* ships
Batavia 42, 43, 46, 47, 48, 49, 52, 63, 76
Bayly, Christopher 10, 109
Bayonne 202
beads 110, 111, 113, 128, 131, 153, 154
beaver, beaver wool 143–44, 147–50,
  154–56
Beck, Ulrich 3
beef 112, 236, 238–39
beer 104
Beijing 25, 58, 65
Beja 202
Belgrade 215
Bengal 10, 11, 14, 161–76, 187
Benson, Mark 114
Ben-Taleb, Abdelkerim 223–25
Ben-Taleb, Muhammad 222–23
Berlin 104
Bhabha, Homi 29, 126
Bible 12, 28
Bight of Benin 14, 112, 181, 183–84,
  187–92
Bight of Biafra 112
Bijapur sultanate 183
Bilbao 89, 202
bills of exchange 114, 116, 200, 204, 237,
  239, 242
bin Azourz, Muhammad ("Mahmet
  Zourzé") 221
Bissau 111, 114
Bissendas 170
Black family 243
Black, Robert 237

blankets 147, 154
Blue Eagle, ship 86
Bolama island 114
Bolivia 13, 72
Bologna 85
Bombay 124, 127, 128, 130, 131, 134, 161
bonnet; *see* hat
Bonny 117
bookkeeping 201
Borchebourde, Daniel 45
Bordeaux 188, 237–38, 241–43
Boston 127, 128, 130, 133, 239
Bourbon, Alexis de 221
Boxer, Charles 52
Brand, Adam 100
brandy 111, 149, 236–37, 242
brass 128
Brazil 144, 149, 154, 184, 187–92,
  199–203, 205, 206, 238
bread 87
Breckenridge, Carol 126
Breton, Francis 80, 81
brigs; *see* ships
Bristol 202
Britain, British 3, 14–5, 26, 103, 110, 112,
  113, 115, 117, 125, 129, 132, 133, 134,
  164–68, 172–75, 213–26, 231, 233–38,
  240–44; *see also* England, Scotland
Brito, Pedro de 73
broker, brokerage 4–5, 7, 28–30, 35, 46,
  52, 79, 161, 168–70, 191, 199, 201–2,
  207; *see also* go-between
bronze 77, 84
Brook, Timothy 67
Broutaert, Johan 165, 169–73
Brown, Benson & Ives, firm 114, 115
Brubaker, Rogers 6
Bruijn, Daniel de 204
Bruijn, Willem de 198, 204–6;
  see also Bruijn & Cloots (firm)
Brussels 83
Brutus, ship 223
Buddhism 44, 46–7, 48, 50, 51, 63
Buenos Aires 78, 87
Bullom shore 108
Bunnag family 44
Burma, Burmese 40, 45, 49, 64, 65, 68
Burt, Ronald S. 7
Burton, Richard F. 130
Busaʿīdi dynasty 126, 127
butter 236, 239
Cà Mau Peninsula 58

Index 253

Cádiz 80, 83, 86, 198, 202, 207, 223, 236, 243
Cairo 9
Calcagno, Gian Carlo 84
Calcutta 4, 124, 127, 130, 203
calico (printed cotton cloth) 108, 128
Calicut 79
Callao 78
Calvinism 46; *see also* Protestantism
Cambodia 12, 43, 56–61, 63–4, 66;
  see also Indochina
cambric (linen textile) 112
Canada 14, 145–46, 151, 155–58;
  see also North America
Canary Islands 166
Canton (Guangzhou) 4, 7, 9, 11, 12, 23–35, 58, 59, 65, 124, 127, 165, 204;
  see also Whampoa
Cape Coast 188
Cape of Good Hope 9, 162, 166
Cape Town 132
Cape Verde 113, 114
capital 6, 147, 162, 165, 203–4, 206–7, 235–37, 117, 127, 147, 162, 165, 235–37, 239; social and political capital 7, 172–74; cultural and intercultural capital 12, 34, 68; human capital 199; capitalism 11, 175
Caracalla, Roman Emperor 51
cardamon 75
Caribbean 27, 156
carpets 123, 131, 132
Carreira da Índia 203
Carrière, Guillaume 221
Casa da Índia 201
cashmere 132
Caspian Sea 100
Castile 77, 83
Catholicism, Catholic 15, 28, 198, 235–37, 239, 243–44
cats 150
cattle 111; *see also* beef
Cauvière, François 221
ceramics 12, 113; *see also* porcelain; earthenware
Ceylon 166
Chakrabarty, Dipesh 126
Chakri dynasty 44
Chandernagore 168
Changchou 75
Chanlay, Nicolas-Joseph Thirion de 165–73, 175

Chanthaburi 65, 66
Chaophraya Plain 59
Chaozhou 56, 65, 66, 68
Chardin (merchant) 189
Charente region 237
Charlemont, Earl of 231
Charles V, Holy Roman emperor 87
Charles VI, Holy Roman emperor 198
Charleston 238
Chester 238
children 29, 45–7, 62, 66
China Seas 1, 57, 162, 203
china; *see* porcelain
China, Chinese 8, 9, 10, 23–34, 42, 43, 56–65, 67–8, 73, 74, 75, 76, 77, 100, 131, 162, 163, 165, 189, 190, 204
Chinsura 169
Chipewyan 145
Chouart, Médart, Sieur des Groseilliers 144
Christianity, Christian 24–5, 28, 47, 87, 168–69, 214, 218; *see also* Catholicism, Protestantism, Franciscans, New Christians; Christian Missions 24–6, 28, 31, 40, 56, 63
Churchill River 145
cigar 7, 13, 99
Cipolla, Carlo 72
Clinkaert, Mathias, Capt 161, 165, 169–72
clocks 128
Clonmel 244
Cloots, Egidio 198
Cloots, Jean-Baptiste 198; *see also* Jean-Baptiste & Paulo Jacomo Cloots (firm)
Cloots, Paulo (the elder) 198
Cloots, Paulo 198, 204–6; *see also* Bruijn & Cloots (firm)
cloth; *see* textiles
cloves 123, 128, 129, 131
Cochin 124, 130
Cochinchina 56–64, 66, 68;
  see also Vietnam, Indochina
Code Maritime 163
coffee 111, 123, 128, 131, 234
Coke, Roger 233
Collins, Samuel 99
colonialism, colonial, colonies 1, 2, 5, 6, 8, 10, 14, 24, 40, 41, 48, 50, 56, 62, 67, 73, 74, 80, 83, 110, 115–16, 124–26, 144, 147, 154, 156, 174–75, 196,

254 Index

199–202, 204–7, 213, 234–36, 238, 242–43; *see also* imperial; postcolonial 4
Columbus, Christopher 82
combs 153, 154
Comoros 128
Compagnie du Sénégal 115
comprador; *see* interpreters
Concord, ship 86
concubine 8, 12, 45, 66
Confucianism 2, 60, 62, 63, 67, 68
Congo 127
Constantinople 9
consumption, consumer 5, 7, 9–13, 83, 94, 99, 104, 105, 108–19, 124, 128–29, 143, 154–56, 206, 232–33; consumer revolution 113, 116, 118–9
contact zone 4–5, 7, 9, 12, 23–4, 27, 33–4, 41, 118
contraband 74, 78, 80, 226; *see also* smuggling
copal gum; *see* gum
Copenhagen 172
copper 41, 72, 75, 77, 84, 98
coral 79–80, 112, 189
Cork (city) 236–37, 243–33
Coromandel Coast 14, 165–70, 172, 174, 181–87, 189, 191–2
correspondence 62, 82, 97, 132, 181, 182, 201, 215, 222, 244; *see also* letters
corsair 83–4, 87, 213, 216, 224, 226; *see also* pirate, privateer
Corsica 84
corvette; *see* ships
cotton 9, 77, 78, 79, 100, 113, 114, 115, 116, 124, 127–28, 166, 183; *see also* calico; guinea cloth, kaniki, merekani
Coursey (merchant) 237
credit 79, 83, 102, 114, 116–9, 128, 149, 189, 201, 206; *see also* debt
Cree 145, 151–52, 157
creole, creolization 1, 5, 12, 64, 65, 67, 126, 130; *see also* métissage, mestizo
Cuddalore 183
Curtin, Philip 3–9, 29, 67, 181
Cusack (merchant) 237

Dahomey kingdom 183–84, 188–89
Dakota (people) 145
Danish Asiatic Company 162, 167, 168, 173, 175
Dantzig 103

Das Gupta, Ashin 197
dates 123, 131
De Bruijn & Cloots (firm) 196–207
de Lolme, Jean Louis 234–35
debt 1, 74, 83, 102, 110, 114, 117, 205–6, 222; *see also* credit
Denmark 94, 100, 172, 183, 185, 186, 219
Deshima Island 24, 26, 27, 77; *see also* Nagasaki
Devon 237
dhows; *see* ships
diaspora 4–6, 60, 63, 67, 109, 116, 117
Diderot, Denis 241
Diemen, Antonio van 49
diplomacy 10, 13, 15, 42–4, 46, 48, 50, 58, 62, 67, 99, 101, 104, 123, 130–32, 135, 174, 184, 213, 215, 218, 226, 235
distrust, untrustworthy 7, 8, 13, 47, 97, 164; *see also* trust
Dodd and Crisp, merchants 101
Domingo, ship 111
Dover 80
Drennan, William 244–45
Drucker, Peter F. 163, 174–76
drunkenness 48, 161; *see also* alcohol
Dublin 237, 241, 244
Dulivier, Pierre 186, 190
Dunkirk 80
Dutch 14, 26, 28–34, 40–52, 73, 74, 75, 77, 78, 79, 80, 82, 92, 99, 100, 103, 104, 144, 146, 147, 164, 167–89, 172, 181, 183–92, 196, 199, 201, 203–6, 217, 224, 225, 233, 236, 244; *see also* Low Countries
Dvina river 101
dyes, dyewood 41, 78, 116, 201; *see also* sappanwood

earthenware 111; *see also* ceramics
East Frisia 164
East India Companies 6, 23, 24, 27, 84, 161–65, 168, 174; *see also* French East India Company, Ostend Company, Prussian East India Companies, Swedish East India Company, VOC; Danish East India Company, EIC
ebony 75
Edo (Tokyo) 25
Egypt 131
EIC (British East India Company) 11, 26, 42, 67, 73, 78–82, 130, 149, 165, 166, 168, 172, 174, 185–87, 190, 192, 202, 203, 204

Index 255

El Majidi ship 134
Elbing (Elbląg) 103
Elbingen 103
elephants 41
Elias, Minas 168, 169
Ellins, William 103
Elmina 188
Elvas 202
Emden 163–65, 173
England, English 2, 13, 41, 42, 73–4,
  77–82, 85, 86, 92–105, 111, 115, 123,
  128, 129, 131, 144–47, 151–53, 157,
  161, 181–92, 199, 203, 204, 213, 216,
  222, 231, 233–34, 238–42;
  see also Britain
Enlightenment 2, 105, 197
Ennis 237
Erzurum 215
Estado da Índia 190
Estremoz 202
Eurafrican, Euro-African 111, 117,
  190, 192
Europe, European 2, 6, 7, 9, 10–1, 13,
  14, 23–7, 31–5, 40, 41, 42, 46, 47, 50,
  51, 59, 67, 74, 77, 79, 83, 87, 94, 109,
  110, 112, 114–8, 124, 125, 127, 128,
  129, 130, 134, 135, 145–48, 150, 151,
  155–58, 161–65, 168–70, 172–74,
  181–92, 199, 201, 204–6, 213–16, 218,
  220–3, 225–26, 243; Western Europe
  10, 124, 212–4, 217; Northern Europe
  15, 196, 202, 212, 214; Southern
  Europe 237–38, 243
Experience, ship 222

fabrics; *see* textiles
Fajardo Chacón, Diego 77
Falconbridge, Anna Maria 108, 111, 115
fashion 108–11, 113–6, 118–9, 143;
  see also taste
Favart, Charles-Simon 241, 243
felt, felting 143–44, 147, 155, 156
Felton, John 100
Fitzgerald banking house 239
flag 168, 216, 219–20, 223, 225;
  see also papers, passport
Flanders, Flemish 76, 80, 82, 83, 85, 88,
  161, 164, 165, 168, 172, 175, 204;
  see also Low Countries
flax 104; *see also* linen
Florence 85
Fort Albany 145, 148, 149, 150, 155

Fort Churchill 145, 149, 150, 155
Fort Saint Joseph 113
Fort St. David 183
Fort St. George 183
fox 148
France, French 14–5, 42, 50, 51, 61, 63,
  67, 80, 82, 83, 104, 110, 111, 112, 113,
  144, 146, 147, 151, 156, 157, 161,
  163–68, 172–74, 181–92, 199, 201, 203,
  204, 213–14, 219–26, 232, 235–42
Franciscans 63
Francisco, Prince of Portugal 203
Frederick II, king of Prussia 163, 175
Frederick William I, king of Prussia 103
Frederiknagore (Serampore) 168, 173
Freeport 117
Freetown 117, 118
French East India Company
  (*Compagnie des Indes*) 67, 165, 168,
  181–83, 185–87, 189–92
frigates; *see* ships
frontier 4, 12, 57, 62, 65–8, 87, 213,
  215–17, 225
Fujian 59, 62
Fula state 114
Fuller, Rose 242
fumi-e 28
Fur, fur trade 4, 11, 12, 14, 143–52,
  154–58
Fusaro, Maria 225
Futa Jallon 116
Futa Toro 112, 114, 118

Galam (Gajaaga) 112
galley; *see* ships
Gallwey (merchant) 237
Gambia, The Gambia 111, 112, 113;
  see also Senegambia
Games, Alison 2, 8, 23
Ganges river 161
gender 26, 28, 30–2
Genoa 82–7, 198, 202, 217
George I, King of Great Britain 103, 104
George III, King of Great Britain 242
Germany, German 82, 83, 100, 104, 125,
  134, 163, 199, 203–4, 234
Ghent 164, 173
Ghobrial, John-Paul 8
Gibraltar 222–23
gift, gifting 43, 46, 65, 123, 130–32,
  148–51, 154–55, 157, 184;
  see also present

256   *Index*

glass 111, 113, 131
Goa 80, 81
go-between 5, 7, 28–30, 34, 51;
    see also broker
Goens, Rijckloff van 46
gold 72, 78, 81, 84, 108, 110, 112, 116,
    118, 132, 190, 199–200, 202–3
Gold Coast (West Africa) 112,
    183–84, 188
Gondaverdy, Merza 170
Goodfellow, Charles 102
Goody, Jack, Capt 86
Gordeon, Patrick Gen 99
Gorée 113, 115, 118
Gould family 237
grain 202
Gran Loggi, ship 86
Grandpré, Étienne Nicolas de 214
Granovetter, Mark 6
Great Britain; *see* Britain
Greek 222
Grendi, Ambrosio 86
Grenville, George 242; 'Grenville
    Programme' 243
Guangdong 58, 59, 62, 65
Guangxi 65
Guangzhou; *see* Canton
Guatemala 87
Guimarães, Manuel de Castro 203
guinea cloth (cotton textile) 112
Guinea Coast 110, 112, 114, 118,
    191, 238
Gujarat 73, 78, 79, 126, 128, 185
Gulf of Siam; *see* Gulf of Thailand
Gulf of Thailand 8, 42, 56–9, 61, 64,
    65, 67
gum 110, 115, 116, 128, 131
gunpowder 77, 82, 112, 128, 131, 133,
    152, 154, 186, 202
guns 74, 82, 112, 128, 131, 133, 147, 148,
    150, 152, 153, 154, 157, 202
Gurnell, Jonathan 237

Hà Tiên 12, 56–68
Habsburg dynasty 72, 83
Hainan 56
hajj 130
Hamburg 85, 103, 124, 134, 198, 202
Hamerton, Atkins 132
Hancock, David 2
Handel, George Frederick 241
handkerchiefs 108, 154
Hanover 104

hare 144
Harper, John 239
Harrison, Edward 186
hats 14, 143–44, 154–56, 238
Hawkins, Joseph 111
Hebdon, John 99
Hébert, Guillaume André 187, 190
Heeck, Gijsbert 45
hides 42, 75, 128; *see also* leather
Hirado 26, 48, 52
Hispaniola 239
Hoca, Ali 222
Hội An 63
Holland; *see* Dutch
Hong merchants 34
horses 131–32
Hudson Bay 145–46, 151–54, 157
Hudson's Bay Company 14, 144–49,
    151–57
Hudson's Bay company 14, 144–57
Huế 58, 60, 63, 64
Hueda kingdom 183–84, 188, 190
Huffon, king of Hueda 184
Huguenot 189
Hurtado de Corcuera, Don Sebastián
    73, 77
Huw, Craig 222–23
hybrid, hybridity 4–7, 9, 11–2, 23, 26,
    28–32, 35, 40, 51, 116, 197, 207,
    239–40, 242–43

identity 1, 4–5, 29, 30, 46, 61, 63, 167,
    231–2, 235, 237, 239–42, 244
imperial, imperialism 1, 5, 8, 10, 11, 14,
    49, 135, 161–62, 174–75, 181–82,
    189–92, 231–32, 234, 236–45;
    see also colonialism
India 6, 8, 13, 41, 42, 73, 74, 78–81, 99,
    110, 113, 114, 115, 124, 127, 128, 129,
    133, 134, 135, 162–75, 182–83, 185–86,
    190–92, 203, 239; *see also* Asia:
    South Asia
Indian Ocean 1, 2, 7, 10, 13, 33, 79, 80,
    123–31, 134, 135, 162, 164, 182, 185,
    192, 197, 203
indigo 129, 183, 234
Indochina 67; *see also* Vietnam,
    Cochinchina, Cambodia
Indonesia 57
insurance 165, 237
Intendencia de Marina 198
interloping 162–63, 174, 202–4, 238
interpreters 9, 27, 30–1, 34, 48, 73, 221

Ireland 10, 15, 216, 231–45
iron 74, 82, 98, 111, 113, 115, 147, 152, 153, 156, 158
Irvine, Charles 165
Isebrand, Eberhard 100
Isham, James 150, 152, 153, 157
Islam, Islamic 2, 9, 27, 42, 43, 47, 114, 117, 214, 219, 220, 223, 226
Isle of Man 242
Istanbul 124, 127, 134, 225
Italy, Italian 13, 74, 82, 84, 100, 199, 213, 222
ivory 75, 110–12, 116–18, 123, 126, 128, 129, 131, 133, 203

Jacob, Margaret C. 2, 197
Jacobite 235
Jahaanke 4
Jakin 184, 190
Jamaica 115, 242
James River 238
Japan, Japanese 6, 10, 23–34, 42, 57–9, 61, 74, 77
Java 77, 129
Jean-Baptiste & Paulo Jacomo Cloots (firm) 198, 201; see also Cloots, Jean-Baptiste; Cloots, Paulo Jacomo
Jeddah 130
Jerusalem 87
Jiangning 77
Jiu, Mo (Mạc Cửu)
Johnson, Samuel 33
joint-stock company 117, 145–47, 150, 156–57
Judaism, Jewish 4, 27, 221, 223, 239
Juma, Muhammad 131
junks; see ships

Kaiser, Wolfgang 212
Kangxi emperor of China 76
kaniki (cotton fabric) 129
Kazan 104
Kearney, Comte de 239–40, 243
Kelly, John 237–38
kente cloth 113
Kenya 134
Kerry 237
kettles 153, 154
Khan Panni, Da'ud 185
Khmer 60, 61
Kilwa, Sultanate 125, 126
King, Gregory 143

Königsberg 87, 92, 103
Kriger, Colleen 113, 114
Kutch 128
Kyushu 74

La Réunion 124
La Rochelle 202
lac, lacquer 42
lace 152, 154, 189
Lally, Thomas Arthur, comte de 240
lançados 110
landlord-stranger relationship 116
language 1, 2, 4, 5, 26, 28, 30–2, 34, 42, 46, 48, 51, 87, 128, 145, 151–52, 157–58, 162–63, 170, 181, 201, 217–21, 243; see also vernacular, interpreters; lingua franca 1, 128; multilingual 162, 225; translation
Lao 45
Lapwing, ship 111
lascars 10
Laugier de Tassy, Jacques Philippe 213
law, legal, illegal 1, 5–6, 10, 14, 15, 26, 34, 42, 46–7, 48, 49, 50, 60, 67, 109, 117, 162, 163, 164, 172, 174–75, 189, 202, 203, 212–15, 217–22, 225–26, 242–43
Lawrence, Richard
Le Mars (ship) 190
Lê Bác Bình 63
lead 41, 112
leather 128, 131; see also hides
Lefroy and Charron, firm 222
Leizhou 56, 58
Lemire, Beverly 109
letters 2, 32, 43, 48, 61, 63, 79–81, 85, 92, 95, 97, 102, 117, 132, 146, 149–50, 152–53, 156–57, 161, 164, 165, 185, 188–89, 205, 215, 217–20, 223, 226, 237–38; see also correspondence
Levant 10, 87, 234
Li Shiyao 31, 65
Liang Zhongluan 62
Lieberman, Victor 68
Liguria 82, 84, 85, 86
Limerick 237
linen 113, 115, 202, 234, 239; see also cambric; flax
Lisbon 14, 115, 169, 175, 196–204, 206–7, 223–24, 236, 238
Lithuania 92; see also Poland-Lithuania
Liverpool 237
Liverpool ship 130

258 *Index*

Livorno 84, 202, 222
Lomellini family 84
London 15, 77, 78, 79, 80, 81, 92, 93, 95,
  96, 102, 115, 124, 129, 132, 133, 134,
  145–56, 148–54, 157, 172, 198, 202,
  220, 232, 237, 239, 243–44
Louisbourg (Cape Breton Island) 239
Low Countries 83, 237, 244;
  see also Flanders, Dutch; Austrian
  Low Countries 163, 172
Lowndes, Thomas 236
Lübeck 100
Lucas, Charles 234
Lyon 202

Maastricht 198
Mạc Thiên Tứ (Mo Tianci) 12, 56–68
Macao 34, 74, 203, 204
Macaulay, Zachary 116, 118
Macauley, Melissa 67
Madagascar 128, 129, 134
made beaver (unit); *see* beaver
madeira (drink) 111
Madeira 166, 205
Madras (Chennai) 4, 166, 181, 183, 185,
  186, 189–91, 203
Madrid 198, 202
Maffi, Davide 83
Majid bin Saʿīd, sultan of Zanzibar 126,
  131, 134
Majorca 86
Makassar 78
Makran Coast 125, 126
Makua 128
Malabar, Malabar Coast, Malabari 131
Malaga 222, 223
Malagasy; *see* Madagascar
Malawi 127
Malaysia, Malay 48, 57
Mali 116
Malines 173
Manchu 56, 63, 74
Mandigoes; *see* Mandinka
Mandinka 118
Manila 63–4, 73–4, 77–8, 82, 186, 189;
  Manila galleon 72–3
Manitoba 145
Maratha 183, 184
marriage 29, 44–7, 52, 56, 58, 63, 67,
  116, 198, 204; *see also* wife, widow
Marseilles 124, 134, 190, 224
Marshall, Peter 97
marten 148, 150

Martin, François 181, 186, 190
Martin, Joseph 95–6, 102
Maskell, John
Massachusetts 129
Masulipatam (Machilipatam) 166, 168
Mauritius 124, 130, 135
Mediterranean 2, 15, 33, 80, 84, 87, 126,
  213–14, 217, 219–20, 222, 225
Meerwijck, Jan van 45
Mekong River 56–60, 64, 66
merchant-banker; *see* bank
merekani (cotton fabric) 129, 131, 133
Mergui 42
mestizo 45, 47, 64; *see also* métissage,
  creole
métissage, métis 5, 116; *see also* mestizo,
  creole
Metteren, de (merchant) 168
Mexico 72, 75, 78, 81, 82, 151
Mexico City 81
Middle East 7, 14, 100; *see also* Levant;
  North Africa
middle ground 4, 12; *see also* contact
  zone; third space
Milan 82, 84, 85
millet 112, 115
Ming Dynasty 30, 56–8, 63–4, 67, 74, 76,
  77, 78
Minh Hương 64
mirrors 131, 152
Missinaibi River 145
Mo Jiu (Mạc Cửu) 58
Mocha 43, 80, 131
Moluccas 11
Mombasa 126, 127, 129, 130
Mon 45, 46
monopoly 6, 11, 23, 27, 43, 73, 92, 93,
  95, 98, 102–3, 118, 161, 183, 201,
  204–6, 234, 236, 243
monopsony 155
monsoon 78, 80, 134
Moor (historical usage) 41, 48, 168,
  223–24, 226; *see also Islam*
Moose Factory 145
Morning Herald, newspaper 123
Morocco 113, 213, 222–23
Morris, James 239
Moscow 13, 92–102, 104–5
Moylan, Francis 236
Moylan, John 236
Moylan, Stephen 236
Mozambique 126, 203
Mu Tianyan 77

Mughal 10, 78, 167, 183–87, 192
Muhammad, Bektaş (Dey) 217–20, 222, 226
Muijden, Jan van 46
Munster 236
Muscat 123, 124, 125, 127, 130
Muslim; *see* Islam

Naan, Mohandas 79
Nagasaki 7, 11, 12, 23–35, 43, 58, 61, 77; *see also* Deshima
Naimbana, king of the Temne 108, 111, 115
Nantes 198, 202
Naples 85, 86, 87
Narai, King of Siam 42, 45, 47
Nasiri ship 130
Neijenrode, Cornelis van 47–8, 52
Nelson River 145
Nesbitt banking house 239, 242
Netherlands; *see* Dutch; Low Countries
networks 5–7, 9, 10, 13–4, 33, 42, 44–7, 56, 57, 59, 63, 67–8, 77, 113, 117, 124–26, 129, 134, 135, 161–63, 165–74, 188, 190, 197–99, 202, 204, 206, 235–40, 242–43
neutrality, neutral 3, 51, 57, 64–7, 184, 187, 213, 217, 225
New Christians 83
New England 114, 124
New Institutional Economics 5, 13
New Ross 244
New World; *see* Americas
New York City 13, 123–5,128–32
Nguyễn lords 56, 58, 60, 64, 66
Nguyễn Cư Trinh 63
Niuminka 113
Norton, Richard 149
Norway 94
nutmeg 128

Ocean, ship 111
O'Conor, Charles 244
Official Standard 147, 148–50, 155
offspring; *see* children
Olivares, Count-Duke of 83
Olive Branch, ship 115
olive oil 202
Oman 123, 125–27, 129, 131, 134–35
Oman and Zanzibar Sultanate 13, 123–27, 129–30, 132, 134–35; *see also* Oman; Zanzibar

Ontario 145
opium 79, 175
Oromo 128
Orrery, Earl of 234
Ostend 237, 243
Ostend Company 162, 165, 174, 175, 198, 204, 237
Oswald & Co., firm 134
otter 150
Ottoman, Ottoman Empire 10, 14–5, 212–18, 220, 222
Ouidah 4, 117, 181–84, 187–92
Oursel, Nicholas 237
Oyo kingdom 183

Pacific 73, 78
pacotille, port-permis 164
Pāli 50
palm oil 116–7
Papels 114
paper (material) 83, 112, 131
Papers, paperwork 85, 164, 167–68, 178, 203, 224, 226; *see also* passport
parasols 113
Parekh, Tapidas and Tulsidas 79
Paris 115, 173, 186–89, 198, 202, 232–33
Park, Mungo 116
Parma 85
Pasley, Robert 169, 175
passports 163, 190, 203, 216–19, 223, 236; *see also* papers; flag
Pate 126
Patriot, patriotic 231, 234, 241–45
Pattani 43, 47
Paulo Jacomo Cloots 198, 204; *see also* Jean-Baptiste & Paulo Jacomo Cloots (firm)
Peace of Münster 84, 85
Peace of Paris 241–42
Peacock ship 130
Peacock, Francis 97
Pearl River 28
pearls 123, 132
Pearson, Robin 117
Peçevi, İbrahim 215
Pegua, Osoet 45, 47
pelt; *see* fur
Pemba Islands 125, 126
pepper 75, 77, 79, 88, 128, 166, 168, 170, 203
Peranakan 64

260 *Index*

Perceval, John, Second Earl of
 Egmont 240
Percival, Joseph 238
Peri, Domenico 84
Persia, Persian, Parsi 9, 27, 41, 42, 44,
 48, 123, 128, 131, 132, 167, 170
Persian Gulf 79, 123, 129, 131
Peru 78, 81
pesos; *see* Piece of Eight
Peter the Great, Tsar of Russia 92, 93,
 100, 102
Petty, William 233
pewter 111
Philadelphia 236, 238
Philip II, King of Spain 82
Philip IV, King of Spain 80, 82, 83,
 86, 87
Philippines 13, 73–4, 77–9
Phnom Penh 57
Phocas, Byzantine Emperor 51
Phoonsen (VOC agent) 187
Pidgin 31–2
Piece of Eight 7, 9, 13, 72–88
pipe (tobacco) 104, 111, 151
piracy 65, 73, 83, 84, 87, 130, 213–14,
 223, 226; *see also* corsair; privateer
Pitt, Thomas 186
Poivre, Pierre 61, 63
Poland, Polish 95
Poland-Lithuania 93, 94, 99;
 see also Lithuania; Poland
Polanyi, Karl 3–4, 5, 7, 9, 11, 23, 26,
 145, 157
Pollock, Sheldon 1
Pondicherry 174, 181–87, 189–92, 240
porcelain 7, 9, 131, 203, 204;
 see also ceramics
pork 236
Port of Trade; *see* Polanyi, Karl
Porto 202
Portonovo (India) 183
Portugal, Portuguese 14, 26, 41, 42, 48,
 73, 74, 78, 80, 83, 110, 111, 113, 126,
 144, 156, 183–85, 187–92, 196,
 198–207, 217, 223–24, 234, 238–39
Potosí 13, 72–87
Prasatthong, King of Siam 46, 48, 49, 51
Pratt, Mary Louise 40
Presbyterian 237
presents 112, 133, 183, 188; *see also gift*
Pret, Catherina de 198
Pret, Jacomo de 198
Pret, Jeanne de 198

Prince Henri de Prusse, ship 161, 165–7
Principal-Agent problems 5, 6, 14, 145,
 146, 164–65, 167, 205
private trade 52, 58, 147, 150, 161–73,
 181–83, 189–92, 200, 204
privateer 214, 221, 223, 236, 238, 241;
 see also corsair; pirate
prostitution, prostitutes 8, 12, 28–9,
 31, 35
Protestantism, Protestant 15, 235–37,
 243–44; *see also* Calvinism, Huguenot,
 Presbyterian
Provence, region 87
Providence, RI 133
Prussia 103, 104, 161, 163–64, 167–70,
 172–75
Prussian East India Companies 14,
 162–64, 174–75; Prussian Bengal
 Company 161–75; Prussian China
 Company 164–65

Qianlong, Emperor of China 59, 65
Qing dynasty 23, 26, 27, 32, 56–9, 61, 63,
 65, 67, 68, 76, 77
Quebec 145
Queen Victoria ship 134
Quinam 75
rabbit 144

RAC (Royal African Company) 187
Rachel or *Rahhel,* ship 223–24
Radisson, Pierre Esprit 144–45
Rama II, King of Siam 44
Ramsey, James
Rannie, David 172
Raşid, Mehmed 215
Recife 199, 202
Red Sea 79, 80
Reid, Anthony 64
religion 2, 4, 5, 14, 24, 25, 28, 31, 32,
 46–7, 50, 63, 67, 83, 87, 162, 181, 212,
 237, 244–45; *see also* Islam; Judaism;
 Buddhism; Confucianism;
 Christianity; Protestantism;
 Catholicism
Renaud 168
Republic of Letters 2
reputation 1, 64, 72, 73, 172–73, 181
Revolution 231, 235, 244;
 see also consumer revolution;
 American Revolution 109, 234–35;
 French Revolution 232, 241

Rhett, William 238
rhino horn 75
Rhode Island 111, 114, 115
rice 41, 42, 43, 46, 59, 75, 111, 116, 124, 166, 234
Rich, E. E. 145, 148, 156
Richardo, David 232
Richardson, David 117
Richmond 172
Ried 170
Riga 92, 101
Rio de Janeiro 199, 202, 203
Rio Nunez 111
Rocky Mountains 145
Rodney, Walter 109, 110
Rokel 116
Ronquillo, Pedro 86–7
Rotstein, Abraham 145, 148, 157
Rotterdam 238
Rousseau, Jean-Jacques 197
Rowe, William 67
rugs; *see* carpets
rum 111, 237
Russia 7, 10, 13, 92–105

Sa'īd, Sayyid, sultan of Oman-Zanzibar 123, 124, 126, 127, 129–34
Safavid Empire 10
Sahara, (Trans-)Saharan trade 111, 114, 117
Saigon 57, 60, 64
Saint Domingue 115, 239;
    see also Hispaniola
Saint Louis 112, 115, 117, 118
sakdina 43–4
sakoku 6, 26
Salem, Mass 128, 129, 130, 133
Salihi ship 130
salt 166, 168, 170, 236, 238
saltpeter 74, 78, 183
Salvador (Brazil) 205
San Thome (India) 166
sandalwood 75
sappanwood 42, 75
Sarsfield family 237, 239
Sarsfield, Dominic 239
Sarsfield, Patrick 237
Saskatchewan 145
Savi 190
Savoy 85
Schiedam 52
schooners; *see* ships

Schouten, Joost 48, 49, 52, 76
Scipione, ship 86
Scotland, Scottish 99, 100, 134, 151, 164, 165, 169, 172, 175, 216, 231, 239, 242; *see also* British
Seahorse, ship 73, 77, 78, 82
Seeman, William 131
Sen, Amartya 232–33
Senegal 111, 112, 115, 117;
    see also Senegambia; Senegalese islands 116
Senegal River 112, 114
Senegambia 113, 116, 118
Serer 111
serraf 78, 79, 80, *82*
servants 9, 12, 27, 98, 102, 170, 172, 219–20; company servants 52, 81, 149, 161–62, 165, 190–92
Seville 81, 85, 202
Sewji, Jairam 131
Shah Allum ship 130
Shah Jahan, Mughal Emperor 78
shahbandar 60
shares, shareholders 145, 147, 149, 161, 163, 203; *see also* stock exchange
Shenandoah ship 134
ships 9, 10, 13, 26, 42, 59, 73–5, 79, 85, 86, 101, 111, 114, 115, 117, 123–24, 128–35, 146, 149, 152, 161, 163–68, 170, 172–73, 181, 186, 187, 190, 201, 203, 204–5, 214, 216–24, 238, 241–42
shirts 116, 154
Shivaji, Maratha leader 184
shoes 108, 113, 128
Shunzhi, emperor of China 76
Siam 8, 12, 40–52, 56–60, 63–6, 68, 76
Siberia 94, 95
Sierra Leone 109, 111, 112, 114, 115, 116, 117–18
Sierra Leone Company 115, 116, 117–18
Sihanoukville (Kampong Som) 57
Siin region
Silesia 104
silk 9, 100, 108, 113, 132, 204
silver 9, 10, 13, 42, 72–88
Singapore 127, 134
Sir Lanka; *see* Ceylon
slavery, slave, slave trade 4, 9–10, 12, 13, 27–9, 43, 44, 109, 110, 112, 113, 115–18, 125, 127–28, 131, 132, 183, 188–90, 203, 219, 238, 245
sloop; *see* ships
Smolensk 92

262 *Index*

smuggling 6, 27, 33–4, 52, 73, 83, 94, 242–43; *see also* contraband
Somalia 127
Sombatthiban, Okya 46
Songtham, King of Siam 41, 51
Sousa de Meneses, Manuel de 190
South Sea 190
South Sea Bubble 239
Southern Netherlands; *see* Low Countries; Flanders; Dutch
Spain, Spanish 13, 15, 42, 49, 72–4, 78–89, 85–7, 103, 144, 156, 186, 205, 213, 217, 222, 234, 235–36, 239, 243–44
spices 9, 43; *see also* pepper; cardamon
Spilman, James 95–6, 102
Splitgerber, David 164
St Catherine, ship 221
St. Bernard, ship 86
St. Helena 124
St. Jago (Santiago, Cape Verde) 114
St. Lawrence River 145
St. Petersburg 104
Staunton, Richard 150
stock exchange 201, 212; *see also* shares
stockings 104, 108, 115, 238
Strasbourg 223
Struys, Jan Janszoon 41
subaltern 8, 10–2, 145–46, 157, 233
Subrahmanyam, Sanjay 162
suftaja 117
sugar 78, 111, 124, 128, 131, 202, 234, 236, 239
Sultana, ship 123–24, 128–35
Sumatra 88, 128
supercargo 27, 161, 164–74, 222–23, 237
Supply, ship 82
Surat 73, 77–82, 84, 86, 161, 185
Swahili, Swahili Coast 125, 126, 128, 129, 131, 134, 135
Sweden 94, 163, 168
Swedish East India Company 162, 165, 168, 172, 174, 175
Sweers, Catharina and Solomon 52
Swift, Jonathan 234
Switzerland, Swiss 213

Tabarka 84
taffety or taffeta (fine textile) 108
Taiwan 74
Taksin, King of Siam 65–6
Tanka 28, 31
taste 14, 84, 105, 109–12, 118, 146, 147, 152, 154, 157; *see also* fashion

taxation 6, 43, 65, 78, 103, 143, 147, 166, 170, 187, 243; tax farming 201, 204–6
Tây Sơn dynasty 66
tea 9, 59, 111, 202, 203, 204, 234, 242
Temne 108, 115, 118
Temple, William 233
Testas and Son (firm) 189
Tetuan 221
textiles 12, 42, 43, 74, 76, 99, 100, 101, 108, 110–16, 118, 126, 128–29, 133, 147, 148, 152, 153, 154, 166, 202, 203, 238, 240; *see also* cotton; silk; wool; flax; linen; calico; taffety; bafts; guinea cloth; cambrics; *kente* cloth; kaniki; merekani
Thailand; *see* Siam
third space 4, 12, 40
timber 238
Timmany; *see* Temne
tin 41, 59
tobacco 7, 12, 13, 92–105, 111, 147, 149, 154, 188–89, 202, 204–6, 234; *see also* cigar; pipe
Tokugawa 26, 31, 32, 77
Toledo 85
tolerance, toleration 61, 87, 93, 212, 225
Tone, Wolfe 244
Tory 242, 244
Toulon 221
Trần Giang (Cần Thơ) 66
Tranquebar 183, 186
transcultural, transculturation 2–7, 23, 9, 12, 15, 40, 51
translation 1, 5, 32, 43, 50, 51, 65, 212, 213, 215, 221; *see also* interpreter; translator 30, 48
treaty 15, 49, 80, 102, 129, 184, 213–20, 223–26; Treaty of Nerchinsk 100
Trinh, Cư 63
Tripoli 214, 221
Trivellato, Francesca 1, 6, 29, 33, 212, 217, 226
Trondheim 238
trousers 116
trust 1, 33, 34, 58, 65, 72–3, 76, 79–81, 83, 86, 88, 181, 186, 192, 239; *see also* distrust
Truxes, Thomas 236, 238
Tucker, Josiah 243
Tunis 214, 221
Tunisia 84
Turin 202
Turkish 216, 217, 222

Index 263

tutenague 166

Udong 57, 58, 60, 61, 64
Ukraine 92, 93, 95, 96, 99, 104
United States of America 123–4, 128–33, 135, 213, 217
Utrecht 93

vakil 170
Van Buren, Martin, President of the USA 123, 131
Vasconcelos, Rodrigo Sande de 204
Vattel, Emer de 213–14, 225
Venice 72, 73, 81, 85, 86, 113, 198
vernacular 1, 3, 5, 11, 162
Victoria, Queen of Great Britain 129, 132
Vietnam 12, 27, 56–8, 60, 64, 66, 68; *see also* Cochinchina; Indochina
Vijayanagara empire 182
Virginia (colony) 99
Vliet, Jeremias van 12, 40, 44–52
VOC (Dutch East India Company) 11, 12, 26, 27, 28, 40, 42–9, 51–2, 62, 67, 73, 74, 78, 79, 82, 161, 165, 172, 174, 185–87, 202, 203, 204
Volga river 104
Vologda 101
Von Glahn, Richard 76
Vora, Virji 79
Vries, Jan de 111, 113

War, warfare: 5, 9, 15, 25, 40, 43, 44, 49, 56, 64, 73, 74, 76, 80, 82–3, 87, 102, 112, 126, 129–30, 163, 184, 191, 213–15, 218, 236, 240–43; Thirty Years War 80, 83; Nine Years' War 181; War of the Spanish Succession 186–9; War of the Austrian Succession 188–89, 214, 240; Seven Years' War 175, 192, 231, 235, 239, 241–43, 245
Washington, DC 123, 130, 132
Washington, George 236
Waterford 244
wax 111, 116

weapons 110; *see also* guns
Weber, Friedrich Christian 104
West Indies 183, 236–38
Wexford 244
Whampoa 27; *see also* Canton
wheat 87, 128, 219, 221, 222–24
Whig 234, 242, 244
Whitworth, Charles 92–104
WIC (Dutch West India Company) 187
Wicquefort, Abraham de 50
widow 167, 189
wife, wives 12, 45–7, 66, 97, 173, 181, 190; *see also* marriage; *see also* widow
William II, Prince of Orange 49
William III of England (William of Orange) 93
wine 188, 236–38
woodchuck 150
wool, woollens 80, 104, 113, 115, 143–44, 156, 202, 234, 236; *see also* beaver
Woulfe family 237

Xeno, Giovanni *also* Yani Ikseno 222–23, 225

Ya'rubi dynasty 126
Yale, Elihu 190
Yangzhou 77
Yao 128
Yemen 123, 128
York Factory 145, 149, 152, 153–55
Youghal 244
Young, Arthur 234
Young, John 165, 166, 168–73

Zanzibar 10, 13, 123–35; *see also* Oman and Zanzibar sultanate
Zaramo 128
zecchina (sequin), coin 72, 81
Zeller, Arnaldo van 204–6
Zeller, Jan van 204
Zeller, Maria Luísa van 204
Ziegenbalg 168, 173

Printed in the United States
by Baker & Taylor Publisher Services